ETHNOGRAPHIC ESSAYS IN CULTURAL ANTHROPOLOGY

ETHNOGRAPHIC ESSAYS IN CULTURAL ANTHROPOLOGY

A PROBLEM-BASED APPROACH

Editors

R. Bruce Morrison
Athabasca University

C. Roderick Wilson
University of Alberta

THOMSON
WADSWORTH

Australia • Canada • Mexico • Singapore • Spain • United Kingdom • United States

To the memory of James A. Clifton,
distinguished scholar, applied anthropologist, mentor, and friend

Edited by Sybil Sosin
Production supervision by Kim Vander Steen
Designed and typeset by Lucy Lesiak Design, Chicago, Illinois

ISBN: 0-87581-445-X

Library of Congress Catalog Card No. 2001135278

Wadsworth/Thomson Learning
10 Davis Drive
Belmont CA 94002-3098
USA

For information about our products, contact us:
Thomson Learning Academic Resource Center
1-800-423-0563
http://www.wadsworth.com

For permission to use material from this text or product,
submit a request online at http://www.thomsonrights.com

Any additional questions about permissions can be
submitted by email to thomsonrights@thomson.com

Printed in the United States of America
10 9 8 7 6 5 4 3

CONTENTS

v

Undergraduate teaching, perhaps especially in anthropology, is character-ized by individuality. We each have a sense of what works best for us. We each have our own fieldwork experiences to draw on. Each of our insti-tutions has its particular resources. So we will not tell you how best to use this text. It will be used differently by each of you.

Nevertheless, some things do need to be said about using *Ethnographic Essays in Cultural Anthropology: A Problem-Based Approach*. As the subtitle indicates, the text uses a problem-based learning (PBL) approach. Case Western University Medical School in the United States developed the PBL approach in the 1950s. It was later adopted at McMaster University Medical School in Canada. The idea behind the PBL approach is that an integrated cur-riculum structured around real-life problems better prepares students to face the challenges of medical practice than does the usual discipline-based cur-riculum. The PBL approach focuses on contextual and cumulative learning. That is, a subject is not learned in depth at a single point in time but is instead introduced repeatedly in various contexts and at varying levels of abstraction.

Several implications follow from these characteristics: (1) Teaching becomes less topic based. In PBL, we do not exhaustively cover one topic this week and another the next. Kinship is not over in the third week; it returns in different contexts. (2) Things keep coming up. Teaching is more about responding to student questions and less about imposing order on an untidy world. (3) Teaching becomes more inductive and less deductive. (4) Classroom activity is less about teaching than it is about helping students learn. (5) Greater responsibility is placed on the teacher. You are not working from a text that contains all the definitive answers.

Since its start in medical schools, the PBL approach has spread to many other disciplines. Richard Robbins' *Cultural Anthropology: A Problem-Based Approach* was the first book to introduce the PBL approach to anthropology. This book differs from Robbins' book not in its approach, but in its content. Rather than drawing on a variety of ethnographic examples in order to exam-ine a problem, our discussion of each problem is embedded in a specific ethnographic context. Each chapter is, in effect, a mini-ethnography. This allows students to explore each set of questions in the context of one partic-ular society and to develop some appreciation for the richness of the society as a whole and for how institutional arrangements tend to support each other.

Is this approach antithetical to more traditional ones? We don't think so. *Ethnographic Essays in Cultural Anthropology: A Problem-Based Approach* can be used with the Robbins' book, can stand alone, or can be used to supplement other anthropological texts by exposing students to the same fundamental concepts within the problem-solving context.

For those intending to use both this and Robbins' books, a glance at the chapter headings will indicate that there is substantial overlap in the problems considered. Indeed, Robbins' table of contents was our starting point. But even those chapter authors using problems nearly identical to those used by Robbins were free to develop the problems their own way. The result is pedagogically interesting: two parallel and mutually interpreting expositions of a single problem.

In other cases, the connection between the two books is less obvious. We did not, for instance, match Robbins' Chapter 2 on the long-term transformation of human societies from hunting-and-gathering bands to industrial states. In its stead is a chapter on indigenous knowledge, both traditionally and in the modern world, a topic implied in Robbins' text. Additionally, our Chapter 5 directly addresses the way in which contemporary small-scale societies interact with states, and other chapters also feature discussion of the topic, so students are exposed to stereoscopic perspectives on complex realities.

The chart that follows illustrates the topical and conceptual range of the text. In reality each chapter's coverage is more complex than the chart indicates, but it does provide a sense of how the traditional topics are covered.

Robbins sought to address the learning process in the classroom by more actively involving students in problem-solving as a way to engage their imaginations as well as to integrate their knowledge. We believe this book also contributes to that process.

Topic-Chapters Correspondence Chart

Topic	Chapter
Agricultural society	3, 6, 10
Applied anthropology	2, 8
Art and aesthetics	1, 2, 9
Belief systems and values	1, 2, 3, 4, 5, 6, 7, 8, 9, 10
Colonialism	1, 2, 3, 5, 6, 9, 10
Cosmology	2, 3, 6, 9, 10
Culture (concept)	1, 3, 8, 10
Culture change	1, 2, 3, 4, 5, 6, 7, 8, 9, 10
Death	1, 3, 10
Economic development	4, 5, 6
Economic relations	1, 2, 3, 4, 5, 6, 7, 10
Education	1, 3, 4, 5, 7, 8, 9, 10
Environmental relations	2, 3, 4, 5, 6
Ethics	2, 8
Ethnocentrism	1, 6
Ethnography/ethnology	1, 8, 9, 10
Ethos	3, 5, 6
Family organization	1, 2, 3, 4, 5, 6, 7, 10
Feuding	4, 5, 6

Fieldwork	1, 6, 8, 9, 10
Food production	1, 2, 4, 5, 6, 7
Gender roles	1, 4, 5, 6, 7
Gift giving	1, 2, 5, 10
Globalization	1, 3, 5, 7, 8
Health	2, 4, 5, 7, 9
Horticulture	1, 3, 4, 5, 9
Hunting and gathering	2, 5
Indigenous knowledge	2
Industrial/postindustrial society	7, 8
Kinship	1, 4, 5, 6, 10
Language and culture	1, 3, 5, 9
Marriage	4, 5, 6
Migrant labor	1, 4, 7, 10
Missionization	1, 5, 6, 9, 10
Oral literature	2, 3, 9
Organization anthropology	7, 8
Pastoralism	3, 4, 6
Political organization	1, 2, 3, 4, 5, 6, 7, 9
Religion	1, 2, 3, 5, 6, 9, 10
Ritual	1, 2, 3, 9, 10
Sexuality	4, 6
Social structure	1, 2, 3, 4, 5, 6, 7, 8, 10
Status and rank	1, 2, 3, 4, 5, 6, 7, 8, 10
Systems of exchange	1, 2, 3, 5, 7, 8, 10
Witchcraft	3, 9

ACKNOWLEDGMENTS

Anyone who has struggled to put a book together knows that the scholarly effort reaches completion only with the dedication and cooperation of more people than could possibly be mentioned. Although we mention only a few, our appreciation extends to all who participated.

The contributors to this volume have endured a great deal of editorial constraint and comment from us. Yet they have managed to produce manuscripts of exceptional quality. We sincerely thank them.

Anthropologists doing fieldwork depend on the goodwill and hospitality of ordinary people who are really extraordinary. They share their lives with us, and they become our teachers. We owe them a great debt and extend our heartfelt appreciation for their support.

This book could never have been written without the generous institutional support of Athabasca University and the University of Alberta.

Dr. James A. Clifton, Consulting Editor for Anthropology for F. E. Peacock Publishers, encouraged us to put together this collection of ethnographic essays. As we survey the results, we are glad that he did. Richard Welna, Vice President and Publisher at Peacock, has provided unflinching support and much-needed advice, for which we are indeed grateful. We are particularly grateful for Sybil M. Sosin's excellent editorial advice. Her professional skills are truly exceptional.

We benefited from the critique of our book proposal by Henry Selby (University of Texas), Carol I. Mason (University of Wisconsin-Fox Valley), and Elvin Hatch (University of California, Santa Barbara). Elizabeth E. Brusco (Pacific Lutheran University) provided particularly useful comments on the finished manuscript.

The wholehearted support of our families has made the task of putting this book together both easier than it might have been and also a wonderful adventure.

Marietta L. Baba (Ph.D. Wayne State University) is Professor and Chair of the Anthropology Department and founding director of the Business and Industrial Anthropology Graduate Sequence at Wayne State University. Her research interests are organizational culture, technological change, and evolutionary process. She is actively involved in both research and consulting with a number of large corporations and organizations, and she is listed in *Who's Who in America*.

Donald M. Bahr (Ph.D. Harvard University) is Professor of Anthropology at Arizona State University. His research interests have focused on the Pima-Papago culture of southern Arizona. His books, which include *Piman Shamanism and Staying Sickness; Pima-Papago Ritual Oratory*; and *Ants and Orioles, Showing the Art of Pima Poetry*, reflect his particular interest in oral traditions.

Marcia Calkowski (Ph.D. University of British Columbia) is Associate Professor and Head of the Department of Anthropology at the University of Regina in Saskatchewan, Canada. She has conducted extensive research on Tibetan exile communities in India and Nepal. Her current research focuses on the practices surrounding the selection of reincarnated Tibetan lamas or *Tulkus*.

Mike Evans (Ph.D. McMaster University) is Assistant Professor at the University of Alberta. As an economic anthropologist, his work has centered on the role of cultural values in shaping contemporary economic practices in Tonga. His current research concerns the effect of Tongan values on international migration and the social, economic, and cultural linkages between Tonga and Tongans overseas.

Sharon Hepburn (Ph.D. Cornell University) is Assistant Professor of Anthropology at Trent University. She is an interpretative anthropologist who has done extensive research in Nepal. Her current research interests include understanding how people in Nepal make sense of the people, things, and ideas associated with modernity; investigating the parallels between people's views of the social world and their views of the physical world; and the historical and ethnographic study of the idea of mortality. She is currently finishing a book entitled *To See the World: Vision, Tourism and Ethnic Politics in Nepal*.

Leslie Main Johnson (Ph.D. University of Alberta) is an independent scholar. She lived in northwestern British Columbia in Gitksan territory near the village of Gitwingax for 12 years before returning to graduate school. Her research interests have included ethnobiology, ethnoscience, subsistence, and concepts of health and healing among northwestern Canadian First Nations. In addition to fieldwork with the Gitksan and Wet'suwet'en of northwestern British Columbia, she has worked with the Kaska Dene of the southern Yukon and Gwich'in of the Mackenzie Delta region of the Northwest Territories in recent years.

R. Lincoln Keiser (Ph.D. University of Rochester) is a Professor of Anthropology at Wesleyan University. He has done fieldwork focusing on the anthropology of violence with tribal communities in Afghanistan and Pakistan and with an African American street gang in Chicago. In addition to numerous articles, he has written three books: *Hustler: The Autobiography of a Thief; Friend by Day, Enemy by Night: Organized Vengeance in a Kohistani Community*; and *The Vice Lords: Warriors of the Streets*. He is currently working on a new edition of *The Vice Lords* in which he examines the group's change from a fighting gang to a drug gang.

Heather Young Leslie (Ph.D. York University) is Assistant Professor at the University of Alberta. She is a feminist and medical anthropologist specializing in the relationship between culture and medical systems. Past research examined mothers' health care practices with specific reference to raising healthy children in Tonga. Her current research, which focuses on indigenous Pacific Islanders who study Western biomedicine, is based on archival and ethnographic work in Fiji and Tonga.

Barbara J. Michael (Ph.D. University of Kansas) is Assistant Professor at Stephen F. Austin State University. She is a sociocultural anthropologist with research interests focusing on gender and economics, particularly in pastoral nomadic societies. Her regional specialization is the Middle East, and she has done extensive field research in Sudan and Yemen. In Yemen she investigated the sociocultural context of traditional medicine. She is also interested in ethnographic film and photography. Her book for young readers, entitled *Meet the Baggara*, is in press.

Ann Miles (Ph.D. Syracuse University) is Associate Professor of Anthropology and Women's Studies at Western Michigan University. She is a medical anthropologist whose area interests focus on South America. She has worked as a public health planner and program evaluator in Peru, and she has conducted extensive field research in the southern highlands of Ecuador. In addition, she is part of a faculty team for the Summer Institute on Migrant Farm Worker Health in connection with the Rural Health Education Program at Western Michigan University.

R. Bruce Morrison (Ph.D. University of Alberta) is Adjunct Professor of Anthropology at Athabasca University. His applied and scholarly interests have taken him to the Caribbean, Southeast Asia, South Asia, and Canada. Most recently he conducted applied, ethnohistorical, and ethnographic research in Nepal and India. He is coeditor with C. R. Wilson of *Native Peoples: The Canadian Experience*. He retired from Athabasca University to devote more time to writing in 1994, and he is currently working on a book about the role of the Sherpas in mountaineering.

Christina Sonneville (B.A. Western Michigan University) has a degree in anthropology and Latin American studies and is the coordinator for the Summer Institute on Migrant Farm Worker Health at Western Michigan University. She is currently completing her master's degree in social work at the University of Michigan.

C. Roderick Wilson (Ph.D. University of Colorado) has done anthropological research among the Navajo and Papago of the American Southwest, the Cree and Metis of Alberta, and pastoral nomads in Kenya. His theoretical interests are related to questions of culture change. He is coeditor with R. B. Morrison of *Native Peoples: The Canadian Experience*.

James A. Yost (Ph.D. University of Colorado) moved to Ecuador with his wife and three children under the auspices of the Summer Institute of Linguistics when he finished his Ph.D. He lived and worked with the Waorani for a decade, and he continues to work with them on projects that they define, most recently on assessing the potential for ecotourism as a sustainable, nonextractive source of income. When he is not working with the Waorani, he is a rancher in northern Colorado.

*A*nthropology literally means the study of mankind or, in contemporary terms, the study of humanity. Anyone watching the evening news on television is aware of the amazing variety of societies around the world. While we notice that these societies have many things in common, we are also aware that differences in beliefs have spawned widely divergent ways to organize our lives. Historically, anthropology has asked questions about what it means to be human in these varied contexts.

A central feature of cultural anthropology is its emphasis on understanding other peoples who live in these varied contexts from an insider's viewpoint—as they themselves understand things. Given that every anthropologist already has a functioning culture, this is not always easy to do, but it is part of what makes doing anthropology challenging and exciting.

Anthropologists have a holistic perspective, meaning that they try to get the big picture that incorporates all the relevant factors. As you will see in this book, most anthropologists pay special attention to one, two, or three aspects of societal interaction. Nevertheless, while examining specific details, their mindset is to keep a broad perspective. You might get some sense of all this by noting the kinds of places in which cultural anthropologists do their fieldwork.

Cultural anthropologists are joined by other anthropologists with different specializations but the same overall orientation. In North America, there tend to be three different specializations besides cultural anthropology. There are archaeologists, who examine cultures of the past. Their methods of data collection are different (it's hard to talk to a skeleton), but they share the belief that much in the present has been shaped by the past. There are also physical anthropologists. Some physical anthropologists study our very ancient evolutionary past, and others study our nonhuman but biologically related "cousins." We share the conviction that our behaviors are to some extent rooted in our biological past as well as in our cultural past, and that it is useful to make comparisons between groups. Finally, there are linguistic anthropologists, who study human languages and who remind us that language—the words we use and the way we use them to think about things—is also a central feature of all cultures.

Anthropologists assembled an amazing amount of information about different societies around the world during the 20th century. In the beginning, they usually studied small-scale societies. Doing anthropological research or fieldwork often involved living and working within the community being studied. In the case of social or cultural anthropologists, they were like children who had to learn a culture from the ground up. They usually learned the language in order to ascertain how one should behave in that particular society. The process often took several years. The accounts of their study were known as **ethnographies**.[1] These early ethnographies were usually comprehensive in nature; that is, they more or less described a complete way of life, including such things as how people made a living, what they believed in, and how they related to one another. As time went on, anthropologists became more focused on specific problems, partly in order to fill in gaps in what was already known. In addition, they began to study more-complex and larger-scale societies.

Whether problems are formally stated at the beginning of the research or become recognized only as fieldwork unfolds, problem formulation is at the heart of anthropological research. This means asking questions. These questions, or some of them, may be asked out loud, or they may be asked silently to oneself, but they need to be asked. Why does one person sit with that other person at a particular event? Why do some people defer to other people? Who makes what kind of decisions? Why are children encouraged to act in a certain way, or why are the dead cremated rather than buried? The number of questions generated in the course of a study sometimes seems endless, but the questions are tools that lead to understanding why the people in a particular society act the way they do.

This book is intended to provide an introduction to the fundamental ideas anthropologists use in understanding cultures around the world. These ideas are presented within the context of descriptions of specific cultures. In each chapter, the authors pose a problem as well as a number of questions that relate to the problem, much in the way one would pose problems and questions in the course of doing research. Just as the field researcher becomes totally engaged in pursuing the answers to the questions and problems, so we hope to engage you in an exciting learning enterprise that is more than just sitting down and learning a bunch of facts about a group of people.

The peoples you will be learning about live in many parts of the world. They possess vibrant cultures that have creatively dealt with a myriad of social, political, economic, and religious issues over time. They, like all cultures everywhere, are changing, albeit at different rates. To get an idea of the range of ideas you will encounter while reading this book, turn back to the table that appears at the end of "To the Instructor."

---

[1] Key terms appear in boldface in the text and are defined in the Glossary at the end of the book.

UNDERSTANDING DIFFERENCES AND SIMILARITIES

HEATHER YOUNG LESLIE
AND MIKE EVANS

PROBLEM 1 *How does anthropology contribute to our understanding of both the similarity and the diversity in people's ways of life?*

INTRODUCTION
Why Can't They Be More Like Us?

All human beings depend on what anthropologists call **culture**. Culture is the way people collectively organize their lives, think about the way in which they live, and act out their lives with others. Like language, culture is an essential attribute of humanness.

Anthropology is about similarity and difference—and how we need to understand and act on both. A fundamental idea in modern anthropology is that all cultures are different and that this difference is the cause of the wonderful variety of human ways of life. But we also recognize that a fundamental similarity underlies the differences: We are all part of the same species, and we all face similar challenges as we make our way in the world.

The research on which this chapter is based was supported by two grants from the Social Sciences and Humanities Research Council of Canada (one each to Young Leslie and Evans), a grant from the International Development Research Council of Canada (Young Leslie), and a grant from the McMaster University School of Graduate Studies (Evans). We acknowledge this help and the help of the people of Kauvai and others in Tonga and Canada, with gratitude.

In anthropology, the description of specific human cultures is called **ethnography**. Ethnography logically comes before **ethnology**, which is the comparison of diverse human ways of life in search of explanations for how people both differ and are the same. The chapters in this book are examples of ethnography. As readers think about them and start to compare and come to conclusions about them, they are beginning to generate their own ethnologies.

Today, as in the past, people live in different kinds of environments; obtain food, shelter, and companionship in different ways; speak different languages; and use different systems for recording and transmitting what they have learned. They also make different rules for ensuring fairness and righting wrongs, and they perceive beauty and ugliness, as well as courtesy and rudeness, in sometimes dramatically different ways. Diversity is something all human beings have in common.

Sometimes it seems that diversity is a barrier to cooperation, understanding, and harmony among different people. But one thing anthropologists have learned from past research is that people who may seem different, strange, or distant can be similar, familiar, and interconnected in interesting if sometimes hidden ways, and that people who seem the same may have quite a range of differing practices.

We have also come to understand that diversity and familiarity are often related to power. What feels familiar and is called normal are the ideas of people who have power. The concept of ethnocentrism points to exactly this issue. **Ethnocentrism** refers to the very common notion that what is normal within one's own society should be normal in all human societies.

Anthropologists teach that where human beings are concerned, there really is no such thing as normal, just current and local ideas of what is acceptable and appropriate here and now. For example, community elders have been revered and given great precedence in such societies as the Native American First Nations, Japan, and Tonga, while aging is devalued and youthfulness is esteemed in much of Canada and the United States. Likewise, there are and have been societies where status is based on amassing wealth, such as the United States and Canada, and others where status comes from giving away as much as possible, such as the Northwest Coast First Nations of Canada and the Mt. Hagen area of Papua New Guinea.

It might seem that human separateness comes from geographical and linguistic differences, but anthropological research has shown that these differences are not the barriers they may seem. Peoples speaking the same language may become bitter enemies, while peoples on the different sides of a mountain or an ocean may become closely and amicably associated.

This chapter uses ethnography to examine the questions of difference and similarity, as well as of distance and interconnectedness, and the power relations that affect both. By examining the lives of people from a small, seemingly distant community we call Fusipala, in the island-based Kingdom of Tonga, we can learn something about what it is to be a human being. The descriptions in this chapter also help demonstrate how anthropology identifies and describes differences with an eye to similarity, connection, power, and the humanity that links the peoples of the world, both past and present.

QUESTIONS ────────────────────────

1.1. What do anthropologists do?

1.2. Where does an anthropologist find culture?

1.3. What is the relationship between culture and the individuals and groups who share it? Who has culture?

1.4. When things change, do they also remain the same?

1.5. When things stay the same, do they also change?

QUESTION 1.1
What Do Anthropologists Do?

Anthropologists work where there are or have been people. Some, who are called archaeologists, generally look at the evidence people from the past have left in order to understand human life in previous times. Physical or biological anthropologists may work on material from past or contemporary people, but always from the perspective of the human body's interaction with the environment. Linguistic anthropologists focus on language, meaning systems, and the human use of symbols in order to explain humanity past and present. Social and cultural anthropologists work with living people, and this book focuses on their work.

Historically, many anthropologists studied human life in the parts of the world that Europeans encountered during the colonial expansion that began in the late 16th century. The very early anthropologists were ethnologists who emphasized the universality of human culture, which they conceptualized as a single entity. They theorized that differences between peoples were a result of differences in levels of cultural evolution. Human culture was manifested in different ways because of variations in the development of technology or systems of thought. In other words, these anthropologists believed that some societies had achieved more culture than others. They studied the process of cultural evolution by comparing societies in terms of how they fit into a kind of culture-attainment scale.

Other anthropologists began to apply these ideas in systematic ways, and more and better information about other peoples was collected. Ultimately, this so-called unilineal evolutionary approach was abandoned. Anthropological research showed that the tremendous variety of human ways of life did not fit neatly on a scale. In fact, it became obvious that the construction of a scale was as much a process of promoting European achievements as of analyzing human evolution. What remained was an appreciation of variety in human cultures and the desire to develop new and better ways to describe and understand each specific culture (ethnography) and compare different ways of living (ethnology).

Anthropologists generally select small societies or social groups encapsulated within larger societies to study. By studying a small group, we can better understand what it is like to be a member of the group. We seek to provide contextually rich descriptions and analyses of the small groups to add to the overall picture of human beings and human life. The diversity of anthropological research reflects the variety of cultural and social formations of which human beings are capable.

Anthropologists have learned that the more time we spend learning the languages, customs, practices, and histories of other people, and the more we invest in the community and make it part of our own personal community, the more likely we are to learn something that is true and valuable not only to anthropologists, but to everyone. Generally, then, an anthropologist spends at least a year learning to live as a member of a host community. Many return to the community for years afterward, albeit for shorter visits. An ethnographer who learns to live as a member of the community is engaging in **participant observation**.

Doing ethnography is not easy. In many ways it is like being an immigrant, especially when the researcher must learn a new language as well as different social practices. Returning home is like being an immigrant all over again, and it can be just as stressful to relearn living in one's own society. But one of the most important rewards of ethnographic research is perspective, the ability to view one's own society and home culture with fresh eyes. Anthropologists tend to use their perspective to make constructive critiques of their own societies and cultural practices.

QUESTION 1.2
Where Does an Anthropologist Find Culture?

Culture provides all people with the capacity to live in the world, reproduce society over generations, and adapt to changing circumstances. Culture is thus universal and part of what we share. But particular peoples practice specific cultures, so one basis of our similarity as human beings is manifest in our differences. We also share this world and its global ecosystem.

Although anthropology has traditionally studied small groups of people, we are increasingly aware that these groups are connected to one another. While intercultural contact has always been a fact of human existence, people have been profoundly interrelated through political and economic structures arising from European exploration and colonization over the last 400 years, and these connections have given rise to new similarities and new differences.

Our ethnographic example starts, as it should, with people in a particular place. The place is an island called Kauvai.[1] It is located in the Kingdom of Tonga.[2] In 1991 we went there with our small daughter, who was then a year and a half old, to do ethnographic research. Tonga is a nation of Polynesian people whose resident population in the last decade of the 20th century hovered at approximately 100,000. In the Kingdom of Tonga, people make use of 170 or more small islands and about 750,000 square kilometers of deep Pacific ocean for farming, fishing, and the manufacture of traditional medicines,

---

[1]Kauvai, the names of its villages, and the names of the people of Kauvai are pseudonyms.
[2]The following references to Tonga are largely framed in the "ethnographic present" of 1991–1993. Our contact with people living in Tonga has been regular, and we returned for brief visits in 1999 and 2000. While we attempt to provide current information, some things may have changed, and the descriptions may not necessarily reflect such changes. This is part of writing about a place and a time; the place and time on which the ethnography is based must be specified. To do otherwise is to suggest that some societies are "timeless," which is not true.

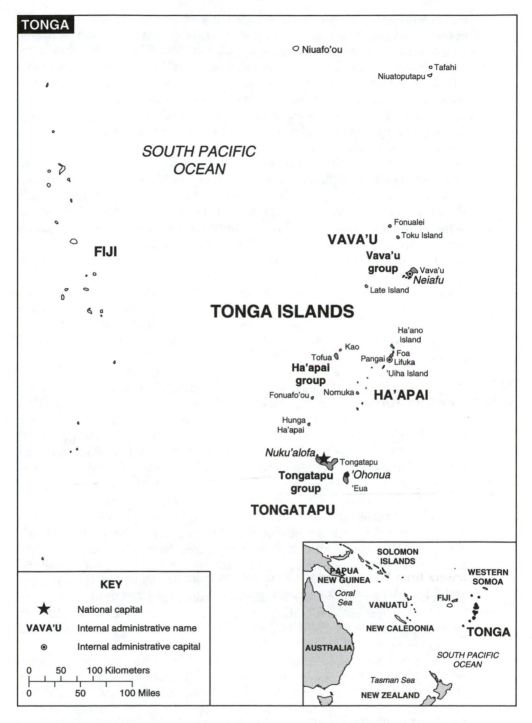

woven mats, bark cloth, and other items. While the land base is quite small, approximately 739 square kilometers, the ocean area is large and productive.

The islands are grouped into four clusters: the Tongatapu group in the south; the far-flung atolls of Ha'apai in the center; the larger islands and deep harbors of the Vava'u[3] Islands in the north; and the tiny northernmost islands

[3]The apostrophe in some Tongan words indicates a glottal stop. Most of us make a glottal stop when saying "Oh oh" quickly.

of Niuatoputapu and Niuafo'ou, which are geographically close to Tonga's northern neighbor, Samoa. The largest piece of land is the main island of Tongatapu, where two-thirds of the population lives. The national capital of Nuku'alofa is on Tongatapu and is the political and economic center of the kingdom. Parliament, major government offices, the highest law courts, the main hospital, schools, businesses, banks, and social elites are most likely to be found in or near Nuku'alofa. Most Tongans who do not live by subsistence farming and fishing are employed in the civil service, tourism, and small businesses located on Tongatapu.

Tonga is not a rich country. In 1989, the gross domestic product (GDP) was just under $160 million for a population of 90,485, or $176.82 per person. Tonga has few natural resources: no mines, no fossil fuels, and no great stands of timber. The main exports are agricultural and marine products and people. With its low GDP and dependence on migration, remittances, and foreign aid, Tonga is sometimes described as having a Third World economy.

As a nation, Tonga labors to mitigate the kinds of economic, educational, medical, and personnel resource disparities that result when regional populations are separated by distance, an ocean, and poor infrastructural links and when a lack of natural resources limits state-based spending. These same problems are faced by much larger nations, such as Canada and Russia, where people live relatively far away from each other and yet expect to have equal access to government resources.

The tiny island of Kauvai, where we lived for 19 months, is situated in the Ha'apai region. Despite being centrally located, Ha'apai is at the economic periphery, far from the jobs and business opportunities in Nuku'alofa. Although Ha'apai occupies an economically peripheral position, it is idealized and mythologized as a cultural center, the place where old-style traditional Tonga persists; as one government official said, "Ha'apai is where the *real* Tongan customs are practiced." Culture change is believed to be less prevalent in small fishing villages like those on Kauvai, and the people of Kauvai refer to Nuku'alofa as *muli*, meaning overseas or a foreign land.

Only 4 square kilometers large and a mere 30 meters above sea level, Kauvai is always at the mercy of the elements, including hurricanes and droughts. The communities on Kauvai prospered historically because of the superb fish resources nearby in the ocean. Three of Kauvai's four small villages form the official estate of Havea, a hereditary chief holding one of the 33 titles established under the Tongan Constitution of 1875. These nobles are part of a colonial-era codification of Polynesian chiefly systems of authority based on European political models, specifically the British monarchy and peerage system.

Fusipala, the largest village in Havea's estate and Havea's hereditary home, is the seat of power for most of the island. Its population varies between 135 and 150 people. The population fluctuates severely and frequently as a result of out-migration for school or jobs. The number of voters registered to Fusipala, and to Kauvai as a whole, is greater than the number of residents because the Tongan system of registration is based on the village of parents' birth, rather than on location of residence. In 1991 roughly 600 people were registered to vote in Fusipala. Many of Kauvai's registered voters live near Nuku'alofa or in Pangai, the regional center for Ha'apai, and a great many more live even farther away.

The fourth village on Kauvai is a government-administered estate, not part of Havea's or any other noble's holdings. Technically, the people living there owe no fealty to any noble. However, all four villages are inhabited by people who have cooperated and interacted on a daily basis for generations.

Kauvai is a tiny island in the middle of the Pacific Ocean, but it is not isolated. Its residents depend on fishing, animal husbandry, agriculture, copra (dried coconut) sales, and textile production for their livelihoods. Textiles, copra, fish, and crops from Kauvai end up in New Zealand, the United States, and Japan. Commodities, fuels, and ideas from overseas also make their way to Kauvai. People make and think about cash expenditures daily, but the monetary amounts are very small, and infrastructural links are too poor to allow greater participation in the **market economy**.

Most people live in two-room wooden houses with corrugated tin roofing that are perched on cement stilts. Behind the typical house is a kitchen house where meals are cooked over coconut-husk fires and eaten sitting on the floor or on benches at a table. A small number of households also have a second dwelling, a coconut palm–thatched house called a *fale tonga* that is used as a spare or boys' house; at puberty, brothers and sisters begin to be physically and socially separated. The tin-roofed houses were subsidized as part of a British relief effort after Hurricane Isaac destroyed all the homes in 1982. More than a decade old now, these hurricane houses, as they are called, still look temporary, a stark contrast to the building boom in the capital, Nuku'alofa.

As is the case for much of Tonga, water is a treasured resource. Groundwater is nonexistent on coral atolls like Kauvai, so inhabitants depend on rainwater. Freshwater may be tapped from seeps on the larger atolls, and a thin layer of rainwater filters through the soil to collect and float on the underlying seawater.

Earlier Tongans dug wells, sometimes puncturing the floor of the atoll to create small, highly prized pools, which frequently figured in stories of chiefly people's adventures. Before the Christian missionaries arrived in the 18th century, rain was considered a major gift from the gods, especially Tangaloa 'Eitumatupu'a, who lived in the sky and who was the divine father of the Tu'i Tonga, the first of the sacred high-ranking chiefs. One of the fears expressed during the missionary era was that the gods would be angry with the Christians and stop the rains.

Today, each village on Kauvai has one or two public reservoirs with corrugated tin roofs and eave troughs for rainwater storage. This was part of a national initiative that began in 1909. Most churches also have water reservoirs, a pragmatic use of the largest roofs in the village, although there were initial qualms about using rainwater from the roof of God's house because it might be taboo.[4] There are no water catchment facilities in the bush where the gardens are. Irrigation is rare and done by hand.

The southern half of the island has brackish wells; the northern half has no wells at all. Numerous attempts have been made to find a well in Fusipala, but the water tapped has always been saline. Most families depend on their roofs and cement storage tanks for drinking and washing water. Generally, one half of the roof has guttering. Reservoirs often leak. Old, cracked water

---

[4]It is interesting to note that our word *taboo* is an Anglicization of the Polynesian *tapu,* which refers to something set aside from normal use because it is sacred.

reservoirs that serve as breeding grounds for mosquitoes and holding tanks for refuse are sentinels to past development projects, memoirs of home sites now abandoned to weeds and pigs, and distant reminders of the people's dependence on forces not human.

There are few modern mechanical conveniences on Kauvai. Four or five families have gas-powered generators that they use on special occasions, such as feasts. No one, not even the government nurse, has refrigeration or other electric utilities that can be used on a daily basis. In 1993 the small generator we brought from Canada was the only generator in Fusipala; since then about five households in the village have obtained generators, and a committee has been formed to consider a diesel-powered electricity system for the island.

Families with insulated coolers can get blocks of ice for a few cents from the Ministry of Fisheries office in Pangai. The half-day trip to Pangai precludes regular use of ice, but it is especially popular at Christmas and New Year's Day for cooling fish, mutton, and such other feast treats such as ice cream. A couple of families have received televisions and VCRs as gifts from overseas relatives. These are popular sources of entertainment at Christmas time.

Many women yearn for "modern" wringer washing machines to replace their tubs and washboard. There are a few propane stoves, which are also reserved for special occasions. Most baking is done in earth ovens.

The most common means of transport is walking, followed by horse and cart and bicycle. The only motorized vehicle on the island is the nurse's small 100-cc motorcycle. Some farmers would like tractors, but it would be difficult to carry these heavy vehicles on 14-foot wooden boats in potentially rough seas and to unload them onto an island with no wharf. From time to time over the last 20 years, people have had short-term access to tractors, but such opportunities have been rare. In 2000, the Governor of Ha'apai arranged for tractors to be driven across the reef at a very low tide. On its return, a tractor was swamped, an expensive lesson in the problems of island development.

There are two solar-powered radiotelephones on Kauvai. Residents of villages without one of these phones who want to make or receive calls must walk to the next village, a trip of 20 or 30 minutes (depending on the weather). The exchange is a simple pick-up-and-wait-for-the-operator-to-answer type. Both halves of the island have designated time slots for making and receiving calls. A schedule of incoming calls is regularly announced on the radio. A resident who hears that a call is coming in goes to the phone and waits. We found the interminable waits excruciating. Local residents don't like them either.

Kauvai is usually reached by an open fishing boat from a neighboring island. Prior to 1980, much of the fishing and travel from Fusipala was done by sail and paddle. Most fishermen now use outboard engines of 15 to 30 horsepower. The boat trip takes about 40 minutes when the sea is calm. A reef causeway allows people to walk from the neighboring island to Lifuka, the main island of the Ha'apai group, or to ride there on a motor vehicle, such as a bus or a passing truck. The causeway is relatively recent (1990), and it occasionally floods.

People who take this trip are generally heading for Pangai, the regional center of Ha'apai, on the island of Lifuka. Pangai has stores, several church-run high schools, a hospital, a police station, a courthouse and jail, a bank, some government ministry offices, fairgrounds, and a royal residence.

From Pangai, travel connections can be made to other islands. While we were there, Pangai was served by Twin Otter airplanes and two ferry boats. The ferries are imported river boats that have been refitted and converted to open sea vessels. The trip to the capital of Nuku'alofa can take 50 minutes or 18 hours, depending on the mode of travel. It takes another 25 minutes by air or 8 hours by sea to reach Neiafu, the regional center for Vava'u in the north and a popular tourist destination.

When we made our way to Kauvai and set up a household in the village of Fusipala in 1991, it took us about three days to get there from southern Ontario, Canada, where we attended graduate school. We arrived in August with one small child, two laptop computers, a small generator, and miscellaneous domestic items. We had assumed that we needed to bring most of what we would be using. With the exception of the computers, we need not have brought any of the purchases. Everything was available in Tonga, and many things were much less expensive than in Canada. At that time there were strong diplomatic ties between Tonga and Taiwan, which meant, for instance, the mosquito netting purchased in Toronto for approximately $80 cost $15 in Nuku'alofa. This was our first lesson about how well connected Tonga is to the rest of the world.

As mentioned earlier, the primary method of ethnographic research is participant observation. This method requires an anthropologist to integrate into the community. The basic idea is that by living with and like everyone else in the village, we can learn what is most important to people, rather than assume that the aspects of life that are important to us are also important to villagers. Integration requires linguistic and cultural competence—knowing how to behave and understanding the meanings behind expected behaviors. Being a participant observer means that nothing can be taken for granted. The switches in mental orientation—in perception of self and normalcy—that result from this immersion process can be radical.

Thanks to the patience and kindness of our neighbors and friends, we gradually learned how, in Tongan terms, a person should *be*. Knowledge of Tongan language and Tongan culture goes hand in hand with integration, and in fact the two happen at the same time. This was the necessary knowledge that preceded our more detailed work on maternal–child relationships (Young Leslie) and the village economy (Evans).

It is important to note that, with the exception of our daughter Ceilidh, we did not "become Tongan." We did learn how to treat people respectfully and properly, and we became adept at acting and thinking like our neighbors. There is a difference between learning a culture as a child and as an anthropologist. Adults maintain at least some distance; they know that they have a home and way of being elsewhere. After spending a year in Fusipala, our daughter had no idea that she was anything other than a Tongan, the same as every other child in the village. Perhaps the most telling evidence of this occurred one afternoon. Speaking Tongan, her language of everyday use, Ceilidh called to us from the doorway, "Heather, Mike, come look, Europeans!" She had noticed two tourists strolling down the road, an unusual event, and her reaction was the same as any other village child: excitement and fear. We, on the other hand, had and continue to have a kind of expanded, bifurcated sense of identity and culture, which recognizes both the social practices and expectations that come from our culture and those we learned from ethnographic fieldwork. This enhanced perspective is not unique to anthropologists, of course, but anthropology has made this kind of experience a central feature of how we come to know what we know.

In the first few months, we also learned about our neighbors and began to form friendships that we maintain to this day. Ethnographic fieldwork requires the cooperation of the people with whom one works, and such cooperation is dependent on the same goodwill as is human cooperation in any other context. Integration into Fusipala was a gift people gave us, and it made possible everything that followed. All the best ethnographic fieldwork is based on the willingness of people to share the problems and solutions of being a human being on a day-to-day basis. The problems are universal, the solutions particular, and ultimately they are the basis of anthropological knowledge and practice.

QUESTION 1.3
What Is the Relationship Between Culture and the Individuals and Groups Who Share It? Who Has Culture?

Culture is in our minds; it seems manifest in the world that we inhabit, and it shapes the way we live and thus re-create culture over time. All of us have a set of flexible and interrelated notions that we use to interpret the world and guide our actions. Culture is something we practice, but the ideas of how to behave, how to do things, and what kinds of practices are to be done are also our culture.

In spite of the fact that we have culture individually, we never really practice it alone. Our lives are dialogues with others, interactive processes in which we act individually and collectively to reproduce, shape, and change culture, which we then use to act again. Both cultural continuity and culture change are products of this repetitive human activity.

When anthropologists talk about culture, we are generally talking about some version of a collective, shared set of ideas and activities that characterize human social life. Within any society with a shared culture, however, there is variation. Children do not know what elders know. Women and men often do and think different things and act in different ways with different motivations. Young men, for example, have different desires, rights, and responsibilities than older women. Even within a group of senior adults, there is individual variation in knowledge, prestige, skills, preferences, and so on that stems from personal experience.

People whose access to wealth, resources, specialized knowledge, or privileged status gives them influence often have a better chance to shape and define expectations, behaviors, and priorities. **Power** is a part of all societies. The lines of access to influence and what is deemed worthy of being influential vary from one society to the next depending on cultural parameters. For example, in North America, wealth, resources, and fame are accepted forms of influence and power. In Tonga, age and genealogical relationships, especially the relationship of a sister to a brother, are sources of influence and power.

Sālote and Tupou are respected elderly women. As mothers, sisters, and accomplished weavers of ceremonial textiles, they have power. That is, they influence community decisions; they direct their children and grandchildren; they guide their church congregations; and they create and provide access to privileges and resources. The power of older and respected women is not unlimited or uncontested, but it is not negligible either. However, even the powerful are shaped by their culture and social position. Sālotē's and Tupou's lives, indeed their very bodies, are shaped by practices and values that they think of as Tongan culture. They are both the creations and creators of this culture, at once products and producers of the men and women stretching from the far distant past to the foreseeable future.

Sālotē's hands are old, fleshy, and strong. Her fingers, like those of many older women, are as gnarled and crooked as the roots of the banyan tree. The end of each finger is permanently hooked. These hands proclaim Sālotē's profession even when they are lying limply in her lap or when she is fanning herself at church. Tupou's hands were the same, if a little leaner, more sinewy. "Look at the hands of a weaver," Losalina said softly to the circle of women as we washed and perfumed Tupou's body for burial. Losalina laid Tupou's slack hand across her own younger, firmer palm and curled her still straight and flexible fingers through Tupou's. There was at least 30 years difference in age between them.

Like several other women of their generation, Tupou and Sālotē are mothers who have lived all their lives, some 60 to 90 years, on the island of Kauvai. These women are easily spotted making their way to church, torsos bent forward at the hips, hands linked at the base of the spine. Twirling a coconut leaf fan as ballast and puffing like old steamships, they waddle slowly, painfully, to prayer.

Sālotē is the oldest woman on the southern half of Fusipala, where she lives on her widow's land allotment. She presides over a network of kin and

Lotoa Fifita holding a kapa (tin blade) while making a mat. (Photograph by Heather Young Leslie.)

affines (people related through marriage) that extends to three households in the village and at least two more in other parts of Tonga. One son-in-law affectionately (but quietly) calls her *Pule* (boss), but her granddaughter calls her by a diminutive, *Lote*.

By Kauvai standards, Sālotē is in many ways an unremarkable woman. Her long hair is gray and soft, with wispy ends and white roots. She usually twists it up into a knot on top of her head. On Sundays, a daughter or granddaughter combs her hair and grooms her, and she looks beautiful despite her sagging body and melancholy eyes. Those eyes are formidable; they are sometimes disapproving, often tired, and bright with tears when she is happy, proud, or sad. Sālotē's tongue is just as formidable, and her sharp commands and retorts are alarming to the uninitiated. Chuckling and shushing as she squeezes juice from a bundle of leaves with one hand, dripping it down her thumb into the open, wailing mouth of the child she holds with the other, Sālotē transforms herself from matriarch to Madonna.

All of Sālotē's nine children are alive, and only two have never married. Three daughters live on Kauvai, and another lives just outside of Pangai, but Sālotē is too afraid to make the boat trip to visit her. Sālotē is more blessed than Tupou, who had no children from either of her two marriages, but fostered two children. She is also more fortunate than Kalistina, whose children have all moved away, some to Tongatapu and others to Auckland.

Kalistina's faded beauty is evident, and her smile is more frequent and radiant than Sālotē's. But she too has tired eyes, and like Sālotē, Tupou, and most of the other women of their generation, Kalistina's lower back is permanently bent, and her hands have hooked metacarpals. These women walk the same walk, leaning forward at the hips with their chins waist high. When Kalistina is walking, she swivels her head sideways to look up. To stand even close to upright, she bends her knees, swings her shoulders up, and sticks her chin out.

Two of Sālotē's daughters, Malia and Lupe, work with Kalistina on a regular basis. There are many cooperative weaving groups on Kauvai, and at least four in Fusipala alone. The group Tupou worked with disbanded for the year after her death as a sign of mourning. In this group, Lupe generally does the starting edge, Malia the closing edge, and Kalistina the middle. Membership in a weaving group is flexible, and sometimes one or two other women join the *toulālanga* on a short-term basis. Sālotē recently retired from this group because she found the pace too exhausting. These days she plaits at home, alone or in the company of Fo'ou, her unmarried daughter.

Pandanus, also known as screw pine, is a plant indigenous to the Pacific. It grows well on windy and rocky shorelines and is thus well-suited to coral atolls. When properly processed, the long and treacherously barbed leaves can be sliced into widths ranging from two centimeters to only a few millimeters. Tongans have cultivated pandanus for centuries; it was the original material for the sails that powered the first voyagers across the Pacific Ocean. Today on Kauvai, women know and cultivate several varieties.

When properly processed, pandanus provides textures ranging from that of firm leather to something more akin to starched satin. Colors of processed pandanus naturally range from khaki to pearly gold, and Tongan women will also use natural or commercial dyes to create even more colors. Processed fibers may be hand woven into large mats suitable as floor coverings and sleeping mats, or into a variety of fancier mats intended to be wrapped around the waist and hips.

Historically, the finest, softest pandanus textiles were decorated with red feathers and worn by chiefly daughters and sons. Some of the best of these garments have the texture of silk and are hundreds of years old. Such special pieces are given names and handed down through generations in the same way that sacred or familial heirlooms of silver, jewelry, or land may be passed on in other societies. These treasures are guarded fiercely, and they must be worn at major ceremonial events. For example, one particular fine mat, as such garments are called, must be worn by a member of the royal family when being crowned; an heir to the throne cannot be crowned king or queen without that mat. In this way, certain mats are equivalent to the crown jewels of Great Britain.

The skills for making and knowing how and when to use particular ceremonial textiles and the responsibility for keeping and safeguarding them lie with women. In fact, these textiles, along with the cloth beaten from mulberry bark, are referred to as "women's wealth." But along with the prestige and privilege come disadvantages resulting from the labor of hand weaving without a loom. Making Pandanus textiles is time-consuming and physically uncomfortable. Women must sit on the floor for hours each day, bent over the multiple strands that they hand weave. A lifetime of such work, which is the major economic and social activity of women on Kauvai, produces bent backs and crooked hands. The weaver's bent back is probably caused by arthritis and/or postmenopausal osteoporosis exacerbated by years of sitting hunched over while hand weaving textiles, as well as by the cultural pressure on women and chiefs to demonstrate proper behavior by remaining seated and unmoving whenever possible. The permanent crook of the index finger seems to develop from picking up the fibers during weaving, and as women get older, arthritis may cause their other fingers to hook.

Malia and Lupe are women in their early forties who have yet to acquire the weaver's bent back, but each does show an early sign of the weaver's

Loutoa Kepueli, Pauline Ngalu, and Mele Finau bring gifts of fine mats and food for the formal leave-taking ceremony of a Methodist minister and his family. Note the prominence of the fine mats in the presentation and the bent walking position of the women.
(Photograph by Heather Young Leslie and Mike Evans.)

FIGURE 1.1. Sālotē's Household

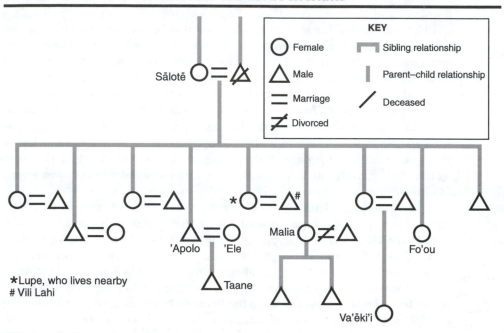

Note: Only persons who live in the village are identified by name.

hand. Malia and Lupe are of the same generation as Losalina, who came to help prepare Tupou for her funeral. Like Losalina, Kalistina, and most adult women on Kauvai, Lupe and Malia spend their days plaiting their textiles, generally working from dawn to late afternoon. When a deadline looms, they work late into the night by the light of a kerosene lamp.

Losalina and Malia live at opposite ends of Fusipala. They are unrelated and attend different churches, but they have much in common. Their households and domestic situations provide fairly typical examples of the lives of many people on Kauvai.

Malia has two sons and has divorced her husband (see Figure 1.1). She lives with her mother, Sālotē, who is the head of the household, her sister Fo'ou, and Va'eki'i, the daughter of Malia's brother, who now lives on Tongatapu and whom the family has fostered. Fostering of children is a common practice in Polynesian societies and is seen as a demonstration of love rather than a sign of inadequate parenting. Malia's sons live in Pangai with a relative of their father. Malia's brother 'Apolo, his wife, 'Ele, and their young son live in Sālotē's household. Sālotē's husband died a few years before, and now she holds title to the house and bush allotment. Since inheritance is legally passed to males according to rules of primogeniture, Sālotē holds the property in trust for her firstborn son, who lives in New Zealand.

Sālotē's entire household, including 'Apolo, 'Ele, and their baby, eat from the same gardens, use the same cookhouse, and share household duties and resources. 'Apolo has become the main food producer for the family since his father died because his two brothers live off Kauvai. 'Apolo does not enjoy fishing, so Sālotē's household depended on her son-in-law Vili Lahi for fresh fish until about 1995, when his boat was no longer seaworthy. Earlier Vili Lahi was an avid fisher, but now age and arthritic knees also keep him on land.

He and Lupe live on a separate property a short walk away and form a separate household, but they eat a lot of their meals with Sālotē. After Tupou's death, her widower, 'Ofa Lelei, was also a frequent guest at meals.

Losalina lives at the other end of the village in the household of her mother, Latulahi (see Figure 1.2). Losalina is close to Malia in age, is widowed, and has two sons who are younger than Malia's sons. Losalina's brother Vaka and his wife, Paea, their young son Si'i, and a toddler daughter share two rooms in the three-bedroom house with Losalina, Latulahi, and Losalina's young son Tolu. The property will eventually be inherited by Vaka. Until Latulahi dies, however, Vaka and Paea are like guests, while Latulahi and Losalina live in the main part of the house. The quarters are cramped, and Losalina and Paea sometimes quarrel, but Losalina's son Tolu is a good brother to Paea's son, Si'i. When Losalina's eldest son attended high school, he lived with her brother near Nuku'alofa, coming home on holidays. Now, he stays with other young, unmarried men in a separate house in the village. Like Malia's brother, Losalina's brother is the main food producer for the household. As governmental agricultural officer for the island, he also draws a small (and rare) salary while living on Kauvai. When Vaka wants to go fishing, he goes with a brother, Maake, who lives nearby.

Both Sālotē's and Latulahi's households are multigenerational, with an extended family ranging in age from over 60 to 6 or younger. Both are headed by women, with some secondary-school-aged children of the house living elsewhere and at least one primary-school-aged grandchild in the household. Both households depend on gardens for their staple and ceremonial foods and on kin-based relations for access to fish. Like all residents of Kauvai, the families have pigs and chickens that they allow to run free. These animals pro-

FIGURE 1.2. Latulahi's Household

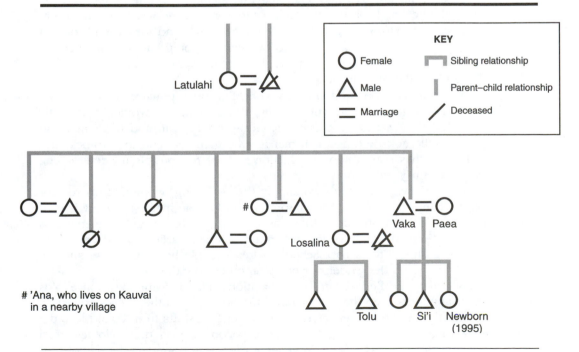

'Ana, who lives on Kauvai
in a nearby village

KEY
○ Female   ▯ Sibling relationship
△ Male | Parent–child relationship
= Marriage   / Deceased

Latulahi — Vaka — Paea — Losalina — Tolu — Si'i — Newborn (1995)

Note: Only persons who live in the village are identified by name.

vide occasional and ceremonial sources of meat. Pigs are also sources of wealth. Along with kava and certain types of root vegetables (especially yams), pigs are the masculine equivalent of women's textiles.

While it is not the cultural norm for women to be heads of households, neither is it abnormal. Sālotē and Latulahi preside over their households like queens. They spend most of their days weaving pandanus at home, and leave only to attend church. Sālotē, like Kalistina and Tupou (before her death), can walk unassisted, but Latulahi must use a cane to negotiate the route to her church. Her back is so bent that her hands and a fan can no longer serve as a counterbalance. She crawls on hands and knees inside her house, and depends on one of her grandchildren to run errands.

The pattern of life is predictable, but not dull. The residents of Fusipala expect the days and weeks to follow a regular pattern. From Monday to Friday, families wake before the sun and say a morning prayer of thanks to God. On Monday, Wednesday, and Friday, the Methodists attend a dawn prayer service (there are three Methodist congregations, one Mormon congregation, and one Seventh Day Adventist congregation in Fusipala, and similar congregations in the other villages). After prayers, sleeping mats and blankets are bundled away, water is drawn, faces are washed, teeth are brushed, and pigs are fed. Men prepare to go fishing or hoe the gardens; young mothers tend to babies and young children; and older women or men begin to prepare the day's main meal. Women slice pandanus strips for the day's weaving, braid daughters' hair, or iron school uniforms. Schoolchildren run errands, visit neighbors, fetch water, or linger at the small village shop hoping for free sweets. Younger siblings tag along or play at home. If children want to eat breakfast, they have cabin crackers, leftovers like taro or cassava, or germinated coconut. Most adults wait until mid-morning, usually around 10 A.M., to eat the main meal of the day.

Most adults are well into their weaving, tilling, or fishing by the time the schoolchildren circle around the flagpole in front of school to recite the morning prayer at half-past eight. When the sun is high and the ground too hot even for feet hardened and callused by years of going barefoot, men sometimes join their wives or nieces in the shade of the weaving house. There they chat and eat the main meal.

Food preparation is often men's work. European practices introduced by Christian missionaries prescribed everyday cooking as women's domestic labor, but this was not the case historically on Kauvai, and both men and women still cook. Because men manage the gardens, tend to livestock, and go fishing, they control food production and are responsible for determining what the family will eat on a day-to-day basis.

On days when they are working at their weaving, women rarely rest for longer than it takes to eat their taro and fish, but the men's company is usually a welcome distraction. Later, as the sun becomes infinitesimally less intense, the men, singly or in pairs, return to their gardens, head out to the reef, or go home for a nap. Schoolchildren straggle home by 3 P.M. and are often sent out to the gardens or on some other errand.

Saturday is called *Tokonaki,* preparation day. On Saturdays, households wash laundry, sweep the grass around the house, burn the week's collection of animal dung and other refuse, fish, gather foodstuffs from coral reefs, dig up extra root crops, bring home extra coconuts, iron dress clothes, read required Bible passages, and, in general, prepare for Sunday, the day of rest.

Finau Sitani, his daughter Lesieli, Heather Young Leslie, and her daughter, Ceilidh Evans, at a small feast given by Finau and his wife, Mele, for their oldest child, Sitani.
(Photograph by Mike Evans.)

Sunday is devoted to church attendance, eating the Sunday meal, studying the Bible, and sleeping. Women teach Sunday school or visit relatives and invalids. Men participate in the kava-drinking circle. Kava, a mildly relaxing herbal concoction made from the roots of *piper methysicum,* is the national drink of Tonga. Although it is consumed casually by men, kava is strongly associated with sacred and ceremonial activities, and Sunday in Fusipala village is certainly a sacred day. Work and such distracting activities as reading novels, writing letters, picking fruit, mending clothes, washing hair, and swimming are forbidden. Sunday is for devotion to and contemplation of God. Usually there are two church services on Sunday, and sometimes there are as many as four.

The regularity of these days and weeks are punctuated by predictable events like Christmas, New Year's Day, special church meetings, the annual agricultural and industrial fair, and large cooperative work projects like building a village fence. And daily life can also be interrupted by unexpected events—like Tupou's death.

QUESTION 1.4
When Things Change, Do They Also Remain the Same?

One of the most challenging events in the life of a group of people is death. Death is change; death is renewal; death is inevitable. In many cultures, and certainly in Tonga, the death of an older person triggers a particularly intense period of social activity.

When they realized that Tupou was dead, Malia and Lupe cried, wailed, and called to her, then dried their eyes and set about organizing her house for the funeral despite the fact that it was about 9 P.M. and pitch dark on a cloudy, moonless night. "Go tell Tevita we need the lamps from the church," ordered Lupe, referring to Tupou's minister. Word of Tupou's death spread quickly, and a party of men and women soon congregated.

With a death, the inside of the house is the women's domain. Tupou's iron bed was dismantled, and all of her and her husband's possessions were removed from the house. Young Leslie helped the women sweep the floor, dust the walls, and line the walls of the back room with white bedsheets. Other women, young and old, arrived, some from other villages on the island. They filled the front room of the house, lending a hand wherever needed— chewing candlenuts to make a sweet-scented emollient, hanging curtains, sweeping away rubbish, crying and singing hymns. In the back room, we prepared scented water and carefully, decorously, bathed Tupou, preserving her dignity and dressing her in a clean, white gown. Outside the front door, men built a shelter of poles and coconut fronds and packed the household's contents away into the cookhouse. It began to rain. The only unoccupied person was 'Ofa Lelei, Tupou's widower, who stood silently in the rain.

As highly charged events scripted by traditional ideals, funerals fuse social and structural obligations with traditional ideals of kinship and appropriate behavior. They are events at which one may observe individual influence and power being enacted and tradition being perpetuated and also modified. To understand people's actions at Tupou's funeral, one must understand Tongan kinship and how personal identity and social status are related.

Tongans trace their kin **bilaterally** (through both mother and father) as far back as memories and record books permit. This kin group is called the *kāinga*. The term is usually translated as extended kin, but it really describes people who are native to a place, blood relatives, and/or social compatriots. The term is used, for instance, to refer to the relationship of persons who live on a chief's estate and to describe the relationship between them and the chief, regardless of whether there are genealogical relationships. Similarly, all the members of the same Christian denomination are known as *kāinga lotu* (family in prayer). The social interactions of *kāinga* are like those of kin and involve displays of affection and mutual obligation. Kinship systems are systems of behavior, not determined by biology. In Tonga, one must behave like kin in order to be kin.

Kinship terminology and the definition of the family are changing. The term *fāmili,* from the English word, is used to refer to the nuclear family and genealogically close relatives. In general usage, *fāmili* is a subset of *kāinga*. *Kāinga* is generally used to refer to distant kin—the relatives one sees only at such major life events as birthdays, weddings, or funerals or those who are emotionally aloof. *Fāmili* is used to mean close kin with whom one is in frequent or comfortable contact, even if they are genealogically distant, and those descended from grandparents' siblings.

A father and his brothers are called *tamai* (father), and mother and her sisters are called *fa'ē* (mother). Persons of the same generation who trace their descent from common grandparents or earlier ancestors consider themselves siblings. As in all of Polynesia, the brother–sister relationship is marked by strong bonds of affection and equally strong avoidance taboos. Brothers demonstrate their affection for their sisters through respect, generosity, and avoidance, while sisters demonstrate it through an acceptance of the authority of their symbolic position and expressions of solidarity with the social and political actions of their brothers.

The people whom English speakers call cousins are considered by Tongans to be brothers and sisters. Those whom we call nieces and nephews are thought of, treated, and expected to behave as daughters and sons. The relations of nieces and nephews to their aunts and uncles, however, is different from anything in North American and European kinship. In Tonga, a father's sister and a mother's brother are especially significant relatives. The father's sister is highly ranked, and her position is imbued with the authority of the father's side of the *kāinga*. She is revered and treated with respect, especially at events like funerals, weddings, and first birthdays. A mother's brother can always be counted on to be supportive, loving, and generous, the epitome of the maternal side of the *kāinga*. For example, Sālote's brother 'Ofa Lelei was a favorite maternal uncle, or *fa'ē tangata*—a "male mother"—to her children, and the children's relationship to him was "easy." If he had been their father's brother, the relationship would have been marked by respectful obedience.

The brother–sister relational pair (or dyad) also underlies rank in Tongan kinship. First gender, then age are the key factors in determining personal rank. Sisters rank higher than their brothers, and this asymmetry is passed down through the generations so that descendants of a sister rank higher than those descended from her brother. Descendants of an elder sibling carry higher personal rank than descendants of a junior sibling. This rank-based skewing and the responsibilities and privileges that go with it mean that sisters and their children are considered *fahu* (above the law). Husbands are superior in rank to their wives and also to their wife's brothers. The correlative is also true, as when wives are subject to the authority of their husband's sisters.

Sālote's daughters treated Tupou with the same kind of easy affection that marks the *fa'ē tangata* relationship. This is because Tupou was the wife of their *fa'ē tangata* as well as their mother's contemporary. Their distress at Tupou's death was no less striking than the distress of Tupou's own sisters, the son and daughter Tupou and 'Ofa Lelei had fostered, and the children of Tupou's and 'Ofa Lelei's own siblings, for whom Tupou was a mother.

In practice, rank means that one should be ready to give without reservation to a father's sister and to take what one desires from a mother's brother.[5] These principles apply to all descendants. A high-ranking and well-respected Tongan woman described the privileges and burdens of the *fahu* system thus: "Mother's side pushes you up, and your father's side pushes you down." This redistribution of wealth according to rank applies to giving at funerals and weddings and also to the movement of the valuables of everyday life: food, textiles, children, money, tools, equipment, and so on.

While the sister–brother dyad underlies Tongan kinship, the model for ranking practices is the chiefly–commoner relationship in which the *'eiki*

---

[5]It should be noted that principles governing behavior sometimes are in conflict. In this instance, the principles of rank sometimes conflict with the principle of independence, and disputes occasionally occur, especially between children's mothers and husband's sisters.

(chief) is high in personal rank relative to other people. Sisters, for instance, are described as being chiefly to their brothers, and the elder sibling is chiefly to the younger. The opposite of being chiefly is *tu'a,* and the *tu'a* are supposed to be supportive and obedient to those who are chiefly. *Tu'a* also refers more broadly to the category of people normally called commoners in English. Kinship aside, the *'eiki–tu'a* relationship characterizes all interactions. Guests are treated as *'eiki* by their hosts; the doctor is *'eiki* to the patient; the deceased become *'eiki* to the living; the King is *'eiki* to the populace; and all Tongans including the King are *tu'a* to God. Rank requires displays of respect, submission, and obedience to those who are of higher rank, and it obligates returns of love and generosity to those who are of lower rank. Ultimately, the behavioral expectations of obedience and generosity embedded in the *'eiki–tu'a* relationship also characterize the historical interactions of government (*'eiki*) and the populace (*tu'a*).

In everyday practice, then, kinship behavior is relative to the situation and the persons present. It is also predominantly affective, expressed through demonstrations of sharing—*'ofa,* or love, generosity, and empathy—and recognition of duty and obligation. Both are demonstrated through the reciprocal flow of acts of kindness, surpluses of food, ceremonial wealth (pigs, textiles, kava, yams), and oratory.

The marking of real or fictive kinship through affection is typical of Polynesian societies. When someone is ill, *kāinga* express their support. When someone dies, their *kāinga* and those of their spouse offer labor, food, hymns, or textiles. Actions are motivated by affection and duty and by the desire to publicly demonstrate both. Funeral gifts are prescribed not only by kinship category (mother's or father's side), but also by personal relationship to the deceased and/or the bereaved. As Cowling says about funerals in Tonga:

> The contemporary elaborate funerary rites and the post-funerary rituals which are maintained by commoners in Tonga can be seen as ways of assuring the dead person that they are honoured and encouraging them to rest quietly and not harbour malevolence towards the living. Generosity in funeral prestations is multi-purpose—it re-affirms relationships, stressing the value of kinship ties, demonstrates respect both to living and dead kin, comforts and assists relatives and friends, and impresses others with the strength of feelings. [1990:83]

Sālotē's role in Tupou's funeral and funeral redistributions demonstrates the importance of emotional bonds in kinship relations. As a sister, Sālotē was superior in rank to both 'Ofa Lelei and Tupou. She therefore had no obligation to give at Tupou's funeral. However, as the person with whom 'Ofa Lelei had the strongest affective bond (despite the formal brother–sister respect), and because her children loved their maternal and now-widowed uncle, Sālotē became a conduit for many of the resources that went into Tupou's funeral.

For example, in order to include horse meat as part of the food and wealth items regularly distributed to guests at a funeral, Sālotē's son 'Apolo traded his lively young horse for an older horse that belonged to Sifa, his neighbor. This trade provides a clear example of the value of kinship connections and of how resources are mobilized through interpersonal connections. Sifa is brother to Vili Lahi, who is husband to 'Apolo's sister Lupe. Since Vili Lahi is the son of Sifa's paternal aunt, he is higher in rank than Sifa and can take anything he wants from Sifa. As brother to Vili Lahi's wife, 'Apolo is Vili Lahi's brother-in-law, and Vili Lahi is obligated to help 'Apolo. So even though 'Apolo gave away his strong young stallion, he did not lose the use of the horse; anytime he needed it, he could ask his brother-in-law to get it for him. But the example also demonstrates the significance of social relations that prioritize love and kindness. Sifa knew the rules of kinship as well as 'Apolo and anyone else. He could have refused to trade the horse, in which case 'Apolo would have probably killed the young stallion. But Sifa agreed to the trade out of empathy for the suffering caused by Tupou's death.

The network mobilized through Sālotē was evident in numerous ways. In addition to trading his horse, 'Apolo also gave pigs. His brother Sione arrived from Tongatapu with a very large sack of flour and another of sugar. Sālotē's daughters Malia and Lupe gave cotton sheets, bark cloth (tapa), food, and labor. Sālotē's son-in-law Vili Lahi contributed pigs, fish, and labor. Tupou's sisters' husbands and their agnates provided pigs, goats, flour, lard, sugar, jam, textile wealth items, labor, and hymns. The distant relatives who had pitied 'Ofa Lelei's and Tupou's childless status and had given them babies to foster also contributed. Throughout the day after Tupou's death, long trains of women from all over Kauvai brought carefully folded bark cloth and purchased fabrics draped over branches of blossoms.

Life on Kauvai is an intertwining of numerous lives in which people fulfill multiple roles. Sālotē, whose hands are old and arthritic, works mostly with the pandanus fiber called *kie* these days because, she says, *kie* is soft and flexible. "My hands are weak now," she told Young Leslie. She handles the slippery *kie* fibers with a confidence born of years of practice. Her textiles are so smooth that it is hard to distinguish the individual fibers. Tupou, too, was working on a textile made from *kie* fiber when she died.

According to Kauvai standards, Sālotē is a typical Tongan woman: a devoted sister and mother, an ardent Christian, and a traditionalist. She can call on a wide net of family and friends to help. She attends church regularly and donates handsomely. Her children are good, dutiful people, and some have well-paying jobs. She can offer access to important social and material resources when necessary. Her family eats well, and she has made many, many pandanus fiber textiles that are laid aside for redistribution at her own funeral. Through her life's practices, Sālotē has created, perpetuated, and maintained the social relations that she was taught to think of as the keys to living well, and in the process she has recreated Tongan culture itself. Although Sālotē's hands are now weak, her reach is still strong.

Tupou's funeral and mourning period lasted seven days. She was laid out for visitors on the first day and buried on the second. For the next five days, visitors stayed with 'Ofa Lelei, and groups of women visited Tupou's grave each evening to comfort her and keep her from becoming lonely. During this time, neighbors, kin, and visitors were fed every morning and night. Women in sooty cookhouses boiled *keke,* the Tongan version of the doughnut (no hole), in lard. In the morning and afternoon, younger girls and boys delivered plates of *keke* with jam and mugs of sweet tea to the mourners and the households of the village. Men slaughtered animals, dug huge pits, and kindled great fires for the earth ovens. Other men, holders of ceremonial titles and church elders, came to drink kava. The ritual of the kava circle helps glorify or elevate an occasion and consequently the person at the center of the event, in this instance, Tupou. One of the workers at the funeral was Lupe's husband, Vili Lahi. He provided taro and other root vegetables from his gardens, prepared pigs for the daily feast, and fished each night. He dressed in a short, ragged woven waist mat, the sign of mourning for someone not too close to the deceased.

This use of textiles is one example of how bodies exist as **signs** of social relations for Tongans. Appearance, silhouette, skin, hair, coloring, size, posture, adornment, and gestures are signs that indicate personal genealogy and the quality of contemporary networks. At a funeral, the pandanus waist mats called *ta'ovala* publicly signify one's relationship or relative rank to the deceased. Since the mats must be bound to the body to be worn, wearing one is seen as binding the person into a ritual status that is unique for each person, since each person is a unique focal point of kinship relations. The persons wearing the longest, oldest, and crudest mats are the mourners closest and lowest in rank to the deceased. They demonstrate their unraveled world with unbound, wildly ruffled hair and heart-wrenching wails. In the pre-Christian past, self-induced lacerations of the skin, finger amputations, and other mutilations were also part of their mourning. Officially, the *ta'ovala* signifies respect for the deceased. It also acts as a sort of protective shield by binding the wearer, whose social world is rent, into temporary wholeness and by making it unnecessary for the deceased person to reach out and touch the wearer because of anger at disrespect (a touch from a spirit is believed to cause a spirit illness).

On Kauvai, *ta'ovala* are worn by nuclear family members and *kāinga* for weeks or months. A widow wears one for a year, until the hair her husband's sister has shorn from her head has grown back, her ritual state of being unconnected is rectified, her social world is reconfigured, and her deceased spouse has settled in the afterworld. This process begins in the feasting, kava circle, ministerial eulogies, cloth wealth gifts, and redistributions of the funeral.

The living are not the only ones whose bodies are signs of social relations. The deceased is also ritually marked: Tupou was laid in state on special and prestigious textiles she herself had woven. The textile wealth demonstrated her capabilities as a woman and marked her as one entering the rank of ancestor. As the saying goes, *Oku 'eiki 'ae taha he'ene mate* (at death, one becomes a chief).

As occasions requiring the demonstration of genealogical relationships, deaths are essentially family affairs in which everyone's actions are prescribed by status and rank. On Kauvai, at least, funerals involve more than family. A funeral encapsulates social and emotional relations into an intensely personal, emotionally laden time and place. Just as death demands reconfirmation of social ties (for the sake of the children if for no other reason), it also creates the need to give or receive emotional support, in the process giving content to kinship roles.

Vili Lahi explained his own rationale for wearing the *ta'ovala* and providing pigs and other food for the funeral despite the fact that he and Tupou were affines rather than blood relatives. He did it for his wife, Lupe, who wanted to be able to comfort her favorite uncle, 'Ofa Lelei, and his wife, Tupou. Anthropologist Shulamit Decktor-Korn (1974) noted that funeral participation among Tongan commoners reflects a relationship to the bereaved. The ritual days of mourning, the mobilization of labor, the prolonged wearing of the *ta'ovala,* the funeral bier of ceremonial textiles, and the disbursements of textiles and foods to kin and neighbors all serve to mark the importance of social relationships that surpass genealogy and extend laterally to as many members of society as possible.

The people connected to Tupou and 'Ofa Lelei gave of their time and resources because they had sympathy and love for 'Ofa Lelei and because they loved Tupou and wanted her to be comforted in her transition from living person to spirit. They gave for honor, duty, and love as extended family and members of the community. Others gave because they knew that 'Ofa Lelei's grief was his sister Sālotē's, too. They included Sālotē's children, who gave because they felt love and empathy and wanted to help their mother and their favorite uncle get through the initial shock of Tupou's death. People from across the island offered hymns, food, labor, and textiles to spread the pain of Tupou's passing as far and as thinly as possible. To bear such a burden alone is too terrible, Malia told one of us; grief and emotional traumas have been known to precipitate illness and suicide. With Tupou's death, people felt the threat of becoming unraveled, the jeopardy presented by the loss of a community member who was a sister, wife, mother, partner in a weaving group, member of the parish, and neighbor. Now, people commented, there was one less person left to help *fua kavenga,* that is, to carry the burden of life on Kauvai.

Because a funeral requires the display, use, and gifting of textiles and foods, and because death is not always anticipated, each death serves to remind people of the importance of having sufficient supplies of women's and men's wealth on hand at all times and of the necessity of good social relations. Like other life crisis events, funerals in Tonga are occasions at which individual influence—the strong and extensive social relations based in years of fulfilling familial and community obligations—becomes the source of and the means for social power. Each funeral provides for and in some ways demands the rebuilding of interpersonal relationships and of the very ideas on which these relationships are built. Each funeral is a product of Tongan tradition and in turn reproduces Tongan culture. From a funeral we learn that people must make culture in both life and death.

QUESTION 1.5
When Things Stay the Same, Do They Also Change?

Contemporary Tongans are descendants of the first explorers of the Pacific and of the originators of Polynesian culture that spread as far as Hawaii, New Zealand, and Easter Island. Historically, Ha'apai people voyaged throughout Tonga, to Fiji and Samoa, and possibly as far as Anuta, and many of the old stories revolve around the theme of heroic voyages. During the 17th century, Tongans adopted catamaran-style ocean going canoes called *kalia* that were capable of carrying 200 or 300 people and that extended and improved their ability to travel and trade. Some scholars speculate that the *kalia,* with its smaller size and new style of sail and rigging, was adapted from boats used by traders in the western Pacific and southeast Asia. The traders never made it to Tonga, but their sailing technology did, replacing the huge voyaging vessels Tongans, Fijians, and others had used in the earlier migrations. Voyaging continued in the 18th century, with Tongans traveling as whalers or missionaries. According to Tongan scholar 'Epeli Hau'ofa (1994), himself the son of Tongan missionaries to Papua New Guinea, the notion of the Pacific as a sea of islands connected by the flow of people between them is both old and contemporary.

Today, there are a few people on Kauvai who have never traveled farther than Pangai or Tongatapu, and many who periodically travel to Tongatapu, but only a few who have been to the other islands in Ha'apai, or as far as Vava'u. While there is probably less intraregional travel than in the past, many women and most men have journeyed out of the country. In the 1970s, many took freighters to Auckland or Sidney by way of Fiji (the cheapest method) to visit relatives or work for a few months and return with cash and any other material wealth they could bring home.

At the beginning of the 21st century, no one uses *kalia* for travel, although the craft appears in the name of the Tongan Internet provider kalianet.to, giving access to a new ocean that young Tongans are surfing with great aplomb. People continue to move in a vast network that stretches from Tonga to Australia, New Zealand, Japan, and Hawaii in the Pacific; Alberta, Alaska, British Columbia, California, and Utah in North America; and as far as Norway in Europe. Not only people, but also material wealth flows through the links formed between Tonga and the Tongans living elsewhere. Bulky shipments of traditional woven pandanus or bark-cloth textiles and traditional foods are sent by container ship to overseas relatives. In return, they send money and bring foreign commodities when they visit.

It is this production and flow of people and wealth, which Tongans refer to as *'ofa,* love, that knits Kauvai people together wherever they are and allows villagers in Kauvai to retain ties with overseas kin. Although the island is not easy to get to, it is not isolated from the rest of the world. The basis for continuing global connections between Tonga and overseas communities is the same network of affection and obligation that creates and maintains life in Fusipala.

Labor emigration is more difficult now than it was in the 1970s because New Zealand, Australia, and, to a lesser extent, the United States and Canada experienced severe recessions, high unemployment, and burgeoning illegal alien problems in the 1990s and have reduced or withdrawn offers of migrant worker's visas. Most of the men who left and returned to Kauvai are currently between 40 and 60 years old, members of the generation after Sālotē's. Today young adults may go overseas for school, sports, musical competitions, or church-based gatherings or to serve as missionaries. Some return; many do not. Kauvai people of both Sālotē's and Losalina's generations have siblings, spouses, children, and grandchildren living temporarily or permanently and legally or illegally overseas. Tonga, Tongans, and Tongan culture are no longer restricted to the islands of the Kingdom; today the globe itself is a sea of islands. While things have changed, they have also stayed the same. One senior woman from Kauvai said: "Tongans can be Tongan anywhere." In fact, she claimed, the opportunities for amassing wealth that exist in Auckland mean that it is easier to be Tongan there than on Kauvai. What holds Tongans together is not so much geography or nationality as a common commitment to life and death framed by Tongan culture.

CONCLUSIONS

This chapter has used an extended example drawn from the Kingdom of Tonga to examine how anthropologists work to understand the diversity and the similarity of human ways of life through time and space. The five questions investigated in the chapter all approach the problem of understanding by asking how human cultures are best examined given the diversity and variety between and within them.

We started by asking what anthropologists do. The various branches of anthropology examine human cultures from antiquity to the present and across the globe. Cultural anthropology is based on participant observation, a method that is particularly well-suited to intensively studying small groups of people. Ethnography, the study of specific cultures using participant observation, allows anthropologists to learn about how people see themselves and think about their lives. Specific ethnographies form the basis of ethnology, the systematic comparison of different cultures to determine the ways cultures are similar and different.

For an anthropologist, culture is more than a particular ritual or art form. Such things are a small subset of the behaviors and beliefs that anthropologists identify as culture. We find culture everywhere. When doing ethnographic work, we focus closely on one place and one culture, while at the same time remembering that peoples and cultures are connected to the global system. Much of what anthropologists find interesting is everyday, unmarked, and in some ways unremarkable behavior and beliefs. Through participant observation, immersion in a place, and establishing cooperative human relationships with members of that locale, we learn by doing. This is much like learning a natal culture, but it differs in that the practice of anthropology always involves the comparison of cultures.

Cultures can be conceived of as systems for living in the world. Though we often talk about a culture as if it were a single thing, individuals learn, carry, and teach culture throughout their lives. Individual variation is to be expected within a culture. The practice of culture brings people into a dialogue that maintains some continuity as well. The answer to the question "Who has culture?" is that individuals do, but that the practice of culture is collective and interactive. It is problematic to talk about some individuals having more culture than others, but it is vital to recognize that there are differences in people's power, prestige, knowledge, and opinions. All of us make and remake culture in the course of everyday existence, but some people have more power to suggest change or demand continuity.

Nowhere is the continuity of social life more at risk than at death: a piece is suddenly missing from the social fabric, connections are sundered, and a void forms. The practice of culture must change when a death occurs, if only because the participants in the dialogue have changed. On Kauvai death is a particularly intense period of re-formation. In the face of death, through culturally prescribed funeral rites and practices, the people of Kauvai actively seek continuity even as they know that change is inevitable.

The use of traditional wealth items and traditional exchange practices in managing death speaks to the profound continuities of contemporary Tongan culture with the culture of the past. There have been vast changes as well. Tonga was once part of a regional system in the western Pacific; today it is part of a vast network of economic and political forces that encompasses the entire globe. Within this network, Tongans residing in Tonga actively use traditional methods of exchange and traditional relationships to extend their connections to communities in New Zealand, Australia, and beyond. In change there is continuity, and in continuity there is change. This is the conundrum but also the wonder of culture and the essence of humans dealing with each other within and between particular cultures as they make and remake the contexts of their lives.

REFERENCES AND RECOMMENDED READINGS

Borofsky, Robert
1987 Making History: Pukapukan and Anthropological Constructions of Knowledge. Cambridge: Cambridge University Press.
> A detailed and careful analysis of the uneven distribution of power and the role of age, gender, and individual ability in affecting processes of cultural change and cultural reproduction.

Counts, Dorothy A., and David R. Counts, eds.
1985 Aging and Its Transformations: Moving Toward Death in Pacific Societies. Lanham: University Press of America.
> An edited volume on aging, death, and dying in Oceania, with several excellent articles on the social and cultural implications of death in different cultures.

Cowling, Wendy E.
1990 Tongan Folk Belief and Healing. *In* Tongan Culture and History. Phyllis Herda, Jennifer Terrell, and Niel Gunson, eds. Canberra: Australian National University.
> Discusses the effect of illness and death on social relationships in Tonga.

Decktor-Korn, Shulamit R.
1974 Tongan Kin Groups: The Noble and Common View. Journal of the Polynesian Society 83:5–13.
> Decktor-Korn's work represents the first thorough examination of Tongan commoners' kinship practices, as distinct from those of the chiefly elites.

Gailey, Christine Ward
1987 Kinship to Kingship: Gender Hierarchy and State Formation in the Tongan Islands. Austin: University of Texas Press.
> A groundbreaking, though somewhat controversial, analysis of the transformation of kinship-based relationships in Tonga after European contact. Unlike many others, Gailey pays particular attention to gender issues and the effect of state formation on kinship and gender. In addition to the work's importance to Tongan studies, it is also a key Marxist feminist text.

Geertz, Clifford
1973 The Interpretation of Cultures. New York: Basic Books.
> In what is arguably one of the most important anthropological works of the last 30 years, Geertz lays out the principles of what is now called interpretive

anthropology. In particular, he addresses the philosophical context of the field-work process and the ways in which ethnographers come to knowledge about a particular society.

Hau'ofa, 'Epeli
1994 Our Sea of Islands. The Contemporary Pacific 6:147–161.
> Written by one of the leading Tongan intellectuals and scholars, this article reflects on the parallels between contemporary migration practices and the long history of extensive trade and contact between Oceanic peoples. The concept of the ocean as a conduit linking, rather than isolating, Pacific peoples has spread very rapidly into a number of other disciplines, including Pacific development studies, fine arts, and history.

Kaeppler, Adrienne
1978 Me'a Faka'eiki: Tongan Funerals in a Changing Society. *In* The Changing Pacific: Essays in Honour of H. E. Maude. Neil Gunson, ed. Melbourne: Oxford University Press.
> Presents detailed descriptions of ritual and social practices in Tonga from a chiefly perspective. Should be read alongside the work of Decktor-Korn.

Philips, Susan U.
1992 Dominant and Subordinate Gender Ideologies in Tongan Courtroom Discourse. *In* Cultural Performances. Mary Bucholts et al., eds. Berkeley: University of California Press.
> This paper examines the role of legal discourse in intracultural conflicts around appropriate gender and kinship relations in Tonga. It is an excellent demonstration of differential access to power and variation in the influence of different types of people within a culture.

Sahlins, Marshall
1988 Cosmologies of Capitalism: The Trans-Pacific Sector of "The World System." Proceedings of the British Academy 74:1–51.

1993 Goodbye to the Tristes Tropes: Ethnography in the Context of Modern World History. Journal of Modern History 65(1):1–25.

1999 What Is Anthropological Enlightenment? Some Lessons of the Twentieth Century. Annual Review of Anthropology 28:i–xxiii.
> These three papers deal with the role of local cultures in the contemporary global system. Sahlins is careful to take the autonomy of local cultures seriously, while at the same time demonstrating system-level linkages. All the papers take up the issue of the how culture change and cultural continuity can be approached at the same time.

Wolf, Eric
1982 Europe and the People Without History. Berkeley: University of California Press.
> Arguably one of the most important anthropological works of the last 30 years, this work integrates local- and global-level analyses in the examination of European colonialism and local reactions to the spread of European political and economic power.

Young Leslie, Heather
1998 The Anthropologist, the Mother and the Cross-Cultured Child: Lessons in the Relativity of Cultural Relativity. *In* Fieldwork and Families: Constructing New Models for Ethnographic Research. Juliana Flinn, Leslie Marshall, and Jocelyn Armstrong, eds. Honolulu: University of Hawaii Press.
> A subtle reflection on the experience of fieldwork and potential conflicts between professional and interpersonal commitments. In particular, the paper examines the implications of cultural relativism for ethnographic practice.

CHAPTER 2

INDIGENOUS KNOWLEDGE AS A BASIS FOR LIVING IN LOCAL ENVIRONMENTS

LESLIE MAIN JOHNSON

PROBLEM 2 *How do people create an understanding of their environment that provides them with the information they need to make a living in an effective and more-or-less sustainable manner?*

INTRODUCTION
Trail of Stories—A Gitksan View of Land

People who live in a wide variety of environments have developed various ways of making their livings. In many places and at different times in human history, these ways of living have seemed to be sustainable—that is, their activities have not seriously degraded the integrity of the environment and have not caused progressive environmental deterioration. How do people create an understanding of their environment that gives them information that allows them to make a living in an effective and sustainable manner?

In the past, some people might have answered this question by invoking instinct or divine guidance as explanations. More recently, scholars have recognized the role of local or indigenous knowledge in guiding sustainable ways of life. Societies in which people live close to the land have a rich knowledge of the land that is integrated with the social system and contains linkages to **cosmology** and moral concepts. This chapter explores the ways the indigenous knowledge of the Gitksan of northwestern British Columbia, Canada, helps shape their relationship to their land and teaches them how to approach and utilize its resources.

The Gitksan homeland is located along the Skeena River and its tributaries in the inner Coast Ranges of British Columbia. These rugged mountains were carved into steep slopes flanking broadened valleys by the glaciers of the Pleistocene era, which also mantled the lower slopes with sediments in the process of deglaciation. The rocky ridges of the Coast mountains have been sculpted by alpine glaciers that have been retreating since the end of the Little Ice Age late in the 19th century. The land is mantled with dense coniferous forests. Five species of salmon and steelhead trout ascend the rivers to spawn, providing a rich and reliable food supply that the Gitksan have depended on for thousands of years. In addition to the salmon of the Skeena's waters, Gitksan have hunted large and small game, including mountain goats, picked the abundant blueberries and huckleberries, and harvested other plant foods to provide a diverse and sustainable way of life.

The Gitksan—the people of the Skeena River—have lived along the river for a long time. Archaeological sites have documented the presence of peo-

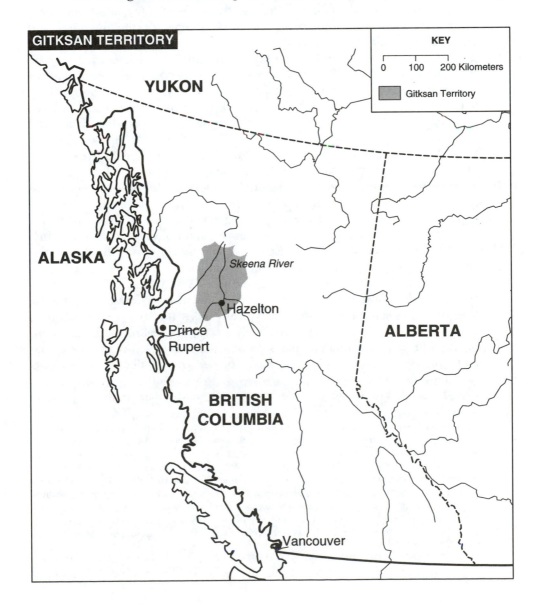

ple with substantially similar cultures about 5000 years ago. Gitksan *adaawak*, or oral histories, detail the migrations and relationships of the various groups of Gitksan who today live in six villages along the central Skeena and its tributaries.[1] Some *adaawak* describe a landscape that differs from today's and that may be what the landscape looked like during deglaciation 9000 or 10,000 years ago. If it is, this suggests that the ancestors of the Gitksan may have been present in the Skeena region for a very long time.

At the time of European contact in the late 18th century, the Gitksan lived in substantial plank houses in large villages. They had an elaborate social structure and well-developed traditions of art and oral literature. The villages were composed of *Wilp*, or Houses. The term refers primarily to the people and not physical structures, although the people who belonged to each House literally lived together in an actual dwelling. The Houses were **corporate** groups. In other words, each existed through time, acted as a legal entity, and owned economically productive territories that included fishing sites, hunting areas, and berry-gathering areas. These Houses were subdivisions of four *Pdeek*, larger groupings often referred to by local people as clans. The Houses, then, can be thought of as localized divisions of clans. Clans are **exogamous**, which means that members of one of group must marry someone from another group. Thus, a Fireweed cannot marry another Fireweed, but must instead marry a Wolf, Frog, or Eagle. At the time of contact, a House was both a corporate group and an actual dwelling within the *Wilp's* village. At present, each House continues to be a corporate group, but the individual members or families live in modern houses rather than sharing a large multifamily dwelling.

The Gitksan were and are a hierarchical society. In the past there were chiefs, commoners, and slaves, who were war captives and the children of captives. At present, there are chiefs and commoners. A male chief is a *Sim'oogit*, and a female chief is a *Sigidimnak*. Each house has a series of chief names, which are really titles. These names are passed to new holders as the previous holders die. Inheritance and House membership is **matrilineal**, which means that it passes in the female line. A son inherits his affiliation or title from his mother, often from one of her brothers. This is especially true of the chiefly class. A person typically goes through a succession of names during a lifetime, beginning with a baby name and perhaps culminating with a highly ranked chief's name. The highest chief's name designates the House as a whole. Under him or her are a series of lesser chiefs and their heirs.

The chief is responsible for the welfare of the members of the House and

---

[1]Gitksan lacks sounds such as *th, ch,* and *r,* but it has a number of *k* and *g* sounds. A *k* or *g* sound that is made at the back of the throat is written as an underlined *k* or *g*. Gitksan also has several fricative sounds we lack in English. The sound spelled with an *x* is closest to the *ch* in the Scottish word *loch* or in the German word *ach*. When this is pronounced further back in the throat, it is somewhat like a French *r,* and it is written with an underlined *x*. Another unfamiliar sound is the *hl* combination, which combines characteristics of *h* and *l*. Apostrophes indicate what linguists call glottalized sounds when they come before a letter, and ejective sounds when they come after it. A glottal stop is the way the *tt* in *bottle* sounds if you are from Brooklyn. Vowels are simple: a single vowel represents a short sound, and a double vowel represents a longer sound.

the lands owned by the House. The chief must also maintain the honor of his or her name by giving *yuukx, or* potlatches, which are feasts at which titles are transferred, names given, debts paid, and ancestors honored. To give a feast, the hosting House and chief amass a considerable amount of goods and food. The chief distributes the goods and food to the invited guests, especially to the other chiefs, whose presence and speeches witness and validate the business transacted.

Each House also owns crests that represent birds, animals, and plants that are iconic representations of events in the history of the House, as well as histories and songs that only the owner may perform without permission. The histories are told and songs performed at public events like feasts. Disputes about ownership of territory are addressed in the feast hall, and the knowledge of oral histories and songs is used to demonstrate ownership. When the Gitksan recently brought the governments of the Province of British Columbia and Canada to court over the issue of aboriginal title (*Delgamuukw v. the Queen*), the chiefs performed their songs and recited their *adaawak* to show their ownership of their traditional territories.

Stories are deeply involved in the Gitksan relationship to land. Histories take place in specific places and are the foundation of an ongoing connection between groups of people and tracts of land. They are regarded as true traditions. Such stories are complex and multilayered; they contain moral reflections and knowledge of human relationships and describe strategies of seasonal subsistence or of defense against enemies. Others are more like fables or folk tales that have a moral point or help explain the nature of the world today. These are called *antimahlaasxw* in Gitxsanimx and are not necessarily regarded as literally true.

As this indicates, the Gitksan landscape is a storied landscape. The names of places serve to locate events in histories. Other names may suggest resources present at the named place or its physical appearance. Besides simply designating a place, therefore, names are a kind of mnemonic peg for a variety of kinds of information. And names are also owned, except those of the most regionally significant features like the river itself, Ksan.

Although the resources of the Gitksan lands and waters are abundant, it is necessary to know when, where, and how to harvest them. This knowledge is gained from experience and imparted in histories and personal reminiscences. In the past, children were often told histories and stories of the House land by a loved *Ts'iits* (grandmother) or *Ye'e* (grandfather) at bedtime. These stories might be repeated many times, with varied emphasis and added information when circumstance indicated the need. Children would be also taken on berry-picking or hunting trips where they would be shown how to travel, what to pick, and how to hunt. The stories reinforced the lessons learned on the land and gained added meaning through experience.

Various kinds of information may be included in stories or shared while on the land. In order to gather or hunt successfully, it is necessary to know the names of plants and animals, how to recognize them, what their habits are, where to find them, what their uses are, and how to gather or hunt them. Specifically, how and where to set nets or traps and when and where various kinds of fish can be obtained are fundamental to traditional Gitksan subsistence. People also must learn how to stay safe while traveling; there are different risks while traveling in the mountains and traveling on the rivers.

It is necessary to be an active listener in order to decipher the messages contained in stories. The stories are oblique, indirect commentaries on events and possibilities, and it is not easy to tease out the lessons and value judgments and to understand their relevance to present circumstances or concerns. What is heard must always be considered in terms of the context in which it was said: by whom, to whom, where, and in response to what actions or situations. Sometimes it may take considerable reflection to understand the meaning of something an older relative has said, or why a particular story was chosen at a particular time. People are also expected to pay attention to their own behavior and that of others and to observe the consequences or results of different courses of action.

QUESTIONS

2.1. When Gitksan people look at the environment, what do they see?

2.2. How is indigenous knowledge of land and living things organized?

2.3. What is the nature of nature?

2.4. Do people without agriculture practice land management or conservation?

2.5. What are the implications of indigenous knowledge for sustainable development?

QUESTION 2.1
When Gitksan People Look at the Environment, What Do They See?

Although languages differ, people everywhere recognize and name the plants, animals, and other features of their environment. People also share their observations about these plants, animals, and environments. Making a living would be impossible without this kind of knowledge. The body of knowledge that people in a society or culture have about the land is known as **indigenous knowledge**,[2] and it is a working knowledge designed for use. Indigenous knowledge about the local environment reflects observable realities and local ways of life, and it reflects the history and language of the people.

Ethnobiologists investigate this knowledge, recording indigenous names and uses for plants and animals and information about people's understandings of habitat and the interrelationships of living things. Ethnobiological research is essentially a comparative enterprise. It allows us to examine the similarities and differences between scientific knowledge and the knowledge of local peoples. Research in other cultures reveals that, for the most part, trained scientists and local experts recognize the same basic kinds of animals and plants.[3] Thus, the tree a trained forester calls a lodgepole pine is *sginist*

[2]*Indigenous knowledge* is also known as *local knowledge* and *traditional knowledge*.
[3]Excluding very tiny living things, like microorganisms, which are likely to be overlooked or more broadly conceived by local people than are larger, more conspicuous plants and animals.

to a Gitksan. A mountain goat is *matx,* and neither a zoologist nor a Gitksan would have any doubt about whether a specific animal is a mountain goat. However, their understandings of the mountain goat's habitat and habits might not be identical. Specific knowledge of hunting strategies in named hunting grounds might be even less similar. And the conception of mountain goats as moral agents and social beings who interact with the humans who hunt them is most unlikely to be part of the zoologist's conception of a mountain goat.

Scientific knowledge is a type of expert knowledge based on empirical, objective, and observable features of the natural world. It is explicitly materialist in its perspective, and it is also reductionist, meaning that it limits the scope of phenomena to be investigated and seeks the simplest causal explanation. Scientific methodology thus attempts to limit complexity in the attempt to tease out causal relationships. Its methodology and requirements for verifying hypotheses are difficult to apply where there are many variables and where the variables may be acting synergistically, that is, where factors interact to produce an effect that would not have been predicted by knowledge of the variables acting in isolation.

Indigenous knowledge, in contrast, is rich and complex. It is embedded in a cultural and social context and born of the experience of individuals and cultures through prolonged spans of time. Indigenous knowledge often transcends the merely material to encompass moral and spiritual values. For example, Gitksan people see mountain goats as sentient beings. Their understanding of mountain goats dates back to the time of Temlaham, an ancestral village near the present location of the town of Hazelton along the Skeena River, which was possibly occupied around 3500 years ago. The goats punished human beings at the time of Temlaham for their moral transgression of taking too much meat, wasting it, and failing to treat the remains of the goats with respect by dancing around in their still wet skins (see the discussions in Harris 1974 and Wright 1962).

According to the Gitksan view, people are successful at hunting mountain goats because the goats decide to give themselves to humans so that people can eat. If a hunter is unworthy because of past failure to respect goats, he will not be lucky when hunting goats; the goats will withhold themselves. A hunter, of course, also must know a great deal about the habits of goats and about the terrain where he wants to hunt them. What time of year will the goats be there? How can the hunter safely reach the goat-hunting grounds?[4] What are the traditional access routes and nearby camping areas? What strategies can be employed in the hunting ground of his House? Without high-powered rifles, goat hunting is not a solitary activity; it takes a group of people acting together to successfully hunt goats. That group is a social group, likely made up of the hunter's relatives.

Indigenous knowledge is not necessarily a unified, logical system or theory. People may shift between perspectives or offer alternative explanations for the same events without believing such explanations to be in opposition or to be mutually exclusive. People think deeply about their own nature and the nature of their world, and they see no contradiction in mixing deep philosophy and moral instruction with highly pragmatic information about fea-

---

[4]Mountain goats have few enemies because they are able to negotiate precipitous cliffs and eat the sparse vegetation found on rock slopes and alpine ridges.

tures of the local environment or details of uses of plant and animal species. Traditional narratives thus often provide information on many levels simultaneously and show linkages between them.

Gitksan people resist placing knowledge in separate categories, but instead believe that true knowledge encompasses relationships and connections. They also believe that all things have purpose and worth and should be accorded respect. Plants that have no purpose for human food are seen as providing food for other animals, for example.

Popular models of science are typified by laboratory investigations in the physical sciences, but there are other scientific traditions that are similar to indigenous knowledge. In its search for connections and its holistic perspective, scientific ecology has some elements in common with Gitksan knowledge. But scientific ecology emphasizes the general and the quantifiable, in contrast to the Gitksan preference for particular knowledge of land and a qualitative social sense of relationship. In the Gitksan world, people are but one of the sentient beings on the earth and must respect the right of others to exist. Animals, plants, mountains, and rivers are believed to have awareness, provide information, and have rights. Western science remains firmly materialist and wholly empirical in its philosophy. Gitksan indigenous knowledge has different underlying paradigms and accepts different types of evidence to validate or verify observations and conclusions.

QUESTION 2.2
How Is Indigenous Knowledge of Land and Living Things Organized?

Indigenous knowledge is complex and multifaceted. It is not a hierarchical alignment of rigidly bounded boxes connected with straight lines and arrows, but rather is more like a net or a circle. It is not reductionist; instead it reflects on relationships and considers linkages on many different levels. It is not designed for general hypothesis testing. It is concerned on the one hand with practical issues, and on the other with the social and moral. And it reflects the universal human desire to understand why things are the way they are. Names of plants, for example, may show the uses of plants. Alder is called *am luuxw*, which means good for neckring, and its bark was used for dyeing cedar bark neckrings red. Neckrings (*luuxw*) were valued ceremonial regalia in the secret societies to which high-ranking Gitksan men and women belonged until the early years of the 20th century. Other names, or perhaps nicknames, link little-used plants with larger, more obvious, or more useful ones. The round-leafed rein orchid is dubbed *hishamooktwt*, or pretend wild rhubarb, and the small licorice fern *hisdemxtwt* resembles edible fern root.

Gitksan name and recognize all of the tree species in their environment and many of the large woody shrubs. Smaller, less significant plants may be lumped into broader classes, and many types are not given individual names. The potential usefulness of plants seems to be important to Gitksan people. For example, they tend to call all wildflowers for which they have no particular use *majagalee*, flower. This tendency to not distinguish and name plants that are not used is not unique to the Gitksan; it is found in the ethnobotany of a number of North American indigenous cultures.

FIGURE 2.1. Gitksan Annual Cycle

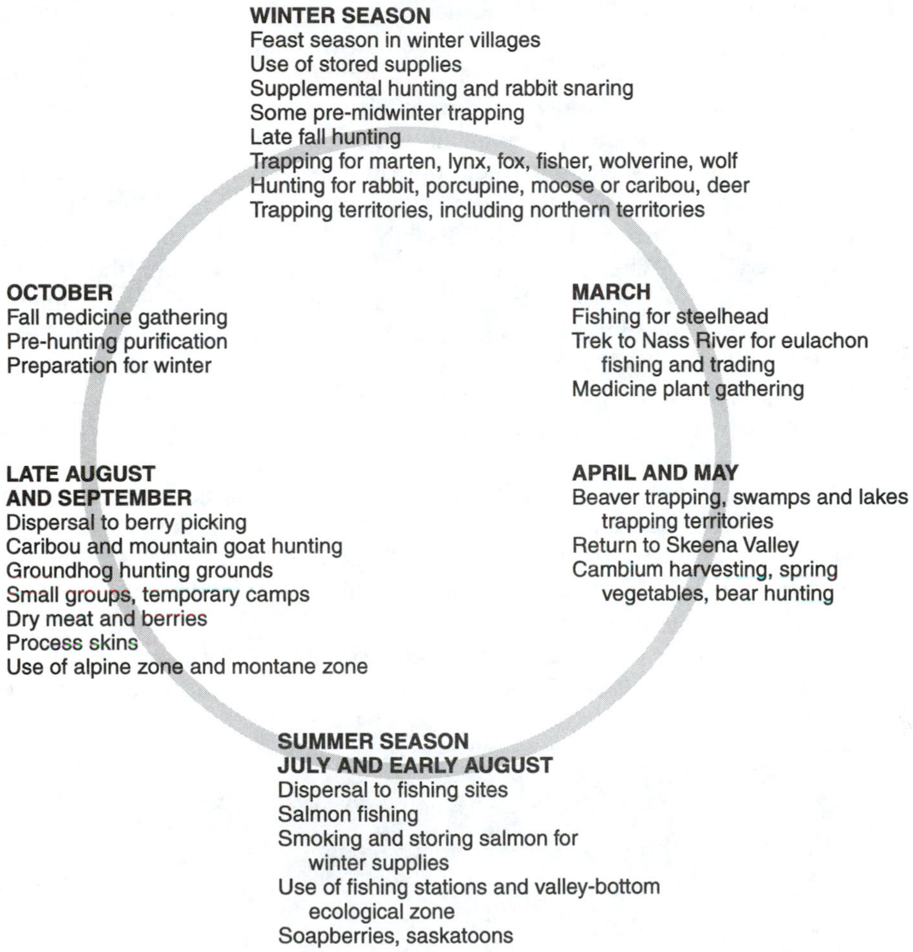

WINTER SEASON
Feast season in winter villages
Use of stored supplies
Supplemental hunting and rabbit snaring
Some pre-midwinter trapping
Late fall hunting
Trapping for marten, lynx, fox, fisher, wolverine, wolf
Hunting for rabbit, porcupine, moose or caribou, deer
Trapping territories, including northern territories

OCTOBER
Fall medicine gathering
Pre-hunting purification
Preparation for winter

MARCH
Fishing for steelhead
Trek to Nass River for eulachon
    fishing and trading
Medicine plant gathering

**LATE AUGUST
AND SEPTEMBER**
Dispersal to berry picking
Caribou and mountain goat hunting
Groundhog hunting grounds
Small groups, temporary camps
Dry meat and berries
Process skins
Use of alpine zone and montane zone

APRIL AND MAY
Beaver trapping, swamps and lakes
    trapping territories
Return to Skeena Valley
Cambium harvesting, spring
    vegetables, bear hunting

**SUMMER SEASON
JULY AND EARLY AUGUST**
Dispersal to fishing sites
Salmon fishing
Smoking and storing salmon for
    winter supplies
Use of fishing stations and valley-bottom
    ecological zone
Soapberries, saskatoons

Note: Annual cycle of movement and subsistence activities of the Gitksan (19th to early 20th centuries); coastal cannery work and fishing omitted.

According to a contemporary Gitksan language expert, *sgan,* the word usually translated as *plant,* carries the connotation of bearing fruit and is connected to the annual cycle of growth, flowering, and bearing fruit. Seasons vary sharply throughout the year in the Gitksan homeland, and many types of knowledge are conceptually related to the annual cycle. Figure 2.1 shows the annual cycle of activities of the Gitksan during the 19th and early 20th centuries. Modern Gitksan live year-round in villages, or in cities outside of their traditional territory. The seasonal activities of fishing for the various salmon species, harvesting the different species of berries, hunting in the fall, and collecting medicines continue to be widely practiced, though people spend less time on the land or at fish camps than formerly. Today, people obtain their eulachon grease by trade or purchase, and roads have made the trade much easier. Most feasts continue to be held in the fall and winter. Only trapping has significantly declined in importance because ecological change and changes in the fur market have made it less productive economically and ecologically.

People who live on the land need to understand annual cycles of snow-fall, snowmelt, avalanche risk, high water, low water, and freeze-up, and of the dormancy, rising sap, flowering, and maturing of fruit. They need to be aware of when bears den up and when they awaken, when moose rut and when they calve, when and where the mountain goats drop their kids, when and where the hoary marmots go into their burrows for hibernation and when they become accessible, and what times of year to hunt beavers. Most important to the Gitksan is when the different species of salmon arrive and where and how to fish for them. When the robins arrive in late March or April, they incessant-ly sing *"Gii gyooks milit, milit,"* which means the steelhead are swimming.

Steelhead spend the winter in lakes and tributary streams. Just as the snow melts and before high water, they begin to head back to the sea. They are the first fresh fish of the new year. Spring salmon (elsewhere known as chinook or king salmon) arrive a little later, slightly ahead of or at the same time as spring high water. In the past, the first salmon run of the season was a sig-nificant event and was marked with a ceremony. Although there are no longer formal village-wide First Salmon celebrations, there is a great deal of excite-ment, and smaller feasts may be held. While the water remains high and full of floating debris, the fish catch will be small; but once the water drops, fish-ing may be quite productive.

In July and early August, there are two runs of sockeye. Gitksan prefer the rich, deep red flesh of the sockeye and use it for most of their smoked

Art Loring of the Gitwangak Lax Skiik (Eagle Clan) and a helper giving out fish at a First Salmon ceremony, July 7, 1994.

(Photograph by Leslie Main Johnson.)

and canned fish. The chum or dog salmon is primarily valued for its roe, and pink salmon is generally not sought. In the fall, coho salmon can be caught. When people worked in the canneries on the coast during the summer season in the earlier years of the 20th century, the fall coho still remained to be caught when they returned to their homes.

Summer is a busy time on the land for Gitksan, as for many northern peoples. During the summer, they put up the summer's abundance for use throughout the year. Even today, when people may have paying jobs and are able to purchase food at the supermarket, many people fish, pick berries, and spend time canning, smoking, or freezing their traditional foods. Many men go hunting in the fall. Today, moose is probably the most important large game animal; but in the past, moose were unknown, and mountain goats, mountain caribou, and bears were the most significant large game animals. There were elders still living in the 1990s who remembered the first time they had ever seen moose.

There is a definite seasonal cycle for plants. Medicinal plants whose bark is used, especially devil's club, can be gathered in the fall after the leaves drop or in late winter. Spiny woodfern rhizomes, a carbohydrate food, were also gathered when the leaves withered, which is when the rhizome is most nourishing. As the sap starts to rise, the saps or cambium of various trees can be harvested for a short period. This is not liquid sap like that tapped from maple trees, but rather a tender, juicy tissue between the wood and the bark of rapidly growing trees. If too old, it becomes woody and indigestible.

In the past, before the introduction of sugar and flour, much western hemlock[5] cambium was collected, pit cooked, and processed into large dried cakes for trade and storage. Forest areas in the upper Skeena show the evidence of this extensive harvest; clear-cut logging has not yet removed these stands of hemlock, allowing us to see the level of harvesting that formerly took place. Knowledge of how to tell which tree would yield large amounts of sweet sap was important, but now has largely been lost. Spring greens like young shoots of cow parsnip or wild rhubarb and the berry-like leaves of a particular stonecrop were also gathered at about the same time.

Wild strawberries and soapberries become available about the end of June. Later in the summer, saskatoons (called serviceberries or shadberries in the United States), blueberries, and huckleberries ripen. Highly productive patches of large sweet black huckleberries form under the right ecological conditions. For the Gitksan, these fruit were *simm'aay,* the real berry, and the condition of good berry patches was carefully monitored. People used to camp at a berry patch for a week or two, and whole groups, perhaps most of a village, would pick and process the fruit into large dried fruit rolls that could be carried back to the village and kept for winter. The resource was valuable enough that people constructed trails in the mountains to ease access, as they did for mountain goat–hunting areas. Today, people are willing to drive long distances in their trucks to productive berry patches where they pick large quantities and bring them home to can or freeze.

In the fall, high-bush cranberries ripen, and medicine-gathering time comes again.

---

[5]A forest tree with edible inner bark, not the poison hemlock of Socrates.

QUESTION 2.3
What Is the Nature of Nature?

Most people in Western society agree that nature is the lands and waters, and the birds, animals, and plants that live on them. Nature is seen as being unaltered by people, a sort of latter-day Garden of Eden uninhabited by Adam and Eve. Nature exists outside of human disturbance. Wilderness—land untouched by human activities, perhaps never visited by people—is the most natural kind of nature. Nature does not include cityscapes or lands cultivated, farmed, and managed by people.

Conceptions of the nature of nature differ among societies. In the past, Europeans viewed nature as uncivilized wilderness. When people of European ancestry came to North America, they perceived most of the landscape as being natural, meaning that it was as God, rather than human beings, had arranged it. Since most of the land was not cultivated, they thought that the inhabitants had not altered the lands or vegetation. They also tended to view the inhabitants as rude or savage, similar to wild animals that wandered in the forest. Such viewpoints persisted into the late 19th and early 20th centuries and influenced such early proponents of wilderness preservation in the United States as John Muir, founder of the Sierra Club. The notion of nature as pristine and divinely inspired also imbued the writings of Thoreau, Emerson, and other transcendentalists. This view is very unlike the understanding that indigenous people of North America had and have of their homelands.

The Gitksan concept of nature leaves no room for a land beyond the influence of people. The entire landscape is their homeland, and people move over it and constantly interact with human, nonhuman, and nonbiological entities. The face of the land bears witness to the history of this continued interaction; it is a constant reminder of human action and of the past. Stories preserve memories of the events of the past and their consequences.

Contemporary economic and other factors, such as compulsory school attendance, have resulted in the concentration of people in the villages for much of the year. As a result, much of Gitksan territory appears unoccupied and wild to Euro-Canadians, who see it as suitable for preservation in wilderness parks or ecological reserves or as ripe for logging and mining. The advertising slogan "Super, Natural British Columbia" projects an image of a magnificent wilderness with towering mountains, swift rivers, grizzly bears, and salmon runs. Missing are the indigenous peoples.

But this is an occupied and humanized landscape. There are many trails, small campsites, and blazed trees. An archeologist would notice numerous regular pits in sandy places near the major rivers. Here and there, petroglyphs, abstract or animal form designs, are pecked into the surface of large rocks at flood level along the rivers. An ecologist might expect to find the hemlock, cedar, and spruce forests normal in this climatic zone when there has been no clearing or burning. Instead, birch, poplar, and pine forests are found in the broad valleys near Hazelton, the result of sustained human activity. The ecologist might encounter a tree with a catface, a triangular scar where the bark was removed. Careful examination would reveal that many of the trees show ax marks at the base of the scar. Someone cut cedar bark here in the past.

Talking to Gitksan, tales emerge. A seemingly anonymous rounded hump of land at the base of a soaring mountain chain is recalled as the place where an ancestor walked and sang a mourning song. The ridge has a name and is part of an *adaawak*, a history. Across the creek is the mountain on which the raft of the ancestral brothers landed after the Flood. Before that they lived on the other side of the mountains. Along the ridge is a place where a now-melted glacier used to be. The place is named *glacier*, a paradox that contains a lesson; according to the late Sim'oogit Tsii Wa, father of the present head of the House of Dinimget: If you walk over a permanent snowfield in the spring, your footsteps can keep melting out, and the glacier may disappear.

The trail reveals places of danger. A name referring to faces carved in standing poles contains the encapsulated knowledge of how to tell when the avalanche danger is low enough to cross old slide areas along the route. A place named for the snaring of caribou recalls the earlier importance of this resource and the tragedy of an argument between two brothers over the catch that ended in a murder. The repercussions of that ancient event affect Gitksan today.

Across the river, amid the mosaic of coniferous and deciduous forest stands, are traditional berry patches that were managed by periodic burning to maintain their productivity. The last burning in the 1920s is recalled. The patches are linked by trails known to the members of the House of Dinimget. Old berry drying racks and bentwood boxes stand against a tree, ready to be used. The trail continues up the ridge above the berry patches, where it passes through areas good for gathering certain medicines, up to a place where goats could be hunted. Sim'oogit Dinimget recalls the location of goat-hunting trails, areas of the best habitat, the strategies used for goat hunting in these areas, and the place people used to make a large camp for hunting and for processing goat meat and hides. A nearby area is good for *gwiikw*, groundhog, hunting. Groundhogs are fat animals with several pounds of succulent rich meat and light warm hides, and a good colony can yield a substantial harvest of meat and skins. They used to serve as a medium of payment in the feast hall. Now people use money, but they still call certain contributions to the potlatch "groundhog."

Where is the wilderness in this landscape, where the histories of the people are written in place names, where the slender threads of trails tie together places where people traveled, hunted, gathered, faced dangers, and remembered the past? The land also contains places of power that continue to affect people. For the Gitksan, there can be no sharp division between places of people and places of nature. People belong on the land. It was given to them by the Creator, who also taught them how to live there. Although some places are more frequently occupied by people than others, more altered by villages and trails, frequently used camps and berry patches, all of the lands and waters are named and owned by the different House groups.[6] These social realities constrain who may hunt where, whether one can pursue an animal over the boundary into the next House territory, and what fishing sites one can use. The Gitksan see a rich tapestry that is at once both natural and cultural. People are one of many kinds of beings in the created world, and have both rights and obligations with respect to the other beings who share the world with them.

[6]In this discussion I am ignoring the recent presence and activities of non-Gitksan who live within the Gitksan homeland.

QUESTION 2.4
Do People Without Agriculture
Practice Land Management or Conservation?

The stereotype of hunters and gatherers who make their living without herding animals or cultivating crops is that they wander across the landscape without altering the lands. This vision has echoes of Eden and draws on the 17th century notion of the noble savage. Although this term is not politically correct, the idea persists in popular culture. Some contemporary rhetoric uncritically characterizes Native Americans and Canadian First Nations in romanticized terms as natural ecologists and conservationists who always live in harmony with nature. Another stereotype is that they are technologically too simple to wipe out fish or game species, especially because their population is relatively small. A further argument implies that many indigenous peoples are not natural conservationists, but instead overexploit and degrade their environments, leading to population crashes. Places like Easter Island are cited in support of this model (although Easter Islanders did grow crops and have domestic animals). None of these scenarios helps us understand what nonherding and noncultivating peoples actually do—or did until their homelands were invaded by people who possessed more elaborate material technologies and did farm or herd.

What can Gitksan people teach us about the conservation and land management of people who are not cultivators or herdsmen? A story helps provide an answer. The people of Temlaham took more goats than they needed, wasted meat, and failed to show proper respect to the hides of the animals they had slaughtered. The goats disguised themselves as high-born human chiefs and appealed to the vanity of the townspeople, inviting them to a feast. Most of the hunters, chiefs, and high-born people of the town followed these strangers, were feasted by them, and were cast off a precipice. One wise man who had resisted the mistreatment of the goats was saved and returned to the town to teach the people who were left the proper way to treat animals (see Harris 1974). Clearly, there is a conservation message here: killing more than you need and wasting the flesh of animals that have given themselves to you is wrong and will lead to retribution by the offended animals. Similar stories warn of the dangers of failing to respect the salmon.

Gitksan do not separate waste from other forms of offending animals or fish; these nonhuman beings must be respected in all ways. The prohibition of playing around with fresh animal or fish remains appears in a number of histories, and transgression is followed by swift punishment. For the Gitksan, as for many other First Nations and Native Americans, death is not instantaneous, but rather a process. It may take several days for the spirits of animals, especially powerful animals, to depart totally from their material remains. Before this process is complete, the animal's spirit is particularly sensitive to how its body is treated. Hence the dire consequences of playing around with fresh animal skins.

The discussion so far has dealt with Gitksan beliefs and practices that have the effect of limiting overhunting and overfishing. In the Gitksan view, other beliefs and practices also affect the abundance of animals and fish and the ease with which people can catch them. Since the animals are regarded as sentient actors, human actions affect the likelihood that animals will offer themselves. This leads to a number of practices designed to avoid offending and alienating animals, generally conceived of as respect. Proper disposal of inedible remains of animals or fish is an aspect of respect. All unusable animal remains should be burned rather than being left around where people might step on them or where they might be eaten by dogs. All waste from fish should be returned to the water.

Other aspects of respect include restrictions on who may eat fresh meat or fish. The Gitksan, like many indigenous people, believe that women have a particular power during their menstrual periods that may offend the spirits of freshly killed animals. If a menstruating woman eats meat killed by a hunter, that hunter's luck with that type of animal will be lost. Menarche (when girls have their first menstrual periods and are just becoming women) is seen as a particularly potent time in a female's life. A newly menstruating girl's power is thought to require careful handling to avoid harm to the girl and to others. In the past, such girls were secluded for a long period, were trained in skills they would need as women, and were taught discipline. It was thought that if a girl this age looked up at a mountain, the mountain would become barren and would support neither game nor berries. Girls at menarche were forbidden to eat fresh meat, fish, or fruit because the spirit essence contained in these things would encounter their as-yet uncontrolled female energy and would be offended, resulting in poor harvests of meat, fish, and berries. Conservative Gitksan still do not want the meat they hunt to be eaten by menstruating women or teenage girls. Who eats store-bought meat is not an issue for Gitksan because such meat is not obtained through a close and reciprocal relationship with the animal.

In common with many peoples, Gitksan regard luck as a consequence of a person's actions or of the actions of others. It is not random, and it can be enhanced or lost by what a person does. Ritual purification, which can involve fasting and bathing in cold pure water, using the sweat hut, or washing with the powerful devil's club plant (an extremely spiny and aromatic sprawling shrub), helps ensure luck. These practices are called *si satxw*. Certain plants can cleanse contaminating influences, erase bad luck, and return a hunter's normal luck.

Gitksan people believe in the reincarnation of people, who may be reborn as children, and of animals and fish, who may come back to give themselves to people as food. If fish or animal wastes are treated disrespectfully, the fish or animal will not come back. People believe that hunting animals and catching fish when they offer themselves shows appreciation and motivates the animals and fish to remain where they are to be appreciated and used. Failure to fish a salmon run might cause those fish to disappear.

This perspective clearly differs from the premises of wildlife management based on population biology. However, it appears that the salmon stocks of the Skeena River remained abundant under the indigenous system and have been depleted only since the introduction of modern industrial means of catching fish for sale in world markets and the biologically unsustainable problem of mixed stock fisheries that eliminate smaller stocks that happen to run at the same time as large stocks.

There is also evidence that Gitksan management of land and plant resources actively enhances populations of desired species. Gitksan people do not usually phrase their activities in these terms, but rather would describe their activities as "taking care of the land." Berries are important carbohydrate foods for the Gitksan. Before the practice was outlawed, the Gitksan used carefully conducted burning to rejuvenate black huckleberry and low-bush blueberry patches that were overgrown or had lost productivity. The timing of burning was determined by the setting of the berry patch. Low-bush blueberry patches at low elevations could be burned off in the springtime just after snowmelt. By the time people could get to the black huckleberry patches on the mountain slopes, the weather was too warm and dry for safe burning, so fall burning was practiced in these areas. A few years after burning, the rejuvenated bushes were producing large amounts of succulent berries, and the Gitksan could harvest much fruit. However, Euro-Canadian settlers, especially forestry officials, did not understand that fire was being used as a management tool. They suppressed burning on public lands and threatened people with fines and jail sentences for "incendiarism," with the result that the traditional berry patches have become overgrown and are no longer productive. People now must pick in natural burns that happen to occur where huckleberries are growing, or in clear-cuts made in the forests. These sites are less stable over time because they are not managed to maintain the productivity and yield of the berries. The Gitksan and the British Columbia Forest Service are considering attempting to restore the indigenous fire regime and to develop huckleberries as a nontimber forest product.

Pruning is a less-extensive form of berry management that stimulates fruit production. The Gitksan use pruning to manage the species *Shepherdia canadensis,* which they called soapberry because of the frothing properties of the fruit. It produces abundant small berries that are used to make *yal is,* or Indian ice cream. Green soapberries are very tedious to pick, so people often lop productive branches to make picking more efficient. This form of pruning also stimulates the plant to produce vigorous new branches that fruit heavily. Similar forms of pruning have been documented by Kat Anderson for California Indians (Blackburn and Anderson 1993) and by Deur and Turner (N.d.) for other indigenous peoples of British Columbia.

Another form of management no longer practiced by Gitksan is the care of root patches. Although the Gitksan did not grow crops, they tended patches of productive vegetables whose underground portions could be harvested. Harvesting large roots and replanting small bulbs or root pieces act to till and aerate the soil, replant the patch, and thin remaining plants so they will grow more quickly. The Gitksan rely on the spiny woodfern root *ax.* Because the perennial rhizomes take years to become large enough to harvest and may never do so in less-productive sites, conservation and management of fern root patches are important.[7] Burning would not enhance these roots because they grow entirely in the surface organic layers of the soil. Burning, tillage, and replanting were probably all used to maintain productive patches of the other root crop formerly gathered by Gitksan, the bulblets of the rice-root lily. Productive patches of these still persist in floodplain habitats that have been subjected to repeated light burning, but they are no longer tended.

[7]The significance of the root is underscored by the fact a prestigious crest called *Wii Ax,* or giant woodfern root, is owned by a Gitksan House. Its image is found on the ceremonial blanket of the chief and on a totem pole standing in the modern village of Kispiox.

Like other nonagricultural peoples of the world, the Gitksan are astute observers of natural processes and have their own understandings of cycles of abundance of plants and animals. The evidence is clear that conservation concepts, some of which are similar to those of biologists, inform their attitudes about the animals and plants of their environment and have functioned to maintain or enhance the animals and plants they have depended on for their livelihood. These hunter-gatherers practiced active management of some species of plants and of habitats by means of landscape burning, pruning, and tillage.

QUESTION 2.5
What Are the Implications of Indigenous Knowledge for Sustainable Development?

As we have seen, indigenous knowledge often informs practices that promote sustainable, nondestructive relations with the environment. The track records of many indigenous peoples are impressive in comparison with contemporary industrial societies. What is the potential for transferring the knowledge that underpins traditional ways of life to other contexts?

Indigenous knowledge occurs in local contexts, both social and environmental, and is adapted to those contexts. Because local Gitksan knowledge and international scientific knowledge are based on different premises, changing some aspects of the cultural context may have unpredictable local results in terms of what we understand as conservation. That is, when people's settlement patterns change and local communities are linked to the global economy and global markets, things change. According to Eugene Anderson (1996) in his exploration of some of the changes that can occur, people may retain their ideologies and continue practices that are sustainable, or global pressures and the influx of outsiders may make it impossible for local populations to live in a sustainable manner. Local ideologies and practices may not be sufficient to withstand internal and external pressures, and resource depletion and environmental degradation follow.

The Gitksan and other indigenous peoples have different perspectives on the causes of fluctuations of animal and plant species than do wildlife biologists and ecologists. The concept of a limited, fixed, and finite stock or population of animals is incompatible with many cultures' notions of the nature of animals or plants. A people that believes that the animal's will is involved in whether it is present and that the hunter's or fisher's appropriate treatment or need pleases or displeases the target species has different prescriptions about what to do when observable or harvestable species' numbers are low. Thus, when fish conservation measures involve closing fisheries, this conflicts with the Gitksan belief that without use the species will disappear from the local area. Catch-and-release sports fishing looks like extremely dangerous and disrespectful fish torture and rejection of their flesh as food. Similar issues arise when parks are created to preserve natural landscapes. The notions of "look but don't touch" and "leave only footsteps, take only pictures" do not make sense in the context of a humanized, social homeland with a network of **reciprocity**—of giving and accepting gifts—in which mutual respect links people to other species.

Conservationists often assume that their interests and desires are compatible with those of indigenous peoples, but the two groups disagree about the fundamental relationship of people with landscapes and of the nature of nature. Their goals may also therefore be irreconcilable. Based on his experiences in New Guinea, Australia, and Oceania, Peter Dwyer (1994) comments that the romantic notion of the innately conservationist nature of traditional cultures is based on faulty premises and that the notion of global conservationists is substantially different from that of local indigenous peoples. Nevertheless, awareness of indigenous knowledge can provide alternative constructions of reality that may well help industrialized global society move toward greater sustainability and may also provide locally specific knowledge essential to avoiding degradation of specific environments or depletion of particular species.

Alternatives to the Unchallenged Notion of the Separation of Human and Natural Realms

One of the most important aspects of Gitksan understanding of the nature of the world and the place of people in it lies in the notion that everything is related to everything else—that there is no separation of the human and natural realms. This perspective is shared with many other indigenous peoples. It means both that people belong in and have a place in nature, and that people have obligations to other biological species and to the lands and waters. Such a perspective prohibits unrestricted self-centered exploitation of other species and despoliation of the environment and gives humans a stake in the health and richness of the environment.

Anderson (1996) sees such holistic, emotional, and spiritual conceptions of the environment as crucial to long-term healthy relationships of humans to the global ecosystem. As he points out, knowledge without caring cannot create the motivation to act. If we regard ourselves as separate from nature, we may not be motivated to do anything about environmental problems because the solutions may require us to compromise our short-term self-interest. As long as we are successful at turning any problems that arise from our activities into someone else's problem while we reap the benefits, we will continue to do what benefits us at the moment. The fact that we are degrading the system that sustains us in the long term is outside of this narrow cost-benefit analysis. The phrase "the tragedy of the commons" is used to describe the situation that arises when most people do what is in their own short-term interest, while resources that belong to no one in particular but are essential to our common well-being are eventually destroyed. The Gitksan view of their environment as a homeland is a useful model to emulate.

Another way indigenous knowledge can enhance sustainable relations with the local and global environments is by providing detailed indigenous knowledge of practices that have worked in particular contexts in the past. This local fine-tuning is necessary for locally optimal dwelling in environments. While such knowledge cannot and must not be transferred piecemeal to other social and biophysical contexts, it can provide guidance in the implementation of workable local solutions in similar contexts.

Who Owns Indigenous Knowledge?

If indigenous knowledge holds important answers for human survival, conservation of biodiversity, and the sustainability of many ecosystems, its preservation becomes urgent. But it is far from clear what preservation of indigenous knowledge may mean. Does it mean bits of knowledge encoded in databases or recorded in scholarly books? Or does it mean the continued viability of knowledge in its local context?

Knowledge means not only power, but also money. It can be conceived of as property. This concept is quite familiar to Gitksan, whose stories, songs, and artistic designs are considered owned property. But modern legal and economic institutions do not include group property, such as the cultural heritage of the entire Gitksan nation or of a Gitksan House, in their definition of intellectual property. Nor do they deal well with traditional property. Intellectual property law offers protection for a limited period of time, and it is designed to protect the monetary interests of known contemporary inventors of new expressions of ideas, artistic productions, and technology. There is no known inventor for indigenous knowledge; nor is it new; nor does it have a defined and verifiable point of origin. And some forms of knowledge are seen by their possessors as being intrinsically incompatible with monetary valuation.

The global indigenous movement is pressing for new definitions of indigenous group or cultural intellectual property. For instance, some parts of the United Nations Convention on Biological Diversity, which is an instrument of international law ratified in 1993, recognize indigenous stewardship of biodiversity and of unique ecological and biological knowledge. As yet, these aspects of the convention have not been applied in Canada, and the United States is not a signatory. The issue continues to gain urgency with increased interest in developing novel pharmaceuticals from indigenous medicinal plants, especially those of the tropics, and in better managing wilderness areas within indigenous homelands.

CONCLUSIONS

The Gitksan have a deep and intimate knowledge of their homeland and of the plants and animals that share it with them. This includes knowledge of features of the landscape and of the habits, behavior, usefulness, and usability of many kinds of animals and plants. This knowledge is similar to Western scientific knowledge in that the same basic kinds of mammals, birds, fish, trees, and shrubs are recognized. In most cases, there is a one-to-one correspondence between scientific species or genera of plants and animals and the kinds recognized by the Gitksan. Smaller, less conspicuous forms are more finely divided by scientific botany and zoology than by the Gitksan. Gitksan lump less conspicuous or salient forms in larger groupings or residual classes, such as flower, bird, or mushroom. Knowledge of the land and of living things also includes a moral aspect, requiring recognition of the rights of other entities and the necessity of respecting them.

Indigenous knowledge forms more of a net than a set of discrete boxes linked by lines or arrows. Knowledge is complex, and biological and landscape knowledge has linkages to many different realms of Gitksan life. Animals are at the same time potential food and crest symbols. Animals are also actors in traditional narratives that teach how to hunt and use their bodies as food or medicine. The narratives also supply moral lessons about punishing such transgressions as disrespect and waste. Plants are similarly respected as sentient beings that can be offended or offer help. People must pray to medicinal plants and leave offerings to enlist their help in healing. An attitude of thankfulness and avoidance of waste are apparent in attitudes toward fish, game animals, birds, food, and medicine plants.

Knowledge is organized, among other ways, by reference to the cycle of the seasons. Land is the scene of histories that link specific social groupings, especially Houses, to particular tracts of land. These linkages are publicly displayed as iconic crests on totem poles and on the ceremonial blankets worn by chiefs in the feast hall.

The Gitksan see their land as a homeland. There is reverent appreciation of the beauty of the land and its gifts, but the land is a social space that records history and requires active engagement and reciprocity with other beings for the mutual good of all. There is no land separate from the realm of humans, no hands-off places where people make pilgrimages to look at wilderness, but not to live in it. Gitksan land was given to the Gitksan by the Creator to be lived in, walked over, used, respected, sung about, and talked about. The different territories of the chiefs cover the lands and waters of the Gitksan homeland. Each person and each group of people belong in certain places.

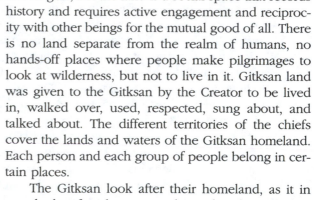

The Gitksan look after their homeland, as it in turn looks after them, providing what they need to live. Gitksan clearly have conservation ideology and do—or did—practice land management. Respect is key to Gitksan conceptions of how to look after the land. Respect for other living beings requires accepting the gift of their substance when offered, sharing it when possible, and not wasting anything. Unusable remains of animals and fish must be properly disposed of as a token of respect and appropriate behavior. This means burning animal wastes and returning fish remains to the water. Animals and fish will come back to those who treat them well. If people refuse the gift offered by failing to hunt or fish when given the opportunity, the animals or fish may abandon places where they are not used and, it is assumed, not needed, resulting in depletion. Use of fire to enhance berry patch productivity was an important form of management. Other practices

Totem pole of Sigidimnak̲ Antk'ulilbixsxw, Kispiox. The One-Horned Mountain Goat crest is at the top.
(Photograph by Leslie Main Johnson.)

include pruning berry bushes, burning to create openings and forage, selective harvesting, replanting, and tillage. Some of these practices are interpretable in terms of scientific paradigms of conservation, and some are not.

Indigenous or local knowledge is most applicable in local contexts, where its specific and fine-tuned nature is in balance both with the environment and particular ways of life. Because indigenous knowledge is holistic and linked to many aspects of social and cultural life, it is difficult to export piecemeal into other social, cultural, and environmental contexts. A proscription on waste, for example, may not have conservation effects when coupled with rapid transportation and an insatiable global market out of balance with the local environment. Similarly, the world conservation movement may admire the traditional adaptations of indigenous people, but may find that worldviews and fundamental assumptions about preservation of landscape and the nature of nature mean that conservationists and preservationists do not seek the same courses of action regarding protected areas and their management as do indigenous peoples whose homeland includes a proposed preserve. Such conflicts over declaration of wilderness parks have occurred in the Gitksan homeland, where notions of wilderness preservation and recreation areas are as incompatible with the Gitksan relationship to their House territories as large-scale mining or forestry development would be.

However, there are lessons to be learned from indigenous peoples, including the Gitksan. A cornerstone of sustainable ways of life is a real commitment to, and reciprocity with, other living beings on the land. Considering relations to the land and its living things to be intrinsically social serves as a corrective to turning virtually everything into commodities. Some Gitksan are not comfortable with objectifying living beings as resources, for example. Adopting their concept could give an emotional and even spiritual commitment to rights and well-being of other living beings. As Anderson (1996) points out, this kind of attitudinal change is probably necessary for sustainable ways of life to be possible in a globalized and industrialized world. The fine-tuned awareness and nuanced response to the environment characteristic of small-scale traditional societies is probably also necessary for appropriately sensitive relationships with the environment and a helpful countercurrent to globalization.

REFERENCES AND RECOMMENDED READINGS

Anderson, E. N.
1996 Ecologies of the Heart: Emotion, Belief, and the Environment. New York: Oxford University Press.
> A geographically wide-ranging examination of the role of emotional commitment and spiritual involvement in promoting sustainable ecological practices in different human societies, with some speculation on how we might move toward sustainable ways of living on a global scale.

Blackburn, Thomas, and Kat Anderson
1993 Before the Wilderness: Environmental Management by Native Californians. Menlo Park, CA: Ballena Press.
> A series of case studies examines ecological relationships and environmental management activities of indigenous Californians.

Deur, Douglas, and Nancy J. Turner
N.d. "Keeping It Living": Indigenous Plant Management on the Northwest Coast.
Unpublished MS, Department of Geography and Anthropology, Louisiana State
University.
> A series of cases presenting indigenous ecological philosophy and land man-
> agement from British Columbia.

Dwyer, Peter
1994 Modern Conservation and Indigenous Peoples: In Search of Wisdom. Pacific
Conservation Biology 1:91–97.
> A critical look at differences in concepts of conservation between the interna-
> tional nature conservation movement and indigenous peoples.

GisdaWa and Delgamuukw
1989 The Spirit in the Land: The Opening Statement of the Gitksan and
Wet'suwet'en Hereditary Chiefs in the Supreme Court of British Columbia.
Gabriola, BC: Reflections.
> This statement by two modern chiefs captures the essence of the Gitksan
> and Wet'suwet'en relationship to land. It is the opening statement of the
> land-claims court case in the British Columbia Supreme Court.

Goulet, Jean-Guy
1997 Ways of Knowing: Experience, Knowledge and Power Among the Dene Tha.
Vancouver: University of British Columbia Press.
> A powerful exploration of an indigenous knowledge system and differences
> from Euro-North American epistemology.

Harris, Kenneth B., with Frances M. P. Robinson
1974 Visitors Who Never Left: The Origin of the People of Damelahamid.
Vancouver: University of British Columbia Press.
> This unique book contains translated *adaawak* or oral histories of a Fireweed
> House, *Wilps Haxbagwootxw,* from the Gitksan village of Gitsegukla. It was
> translated by the current chief Sim'oogit Haxbagwootxw, known in English as
> Ken Harris.

Johnson, Leslie Main
2000 A Place That's Good: Gitksan Landscape Perception and Ethnoecology. Human
Ecology 28(2):301–325.
> This article explores ethnoecology of the Gitksan, combining an analysis of
> Gitksan landscape terminology with the perspectives revealed by traditional
> narratives and as articulated by modern Gitksan.

Johnson Gottesfeld, Leslie M.
1994 Conservation, Territory and Traditional Beliefs: An Analysis of Gitksan and
Wet'suwet'en Subsistence, Northwest British Columbia, Canada. Human Ecology
22(4):443–465.
> A review of Gitksan and Wet'suwet'en beliefs and practices that affect conser-
> vation or management of significant plant, fish, and animal resources. This arti-
> cle, paired with Dwyer's, helps provide a specific local case to illustrate differ-
> ences between global conservation and local conservation practice.

Nabhan, Gary
1982 The Desert Smells Like Rain: A Naturalist in Papago Indian Country. San
Francisco: North Point Press.
> A powerful evocation of the interconnected and intimately detailed nature of
> indigenous knowledge set in the desert of southern Arizona and adjacent
> Mexico.

Nelson, Richard K.

1983 Make Prayers to the Raven: A Koyukon View of the Boreal Forest. Chicago: University of Chicago Press.

> Dick Nelson's classic study of environmental knowledge of a Boreal Forest Athapaskan people from western Alaska; wonderfully readable and detailed, it explores linkages of the practical and spiritual.

People of Ksan

1980 Gathering What the Great Nature Provided. Vancouver: Douglas & McIntyre.

> This locally produced book is a readable compilation of Gitksan indigenous knowledge about gathering and preparing food plants. Facilitated by the late Polly Sargeant, it records the carefully reviewed words of a number of Gitksan elders, many of whom have since passed away.

Additional References Cited

Hallam, Sylvia J.

1989 Plant Usage and Management in Southwest Australian Aboriginal Societies. *In* Foraging and Farming: The Evolution of Plant Exploitation. D. R. Harris and G. C. Hillman, eds. Pp. 136–151. London: Unwin Hyman.

Wright, Walter, with Will Robinson

1962 Men of Medeek. Kitimat, BC: Northern Sentinel Press.

CHAPTER 3

THE SOCIAL AND CULTURAL CONSTRUCTION OF REALITY

MARCIA CALKOWSKI

PROBLEM 3 *Why do people believe different things, and why are they so certain that their view of the world is correct and other views are wrong?*

INTRODUCTION
Mountain Gods, Lake Goddesses, and Adjustable Destinies

Why are we here? Why do bad things happen to good people? What is the meaning of life? These questions, at least one of which sounds like the title of a best-selling book, have confronted people across the globe and over time. Today North Americans face a bewildering array of conflicting answers to them. Society is changing rapidly, and so are ideas about what life is about. Some of people's responses to perceptions of rapid change include the rise of Islamic and Christian fundamentalism and Western fascination with the Dalai Lama and Tibetan Buddhism.

Anthropologists have long been interested in how people raised in different cultures answer these questions. Initially, they were more concerned with the derivation of beliefs about reality than they were with how meaning is constructed. Thus, early anthropologists such as Sir Edward Burnett Tylor, the "father of ethnology," tried to explain the origin of religious beliefs. Tylor argued that religion was essentially the product of human reason; he theorized that early humans accounted for the difference between the living and the dead by developing the notion of a soul and concluding that the soul led a separate existence from the body after death. Tylor held that this distinction eventually led to belief in ancestor spirits and spirits that inhabited animals, plants, and aspects of nature, and, ultimately, to beliefs in deities.

The French sociologist Émile Durkheim (1969) was also concerned with the question of the origin of religion. He hypothesized that the worship of

50

totems (animals, plants, or natural phenomena) was probably one of the earliest forms of religious practice. Since totems were held to be clan ancestors by the people who worshiped them, Durkheim argued that a totem symbolized the clan itself, and he concluded that the worship of symbols of social groups such as clans was actually the worship of society. Durkheim proposed that the social order served as the model for people's beliefs about the cosmic order. For example, societies organized around membership in kinship groups defined by descent from a common ancestor would be likely to practice ancestor worship.

Although anthropologists today do not pursue the question of the origin of religion, those who take a more meaning-centered approach to the question of how people construct reality draw on Tylor's argument that many beliefs about supernatural phenomena such as witchcraft and magic are the product of human reasoning. Equally, these anthropologists follow Durkheim in emphasizing the importance of symbolic representation and in suspecting that a people's notions about the supernatural realm are likely to be modeled after aspects of their social order.

The construction of meaning is a fundamental human activity. When we encounter something with which we are not familiar, we try to make sense of it—that is, give it meaning—by associating or contrasting it with something that is familiar. For example, when Tibetans first saw an airplane flying over and landing in Tibet, some reportedly identified it as an *iron bird*. The label iron bird makes sense of an airplane both in terms of its apparent material composition and in terms of its movement through the sky and to the ground. Here, meaning is constructed by the use of metaphor, what the anthropologist Claude Lévi-Strauss (1966) considers to be a universal logical principle. A metaphor establishes that one thing can be associated with another thing because the two share some similarity.

Another universal way to construct meaning, according to Lévi-Strauss, is to associate things because they are juxtaposed in time or space. For example, many people from Borneo hold that orangutans evolved from human beings who left society to live alone in the jungle and became wild animals. Lévi-Strauss's assertion that people are continually engaged in order-creating activity is a powerful tool for understanding the construction of meaning. Lévi-Strauss insisted that people everywhere rely on the same intellectual tools or logical principles to create order and that people from different cultural and physical environments do not construct the same reality because they do not order or make sense of the same environment.

Other anthropologists, however, suggest that we need to uncover the social and cultural dimensions of order if we are to gain a better understanding of meaning. In other words, they argue that **enculturation**—the ways in which people acquire culture—encourages us to perceive the world in certain ways and not others. Enculturation is accomplished through communication. For example, children in Western cultures are likely to be told by adults that belching is unacceptable at the dinner table and that keeping their mouths closed while chewing is essential dining etiquette. This is how we learn to assign specific meanings to types of behavior. We learn to identify some actions as moral (which means that they are socially approved) and to recognize certain modes of social organization (such as polygyny, a marriage of a man to two or more women) as inappropriate. In other words, the social and cultural dimensions of order include the assigning of value, the association of emotions with designated objects and events, and even, as Victor Turner (1967) has shown, the use of ritual symbols to effect social action. A ritual symbol, according to Turner, is a unique form of representation that brings together many different meanings at once, which enables the symbol both to arouse desires and feelings and to reflect social values.

According to Clifford Geertz (1973), religion plays a pivotal role in the construction of reality because it brings a culture's **ethos** into a meaningful relationship with that culture's **worldview**. By *ethos* Geertz means a culture's values or its moral and aesthetic aspects. *Worldview* means how people believe things actually are. What religion does, says Geertz, is to make worldview emotionally acceptable by presenting it as the absolute truth, the only way that things can be, and to make ethos intellectually acceptable by presenting it as the natural outcome of the way things are. For example, the Balinese may express joy on the occasion of a family member's cremation not because a relative has died, but because the cremation is believed to release the soul to be born again. From Geertz' definition of religion, we can see how people can come to invest strong emotions in the ways they understand the world, and why they may find alternative views of the world, which essentially challenge the order in which they have so much invested, unacceptable.

We must also consider that a people's worldview and ethos may change. Changes occur when ethos and worldview no longer reinforce each other. Many factors may be responsible. For example, social **norms** and **values** may alter dramatically if a society is destroyed through conquest—in other words, if the familiar patterns with which people organized themselves are replaced with alien patterns. Social norms and values may also be transformed by drastic shifts in the natural environment that make it impossible for people to pursue traditional subsistence strategies, or if people cannot accommodate or make sense of new phenomena. Attention to these possibilities and to the roles played by society and culture in the construction of reality distinguish anthropological approaches to the study of religion and belief systems from those of religious scholars.

This chapter addresses the social and cultural construction of reality in two ethnographic contexts: traditional Tibetan society before Tibet and Tibetan cultural areas were annexed to the People's Republic of China in 1951, and the society of refugee Tibetans in India. For Tibetans, both sacred and secular constructions of reality have always been embedded in landscape, in their sense of geography.

The Tibetan Landscape

Tibet features one of the world's most dramatic environments. Bounded to the north, west, and south by most of the world's highest mountain ranges, Tibet has been often referred to as "the roof of the world." The average elevation of the Tibetan plateau is 13,000 feet. The Himalayan range that forms Tibet's southern border with Nepal soars as high as 29,000 feet. Strong winds that sweep over the Tibetan plains cause the temperature to shift from intensely hot to below freezing within a few hours. Dense near-tropical forests are found in southeastern Tibetan regions.

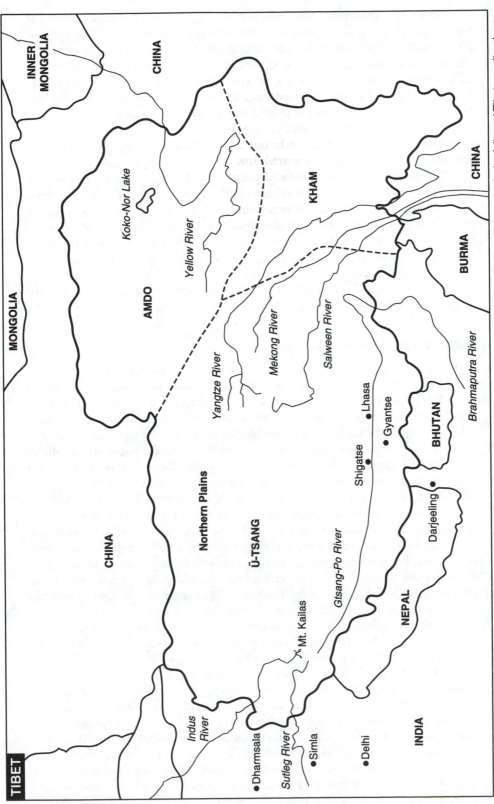

Note: This map incorporates ethnographic Tibet, the region inhabited by people who have historically spoken Tibetan dialects and who followed Tibetan cultural practices. Ethnographic Tibet corresponds to what historians refer to as Ancient Tibet. Most of Central Tibet (U Tsang) comprises what is currently called the Tibetan Autonomous Region in the Peoples Republic of China. Amdo has been incorporated as the Chinese province of Gansu. Kham has disappeared from current maps. Much of it was incorporated into the Chinese province of Sichuan; some is now included in Yunnan.

Tibet's mountains are the source of most of Asia's greatest rivers: the Brahmaputra, the Indus, the Sutlej, the Mekong, the Salween, the Yangtse, and, from the northeastern Tibetan cultural region of Amdo, the Yellow River. The valleys of these great rivers provide the most fertile land for agriculture. Tibet's vast arid plains supported the pastoral nomads' herds of yak, sheep, goats, and horses as well as a rich array of wild animals. Both farmers and nomads commonly engaged in trade, some traveling as far as Nepal, northwestern India, or even Calcutta, bringing wool, salt, borax, skins, and animals to exchange for sugar, cloth, iron, and copper from India and brick-tea, silk, and porcelain from China.

Traditional Tibet was sparsely populated. It has been estimated that approximately 6 million Tibetans inhabited an area of about 500,000 square miles. Nomads, traders, and pilgrims expected to travel great distances and to traverse high mountain passes, risking avalanches, bandits, and other perils. Tibetans understand that they are not the sole occupants of the land. They recognize particular geographic locations as home to a variety of sacred or spiritual beings, having what Bruce Morrison (personal communication) calls a "sacred ecology." The Tibetan construction of reality links human beings, spiritual beings, and ideas of place with time and history.

Historical and Social Context

Until the mid-ninth century A.D., Tibet was a great Central Asian empire ruled by a monarchy. Prior to the seventh century, Tibetans worshiped mountain gods (identifying some as clan ancestors who had originally descended from the sky) and lake goddesses, and propitiated a host of supernatural beings who inhabited various aspects of the landscape and could be either helpful or harmful. Some of these beings, such as the *lu,* who are believed to inhabit bodies of water, and the *sa-dag,* the lords of the soil, were associated with agricultural fertility. The early Tibetan monarchs followed a religion called Bon. Some scholars believe that it was the elite religion of the Tibetan court, in contrast to shamanism, which they consider to have been the popular religion of the countryside. Anthropologists have long understood a **shaman** to be a religious practitioner who is able to communicate with deities and spiritual beings by entering a trance state. Recent scholarship argues that shamans were intimately linked with the political structure of early Central Asian kingdoms. Critical to understanding Tibetan religion is that Bon and Buddhism competed to be the religion of the Tibetan elites.

Buddhism had most likely already entered Tibet from India prior to the seventh century, but Tibetan chronicles stress the roles of the Nepalese wife and Chinese wife of the great Tibetan king Songsten Gompo (605–649 A.D.) in establishing Buddhism as Tibet's state religion. Some 100 year later, the great Indian Tantric Master Padmasambhava (the lotus-born one) traveled throughout Tibet and, according to legend, subdued the Tibetan deities and demons he came across, transforming most of them into protectors of Buddhism. Padmasambhava slew the Tibetan demons that resisted this transformation and directed their souls toward a better rebirth. Other supernatural beings, such as the *lu* and *sa-dag,* were swayed to a more Buddhist orientation and made susceptible to being manipulated by Buddhist rituals. In this way, Tibetans accounted for the fact that the cults of Tibet's mountain gods and the ancient strategies for dealing with demons and difficult spirits were incorporated into the Buddhism of Tibet.

Songsten Gompo's successors continued to be patrons of Buddhism until the ascent to the throne in 838 of Lang Darma. A follower of the Bon religion, Lang Darma was known as the Ox King in part because his name, *Lang,* means ox, and also because the Buddhists he persecuted claimed that he had two horns growing from his head. In 842 Lang Darma was slain by a Buddhist monk. Since rival noble families could not agree on his successor, Lang Darma's death marked the end of the monarchy. To this day, many Tibetans continue to greet strangers by sticking out their tongues to show that since they do not have black tongues like oxen, they are not like Lang Darma and, hence, are Buddhists.

With the loss of its monarchy, Tibet ceased to be a great empire. As the Tibetan state broke up into a number of unrelated princedoms ruled by various noble families, Buddhism continued to flourish, and monasteries were established. Tibetan scholars traveled to India to study under Buddhist masters, and several Indian Buddhist masters traveled to Tibet. While some Tibetan Buddhists followed the spiritual lineage of Padmasambhava and came to be known as Nyingmapa, others became the devotees of spiritual masters who were developing new schools of Tibetan Buddhism. By the 15th century, there were four major sects of Tibetan Buddhism: the Nyingmapa, Sakyapa, Kargyupa, and Gelugpa. Different noble families patronized different sects, and great rivalries arose between some of them.

During the campaigns of the great Mongolian Genghis Khan to conquer Tibet's neighbors in 1207, the rulers of the principalities that made up Tibet and the abbots of Buddhist monasteries offered their submission to Genghis Khan's overlordship. Kublai Khan, grandson of Genghis, made the Sakya monk Phagpa vice-regent over Tibet and charged him with the temporal duties of revising Tibet's administrative and revenue system. This assignment set a precedent for the type of authority that would later be vested in the Dalai Lamas as spiritual and temporal rulers of Tibet.

Tibetan Buddhists believe that great spiritual teachers choose to be reborn in order to help others attain enlightenment. It was established practice in the Kargyu sect and the Sakya sect to recognize the rebirth or reincarnation of a great spiritual teacher. The Gelugpa sect of Tibetan Buddhism, which originated with the teachings of Tsong Khapa (1357–1419), followed this practice by seeking the reincarnations of leading Gelugpa masters. In 1578, one such reincarnation, Sonam Gyatso, visited Mongolia and converted an important Mongol prince, Altan Khan, to Buddhism. Altan Khan bestowed the title Dalai Lama on Sonam Gyatso. *Dalai* is a Mongolian term for ocean, and the meaning conveyed by the title was ocean of wisdom. In addition, Sonam Gyatso was perceived as the incarnation of the compassionate aspect of Buddha. Although he was the first to receive the title, Sonam Gyatso was known as the Third Dalai Lama, or the third incarnation of the Dalai Lama. Considering Sonam Gyatso to be the third Dalai Lama augments his status by providing him with an enhanced spiritual legacy.

In 1642, an intense rivalry between the Fifth Dalai Lama and the head of the Kargyu sect, who was affiliated with the king of the Tibetan region known as Tsang, was resolved when the Mongol prince Gusri Khan killed the king of Tsang, displaced the head of the Kargyu sect, and made the Fifth Dalai Lama ruler of Tibet. When Gusri Khan died in 1655, the Fifth Dalai Lama ruled alone and transformed Tibet into a theocratic state.

China gained a toehold in Tibet around 1720 when the Tibetans sought Chinese assistance in their dispute with the Mongolians over the identity of the 7th Dalai Lama. In 1912, the 13th Dalai Lama reestablished Tibet's complete independence from China. After the victory of Mao's People's Liberation Army in China in 1949, the Chinese assumed that Tibet was a rightful part of their empire. The People's Liberation Army invaded eastern Tibet in 1950, killing thousands of people and destroying monasteries and villages. Although Tibetans put up a fierce resistance, they were overpowered. By 1951, the Tibetan government signed an agreement that seemingly promised Tibet's autonomy within a greater Chinese state. The Tibetans feared that if they did not sign this treaty, the People's Liberation Army would invade Tibet in great force and slaughter its people.

While the People's Liberation Army was busy consolidating a new government in China, they maintained a presence in Tibet but appeared to respect Tibetan autonomy. However, tensions were building in eastern Tibet; guerilla armies were mounted; and by 1958 refugees from eastern Tibet were flooding into Lhasa to escape the People's Liberation Army. The pivotal point was reached on March 9, 1959, when a Chinese commander in Lhasa "invited" the Dalai Lama to come on his own to a theatrical performance. Thousands of Tibetans surrounded the Dalai Lama's summer palace in an effort to protect him from the Chinese. On March 10, 1959, the Dalai Lama left Lhasa in disguise and escaped to India. The Chinese shelled the Dalai Lama's summer palace amidst a tremendous uprising of the Tibetan people in Lhasa. About 100,000 Tibetans managed to flee Tibet. Some went to Bhutan and some to Nepal, but most went to India.

Traditional Tibetan Society

Traditional Tibetan society was a society of aristocrats and commoners, of monks and nuns and high lamas. The government was technically owner of all land, but great estates were assigned to the hereditary nobility and to monasteries. The nobles had to render both revenue and their services to the Tibetan government.

The great estates were worked by peasants. Some peasants farmed a parcel of land rent-free while also working the estate land for the landlord and providing such services to the government as building roads, providing animals for transport, and serving in the military. Other peasants were small holders of land in their own right and paid taxes directly to the government. Nomads either took charge of herds for specific estates or owned their own herds, thus paying taxes directly to the Tibetan government. Many Tibetan farmers and nomads were also traders, which required them to travel great distances. Nomads organized caravans of sheep and goats to carry salt and other trade goods to India, where the animals and their burdens could be sold.

Tibetan monasteries, nunneries, and religious orders were also organized hierarchically. Abbots and important reincarnate lamas occupied the highest positions, and ordinary monks and nuns were below them. An interesting aspect of monastic society was the possibility it afforded commoners to rise in the ranks of religion. Since the theocratic Tibetan government incorporated a bureaucracy composed of both secular and lay officials, commoners who achieved high monastic status could hold the equivalent rank of aristocrats in the Tibetan government itself.

QUESTIONS

3.1. How do worldview and cosmology enable us to navigate an unpredictable world?

3.2. How does language affect the meanings people assign to experience?

3.3. How does symbolic action reinforce a particular view of the world?

3.4. How do people justify their beliefs?

3.5. Since cultures are rooted in environmental and historical contexts, would taking people out of these contexts pose a fundamental challenge to their worldview?

QUESTION 3.1
How Do Worldview and Cosmology Enable Us to Navigate an Unpredictable World?

The creation of order, which anthropologists have claimed as both intellectual and psychological functions of religion, is a major aspect of worldview. **Cosmology** provides a map of the universe that identifies different beings, such as deities, animals, and demons, and their lifestyles and location in relation to us and to one another. Cosmology thus organizes the universe for us. Another function is its contribution to our understanding of how things come to be what anthropologists refer to as theories of causality. In other words, cosmology helps explain good and bad luck, how we make sense of space and weather, and how we understand time.

How Do We Explain Good and Bad Events?

Tibetan Buddhism, the major religion followed by Tibetans, subscribes to the doctrine of rebirth and the law of karma. A person's karma is the sum total of his or her positive and negative actions in previous lives. Karma in some ways resembles our notion of fate or predestination since it is the relative balance between good and bad deeds that determines the circumstances of a person's future life. Buddhism holds that all existence is suffering, that suffering arises from ignorance and desire, that one can escape from existence and its attendant suffering by attaining enlightenment, and that enlightenment can be attained if one follows the eight-fold Buddhist path.

Buddhist cosmology links existence to a cycle of rebirth that is known by the Sanskrit term *samsara*. *Samsara* is divided into six realms. When a person who is not enlightened dies, he or she is reborn in one of these realms.[1] The realms are arranged hierarchically in terms of more and less auspicious

---

[1] When an enlightened person dies, he or she has the choice of ending the cycle of rebirth or of returning to help others. In the latter case, the person is known as a Bodhisattva.

rebirths, but they are represented pictorially as a circle or wheel of life. The apex of the hierarchy is the realm of the unenlightened gods. The life of a god might be viewed as immensely desirable since gods live for a very long time and enjoy all manner of pleasures. However, Tibetans say that in the last week or so of existence, a god falls sick, grows old, and loses friends who are horrified at the transformation. In this last week as a god, the individual finally realizes that he or she has been deluded about the nature of existence, that a god's existence does not transcend suffering, and that he or she will be taking rebirth in another realm with its own attendant suffering.

Below the realm of the gods is that of the demigods who enjoy all the pleasures indulged by the gods save one. A cosmic tree grows through the six realms of rebirth. The gods at the top of the hierarchy have access to the wish-fulfilling fruit produced by this tree. The realm of the demigods does not quite reach this fruit, which, of course, makes the fruit infinitely desirable to the demigods. They constantly wage a war they cannot win against the gods for possession of the fruit.

The third realm, in descending order, is that of humans. Although the human realm falls in the middle of the hierarchy of rebirth, Tibetan Buddhists claim that it is the most desirable into which to be reborn since the individual can achieve enlightenment only from a human birth.

Just beneath humans is the realm of animals and *lu,* nonhuman beings who are iconographically depicted as half-man or half-woman and half-fish or half-serpent and whom Tibetans recognize as frogs and snakes. The *lu* are associated with agricultural fertility and needed rain and are also the guardians of great treasure. They are quick to take offense if their environment is polluted, and they retaliate by making the polluters ill.

The fifth realm of rebirth is that of the hungry ghosts, who are described as having enormous bellies and extremely thin necks. Their enormous bellies ensure that the hungry ghosts will always be ravenous, and they are surrounded by all sorts of tantalizing food. However, their necks are so thin that the only thing hungry ghosts can swallow is their own mucus. The lowest realm of rebirth offers a selection of eight hot and eight cold hells into which one may be reborn.

Some of these rebirth possibilities are clearly more desirable than others, but the message Buddhism emphasizes is that any existence entails great suffering and is also temporary. An individual can eventually find a way out of any of the hellish rebirths, but one is nonetheless doomed to be reborn and to suffer again. Buddhists (and Hindus) invoke the doctrine of karma to explain why someone takes rebirth in one of the six realms of *samsara* and the particular circumstances of the person's existence in that realm—social and economic status, physical appearance, and general well-being. However, Buddhists believe that an individual's actions can improve or impair karmic position. In this way, Buddhism emphasizes that a person exercises individual choice with respect to the future. If the immediate effect of good works is not apparent in the present, it will be in a future life.

The law of karma and the doctrine of rebirth serve as a general guide to Tibetan theories of causality, how things come to be. However, it appears to be a rather generic explanation and possibly not terribly satisfying; I rarely heard a Tibetan invoke karma to account for a particular set of circumstances.

Rather, I heard Tibetans frequently refer to *sonam* (merit), *lungta* (which is similar to luck), and *wangtang* (power) to explain events. According to Buddhist doctrine, merit is acquired through right action, and it improves the nature of one's rebirth. The most desirable rebirth is one that will enhance the chance to attain enlightenment. Merit, perhaps, is a causality that most closely resembles karma.

Lungta explains good fortune in a distinct way. Someone may be generally regarded as an altogether miserable individual with no redeeming qualities. Karma would not be a "comfortable" explanation if this awful person were to win the lottery, but *lungta* would. *Lungta* is dispensed by the older mountain deities of Tibet who were recruited by the great eighth-century Indian guru Padmasambhava to be guardians of Buddhism. Although Tibetans have specific means to try to increase their *lungta,* they never know if they possess a sufficient quantity of it. *Lungta* constantly fluctuates. If one has been successful in some venture against all odds or if one's team has won a sporting event, then one knows one has high *lungta.* Whether one possesses *lungta* is essentially known after the fact as the assessment of some outcome. Thus, *lungta* serves, as Mary Douglas (1970) puts it, as a means to rationalize success.

Wangtang is essentially spiritual power and is obtained through the receiving of initiations (*wang*) into Buddhist teachings. Tibetan Buddhism stresses that an individual follows a graded path of teachings towards enlightenment. Each level of teaching gives one access to more esoteric knowledge and greater spiritual empowerment (*wangtang*). Tibetans describe an individual who possesses a great amount of *wangtang* much as we would describe someone who is very charismatic. In other words, a person who possesses a great amount of *wangtang* is easily able to influence others (to overpower them mentally).

Wangtang serves as a theory of causality on several levels. A Tibetan lama or religious teacher may be called on to perform ritual curing, often the exorcism of evil spirits that have been making someone critically ill or harming that person in other ways. Only a lama who has received higher levels of spiritual empowerment will attempt the exorcism of powerful demonic spirits because the spirits can conquer the lama should the lama's *wangtang* be less than that of the spirits. This view of a Tibetan exorcism as a kind of power battle indicates something very significant about *wangtang*—namely, that it is conceived of as independent of morality (in the Tibetan case, of merit or *sonam*) as well as of *lungta.* Although Tibetan Buddhism holds that *wangtang* is deliberately and systematically acquired through the individual's passage from one stage of spiritual teachings to the next, Tibetans insist that this spiritual power must be balanced with right or moral knowledge, implying that some may acquire the empowerment from a Buddhist initiation without proper knowledge of the teachings. Tibetans cite examples of lamas who commit bad deeds as having *wangtang* that is not sufficiently balanced with knowledge.

The concept of *wangtang* also attests to a general flexibility in the Tibetan conception of destiny. For example, Tibetans believe that a Tibetan astrologer can forecast a person's death and the nature of that person's previous and future life. Such a forecast is linked by Tibetans to the person's karma. However, should an individual live well beyond his or her designated life span, Tibetans would not suggest that the astrologer had made faulty calculations, but rather that the person possessed so much *wangtang* that he or she was able to live beyond the predicted life span. This argument suggests that *wangtang,* like *lungta,* is independent of *sonam* (merit) and, therefore, of karma. Although Buddhist scholars might insist that everything is eventually attributable to karma, as an anthropologist I am interested in which theory of causality Tibetans invoke in a specific context. What one can draw from Tibetan theories of causality is that they allow considerable flexibility in explaining events and a person's situation in life. This flexibility serves to rebuff challenges to the Tibetan worldview.

How Does Cosmology Help Make Sense of Geography and Climatic Conditions?

For Tibetans, the mountains are home to distinct gods whose good auspices must be sought if one hopes to travel safely through the high mountain passes that mark the routes of so many Tibetan journeys. The Tibetan trader, pilgrim, or modern-day mountaineer offers the scent of burning juniper, which is believed to be especially pleasing, and raises prayer-flags to these gods. Prayer-flags are cloths or squares of paper stamped with wood-block prints of auspicious animals and prayers. The most common animal is a horse carrying wish-fulfilling jewels on its back. Tibetans believe that when the wind catches the prayer flags, it sends the horse with people's prayers up to the gods. Hence, the name for the prayer flag is *lungta,* which also means wind horse. If the gods are pleased with these offerings, they will convey *lungta,* meaning good luck, on those who raised the prayer flags.

No one knows for certain whether the gods will look favorably on the people who made the offerings. *Lungta,* so to speak, is literally up in the air. An important consideration in raising prayer flags is to find the highest possible place to do so. Tibetans typically string prayer flags from the highest accessible points of trees near their dwellings, and they will also trek up to mountain ridges to make offerings on important occasions. Thus, Tibetans expect that their chances of gaining the mountain gods' attention are greater the closer they can come to these gods. Although *lungta* is invoked to account for many different occurrences, the specific ways in which Tibetans try to obtain it indicates that it serves to create and reinforce the notion of a sacred geography.

The mountain gods naturally oversee their specific domain and its weather, but Tibetans conceive of climate generally as being the responsibility of the *lu.* As mentioned earlier, the *lu* occupy the realm just beneath that of humans in the hierarchy of existences in the cycle of rebirth, and they are intimately associated with watery places. They live in watery domains such as rivers, oceans, lakes, springs, and wells, and also in terrestrial domains such as trees or unusual rocks. Tibetans respect frogs and snakes as potential *lu* and regard thunder as the crying of dragons who, although *lu* themselves, may travel through the clouds. The *lu* are guardians of agricultural fertility and wealth—in other words, of prosperity—in large part because they are responsible for rainfall. Important lakes in Tibet were commonly thought to be the homes of *lu-mo,* or lake goddesses, who controlled regional fertility and would cause drought, crop failure, and sickness if angered by such actions as the polluting of their watery dwellings. People who cut down too many trees might also fall sick because of the retaliation of angry *lu.*

A *spring in Dharmsala, India, known to be a* lu *dwelling, identified by the emblem of a snake.*
(*Photograph by Marcia S. Calkowski.*)

Protector deities specifically associated with the particular regions in which people are born are known as *kye-lha* (birth gods) and may be mountain deities or lake goddesses. One famous *kye-lha* is Palden Lhamo, who is the *kye-lha* of Lhasa, the capital of Tibet, and the chief protector of the Dalai Lama. Palden Lhamo is a female deity believed to dwell in a famous well in the city of Lhasa. In ritual processions held in traditional Lhasa, Palden Lhamo was represented by a monk wearing a mask resembling the face of a frog.

The hierarchy expressed by the relative values placed on various rebirth possibilities within *samsara* does not equally apply to Tibetan sacred geography. Although the mountain deities and lake goddesses may be viewed as representing distinct levels of a natural geographical hierarchy, their contribution to agricultural fertility and the survival of livestock is equally significant. Tibetan sacred geography thus affirms the Buddhist practice of respecting beings who are either more or less highly placed than oneself.

QUESTION 3.2
How Does Language Affect the Meanings People Assign to Experience?

Language serves many important functions. It enables us to provide names for things; to describe things, actions, and events; to refer to the past, present, and future; and, of course, to communicate with one another. To understand how language affects the meanings people assign to experience, we must focus on how language constructs and reinforces social reality and the relationship of language to our understanding of the cosmos. In other words, we can think about language as a kind of practice, which is precisely what J. L. Austin (1962) encouraged us to do when he developed speech act theory. According to this theory, the act of speaking has three dimensions. The first concerns what the speaker intends to communicate; the second, what the speaker actually says; and the third, what is actually accomplished by the speech act, including how the audience interprets what the speaker has said.

How Does Language Reflect Social Relationships?

What we consider to be social reality has everything to do with how we perceive social relationships and the values we attach to them. Traditional Tibet was a hierarchical society that recognized status distinctions according to several different criteria. For example, the great land owners who could trace their ancestry to Tibet's ancient nobility or to the immediate families of previous Dalai Lamas were at the apex of the socioeconomic hierarchy. Tibetan Buddhists also recognized a social hierarchy based on spiritual status that ranged from the Dalai Lama and the heads of the four Buddhist sects to ordinary monks and nuns. This kind of hierarchy was recognized as well by followers of Tibet's ancient Bon religion, who, of course, gave precedence to their own spiritual leaders. Another criterion Tibetans applied to construct a status hierarchy was age.

The recognition of status differences in these hierarchies is reflected in the use of the honorific and common forms of the Tibetan language. Honorific Tibetan has a distinct vocabulary, which means that people have to learn at least two sets of nouns and verbs in order to communicate in both forms. Lhasa aristocrats would frequently resort to an even more refined vocabulary than standard honorific Tibetan.

The fact that a Tibetan knows and can communicate in both forms of language indicates that he or she is not from the lowest class. The choice of honorific or common Tibetan acknowledges the speaker's estimation of her or his status in relation to that of the person addressed. Tibetans employ the common form when speaking to people of decidedly lower status or to siblings and cousins or close friends. Honorific Tibetan is used to address people of superior social or spiritual status as well as those of equivalent social status with whom close relations are not shared. A Tibetan's social superior replies to social unequals in common language, whereas a social equal would have to reply in honorific language. While Tibetans expect social superiors to respond in common language, they are affronted if a social equal attempts to claim superiority in this way.

Respectful address in Tibetan is not restricted to the use of an honorific vocabulary. Tibetans typically add the honorific suffix *la* to the names of friends, acquaintances, and social superiors when greeting or conversing with them. For example, one would address a friend named Sonam as *Sonam-la*. To do so marks the speaker as someone who is well-mannered and wishes to show respect for the person being addressed. The honorific suffix may also be added to kin terms. In Tibetan, one refers to one's mother (*ama*) as *ama-la* and one's father (*pa*) as *pa-la*. Whether Tibetans address their siblings by kin terms to which the suffix is added often depends on whether the sibling is elder to the speaker. When Tibetans wish to speak to strangers whose names are not known, they gauge the age of the stranger in relation to themselves and address the stranger as grandmother or grandfather, mother or father, or sister or brother. In such cases, the honorific suffix is added to the appropriate kin term. If the stranger to be addressed is a child, Tibetans refer to him or her as "boy" or "girl" and do not add the honorific suffix.

The specific vocabularies Tibetans employ, whether honorific or common, serve to reinforce and establish status hierarchies, and a speaker's knowledge of these vocabularies and the specific contexts in which they should be used asserts the speaker's own status claims. Establishing status hierarchies can be a touchy business when status distinctions are not obvious.

When a person who employs an honorific vocabulary to speak to a near-status equal and is replied to in a common vocabulary takes offense, the reason is largely that the person who is trying to claim superiority is being too obvious or direct about his or her intentions. Central Tibetans generally hold that the more refined and higher status a person is, the more indirect he or she will be when criticizing others. Some young Tibetans who attended English medium schools in India, for example, compared the speeches of certain Tibetan politicians to Brutus's praise of Caesar in Shakespeare's *Julius Caesar*. Their point was that a Tibetan political speech often begins with praise of the very person or thing the speaker intends to criticize later. The following Tibetan story is an excellent example of the importance of indirect communication:

> One day a man came to a well, which was a known dwelling of *lu*. The man defecated on the edge of the well and called down to the *lu* below, announcing that he had given them a golden *phumba* (a silver vessel used to store holy water in the performance of certain Buddhist rituals) as an offering. He went away and another man came along. The second man was shocked to see the feces on the edge of the well and asked out loud who could possibly do such a thing. He then cleaned the edge of the well. But the second man quickly fell ill from a disease caused by the *lu*.

The second man became sick because until he expressed his shock at the way the well had been polluted, the *lu* had absolutely no idea that their environment had been so insulted. The *lu* retaliated against the second man because it was he who spoiled their illusion that they were the benefactors of a golden *phumba* and it was he who was thoughtless enough to inform them that they had received excrement. Note that the second man in the story would probably have been rewarded in a Western parable because he told the truth.

Another illustration of the value Tibetans place on indirection may be seen in the following tale, which describes a conversation between a Lhasa merchant and a member of a pastoral nomadic tribe known as Abuhor. Like cosmopolitan city-dwellers everywhere, Lhasa residents tended to assume that they were far more sophisticated than their rustic countrymen and countrywomen, who would presumably have little knowledge of honorific Tibetan and the etiquette of indirection.

> Once an Abuhor came to Lhasa and approached a merchant, asking in his rough nomad dialect what was in a bag that was full of sugar. The merchant replied that the bag was full of poison. On hearing this, the Abuhor reached into the bag and scooped up handfuls of sugar, which he promptly stuffed into his mouth. While relishing the sugar, the Abuhor proclaimed that he would die that very night of poisoning.

In this case, the Lhasa merchant thought he would have some fun by demonstrating that the Abuhor was so provincial that he was not even familiar with sugar. The Abuhor, however, countered with a masterful display of indirection by accepting the merchant's definition of sugar as poison while at the same time enjoying a free treat. Since the merchant could not demand payment for the cause of the Abuhor's death, the merchant would have to admit his lie if he wished to charge the Abuhor for eating sugar.

Can Language Transform Reality?

We tend to think that the primary function of language is communication. But might language or speech influence the universe? In the Hindu and Buddhist traditions, the uttering of certain sequences of sacred syllables and/or words is believed to exert a profound effect on the speaker, or even on the world itself. These sequences of sacred syllables and/or words are known as mantras in the Hindi and Sanskrit languages and as *ngag* in Tibetan. Every Tibetan Buddhist is familiar with several mantras. The most common is *om mani padme hum,* which is dedicated to the Buddha of Compassion and believed to enhance one's future rebirth. Since the number of recitations is thought to directly affect the quality of one's rebirth, many Tibetans have recited the mantra hundreds of thousands of times. Buddhist scholars do not regard this mantra as a form of communication with the Buddha of Compassion, but rather as a means to focus and purify the mind. According to Buddhist ideology, a focused and purified mind will naturally obtain a better rebirth. In this way, the uttering of a mantra is understood as having an important effect on the person who utters it.

Some mantras employed by Tibetan lamas in Buddhist rituals are esoteric, meaning that they are taught only to people who have attained higher stages of spiritual learning. The knowledge and use of these mantras is restricted to those who are believed to be properly empowered to use them, since to utter them is to manipulate sacred powers. The ritual specialties of certain Tibetan lamas include stopping hailstorms, stopping rain, and inducing rain. The weather-making ritual specialty was critical to traditional Tibetan agriculturists, who sought to prevent weather disasters by hiring lamas to control the weather. Weather-making rituals entail the lama's use of esoteric mantras to redirect the impulses of the *lu* responsible for general weather conditions. If, for example, a Tibetan lama ensures that the weather will be pleasant for a particular period of time, such as for a major public ritual, Tibetans expect the weather to be particularly nasty immediately after the ritual. Such dramatic weather changes are attributed to the *lu's* displeasure that they were forced to relinquish their control of the weather. Another example of the use of esoteric mantras is their invocation in Tibetan Buddhist rituals of exorcism. These rituals are directed at subduing evil spirits and the consequences of malicious thought that afflict people. In such ritual contexts, esoteric mantras are believed to compel Buddhist protective deities to exercise their powers to control evil spirits and to empower prayers.

Mantras are not the same as prayers. Prayers are an attempt to communicate with the deities. The critical difference is that the act of uttering the mantra is more significant than anything that the mantra may or may not communicate.

Does Language Restrict Our Perception of the Universe?

Anthropologists have engaged in substantial debate over whether language controls worldview or worldview constrains language. Tibetan Buddhists and Tibetan followers of the Bon religion believe in reincarnation—specifically in the reincarnation of what is translated as the "transmigrating consciousness." A very young child is a very new embodiment of a very old consciousness. Tibetans say that a very young child recalls its past life and also has the ability to perceive cosmic beings such as deities and demons. This ability explains infants' sudden mood shifts; Tibetans hold that the infants are reacting to the beings that older human beings can no longer see. Once a child begins to acquire speech, she or he forgets past lives and loses the capacity to recognize cosmic beings.

Is Intention More Important Than the Content of Speech?

A famous Tibetan story tells about an old man who circumambulated a sacred shrine near a monastery in Tibet every day, reciting a mantra to the Goddess Tara with great devotion. Several monks from the monastery overheard the old man's utterances and realized that he was repeating the mantra incorrectly. They tried to correct him, to no avail. One day the monastery's abbot happened to look out toward the shrine from the roof of the monastery and noticed the Goddess Tara herself floating above the old man as he made his devotions and recited his version of the mantra. This anecdote makes the point that despite the great emphasis Tibetan Buddhists place on strict adherence to precise speech, utterance, and action in ritual contexts, the intention of the practitioner is of supreme importance. It also suggests that intention is directly related to what is actually accomplished by the utterance.

QUESTION 3.3
How Does Symbolic Action Reinforce a Particular View of the World?

Symbolic action may also be viewed as a form of communication. Like language, it can express social relationships. Like the use of mantras, it can offer people a sense of control over others and the environment.

How Does Symbolic Action Express Social Relationships?

One of the most common ritual actions among Tibetans is the offering of white scarves called *khatag*. The material used to make these scarves ranges from cheesecloth to several grades of silk. The white color represents purity of intention. To give a *khatag* to someone or something is to express respect. Friends and/or family members drape *khatag* around the necks of people who are about to depart on or have just returned from long journeys. In the exile community, the customary wedding gift is an envelope containing money, which the wedding guest presents to the bride and groom while draping their necks and the necks of their immediate relatives with *khatag*. By the time they have received several wedding gifts, the bride and groom are almost obscured by the number of scarves covering them. *Khatag* are presented to individuals being honored at other occasions, such as performers who have just completed an eight-hour Tibetan opera, lamas from whom people wish to obtain blessings, monks who have come to individual homes to perform rituals, and oracles who have given predictions. They are placed on the bodies of deceased individuals. *Khatag* also adorn photographs of lamas that are placed on altars, scroll paintings that depict various Buddhist deities and sacred realms, various effigies constructed by Tibetan lamas to lure evil spirits, and stones inscribed with the mantra *om mani padme hum,* which are customarily placed along important circumambulation paths. During Tibetan New Year celebrations, which generally occur in February but do not always coincide with the Chinese New Year, *khatag* may be seen on water taps as offerings to *lu,* atop stacks of sweet fried bread on the altars in Tibetan homes, and on poles used to fly prayer flags. These examples signify that the giving of a *khatag* is a gesture of respect.

Does the presenting of *khatag* to human and cosmic beings symbolize something beyond respect? We might take a cue from the ritual presentation of *khatag* to Tibetan lamas by people seeking their blessings. The practice is for the lay or spiritually subordinate person to stretch the *khatag* out between two hands while approaching the lama with head bowed respectfully. The lama takes the offered *khatag* and immediately drapes it around the presenter's neck. The ritual act of presenting and then being presented with a *khatag* possibly symbolizes that the giver and receiver are respectfully bound to each other. If this is the case, then draping a *khatag* around a water tap could be an offer to respect the *lu* and their watery dwelling in return for a dependable supply of water for the coming year. The emphasis on the interconnectedness of the universe is, of course, a quintessential Buddhist concept.

Tibetans also use *khatag* to symbolize breaking a relationship. A compelling illustration of this symbolic action is the response of some Tibetan refugees living in India to President Jimmy Carter's 1977 visit to Delhi. Because President Carter had included human rights as a major plank of his campaign platform, Tibetans in exile had entertained high hopes that the Carter Administration would significantly further the Tibetan cause. In fact, Tibetans had made a pun of the president's name, referring to him as *Jigme Khatag*. In Tibetan, *Jigme* means fearless, so Carter was being referred to as "Fearless Honorific Scarf." The exiled Tibetans quickly learned that their concerns were not a priority to the Carter administration, and some of them lined up along President Carter's route in Delhi and held out black *khatag* as a symbolic expression of their feelings. What the Tibetans meant was that President Carter had broken faith with his promise and had broken the essence of a social relation between himself and the Tibetans. The sole ritual use of black *khatag* is in exorcism rituals, where they are draped over the effigies of the most evil demons.

Tibetans use numerous ritual activities to protect against other negative aspects of social interaction, such as envy. Wealthy people who construct tall buildings are particularly concerned that they and/or their buildings might be victims of the evil eye. The concept of an evil eye, which is found in many cultures, implies that a person who consciously or unconsciously envies someone or something can harm that thing or person by simply casting eyes on him, her, or it. The Tibetan solution to counteracting evil eyes that might notice an imposing building under construction is to fashion a large phallus and attach it near the top of the unfinished building. The reasoning behind this symbolic action is that anyone who looks up to view the building will immediately avert his or her eyes in embarrassment. This practice is inspired by an event that occurred when a great monastery was under construction hundreds of years ago in Tibet. Monks labored all day to raise the walls of the monastery, and female witches destroyed their work at night. Finally, the abbot decided to affix a large phallus to the top of the walls, and this strategy succeeded in driving the witches away.

Tibetan symbolic actions are sometimes designed to utilize envy or greed against itself in order to deflect negative effects. Just prior to the onset of the Tibetan New Year, for example, a Tibetan householder fashions a small effigy of the mother of the house out of dough. If possible, the effigy is placed at the intersection of two or more paths or roads. A Tibetan mother is frequently found in her kitchen. Evil spirits that have strayed into the house during the year are naturally attracted to the mother since they view her as the dispenser of good food and loving care. They thus are believed to prefer to hang about in the kitchen. The tactic, then, is to confuse the spirits during the household cleaning prior to the New Year by convincing them that they are being presented with the mother herself. Since, in perfect keeping with Buddhist teachings, evil spirits are not terribly bright, they readily accept this ruse. Their greed causes them to pursue the effigy and thereby to be cast from the household.

How Does Symbolic Action Offer People a Sense of Control?

Victor Turner (1967) theorized that symbols are effective because they combine ideological meaning (the arrangement of social values and norms) with sensory meaning, which arouses desires and feelings. Ritual is a major context for symbolic action, and Turner noted that it is very similar to a drama whose characters are in one situation at the beginning and in an altogether different situation at the end. Ritual essentially indicates that the state in which people find themselves or their world before its enactment will undergo a transformation by the conclusion. Ritual transformation is accomplished through the dramatic sequencing of symbols and often through the dramatic participation of those who would transform themselves and/or their world.

Tibetans about to set out on long journeys may consult astrologers or obtain divinations from lamas to learn what dangers might lie ahead. The astrologer's or lama's forecast might predict that major obstacles will beset the traveler. Does this stop a Tibetan from undertaking the journey? Of course not. Tibetans seek these divinations because they wish to be prepared for what they will encounter. Once the dangers are known, they can take measures to counteract them. One measure is to obtain an amulet from a lama that protects the wearer from specific dangers. A Tibetan amulet is composed of a wood-block print on paper, which is folded into a small square, wrapped with various designs of threads in the five elemental colors of the universe, placed in a charm box encased in silk or simply attached to a blessing thread, and worn around the neck. The wood-block print typically depicts a demonic being who has been chained and constrained by magical barriers and the power of mantras. The multicolored threads wrapping the folded print symbolize additional magical barriers. The wearer of the amulet believes that the evil forces that might be encountered will be trapped and incapacitated within the amulet as indicated by the print.

Tibetans also obtain divinations from lamas and, less frequently, from astrologers to determine causes of illness. One serious illness amenable only to ritual is soul loss. The soul in question is not the one that goes on to rebirths, but rather a kind of secondary soul that exists only for the lifetime of its possessor. Sorcery can cause a person to lose this soul, as can being suddenly frightened. The sufferer may become very depressed and waste away. In the cases I encountered, victims of soul loss tended to consult several different types of medical practitioners and try their prescribed remedies, to no avail. They often consulted a lama as a last resort, but once they obtained the diagnosis of soul loss and underwent the prescribed ritual, they recovered.

In the Tibetan exile community in India, Tibetans seek divination from a lama to learn where to go to sell sweaters. Selling sweaters to Indian tourists in Indian hill stations has been a fairly profitable venture for many refugee Tibetans. But the presence of too many sweater-sellers in the same place at the same time severely inhibits profits. Thus, to consult a lama about where to conduct business can be seen as both a randomizing device that sends sweater-sellers off in varied directions and as a means by which individuals gain the assurance that their extensive travel and labor will be worthwhile.

Tibetan Buddhists believe that they can improve their future karmic circumstances by acquiring *lungta,* or merit. Besides being acquired by observing Buddhist precepts and sponsoring monks and monasteries, merit is also obtained from the recitation of mantras and the turning of prayer wheels. The turning of prayer wheels is related in a sense to the circumambulation of sacred Buddhist shrines, which include temples, monasteries, mountains, caves, and places associated with miraculous signs of a divine being's presence. Tibetan Buddhists circumambulate these shrines by walking around them in a clockwise direction. The more circumambulations an individual completes, the more merit he or she attains. The greatest circumambulation path in Tibet encircles Mount Kailash in far western Tibet, which is sacred to both Hindus and Buddhists. Tibetans especially venerate it as what they believe to be the source of four of Asia's major rivers.

A prayer wheel is a metal cylinder attached to a rod so that the cylinder can spin about the rod. On the circumference of the cylinder are inscriptions of the mantra *Om mani padme hum.* Elderly Tibetans can frequently be seen spinning their prayer wheels while walking, resting, or even conversing with others. Tibetan Buddhists believe that the recitation of this mantra hundreds of thousands of times will enhance their future rebirth, and they also believe that spinning the prayer wheel is equivalent to reciting the mantra. Since the circumference of the cylinder may accommodate several successive inscriptions of the mantra, Tibetans believe that each complete revolution of the cylinder releases that number of inscriptions. Thus, in the time it takes to spin the prayer wheel through one revolution, a person may launch many more repetitions of the mantra than could actually be uttered.

Some Tibetans have engineered improvements in the prayer wheel design to create even more efficient generation of mantras. For example, mill wheels powered by streams may be inscribed with mantras. In India, some Tibetans devised a kind of reverse prayer wheel by painting used milk tins with a mantra and then inserting drill bits through the vertical axis of the tins. One can then spin the drill bit to generate mantras. Although mill wheels, drill bits, and even prayer wheels might appear to be impersonal means of reciting mantras, in each case, someone is responsible for setting the wheel in motion. There is a significant Buddhist message in all of this. The wheel also refers to the wheel of life, to *samsaric* existence. The basic precept of Buddhism is that we are ultimately responsible for our suffering and our existence, and we are also responsible for our potential enlightenment. Thus, the prayer wheel, circumambulation, and the wheel of existence are what we ourselves turn.

QUESTION 3.4
How Do People Justify Their Beliefs?

The question of how people justify their beliefs can be looked at in two ways. The first is how people distinguish between the miraculous, sacred, or supernatural and the everyday. The second is how people account for apparent contradictions in their worldview.

How Do People Distinguish Between What Is Authentic and What Is Fake?

From the perspective of Westerners, Tibet and things Tibetan have long been associated with Shangri-La,[2] magic, and mystery. As we have seen, the Tibetan worldview entertains a far greater variety of what Westerners would term the supernatural than is generally found in a Western worldview. But Westerners should not assume that Tibetans are less discriminating than Westerners in their perception of what constitutes reality.

For example, Tibetans have a longstanding tradition of oracles. The ancient Tibetan monarchy and later the theocracy of the Dalai Lamas regularly consulted the highest-ranking oracles known as state oracles. Oracles are human beings who, in given contexts, are possessed by deities who utilize them in order to speak to and listen to other human beings. In Tibetan culture, people do not choose to become oracles. Rather, deities select certain individuals to be their mediums. Tibetans are aware that some individuals may fake being possessed in order to turn a profit, to attempt to persuade people of a certain point of view, or simply to gain status. Tibetans also believe that false oracles may be created by ambitious spirits who wish to pass themselves off as deities. Consequently, Tibetans apply various means to test the authenticity of would-be oracles. In the case of state oracles, the verification of a new medium is of extreme importance, and the medium, while in trance, might be asked what message a letter in a sealed envelope contained. With respect to lesser oracles, I have frequently heard Tibetans attest to the genuineness of a medium's possession by observing that the medium speaks in a dialect when possessed by the deity that the medium in his or her normal waking existence neither speaks nor comprehends. Moreover, Tibetans note that the human

---

[2]Shangri-La is a fictitious Tibetan paradise popularized in James Hilton's novel *Lost Horizon*.

medium has no recollection of what was said by the possessing deity at the end of a trance.

Another example of Tibetans' distinction between the supernatural and the natural may be seen in their perception of *ro-lang,* which means walking corpse. Tibetans believe that some evil spirits are constantly seeking a human body to inhabit because their ethereal existence seriously inhibits their ability to act in the world to their own benefit. A human body is available to them only when someone has recently died and the corpse is still fresh. A spirit may then take possession of the body and become a kind of zombie with the capacity to harm human beings. Tibetans sometimes break the spine of a new corpse in order to prevent its being possessed by evil spirits. A *ro-lang* has to adjust to a new body, so it can be identified by the stiffness of its movements. The doorways and windows of Lhasa houses were often built somewhat short of an average adult's height so that a *ro-lang,* being unable to bend, could not enter. When asked how a Tibetan returning home after a long journey could know whether an individual is an old friend suffering from rheumatism or the body of a deceased old friend now possessed by a spirit, one answer is that if the old friend has suddenly become much more intelligent, it is probably a *ro-lang*.

The discovery of the rebirth or reincarnation of a spiritual master is often an exacting process involving a series of divinations by high lamas, the search for miraculous signs, the inspection of the antics of two-year-old children, and the posing of tests to the most promising candidates. In the case of very high-ranking reincarnations, or *tulku,* many Tibetans are aware that there may be a host of candidates, each with his own supporters. The supporters often have vested interests in their candidate's recognition, since important *tulku* in traditional Tibet owned considerable estates, wielded significant authority, and potentially furthered particular political agendas. Thus, the selection of one candidate over another typically required the covert collecting of intelligence about the candidate and reticence about the progress of the search for information while it is going on. In the case of some of the Tibetan Buddhist sects, the selection of the reincarnation of a deceased *tulku* was informed solely by the predictions of very high-ranking lamas.

How Do People Rationalize Apparent Contradictions in Their Belief Systems?

Buddhism locates the origin of suffering in desire. The law of karma accounts for the circumstances of present existence. But as we have seen, Tibetan Buddhists incorporate a number of alternative causalities to explain suffering. Irritated *lu* may cause people to fall sick; angry mountain gods might send avalanches down on unsuspecting travelers; and, despite a propitiator's best efforts to burn juniper branches and hoist prayer flags, the deities may not be in the least inclined to bestow *lungta* no matter how much merit he or she might have attained. Moreover, although the central concern of Tibetan Buddhism is to develop one's capacity to attain enlightenment, Tibetan Buddhist texts also include a host of prescriptions for dealing with nasty spirits and securing the assistance of powerful, but not supremely enlightened, deities to relieve the immediate causes of suffering.

Do these examples represent fundamental contradictions in Tibetan Buddhism, or are they simply different contexts to be addressed? Tibetans would assert that appeasing *lu* and refining consciousness in order to achieve a Buddha nature are complementary, not contradictory, practices. Working to achieve a Buddha nature is, of course, the most important exercise any Buddhist can undertake, but the relationship between appeasing *lu* or the mountain gods and refining the consciousness can best be understood as different orientations toward time. Tibetan Buddhists anticipate that enlightenment can be attained only after thousands, or even hundreds of thousands, of rebirths, but they believe that what one can accomplish within a single lifetime is an invaluable contribution toward this goal. Those who die before they have reached old age lose the full opportunity provided by a human rebirth to attain merit and, possibly, to gain enlightenment. Such practices as appeasing *lu,* then, have what Tibetans understand as the more-immediate goal of maximizing the length of individual life spans. In this way, appeasing *lu* ultimately assists the goal of attaining enlightenment.

For Buddhists, the greatest sin is to kill, yet symbolic killing is a critical practice of certain Tibetan Buddhist rituals of exorcism, and meat was one of the staple elements of the traditional Tibetan diet. How do Tibetans explain these seeming contradictions?

According to Tibetan Buddhism, numerous supernatural entities are responsible for causing harm. One is the *lu,* who generally cause people to be sick in retaliation for the pollution of their domain. (Retaliation is not a proper Buddhist motivation, but the *lu* are not enlightened beings.) Other types of spirits are generated by the festering of malicious thoughts and feelings and the aftermath of evil deeds. Tibetan Buddhist lamas prefer to employ the gentlest means to redress the harm caused by these entities, but the specific ritual performed must conform to the nature of the entity. In the case of *lu,* the ritual often prescribes appeasing the *lu* by apologizing and giving gifts. Appeasement does not work in the case of festering spirits. Instead, the spirits must be caught and, because they are immaterial, coaxed into a body—a small human-shaped effigy made from dough. The exorcist dismembers the effigy with a ritual ax. The logic of the ritual is that the evil spirits must be embodied so that they can be slain. Thus, they are symbolically killed, but only because they are beyond any other sort of appeal and would cause even more harm were they permitted to continue. Tibetan lamas explain this slaying of evil spirits as sending them on to a better rebirth, thus interpreting the ritual action as an act of compassion for evil spirits who would have no possibility of redemption if they remained in their present existence.

In the case of Tibetans' fondness for meat, eating meat is not a sin according to Buddhism. Killing the animal that provides the meat, on the other hand, is. In traditional Tibet, meat was essential for survival. Few crops grow at high altitudes, and vast areas of Tibet are suited only for pastoral nomadism, not for agriculture. But Tibetan Buddhists are reluctant to slay an animal. One way they could avoid sin was to have someone else, such as a servant, kill the animal. Another way was to arrange the animal's death without actually doing the killing. For example, an animal that is driven off a cliff is not, according to Tibetans, killed by humans. In Lhasa, which was home to a small Tibetan Muslim population, people could seek out a Muslim butcher. Although killing animals was necessary for many Tibetans' survival, they tended to regard such killing as an "insufferable truth." One rationale is that it is better to kill one large animal, such as a yak, to feed many people, than to multiply sin by killing many smaller animals to feed the same number of people.

When the Dalai Lama escaped from Lhasa, some monks left their monasteries, disrobed, and took up arms to protect him on his journey to India. Several of these monks told me that although it had been extremely difficult for them to renounce their monastic vows, their highest priority was to serve the Dalai Lama, not to increase their personal stock of merit. But perhaps we should reconsider this: If an individual commits an act of demerit to preserve the existence of someone who has the capacity to benefit all sentient beings, then is the act of disrobing and taking up arms really unmeritorious?

QUESTION 3.5
Since Cultures Are Rooted in Environmental and Historical Contexts, Would Taking People out of These Contexts Pose a Fundamental Challenge to Their Worldview?

Tibetans taking refuge in India in 1959 found themselves in a new climate, a new landscape, and a new linguistic, social, and cultural environment. Merchants who traveled between Calcutta or Darjeeling and Tibet; pilgrims who had visited the most sacred of Buddhist sites, Bodhgaya, where the Buddha attained enlightenment; nomads who traditionally mounted trading expeditions to India to sell their sheep, goats, and salt; and aristocrats who attended schools in India did not find the terrain unfamiliar. But the majority of refugee Tibetans knew of India mainly as the land that was the source of Buddhism.

Tibetans crossed the border wearing sheepskin and woolen garments and were detained in transit camps where the scorching heat persuaded many of them to temporarily adopt Indian cotton clothing. Once they were resettled, they had the *chupa,* a kind of belted robe that was their traditional garment, made from Indian woolen cloth or, for special occasions, from silk. Many refugee men adopted Western dress for everyday wear and reserved their chupa for religious or festival occasions. Tibetan women were less likely to wear Western or Indian clothing and had *chupa* made from cotton to suit the climate.

Living among Hindus, Tibetans had to forego overtly eating beef as a substitute for yak meat, but since beef is cheaper than the more readily available mutton, they discretely purchased it from Indian Muslims on occasion. Most Tibetan men cut their long hair, which they had customarily worn in braids, in order to accommodate themselves to the Indian climate and social environment. Many Tibetan children were sent to schools established through the cooperation of the Dalai Lama's office and the Indian government, separating them from their parents for unusually long periods.

What changed most radically was the way most Tibetan refugees made a living. Former nomads and farmers first became road builders and then farmers on scrub land in the south of India that was leased to the exile government. Others became shopkeepers, exile government workers, schoolteachers, sweater-sellers, carpet weavers, scholars, and soldiers in the Indian army.

These Tibetans faced the challenges of making sense of their new environment and of the cultures they encountered in that environment and of trying
to sustain their own culture in the process.

How Do People Make Sense of New Environments and Unfamiliar Cultures?

Some regions of the India, such as Ladakh and part of the Indian state of
Himachal Pradesh, are geographically very similar to Tibet. Dharmsala, a former British hill station in the state of Himachal Pradesh, became the exile residence of the Dalai Lama and the seat of his government in exile. Although
Dharmsala was not intended to be a major residential area for the 100,000
Tibetans estimated to have taken refuge in India, about 8000 Tibetans lived
there in the 1970s and 1980s. Dharmsala is perched on a ridge over 5000 feet
high that abuts the Dhauladar range, one of several distinct mountain ranges

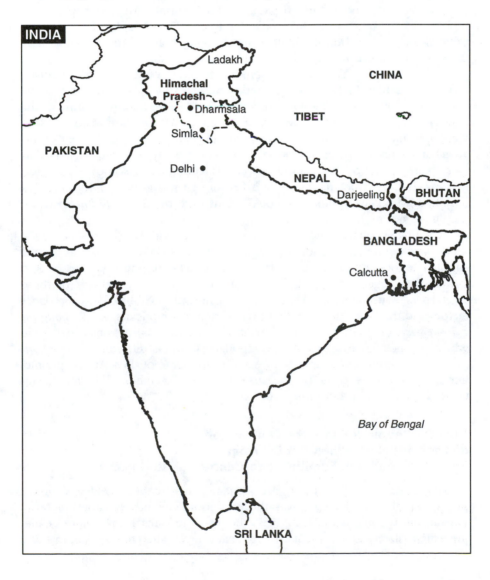

in what Westerners refer to generically as the Himalayas. It is surrounded by pine forests and rhododendron groves and is within walking distance of a waterfall, a hot spring, and a river, and it offers fine views of the mountains as well as of the plains of Himachal Pradesh.

This environment, coupled with the fact that Buddhism and Hinduism share the same understanding of the potential rebirths within *samsaric* existence, easily accommodates much of the Tibetan cosmology. Tibetans living in Dharmsala identify specific rocks and springs, for example, as dwellings of *lu*. One difficulty in dealing with these *lu* was, as a Tibetan who had fallen ill due to his inadvertent aggravation of a local *lu* explained, "We don't know what language these *lu* speak, so I apologized in Hindi, Tibetan, and English." Since the mountain gods of India would not be the deities of specific locales traditionally propitiated by Tibetans, refugee Tibetans would not have specific rituals to address them. However, Tibetans leave their customary travelers' offerings to mountain gods, bringing stones from far places and piling them into cairns along the mountain paths near Dharmsala. Moreover, parties of monks and lay Tibetans in Dharmsala trek to a 9000-foot-high pass to find the optimal location for burning juniper and hoisting prayer flags on particularly important occasions to make their offering to the deities.

Although many Tibetans had some knowledge of India and Hinduism, those who settled in Dharmsala found themselves living in the midst of the Hindu pilgrimage destination of hot springs held to be a sacred shrine of the Hindu god Shiva. Among these pilgrims were *saddhus,* Hindu ascetics who have renounced their former lives, wander in search of the attainment of nirvana, and exist by begging. Tibetan refugees quickly learned that *saddhus* were believed to possess magical powers. Tibetan lamas also possess magical powers. But lay Tibetans were often fearful of the *saddhus.* They said that they had no power against malicious actions performed by *saddhus* because they were not in their own country.

The first encounters most Tibetan refugees had with Westerners were with those working for international relief agencies. The United States was a chief supplier of food aid in the form of such staples as flour and soybeans packed into burlap bags. Expressing their amazement at the sheer size of these Westerners, some Tibetans refugees drew a metaphorical link between benefactors and the food they supplied by referring to Americans as *USA phag-pa gyuma* meaning USA pork sausage. Another humorous reference to people who were not Indian or Chinese categorized them as different colors of *lu*. This is an interesting metaphorical relationship: Some of these "new" people, like *lu,* were benefactors, but because they were members of different cultures, they were unpredictable benefactors.

How Do People Sustain the Central Core of Their Ideology When Cut Off from Their Native Place, Families, and Central Institutions?

Several factors contributed to the resilience of the Tibetan worldview amidst the upheaval of exile. One was the establishment and reestablishment of Tibetan institutions in India. In 1959, the year the Dalai Lama entered exile, the exiled Tibetan government formed what is now called the Tibetan Institute of Performing Arts (TIPA). It was assigned the tasks of preserving and promoting the Tibetan performing arts. Young children recruited for the school studied with former Tibetan opera stars, famous Lhasa musicians, individuals well-versed in Tibetan folk songs and dances, and monks expert in performing sacred monastic dances. The TIPA troupe put on operas, gave musical performances, and performed historical plays recounting events of great religious significance in Tibet's history as well as Tibetan uprisings against the Chinese in the 1950s. TIPA regularly performed in Tibetan settlements throughout India and went on the first of many international tours in the mid-1970s. Former artists organized local opera troupes in some Tibetan settlements.

Many of the Tibetan schools established by the exile government in cooperation with the government of India were residential. Children who attended these schools were separated from their parents for months on end, but they learned to read and write Tibetan, Hindi, and English, studied Tibetan history, and, very importantly, acquired a sense of national identity. Stories in their readers also introduced Tibetan schoolchildren to the animals, environment, and daily activities of Tibetans living in traditional Tibet.

Many of the major monasteries in Tibet were rebuilt in India and continued to receive young boys sent by their parents to be educated as monks. These new monasteries were thus able to continue the Tibetan curriculum of religious education and to supply the monks needed for the performance of Tibetan religious rituals. The Library of Tibetan Works and Archives was built in Dharmsala to house valuable manuscripts brought from Tibet, to attract local and international scholars, to publish Tibetan works, to serve as a museum, and to offer classes in Buddhism and the Tibetan language to Westerners.

The Dalai Lama delivering his annual March 10 address in Dharmsala.
(Photograph by Marcia S. Calkowski.)

Also associated with the library were classes in traditional religious painting and sculpture. Monasteries in other parts of India also carried out the training of young Tibetan artists. Dharmsala was the location of a Tibetan Medical Institute where Tibetans could study traditional medicine, pharmacology, and astrology. Dharmsala became known as Little Lhasa because it was the residence of the Dalai Lama and his government and also because, in drawing together Tibetans from throughout the country, it became a cosmopolitan center of Tibetan culture.

A second factor contributing to the resilience of the Tibetan worldview stemmed from interactions between Tibetans and the Westerners who began to visit Tibetan centers such as Dharmsala in increasing numbers and for a multitude of reasons. Some of these Western people were tourists, some were scholars, and some were students of Buddhism. Even those who had embraced the fanciful image of Tibet as Shangri-La were curious about Tibet and things Tibetan.

They eagerly inquired about Tibetan customs and religion. Thus, not only were Tibetan cultural institutions replanted in exile, but many Tibetan refugees also received the message that their culture and religion were valued by outsiders. Most other refugee groups have not received this message.

A third factor contributing to the maintenance of the Tibetan worldview is the Dalai Lama, who both symbolizes a unifying principle for Tibetans and is an international and interfaith spiritual leader. To receive a blessing from or to be spoken to by the Dalai Lama is understood to be a very significant event in the life of a Tibetan refugee, even one who is not a follower of the Dalai Lama's Gelugpa sect of Tibetan Buddhism. The Dalai Lama is clearly identified by Tibetan refugees as a symbol of the nation. The Dalai Lama's Buddhist approach to the dilemma of his people has earned him various international humanitarian awards, including the Nobel Peace Prize in 1989. The world significance achieved by the Dalai Lama confirms the value of their worldview for Tibetans.

CONCLUSIONS

This chapter has reviewed significant anthropological perspectives about how people construct their view of reality. These perspectives include cognitive, emotional, and experiential approaches to the problem of meaning, the relation of worldview to ethos, and a consideration of how a people's understanding of reality may change. To put these perspectives into an ethnographic context, the chapter looked at how Tibetans in traditional Tibet and refugee Tibetans in India construct reality.

The local Tibetan cosmology reflects what Lévi-Strauss (1966) called "order-creating activity" by associating specific supernatural beings with particular ecological niches. This sort of ordering enabled agriculturists, pastoral nomads, and traders living in a spectacular, mostly arid, high-altitude environment to make sense of dramatic climate changes and hazardous mountain passes in terms of the moods of supernatural beings. A cosmology acquired from India through the importation of Buddhism and the theory of karma enabled Tibetans to explain, among other things, why they might happen to encounter moody supernatural beings in the first place. In other words, the blending of Buddhism with their indigenous ideologies created complex theories of causality that explained and suggested ways to prepare for untoward events in their lives. Tibetans could thus draw on several different rationales to account for good and bad fortune, illness, and why people live beyond their allotted life spans. The theory of karma is a fine example of making worldview, as Geertz (1973) argued, emotionally acceptable by presenting it as the only way things can be.

The contribution language makes to the construction of reality extends far beyond issues of vocabulary, locating actions in time, or even basic communication. Tibetans use language to indicate status differences, to compel supernatural beings to obey human commands, and, through the utterance of mantras, to transform the world. These are illustrations of order-creating activity and Victor Turner's (1967) notions of symbolic action. Tibetans understand that language has its limitations. They note, for example, that children lose their ability to recall past lives once they acquire speech, and they hold that a person's intention is more important than what is actually said. The concept that language can limit understanding is entirely consistent with the Buddhist worldview. Placing a premium value on intention reflects Geertz's theory that religion makes ethos (cultural values) intellectually acceptable.

Symbolic action reinforces a particular view of the world by expressing social relationships and giving people a sense of control. In Tibetan culture, symbols may be used to express both positive and negative social relationships. The presentation of honorific scarves, for example, usually indicates a desire for establishing or continuing positive social ties between individuals and other people or sacred beings. Other symbols are used to ward off negative social relationships aroused by envy and greed. Tibetans achieve a sense of control over their environment and circumstances by obtaining divinations from lamas, wearing protective amulets, flying prayer flags, and symbolically undertaking the turning of the wheel of life. All of these are examples of Victor Turner's (1967) notion that symbols can arouse desires and feelings and effect social action.

Although the Tibetan world is replete with what Westerners typically perceive as magic and mystery, Tibetans themselves are typically skeptical about professed miracles. For example, they take pains to validate the legitimacy of oracles and the recognition of reincarnate lamas. Refugee Tibetans might find themselves justifying religious practices to Westerners who assume that the appeasement of household spirits is incompatible with "true" Buddhism. Tibetans tend to point out that the goals of attaining enlightenment and of satisfying spirits who might make one sick are informed by distinct but complementary time frames: the one concerned with ultimate destiny; the other with improving one's immediate situation in order to be able to work more productively towards the ultimate destiny. Tibetan examples also illustrate that the apparent moral contradictions in certain practices disappear when one considers those practices in terms of relative degrees of compassionate actions. This sort of reasoning illustrates what Geertz (1973) would consider a meaningful relationship between ethos and worldview since it provides a way in which emotional interests can be reconciled with spiritual goals.

Exile meant that Tibetan families were decimated; people's means to secure their livelihood were lost; monasteries and their sacred texts, images, and persons were destroyed; and many people experienced severe psychological trauma. Some monks renounced their vows and took up arms to guard the Dalai Lama during his escape. On arriving in India, Tibetans had to adjust to a new climate, a new diet, often to new occupations, and to the varied cultures of India and the West. What is remarkable is the resilience of their ideology in the face of this upheaval. Major factors contributing to this resilience include the establishment and reestablishment of Tibetan monasteries, cultural institutions, and schools in India; the broadening interest in Tibetan religion and culture throughout the world; and the fundamental importance of the Dalai Lama to Tibetans as a spiritual and political leader and as a symbol of the Tibetan nation. The international renown achieved by the Dalai Lama furthers refugee Tibetans' understanding that their worldview is valued by the world.

REFERENCES AND RECOMMENDED READINGS

Craig, Mary
1997 Kundun: A Biography of the Family of the Dalai Lama. London: Harper Collins Publishers.
> Craig provides fascinating insight into the rise of a simple peasant family to the status of royalty and its role in Tibet's turbulent history based on extensive interviews with members of the Dalai Lama's immediate family.

Evans-Pritchard, E. E.
1987 [1937] Witchcraft Oracles and Magic Among the Azande. Oxford: Clarendon Press.
> An anthropological classic, this book probes the logic constructing the Sudanese Azande's beliefs in witchcraft, oracles, and magic.

The Dalai Lama
1983 [1962] My Land and My People: Memoirs of the Dalai Lama of Tibet. New York: Potala Corporation.
> The Dalai Lama's autobiography.

Goldstein, Melvyn C.
1989 A History of Modern Tibet, 1913–1951. Berkeley: University of California Press.
> An anthropologist utilizes oral history, written accounts by eyewitnesses, and archival materials to describe the history of Tibet from the time of the 13th Dalai Lama to the end of Tibet's existence as a sovereign state in 1951.

Knaus, John Kenneth
1999 Orphans of the Cold War: America and the Tibetan Struggle for Survival. New York: Public Affairs.
> A former CIA officer recounts American covert operations to train and supply Tibetan resistance fighters who waged guerrilla warfare against the Chinese occupying Tibet in the 1960s and early 1970s.

Norbu, Dawa T.
1998 [1986] Tibet: The Road Ahead. London: Rider.
> A Tibetan political scientist draws from his own and his family's experiences to compare commoners' lives in Tibet prior to and after 1959.

Norbu, Thubten Jigme
1986 Tibet Is My Country: Autobiography of Thubten Jigme Norbu, Brother of the Dalai Lama, as told to Heinrich Harrer. Edward Fitzgerald, trans. London: Wisdom Publications.
> An autobiography of the Dalai Lama's eldest brother, who was also recognized as a reincarnate lama.

Norbu, Thubten Jigme, and Colin M. Turnbull
1968 Tibet. New York: Simon and Schuster.
> In collaboration with an anthropologist, the Dalai Lama's eldest brother describes Tibetan lifestyles, history, and religion.

Richardson, Hugh E.
1984 [1962] Tibet and Its History. 2nd edition. Boston: Shambhala.
> The former British representative to Tibet gives an overview of Tibetan social organization, history, and an appendix of treaties and agreements to which Tibet was a signatory.

Shakabpa, Tsepon W. D.
1967 Tibet: A Political History. New Haven and London: Yale University Press. Translated from Tibetan, this book traces the history of Tibet from its ancient monarchy to 1950 and describes significant factors that contributed to the construction of Tibet as a theocratic state.

Shakya, Tsering
1999 The Dragon in the Land of Snows. London: Pimlico.
A Tibetan scholar's history of Tibet from 1947 to the 1990s, this book focuses on Chinese reforms and repression in Tibet and the political efforts of Tibetan refugees.

Stein, R. A.
1972 Tibetan Civilization. Stanford, CA: Stanford University Press. An excellent overview of Tibet's ancient monarchy and empire, its ancient religions, the establishment and development of Buddhism in Tibet and Tibetan ways of life, festivals, arts, and literature.

Thurman, Robert A. F.
1995 Essential Tibetan Buddhism. San Francisco: Harper. A fine introduction to the basic principles and practices of Tibetan Buddhism.

Additional References Cited

Austin, John
1962 How to Do Things with Words. London: Oxford University Press.

Douglas, Mary
1970 [1966] Powers and Dangers. *In* Purity and Danger. Pp. 114–136. London: Pelican Books.

Durkheim, Émile
1969 [1915] The Elementary Forms of the Religious Life. Joseph Ward Swain, trans. New York: The Free Press.

Geertz, Clifford
1973 Ethos, World View, and the Analysis of Sacred Symbols. *In* The Interpretation of Cultures. Pp. 87–125. New York: Basic Books.

Lévi-Strauss, Claude
1966 The Savage Mind. George Weidenfeld and Nicolson Ltd., trans. Chicago: University of Chicago Press.

Turner, Victor
1967 The Forest of Symbols. Ithaca: Cornell University Press.

Tylor, Edward Burnett
1958 [1871] Religion in Primitive Culture. New York: Harper.

CHAPTER 4

PATTERNS OF FAMILY RELATIONS

BARBARA J. MICHAEL

PROBLEM 4 *What do we need to know before we can understand the dynamics of family life in other societies?*

INTRODUCTION
Relatives Are Relative

If you are a North American, chances are that you grew up in a **nuclear family** composed of only yourself, your parents, and your siblings. Your family was probably identical in composition to your **household** (the people living together under one roof). In many other cultures, though, multigenerational households are typical. In places like Yemen and India, the **extended family** (three or more generations of blood relatives) would usually include people related to you only through your father. Among the Hopi, the extended family would be related to you only through your mother. For most North Americans, a grandparent who might come to live with you and your parents could be related through either parent. That is because most North Americans practice what anthropologists call **bilateral kinship** and **descent**, with the mother's and the father's sides equally determining kinship, descent, and inheritance. Yemenis, other Middle Easterners, and East Indians have **patrilineal** kinship and descent, counted only through a person's father's side, while the Hopi base their kinship and descent systems on **matrilineality**, reckoning relationships through a person's mother's side.

The kin group is a culturally defined set of people who consider themselves relatives, and the way in which people trace relatives back to previous generations (descent) is also culturally defined. The manner by which we determine kinship and descent will likely influence the formation of households and families. And it's all relative—that is, who your relatives are is relative only to your own culture. Genetics may be universal, but relatives are cultural.

These patterns not only influence the formation of households and families, but may also identify our most important social circle and tell us whom we can count on. Cultural patterns tell us who are our kin. How we view our various relatives helps us organize our social lives, identifying whom we live with, who our friends or enemies are, whom we can partner with in various sorts of cooperative activities, and perhaps even whom we can marry. Human beings organize themselves into many types of groups with a wide variety of rules about how people can be members. Membership in a kinship group is based on biological relationships, but different cultures view different aspects of biological relationships differently and choose to emphasize different aspects of those biological relationships. This chapter examines these and other questions through the ethnographic case of the Hawazma Baggara, pastoral nomads in the Sudan.

How Kinship Fits into Other Aspects of Culture

The various types of kinship and descent may influence aspects of life in a particular culture other than with whom a member may live. Other aspects of a culture may influence these patterns as well, in a sort of two-directional interaction. Anthropologists say *influence* rather than *determine* because every cultural or social rule includes leeway for members to break, or at least bend, it.

Economic patterns—the way people support their lives—may influence family organization and dynamics. In industrialized North America or Europe, when a parent takes a new job in a different part of the country, generally only a nuclear family is affected and has to move. Imagine moving a three- or four-generational patrilineal Yemeni family: grandparents, parents, unmarried children, and married sons with their families. Twenty or more people would have to move. For a family of Hindu Indian farmers, having a large extended family to provide farm labor is an economic advantage. Of course, neither the Yemeni nor the Hindu families, especially if they are farmers, would likely consider moving because their economic lives are tied closely to the land. In fact, families and places become so closely linked that knowing a person's name may be all that is needed to identify where the person is from. A Yemeni whose name includes "Kawkabani" or "Hadrami" is quickly identified as belonging to a family from the village of Kawkaban or from the Hadramout region. Even if names do not actually incorporate a place name, certain groups of names may be recognized as having their origins in a particular place. This is partly due to the way people think about where they should live in relation to their kin. Unless there are forced migrations as a result of conflicts or famines, or economic pressures make it necessary to disperse, people from many cultures assume that they should live their lives—for many, many generations—in clusters among their kin.

The influences of family organization can also be seen in language and belief. In Victorian England you would have claimed your identity through recognition of both of your parents, but only the eldest son would have inherited any property or a title of nobility from your father. As a North American, you and any or your siblings, male or female, can inherit property from either or both of your parents. But the family name by which you identify yourself typically comes from your father and his father.

Labeling Kin

There are other patterns, many of them linguistic, that indicate the importance of a particular family organization or descent system. You probably address both your father's and your mother's brothers as *uncle* and their sisters as *aunt*. Hawazma Baggara, who emphasize patrilineal connections, address their father's brothers (FB in anthropological shorthand) as *ami* and father's sisters (FZ) as *amti*. Cousins on their father's side are called *ibn 'aam* if they are male and *bint 'aam* if they are female. There is a parallel linguistic pattern for relatives on their mother's side. Her brother (MB) is addressed as *hali,* and her sister (MZ) is addressed as *halti.* Cousins on the mother's sides are either *ibn hal* or *bint hal.*

The chapter also shows how language may help foster a strengthening of certain kinship relationships that are socially or culturally important. Other factors besides economics may also influence family organization or marriage practices. The chapter examines how this works by looking carefully and closely at Hawazma Baggara patterns of family relations.

You may wonder why anthropologists use so many labels for different kinds of families and kinship patterns. Anthropology tries to understand humanity not only by looking in careful detail at a particular culture but also by comparing the practices and patterns of one culture with another. We have already seen that there is a big gap between what you and I mean by *cousin* and what a Hawazma Baggara means. Actually, a Hawazma Baggara cannot really talk about cousin without specifying a particular type of cousin. Terms such as *patrilineal, matrilineal, nuclear,* and *extended* and notations like *FB* for father's brother, and *MZ* for mother's sister make relationships clear. They are analogous to the Latin names botanists use for plants to overcome the confusion of many different local names for the same biological specimen. We use some kinship terms in this chapter, but the most important thing is to understand how different aspects of systems of kinship and family organization function to maintain a set of particular cultural patterns.

The Hawazma Baggara

The Hawazma Baggara are **pastoral nomads** who live in an area called the Nuba Mountains in the Sudan. Anthropologists say that the Hawazma Baggara (whom we call the Hawazma) are a **tribe** because of the way their groups are organized. They are one of five major tribes that together constitute a confederation known as Baggara.

While there are variations between one Baggara tribe and another, they all share certain cultural and social features. They are all nomadic; they depend on livestock for their subsistence; and they are patrilineal. They all share the same belief system and are Muslim. Most importantly, members of each of the tribes believe that they share several common ancestors with the

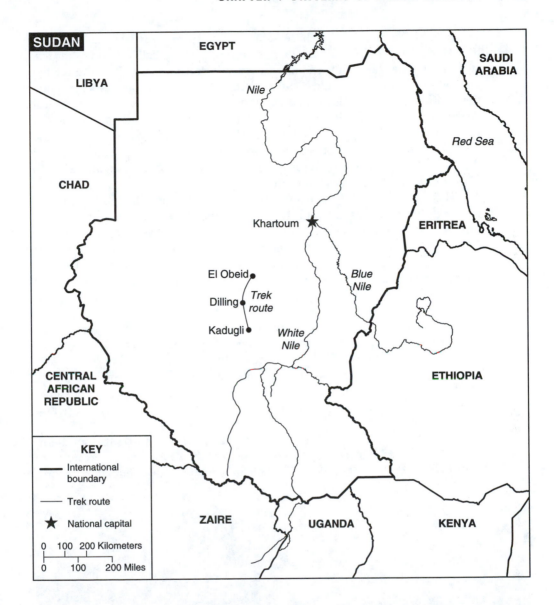

other tribes as well as with members of their own tribe; that is, they believe they are all descended from the same three or four men hundreds of generations ago.

The Hawazma raise cattle as their primary herd animal, although they also keep goats, sheep, and chickens. Like many nomads, they raise some crops: sorghum, sesame, and cowpeas. Some men also travel away from home to undertake wage labor, often in places like Saudi Arabia where, although the risk is high because they often work illegally, the wages are also high. Even though the Hawazma participate in a number of economic activities that are not directly pastoral nomadic, all the economic activities foster or support pastoral nomadism in some way.

The ecological zone occupied by the Hawazma is savanna, where the landscape varies from flat plains to rolling hills. Other groups, some of them settled farmers, also inhabit these same zones. Historically, the main groups the Hawazma share this territory with are the so-called Nuba groups. Westerners who had early encounters with these tribes, which are unrelated groupings of related peoples, called them all *Nuba* without understanding their differences. The Hawazma and the Nuba utilized the same ecological zone in two very different ways. Nuba farmers tended to live on the tops of hills and to raise crops on the hill slopes. The Hawazma used the plains at the foot of the hills, as it is not easy to graze cattle on the slopes. The Nuba and the Hawazma still share the territory, though many Nuba are moving down to plant on the foot slopes or even on the plains.

The plains are cut by wadis (Arabic for stream beds), though even in the rainy season the wadis run with water only during or immediately after a rain. The rainy season is short, lasting from June to October at most. Annual rainfall ranges from only about 200 millimeters in the northern part of Hawazma territory to about 600 millimeters in the southern part. Sparse rainfall makes for sparse vegetation. There are various kinds of grasses, thorny shrubs, and small, thorny trees. The only really large trees are baobabs, which are found only in the northern part of Hawazma territory.

Unlike some pastoral nomads who move to new pastures and new campsites every few weeks, the Hawazma make major moves only twice a year, at the beginning and end of the rainy season. If you look at the map, you will see that the line of Hawazma movement is almost directly north and south. The Hawazma go north when the rains begin and south when the rains end. The distance is about 200 miles, and a move is done in stages over a period of about a month.

The Hawazma consider their home territory, or *dar,* to be the southernmost part of the area. During the rainy season they move north, away from their home territory. They describe their movement and its direction accord-

The rainy season trek—moving herds and households to seasonal pastures.
(Photograph by Barbara J. Michael.)

ing to the soil types they cross. They begin from the *tiin* (clay) of their home territory and cross the *gardud* (mixed sandy clay). Their goal is to reach the *qoz,* or sandy soils. The highest annual rainfall is in the *dar* in the south, and the least rainfall on the *qoz* of the north that borders on the Sahara Desert.

There are many reasons to move out of the zone of higher rainfall during the rainy season. The clay soils get extremely sticky when it rains, so much so that cattle can literally sink to their "armpits" in the mire. Hordes of small insects move in clouds that can block the nasal passages of cattle, causing them to suffocate. The mosquitoes that carry malaria are also more prolific. While there are malarial mosquitoes in the northern part of the territory, they are not as problematic as in the wetter southern zone.

The clay soil of the south makes it possible for pools of water to form and to remain standing for the better part of the dry season, during which there is no rainfall at all. The grasses in the clay zone also grow tall and form standing hayfields that can be grazed during the dry season. Grasses are short on the sandy soils of the north, and they virtually disappear during the dry season, leaving nothing to graze. Water does not pool on sandy soils, but runs off or seeps into the earth as groundwater. Moving north during the rainy season allows the Hawazma to use resources that will not be available in that area after the end of the rains, saving resources in the southern zone that will last for the remainder of the year.

The Hawazma's ability to utilize these different landscapes and to maintain their subsistence as pastoral nomads is enhanced by their family organization and relationships and by a tribal organization that parallels their family organization. Their kinship and family patterns are both biological and culturally relative.

QUESTIONS

4.1. What is the composition of the typical family group?

4.2. How is the family formed and the ideal family type maintained?

4.3. What are the roles of sexuality, love, and wealth?

4.4. What forces threaten to disrupt the family unit?

4.5. How does the pastoral nomadic lifestyle continue to fit into the modern world?

QUESTION 4.1
What Is the Composition of the Typical Family Group?

Two men walking across the Sudanese savanna meet. They do not recognize each other, but they greet each other politely. The first thing they ask each other is "What is your **lineage**?" They recognize each other as Hawazma by subtle clues in their manner and dress, but they need to know more. They can locate each other within a specific kin group once they know that the other man's lineage is Oulad Nuba, Dar Nyla, or Dar Sholongo, for example. When their lineages have been established, they ask each other "Whose camp are you from?" (that is, who is your sheikh or leader?) and "Who is your father?" Both questions lead to information each needs in order to relate to or deal with the other. Least important is knowing each other's given names, though once they have determined that they should be on friendly terms, their personal names become important, just as a personal relationship may become important. But what is most important at the beginning is the question of how their kin groups relate to each other, because each Hawazma man and woman must relate to people within his or her own group and to particular other groups in certain ways that have been established by group consensus and backed by kinship. Thus, each man must establish whether his group is cooperative, friendly, actively feuding with, neutral toward, closer to, or more distant from the group of the man he just met. The answer will dictate how he interacts with the man. Will they fight? Will they become aloof and go their own ways with no further words? Will they inquire politely about their respective sheikhs? Will they clap each other on the shoulder, sit down for a long chat, and exchange information about grazing conditions or markets?

How Kinship Frames Relationships

We already know that the Hawazma have a patrilineal kinship system. The first thing the men in the paragraph above have established is that they are members of the same tribe of Baggara. They then identify the next level of kinship, their lineage, which is also based on relationships of male ancestors. Identifying their fathers places them within a more specific set of male relatives and may even tell them whether they have any relationship to each other. What we see in this example is that personal identity is subsumed within group identity. This characteristic of Hawazma society provides some clues about how individuals may behave, particularly in situations where group good takes precedence over individual preferences.

Let us imagine that the men have established that although they are from different lineages, their lineages are on friendly terms. They become good friends and frequently visit. One year there is very little rainfall, and the herdsmen are tense and worried about the condition of their animals. The brother of one of the men is at a shallow well, trying to draw up enough water for his thirsty herd. A close cousin of the second man comes along with his herd with the intention of using the same well. The animals press in on each other in confusion and thirst. There are strong words; the tension escalates; and the brother of the first man kills the cousin of the second man. The dead man is the second man's father's brother's son (FBS in anthropological notation). Now the two lineages are no longer on good terms. In fact, they are now involved in a blood **feud**, meaning that one way to resolve the problem created by the killing is for revenge to be taken. The cultural expectation is that all the members of the dead man's lineage will now stand opposed to all the members of the killer's lineage.

Now the two friends are again out walking alone. The cousin of the dead man recognizes his friend. Will he call out a greeting? Personally, they are good friends. But his cousin was killed, and the killer was the brother of his friend. This time the men are duty-bound to operate as members of their respective groups, not on the basis of their personal relationship. The cousin of the dead man is bound by his membership in his lineage to take revenge on this person who belongs to and therefore represents the lineage of the killer. Moreover, the rules for blood revenge specify that the death of a brother or a cousin of the killer will neutralize the first killing.

Imagine a different scenario. The two men have established their group identities and have determined that their lineages are friendly, but they do not become personal friends. They see each other occasionally, but that is all. Men from another tribe of nomads who are not Hawazma or Baggara start pushing their herds into the territory traditionally used by the lineage of one of the men. There are skirmishes, and several men from that man's lineage are killed. That man's *omda,* or paramount sheikh, goes to the paramount sheikh of the other man's lineage.[1] The two paramount sheikhs agree to support and defend each other from the intrusions of the other nomads. There is really no other possibility because both lineages are Hawazma and the intruders are not even Baggara. Shortly after the agreement is reached between the two paramount sheikhs, a scout from the first man's lineage spots a camp of the other nomads. A meeting is held, and a plan is made to attack the intruders and drive them out of the Hawazma lineage's territory. In the ensuing battle, one of the men from that chance meeting on the savanna finds himself surrounded and cut off from the other men of his lineage. The other man from that chance meeting sees what has happened and rallies his lineage mates to risk their lives to go to the first man's rescue. The second man is not acting out of friendship, though they become friends after this, but out of the obligations to which he is subject because of the relationship of his lineage to the lineage of the man he rescues.

Each of these scenarios is summarized in the proverb, common throughout the Middle East, "I against my brother; my brother and I against our cousin; my cousin and I against the world." But if I am Hawazma, who is my brother and who is my cousin? The answer seems to be biologically based, but this chapter examines that assumption. Also important is the matter of how I draw the boundaries between myself and my group and the rest of the world.

We begin the investigation of how Hawazma family groups are composed with a description of the relationships between larger groups called lineages and tribes because it's all relative. For the Hawazma, political groups are also kinship groups. Before we can fully understand how smaller units like households and camping units are formed, we have to understand the interlinking of the smaller units with the larger units that are both kin groups and political groups. The goals of each must serve the goals of the others.

The Baggara Family Tree

Figure 4.1 is a family tree, or genealogy, of groups that illustrates a kinship relationship between Baggara tribes and Hawazma lineages, sublineages, and patrilines (smaller groups of men quite closely related through their fathers). The tree is turned on its side so that we can look at the tribal genealogy as a time line or continuum. The name at the far left is Baggara, the confederation

---

[1]Each group, whether large or small, must have a leader, although among the Hawazma, a leader acts only after gaining consensus among all the men in his group. Since the lineage is divided into smaller parts, each with its own sheikh, the entire lineage also has a paramount sheikh recognized by men from all the segments.

FIGURE 4.1. Genealogy

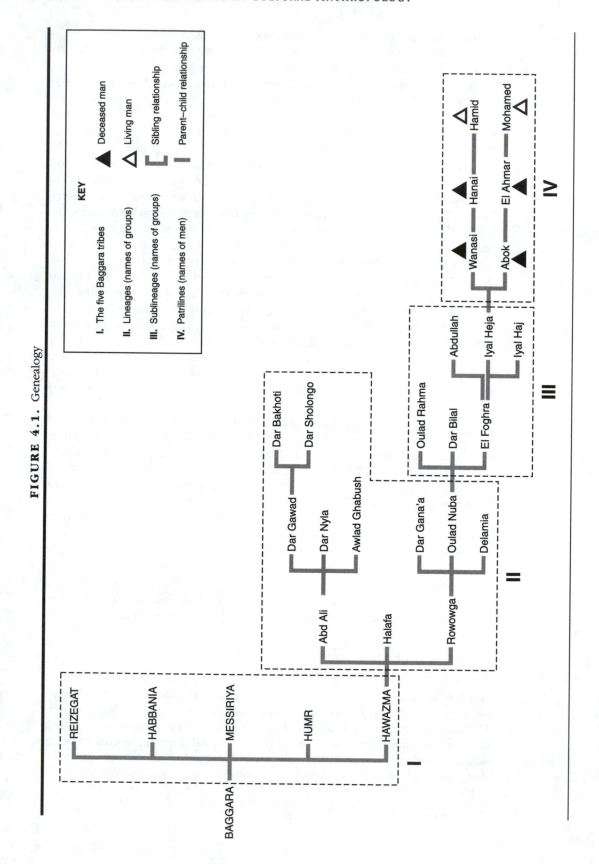

of five tribes. Next are the five tribes, then lineages, then sublineages, and finally patrilines representing three generations of male descendents. Camping units are small localized groups representing two or three patrilines. I worked with a camp composed of the two patrilines shown in the figure, plus one other.

This same diagram could represent the United States, for example, with the whole country or maximal political unit on the far left. The states would be next, with ever-smaller units on the right along the continuum, down to towns. In this example, the units are solely political, formed on the basis of geography and legal processes like incorporating a town. The units on the Baggara tree are also political units, but the political units are formed on the basis of kinship or asserted kinship. (We discuss asserted kinship later.) Large political entities, whether Baggara or the United States, cannot always act as a total unit. So there must be a mechanism to break the total unit into smaller units for other purposes.

The Baggara unit breaks down, or segments, to the smallest unit, the camping unit (*fariq*, as it is called in Arabic). Because the Baggara are pastoral nomads and base their economy on animal husbandry, the smallest units are not only political units but are also management units. In a savanna environment it is not possible to have huge cattle ranches. An area can support only a certain number of animals, which varies according to the availability of grazing and water. Additionally, it is impossible to manage a herd beyond a certain size. There are no barbed wire enclosures in Hawazma territory, and farmers use the land for crops as well. The Hawazma have to be able to keep track of their animals and control their movements. Each family typically has between 50 and 150 head of cattle, plus sheep and goats. Each camping unit consists of, on average, ten families or households. Thus a camping unit may have as many as 1500 cattle associated with it. Each camping unit must be sufficiently distanced from the others so that there is adequate grazing and water and to keep herds from mixing, bulls from fighting, and animal diseases from spreading.

Small camping units are often too small for political action. So they can coalesce into sublineages. Sublineages may also be too small, so they can join together as lineages. In some political circumstances, action may be necessary at the tribal level, and there might be circumstances when all Baggara need to stand together. Anthropologists call these **segmentary lineages**. They are **corporate** units that generally act independently in everyday affairs, but can come together or break apart as the need arises. Actually, according to the circumstances, each segment, whether a camping unit, lineage, or tribe, can act as a corporate unit. This type of social and political organization gives the Baggara the flexibility to deal with environmental and political factors at various levels. It provides a mechanism for efficient management of daily affairs and for collective action in larger political affairs, either internal to the Baggara or with external entities, like the government of Sudan.

All of these units are viewed by the Hawazma as being related through a line of males. Whether we are talking about political units or particular sets of families, we are essentially talking about a patrilineal kinship system with tribes, lineages, sublineages, and camping units descended from the maximal unit, Baggara, through the male line. Thus we see that Hawazma political units and kinship groups are intertwined differently than in our own system, in

Men from several camps discuss issues and petitions to the government of Sudan at a lineage meeting.
(Photograph by Barbara J. Michael.)

which bilateral kinship units do not have a direct or overlapping relationship to towns, states, or the nation.

There are advantages to an overlapping relationship, particularly if we give credence to the proverb "Blood is thicker than water." The Hawazma do not have to negotiate loyalties at the lineage or tribal level; the loyalties are already there as a result of kinship loyalty. There are different levels of loyalty, depending on the context and circumstances. The adage quoted earlier—"I against my brother; my brother and I against our cousin; my cousin and I against the world"—not only invokes kinship obligations; it also embodies political loyalties and action from the smallest to the largest units of Hawazma political organization.

Within this political organization is nested family organization and membership. Families must be organized and formed in a manner that maximizes the kinship relationships required when the various units are acting as political units. Ideologically, there is no room for outsiders who do not fit into the genealogy. That is, the cultural understanding is that each unit at every level, from a newly formed household created by a new marriage up to the maximal unit, must reinforce and solidify kinship relationships.

When I first began working with the Hawazma, I collected genealogies to help me learn who people were and how they were related. I might, for example, ask a man, "Who is that, and how is he related to you?" Frequently I would be told, "He is my brother," or "He is my cousin." But when I sat with each of the men to construct a genealogy, they did not cite a common father or uncle. What I learned was that the Hawazma claim kinship as a way of informing outsiders—whether anthropologists, members of other lineages, or the government—that they would act with the loyalty of brothers or cousins. In a segmentary lineage system, all the men in a camping unit are expected to be related as brothers and/or cousins. The reality is that some men from a different lineage may have decided, for one reason or another, to live with a lineage other than their own. Unresolved arguments, for example, might be a reason for deciding to live in another lineage.

This kind of created kinship affiliation occurs at all levels of the segmentary lineage system. In fact, although the Hawazma claim to be descended from 'Atia, the forefather of all Baggara, studies of disease and blood characteristics suggest that the Hawazma, or at least some sections of the Hawazma, are of non-Arabic origin and have no genealogical relationship to other Baggara. Rather, they represent a political confederation grafted onto the genealogy to look like a kin relationship, and they have been accepted and have come to have the status of blood brothers and cousins.

It's all culturally relative. Your relatives are who you choose to claim as relatives. You may not be able to manipulate your genes, but you can manipulate your genealogy to make it support whatever kinship claims you want to make. When the genealogy is manipulated, it is to allow you to act as if the postulated relationship is real. A brother is someone who acts as a brother.

QUESTION 4.2
How Is *the Family Formed and the Ideal Family Type Maintained*?

In addition to procreation and the replication or maintenance of Hawazma society, there are at least two other goals to be accomplished by the formation of new families. One is the maintenance of the political strength of the tribe, which is accomplished by maintaining strong links of kinship among all the members of the political group. The second goal is economic. Hawazma family organization and the formation of new families are often linked to the pastoral nomadic system and strategies for maintaining that economic system. There are a variety of ways in which these goals might be accomplished.

Multilayered Kinship

Both political solidarity and economic strength can be maintained by keeping everything in the family. One of the primary ways societies accomplish this is by a marriage pattern known as **endogamy**, or marrying only someone from within the group (as opposed to **exogamy**, marrying outside the group). Endogamy is culturally defined and may mean from within one's own village, one's own social status or caste, or one's own kin group. Endogamy creates multiple or layered linkages. In North America, we say that marriages bring new members into our families. In an endogamous system, the same members or kinsmen take on additional roles. In the case of the Hawazma, the preferred form of endogamous marriage is marrying a close cousin. The preferred first-marriage partner for a young man is a young woman who falls into the category of FBD, or father's brother's daughter. Other permutations, such as FFBSD, are possible and have the same result.

In North America, marriages of cousins are often forbidden by law. Our North American prohibition on marrying cousins is arguably a reaction to knowledge of the results of inbreeding. Problems arise from cousin marriages when this type of marriage is repeated over and over with no variation. But there is probably no FBD available for a high percentage of Hawazma young men seeking marriage partners. If a young man marries his FFBSD, the genetic or biological relationship between the two is more distant. Here we see the incongruity between a cultural rule or preference and actual behavior, between the ideal and the real.

If no FBD or equivalents can be found, what are the other preferred choices? The next best marriage partner is someone who is MBD. The same permutations apply, and it might be MMBSD. Of course, the reality is that a young man might marry someone from outside any of these preferred categories of partners. He might marry a woman from a different lineage or from a different tribe of pastoralists, or he might marry the daughter of a settled farmer from another ethnic group.

Endogamous marriages can strengthen economic viability. In order to negotiate a marriage, a young man's family must give **bridewealth** to the young woman's family. The Hawazma pay much of the bridewealth in cattle. If a young man proposes to marry someone from a different lineage, cattle will move out of his lineage. If, however, he marries someone from the preferred category of FBD or even MBD, and assuming that his parents were both from the same lineage, the cattle will simply shift location within a close kin group. This is desirable because pastoral nomads must maintain a minimal herd size to remain economically viable. There should be adequate numbers of milk and meat animals, and the herd must be reproducing at an acceptable rate. Animal pastoralism is a very risky business, and it may be difficult to maintain a minimal herd. In savanna environments, herds can be decimated by disease and drought, and it takes a long time to reconstitute a herd by natural reproduction.

Suppose a young man's family contracts a marriage for him with a young woman from another lineage. The agreed-on number of cattle move to her lineage. Then herds in the young man's lineage are subjected to a debilitating disease like bovine pleuropneumonia, and many animals die. Herd numbers might become so low that the economic security of his family is threatened. When the animals paid for bridewealth are kept within the same sublineage, relatives are obligated to support each other and can rally to the support of a kinsman whose herd is so reduced by shifting animals around. Herds are a pastoralist's walking bank account. Losing animals is like having the cash you hid in your mattress burn up in a house fire, with one major difference. If a breeding pair survives, or if you have access to a breeding pair from one of your close relatives, you can begin to regenerate your herd.

Matchmaking

With these goals consciously or unconsciously in mind, how does a young man go about finding a wife? Hawazma believe that the older generation should arrange marriages for young people. A young man may indicate to his mother, his father, or his 'aam (cousins) that he is interested in a particular young woman. Indeed, the young man and the young woman may have managed to meet and to indicate mutual interest in one another. But the final decision is made by the young man's and the young woman's parents.

Parents take the kinship relationship of the proposed pair into consideration. They consider whether the young man appears to be responsible and a potentially good herdsman. The young man's mother will likely know whether the young woman appears to have learned the tasks necessary to running a household, managing and milking a herd, and astutely marketing milk and milk products. The character of each will also be considered. If the young woman seems to be a suitable partner, a male relative of the young man will discuss the possibility of marriage and what will be included in the bridewealth with a male relative of the young woman.

Once negotiations are completed, arrangements will be made for the ceremony cementing the contract. A religious sheikh presides over the ritual of the contract, which is a verbal agreement, Hawazma society having been non-literate until fairly recently. After the contract is made, it usually takes several months or a year for the bridewealth to be gathered. The young man's family will be expected to give the young woman gifts of clothing, perfume, or jewelry several times during this period. Clothing is also a part of the negotiated bridewealth, and it is gathered and ceremoniously brought to the prospective bride's home and to her mother. On one such occasion, I witnessed the bride's mother decide that the gift was inadequate and refuse to accept it. The woman representing the young man's family had to carry the gift back home, and the "insulting" gift was a topic of discussion at women's gatherings for some time.

The bridewealth is often collected from male relatives in addition to the young man's father, especially from his FB. There are many reasons for this. Taking all the bridewealth from his father's herd might leave the herd much diminished, threatening the father's wealth and economic viability. Collecting from each of his FBs spreads the burden among several herdsmen. It also reinforces their kinship relationship. They are obligated to help because they are close kinsmen; their joint contribution also underscores their kinship commitment. Collecting from several male relatives puts the young man in a position of obligation to these FBs, without whose support he might not have been able to be married.

The bridewealth cattle go to the young woman's father, though some may be distributed to his male relatives. This puts the young woman under obligation also, primarily not to be divorced. Should a divorce occur, the bridewealth cattle must be returned, perhaps placing hardship on the young woman's family.

Arranging Marriages

Most of the marriages I recorded do not fit the FBD pattern, though the marriage partners were "close cousins." It does not really matter that the cultural rules were not followed exactly since the goals of endogamous marriage were met.

Hamid, the son of the sheikh of the camp in which I lived, married Naima, his FZD (father's sister's daughter). This was considered to be a good marriage for both partners. Naima's father had been killed in a lorry (truck) accident some years earlier, and the sheikh had taken responsibility for looking after the family. Among the Hawazma, brothers have lifelong responsibility for their widowed or divorced sisters. At the time of his sister's husband's death, the sons of the family were still young, and though they could serve as herd boys, they were not capable of managing the herd they would inherit. Though I was not present when Hamid and Naima were married and did not learn the details of their negotiations, it is probable that the bridewealth payments were minimal since Naima was so closely related to her prospective husband, and his father had been her family's male protector.

At the time of the marriage, the sheikh already had two sorts of roles in relation to his prospective daughter-in-law: he was her maternal uncle (MB) and her male protector. When Hamid and Naima married, the sheikh also became her father-in-law. The marriage strengthened the ties between him and his sister's family. The sheikh was not the only one who took on multiple roles. Cousins were now husband and wife, a niece was now a daughter-in-law, and Hamid's maternal aunt was now his mother-in-law. This is a virtual web of interlinking and overlapping kinship relationships. Roles bring obligations, and so the obligations that each had to the other also multiplied and solidified. All served, consciously or unconsciously, the political and economic goals of the group.

While Hamid and Naima's marriage might not have been calculated in terms of achieving group goals, some marriages do consciously set out to accomplish a political or economic goal. Nur, for example, first married Fatna, from his own lineage, the Oulad Nuba. Fatna is Nur's FBD and fits the preferred marriage pattern. Then, he married a woman from the Dar Sholongo lineage. Since lineages may come into conflict, marriages between lineages may foster amicable relationships between them.

Some years later, one of Fatna's sisters married a Dar Sholongo man from the same *fariq* or camp as Nur's second wife. These marriages were described as a sort of exchange, an Oulad Nuba woman for a Dar Sholongo woman. The members of the camps of the two lineages considered themselves friends, and the two marriages reinforced the bond.

In another case, Ahmed had already married two Oulad Nuba women when he decided to marry a third time. His first wife had died in childbirth, so he had but one wife at the time of his third marriage. His new wife was the daughter of a merchant from the Bederiya tribe and not Baggara at all. Ahmed was a merchant with a small shop in a village area where a number of Oulad Nuba had established sedentary households. He had frequent dealings with the Bederiya merchant before his marriage to the man's daughter. Ahmed's first two marriages had been within the preferred marriage pattern, so his third marriage could foster other ends.

Another purpose of a marriage might be to change identity. We discussed earlier how genealogies can be manipulated. Manipulation of the tribal genealogy made the Hawazma look like original Baggara, although they probably became Baggara through political confederation. The same sort of genealogical manipulation can take place at a lower level. One family in the camp I worked with was from the Showabna tribe. For reasons I never learned, Yahya had decided that he and his wife and children would join the Oulad Nuba camp of Sheikh Yunis, and they had been living and herding with the camp for many years. His household and thus his descendants were moving toward becoming Baggara, and this was taking place through marriage of his children to Oulad Nuba. One of Yahya's daughters had already married an Oulad Nuba man, and his other children would probably follow suit.

Permanent links to the Oulad Nuba were being created so that "genealogical amnesia" would result in the grafted members being redefined as full Oulad Nuba and Baggara within several generations.

How Polygynous Marriages Solve Many Problems

Marriages can also be a part of an economic strategy. In many of the cases of **polygynous**[2] marriages I recorded, one wife and her children would be living in the nomad camp and engaging in animal husbandry. A second wife and her children would be established as a settled agricultural family and would be engaged in raising crops, or like Ahmed's family they would be living in a village hamlet and involved in trade.

Usually, each wife and her children would be involved in either agriculture or herding. But there was also a great deal of movement of individuals between sedentary and nomadic activities over one or more annual cycles or throughout their life cycles. Sons of the agricultural family would typically help the herding family with tasks that required more manpower, like vaccinating the cattle. Sons of the nomadic family might help out with harvesting. School-age nomadic children often live with their father's settled wife in order to be closer to a school, particularly because the trekking season coincides with part of the academic year. A pregnant nomadic wife might live with relatives in town during the trekking season because trekking is physically taxing and might have negative consequences for her pregnancy.

During one trekking season, 'Aisha, who had been living in the village hamlet, joined the nomadic camp in the hope that doing so would help her young daughter, who had nearly died from severe diarrhea, recover her health. There is a strong belief that a nomadic life is healthful because there is a lot of milk available and because the air is better and the camps cleaner than in settled hamlets. It worked for 'Aisha's daughter, Maryiam, who overcame the effects of mirasmus, a form of malnutrition that had so weakened her that she was unable to hold up her head.

Besides allowing movement between nomadic and settled households to solve short-term problems, polygynous marriages constitute a strategy for flexibility and survival in an economic system subject to environmental vagaries. All of a man's children derive their identities through him, so in one sense all of a man's children, regardless of who their mothers are, belong to one family. All—full siblings and half siblings—have obligations to one another. Therefore, all of them benefit by living in households focused on different economic activities. Each has access to a broader range of products than would be available if all were doing the same kind of thing. Nomadic households cannot produce enough grain, which is a staple food, even though they plant some crops before leaving on trek. Sedentary households, whether Baggara or not, rely on nomads for milk and meat. When the two sorts of economic production are undertaken by different segments of the same family, a wider range of products becomes available to each. In the short term, this means that nei-

[2]Polygyny is the form of polygamous marriage involving a husband and more than one wife. It is by far the most common form of **polygamy**. In the Hawazama case, with bridewealth being requisite to marriage, it is not the law that limits multiple marriages so much as it is economics.

ther a nomadic nor a sedentary household must purchase all its grain or all its animal products. They trade. The nomadic household provides milk cows to the sedentary household, and the sedentary household provides at least a part of the grain required by the nomadic household. Over the long term, it means that if too many animals are lost to drought or disease, there are links that allow a man to survive as a farmer. Or, if crops fail, the sedentary family can become nomadic for a time. Thus, a nomadic man might choose to have both nomadic and sedentary households as a longer-term strategy.

Deciding Where to Live

After marriage, the new couple most often goes to live in the camp of the husband's family (what anthropologists call **patrilocal** residence). The new wife will usually build her house next to her mother-in-law's house. Her mother-in-law is usually also a paternal or maternal aunt. Hawazma households are never really extended households in which multiple generations share common meals and living space and pool resources. Each woman owns her own house and its contents and has her own cows. Meals may be shared with a neighbor, but the preparation is not communal unless there is a feast or other celebration. After the first year or so of marriage, a young man might decide to herd his animals with another camp, or his wife might decide to build her house next to a woman who is her friend.

Other members of the group may also vary their living arrangements, depending on either the needs of economic production or life-cycle circumstances. A widow might decide to maintain her house in her husband's camp or to live near a brother. Elderly people unable to live alone might join the camp household of a daughter or son or live with or near relatives in town. Children might also change their living arrangements before they are grown, particularly if they are in school. Or a grandmother might want to have a granddaughter live with her to help with chores.

Solving Marital Discord

Both families will go to great lengths to preserve a marriage. Even if there is merely an argument, kinsmen from either or both sides may intervene to convince the couple to find a solution. If one partner is seen as being at fault, male relatives, particularly, will strongly lecture that partner.

Hawazma women who have marital problems always have the recourse of returning to their natal home. If her husband is in the wrong, a woman will generally have support from her father and her brothers. One indicator of the strength of a woman's lifelong natal ties is that she does not take her husband's name when she marries, but continues to be identified through her own patriline.

In one case, Younis' young wife Zahara ran away because she was angry with him. She was newly married and inexperienced. The day before, she had had to work under a burning sun to reconstruct her house, which had blown down in a rainstorm. She also had cows to milk and meals to cook. Running away was how Zahara brought attention to her situation. If the problem was left to fester, she might have returned to her mother's house and asked for a divorce. Younis' older cousins and an uncle looked for her, and they found her napping under a tree not too far away from the camp. Zahara had probably wanted to be found; with any determination she could have been much farther away. The men brought her back to camp and spent an hour or so asking her what was wrong and chastising her. Both Younis and his father stayed out of the discussion, though her father-in-law talked to her later to assure Zahara that she was a part of the household, though, of course, he wanted her to behave properly. He was also concerned about his son's behavior, because if his son was not behaving as a good husband, that news would soon spread and would affect the family's reputation.

In another case, Naima seriously threatened to divorce Hamid, a threat she underscored by leaving their house and staying away for more than a week. Hamid was clearly in the wrong. He had been away attending wedding celebrations for several days, behavior many people thought irresponsible for a married man. He created a bigger problem by returning home late one evening and demanding that Naima cook him a meal. Wives are supposed to cook for their husbands, but it was many hours after the time of the regular meal. Naima refused, as was her right in these circumstances, and Hamid hit her. When Naima ran away, everyone was outraged at Hamid. The older women exercised indirect social control by gossiping about Hamid and talking loudly about his bad behavior where his father could hear them. Hamid's uncle, his father's brother, lectured him on more than one occasion about hitting a woman. The intervention of kin reined in inappropriate behavior that might in time have led to a divorce.

QUESTION 4.3
What Are the Roles of Sexuality, Love, and Wealth?

Not only is the choice of a young person's mate allocated to adults, but the way interaction between the sexes is organized also limits a young couple's ability to get to know each other. Although all societies and cultures have **norms**, or rules, that everyone is expected to follow, they are not always followed exactly, and there is cultural leeway for variation or allowances for "human nature."

Daily activities in a Hawazma camp are divided into male and female spheres both according to norms and in actual practice. It is not that women's activities are circumscribed by restrictions, but that men and women rarely work in tandem on the same task in the same location at the same time. Young girls and boys play together, but once they reach the age of eight or so, life begins to be much more gender-segregated. Girls begin helping their mothers more, and boys may be sent out to herd goats and sheep or calves. Older boys are given more responsibility for herding cattle, and older girls take on more and more of the household chores, including fetching wood and water, cooking, and marketing milk.

Many women's activities are concentrated around their houses. The cooking hearth is directly in front of the door, and cows are milked just beyond the main living area. Women go far away from camps to gather firewood or house-building materials or to fetch water, and they may travel long distances on foot to sell milk and milk products or to go visiting. They may go with their husbands to help with the harvest. But instead of cutting sorghum stalks side-by-side with their husbands, they prepare meals and fetch water.

Men gather at a place in the center of the camp or at a point along its periphery where there is a tree or other shelter under which they can sit. They chat or make plans for herding or trekking, receive male visitors, or sleep where they can guard the cattle. Men share their meals with other men and their older sons at their tree. Each man's wife brings or sends a bowl of food she has cooked to the tree, where all the men will share the food sent by all the women. While a woman may carry a bowl of food to the edge of the cir-cle of gathered men, she will not engage in any but terse conversation and will never sit down to chat or to share a meal.

Women share meals with one another in front of or inside one woman's house. Men will not come to a woman's house during the day to sit and chat or to take a meal with the women. Perhaps if a man is a very close relative, such as a brother, he might stop by for tea and a short chat. Even a woman's husband will not hang around the house unless he is very old, and even then he is more likely to hobble over to the men's tree.

Young people past the age of about nine or ten are expected to follow these patterns. While very young boys and girls play together, and no one takes note or offense when they are romping naked together, young adoles-cents are expected to be more circumspect. Girls of twelve are considered to be ready or nearly ready for marriage. Although the age of marriage is rising, young women must comport themselves properly around their potential mar-riage partners.

The actual behavior of adolescents does not always conform to the norms. During my first nights in a Hawazma camp, I fell asleep to the laughter and singing of adolescents and young unmarried adults who had gathered just out-side the edge of the camp to dance or, as they called it, play. Groups of young people might also gather near some woman's house where they would chat, tell stories, joke, or gossip freely in her presence. This behavior is one of the enigmas of culture. Because these young people were all close cousins, they could be relatively free with each other. (If the young men had brought unre-lated young male friends to visit, their female cousins would not have joined in.) Yet these very cousins were potential marriage partners who should not, according to the norms, interact too freely or closely.

Young people might also go to a wrestling match together. The young women dressed in their finery would be the cheering section, singing songs they improvised about the prowess of the young men from their camp. Four or more of the young men might actually participate as wrestlers, while the others would go as spectators. The wrestling matches would draw hundreds of people from nearby camps. As you can imagine, wrestling was not the only item on the agenda. Such occasions give young people a chance to look each over with an eye to finding a partner. Encounters are under the chaperoning eye of the whole group; the young men and women all look out for each other's behavior to a certain extent. Nevertheless, a shy smile is noted, or a glance from an appreciative eye is met. Inquiries can be made: whose son is that, whose daughter is over there?

Ceremonial occasions offer other opportunities for young people to meet

Putting the finishing touches on a wedding house built for a new bride and groom. Only wedding houses have colored mats on the outside. (Photograph by Barbara J. Michael.)

and find ways to get to know each other. Anthropologists have frequently found that ritual occasions offer opportunities to bend rules or to temporarily abandon them. Weddings are particularly good occasions for meeting eligible partners or experimenting with opposite-sex relationships. Kinsfolk from many different camps gather to celebrate the establishment of a new household, and adult men and women can be much freer together. Some of the norms seem to be purposely broken as a means of expressing everyone's interest in and support of a new family. For example, when a new camp is established, only women build houses or collect the materials for their construction. At wedding ceremonies, men and women work side-by-side to gather materials and construct a new house for the newlyweds. This joint project seems to be a symbolic expression of solidarity toward the new couple. On one occasion, I saw men, women, and children huddled together, gleefully looking at family photographs one man had brought.

Since there are so many people to cook for at ceremonial occasions, there are often many fires going, many pots boiling, and a lot of food preparation going on almost all the time. Most of the women help out with the cooking. The cooking takes place in a large open area, and often all—male and female, young and old—gather around the evening cooking fires, where they laugh, tell stories about each other, or talk about events. Young women and men intermingle, cluster together, and form pairs that sometimes edge farther and farther away from the circle of light cast by the fires. Soft voices and laughter can be heard from the dark distance. The parents who notice do not mind.

Sometimes young people who have come to know each other do marry each other. A young man might tell an adult who would be part of marriage negotiations that he is interested in a particular young woman. Even so, the marriage will not take place without the proper negotiations and the agreement of adults about the character, worthiness, and suitability of the partners and the conditions of the marriage, including the bridewealth. Love, pheromones, or attraction might play a part in a few marriages, but generally speaking, Hawazma parents arrange marriages for their offspring for pragmatic reasons, including what they want their genealogy to look like in the future. That is, marriages are arranged with an eye to strategic and political planning for economic purposes or the way they want their relationships to look in tribal history.

In spite of the norms and all the chaperoning, premarital sex is not unknown, and out-of-wedlock children are born. In some such cases, the young people are quickly married to each other or to others. The next section examines some of the effects of premarital sexual relations and illegitimate children on the group and how these issues are dealt with.

Even though the lives of women and men are generally separate in terms of activities and interaction, this is not to say that Hawazma women and men have differing agendas in terms of the goals of their productive activities. Everyone's activities support the goal of success as pastoral nomads. Both men and women work to generate a satisfactory standard of living and also to generate wealth. Wealth is largely measured by the size of herds. It is also measured by the amount of milk that is available to sell as surplus and to some extent by what can be purchased. However, one cannot assume that a Hawazma man wearing a worn *gellabia* or long shirt is poor. He may simply be putting his wealth into herds in order to be able to provide generous bridewealth or an inheritance for his sons.

QUESTION 4.4
What Forces Threaten to Disrupt the Family Unit?

Social, political, and environmental factors can intervene to disrupt Hawazma families. Suppose that a husband and wife came from feuding lineages. It is likely that they would be residing in the husband's camp,[3] whose members would be in opposition to the members of the woman's lineage. Although descent and inheritance are counted through the father, the sons of this couple would find it uncomfortable to have to take a hostile pose toward members of their mother's lineage. The woman would also be in a difficult position: loyal to her natal group, supposedly loyal to her husband and therefore to his group, and perhaps suspect because her loyalties would be perceived to be conflicting.

I met a couple who had faced such a dilemma. The husband was from the Dar Sholongo lineage and the wife was from the Dar Nyla lineage. Their solution was to move to a camp of the Oulad Nuba, a third and neutral lineage. The consequences included being isolated from the supportive networks of their kin. Although all three lineages are Hawazma, this couple never became full-fledged members of the Oulad Nuba camp. Their sons might have married into the Oulad Nuba, and the genealogy would have been manipulated in a few generations so that it would appear that they were all Oulad Nuba. But the one unmarried son who might have been the mechanism for such a move was responsible for the premarital pregnancy of an Oulad Nuba girl.

[3]Most strongly patrilineal people think that patrilocal residence "seems right."

Consequences of Breaking Rules

Premarital sexual relations or pregnancy can disrupt families even when the partners are both from the same lineage or camp. In the case above, getting married would have solved the problem for both the young people and their parents. But the young man's parents would not permit him to marry the girl, and their refusal made it necessary for them to move away. The girl's parents were still faced with a problem: not only had there been a premarital affair, but now there was an illegitimate child. Since his biological father would not recognize him, some way had to be found to give the child an identity.

Traditional Arab naming gives a person an individualistic first name and his or her father's and grandfather's given names. This child was given a personal name and his grandfather's and great-grandfather's names, so that on a future genealogy, after everyone would have forgotten the circumstances, he would appear to be his grandfather's son. The problem of the unwed mother was solved by her becoming the third wife of a sheikh shortly after the child's birth.

When we speak of disruption of the family unit, we must think of the broader family unit; not simply the nuclear family. All sorts of arguments can disrupt Hawazma families. Some may be resolved amicably, but others, like the case just recounted, cannot. Various dissatisfactions had been festering in the Oulad Nuba camp where these events took place. When I joined the camp, some members were already distanced from each other. In a nomadic camp, distancing can be expressed physically through the placement of houses, and the houses of the young woman's parents and a married daughter were clustered outside, though near, the primary camp circle.

Problems between a wife and husband can also disrupt families. Either might ask for a divorce, and other members of the camp might have different ideas about how the problem should be resolved. Among the Hawazma, the families were relatives before the marriage, so a problem between two married persons is more than likely to be a problem between members of the sublineage or lineage. Before the premarital pregnancy problem occurred, problems in the relationship of another Oulad Nuba couple had already caused the beginning of a rift. Sides had been taken. Although almost everyone agreed that the young husband had acted badly, there was disagreement about the wife's role in the problem and antagonism toward the people who supported her. The premarital pregnancy served as a catalyst, and the camp began to separate more. Another segment pulled out of the main camp circle and erected houses apart from it. When I revisited the camp five years later, the young woman's family had joined another camp, and the remaining families were becoming ever more distanced and independent in their movements.

Environmental and Political Pressures on Families

For pastoral nomads, environmental factors and the combination of environmental and political factors constantly threaten families as well as the entire system. We discussed how the Hawazma strategically place segments of their polygynous families in differing economic settings in an effort to maximize all options and to have a fallback position should environmental factors cause staggering economic losses. Sometimes a family cannot recover herds lost as a result of environmental factors, and they must pursue either sedentary agriculture or try to exist as wage laborers. Maintaining identity as a member of a group necessitates participating in some of its activities. Once family members are scattered into nonherding, nonpastoral nomadic occupations, they are likely to be physically scattered as well, and it becomes almost impossible to participate.

The Hawazma must also operate within the state system of Sudan. At various times in recent history, the government of Sudan has taken different and opposing positions about allowing pastoral nomads to continue their way of life. Sometimes they have wanted to settle all pastoral nomads. At other times, the role of the pastoral nomads in the broader economic system of a savanna region has been recognized, resulting in encouragement of their enterprises and permission to maintain their own political organization. Such pressure from the national government poses a threat to the viability of pastoral families.

The longstanding and periodically erupting civil war in Sudan escalated in the mid-1980s, and it has had a major effect on the Hawazma since then. Caught between government forces from the north and rebels from the south, the Hawazma have been subjected to raids on their herds and attacks on their people. The war has limited access to dry-season campsites and cropping fields and has made trek routes dangerous. Many of the Nuba have been forcibly resettled in desert regions farther north. Town life and markets have also been disrupted, making it more difficult for the Hawazma to sell milk products and animals.

The Risk of Educating Sons

Another strategy Hawazma families use to optimize their economic position in a difficult environment is to try to give at least one son training in the skills necessary in an urban context. Previously, completing a secondary education, or even more than six years or so of formal schooling, was not seen as necessary or desirable. Today the Hawazma recognize that a family may not have enough cash income unless at least one son is able to hold a job that requires a secondary education.

Determining whether to send a son to secondary school is a difficult decision to make. Doing so means separating the boy from animal husbandry, which is not taught at school, and thus denying him knowledge that would make him a successful herdsman. Additionally, his father loses his labor not only for all the years he is in school, but possibly forever.

Typically, the oldest son will receive some formal education, but he is not sent to pursue secondary education. He and perhaps another son or two will focus on learning animal husbandry from their father. A younger son is more likely to be selected to gain further education.

The two sorts of education are almost mutually exclusive. Unfortunately, the result is that young people who receive a secondary education often find themselves in a sort of no-man's land between pastoral nomadic and urban lifestyles. Ahmed was one such young man. After he finished secondary school, he found employment as a clerk, but for only a short time. When he came back to live in the camp, he did not know as much about herding as either his older or his younger brothers. He did not fit in very well, nor did he fit in an urban environment. In camp he had links to and yearnings for an urban setting that his family neither desired nor understood. A parallel dilemma existed in town. He was not a cosmopolitan young man whose family had always been clerks or businessmen, and he had links to a lifestyle most urban Sudanese tended to look down on.

I do not know what finally happened to Ahmed, but almost certainly his loosening link to his pastoral family affected the solidarity of the family. When a Hawazma man or woman breaks away from the pastoral nomadic system for whatever reason, the action poses a threat to the continuity of particular pastoral nomadic families and for pastoral nomadism as a lifestyle and economic system.

QUESTION 4.5
How Does the Pastoral Nomadic Lifestyle Continue to Fit into the Modern World?

Like pastoralists elsewhere in the Middle East and Africa, the Hawazma are embedded in a modern nation-state. Their ability to maintain their lifestyle is thus not entirely dependent on their own inclinations and skills. Many factors have enabled the Hawazma pastoral nomadic lifestyle to continue. These include circumstances in the Sudan that have made it possible for the Hawazma to be active contributors to the national economy. Sudan's place in a regional international economy facilitates the maintenance of their lifestyle.

Although Sudan is the largest country on the African continent, it is one of the poorest Third World nations in the world. Environmental conditions in this country of savanna and desert make large-scale intensive agriculture difficult. Like other countries in East Africa, Sudan is periodically subject to severe drought. Even in nondrought years, there is not sufficient water for intensive irrigation of farmlands. The soil will not tolerate intensive cultivation year after year without substantial use of fertilizers. A large region in northern Sudan is the sandy desert fringe of the Sahara, where only small patches of watered land are arable. The infrastructure, which might ameliorate the harsh environmental conditions, is weak. There are not many miles of paved roads, and in some regions no roads link one agricultural area to another. The railroad is unreliable. As in many other Third World nations, resources that might have been allocated to development have been siphoned off by internal conflicts.

A growing population, especially a growing urban population, requires more meat and milk, but the environment cannot tolerate ranches for the intensive raising of beef and dairy animals. Under the combined circumstances of a harsh environment and a poorly developed infrastructure, pastoral nomads like the Hawazma are in a good position to produce and supply meat and milk, as well as hides and some fertilizer. Although harsh environmental conditions result in sparse vegetation, pastoralists can move their herds to areas with grazing and water. They do not need roads to move from pasture to pasture or to get their products to market. Although the animals lose conditioning, they can be trekked to market. Milk is quickly made into cheese, which can be stored for a year or so and taken to market when fuel and vehicles are available. In other words, the Hawazma can be seen as necessary to the economy of the nation. So, even though government policies have vacillated between strongly encouraging **sedentarization** to encouraging larger herds, pastoralism remains the best means to produce needed meat and milk.

Being embedded in a wider economy has offered other means for the Hawazma to expand their herds. Young men have discovered wage labor. There is some internal wage labor, but international wage labor is more profitable in a shorter period of time. Other developing nations in the region, primarily Saudi Arabia, cannot fill all their labor requirements internally. Many Hawazma young men go to Saudi Arabia to work for a year or two and save enough money to start new herds or substantially increase existing ones. They can earn 10 to 15 times as much in a year in Saudi Arabia than they can earn doing low-paid internal wage labor. Their wives can support their households from milk sales, and they and their children will be watched over by other men in the kin group. This is the only way some young men from polygynous agricultural households can become herdsmen. It is a circular interaction. The family system easily supports the absence of some men for even an extended period of time, while access to wage labor supports the continuance of the Hawazma pastoral nomadic family.

CONCLUSIONS

This chapter investigates the central question of how we can understand the dynamics of family life in other societies by looking carefully at Hawazma Baggara family organization and composition. Why is it informative to pose that question about a pastoral nomadic type of society that seems to be disappearing from the modern world? Pastoral nomads have developed a lifestyle that enables them to utilize resources in parts of the world that are inaccessible or not productive to other food-producing systems. The organization of Hawazma Baggara families is a significant factor in their success as pastoralists and as managers of marginal environments. Other planners and development workers can learn from them. Even if they were to choose to abandon pastoralism in favor of an easier way of life, it is important for the environmental knowledge on which pastoralism is based not to be lost.

Studying pastoral nomadic societies also informs our understanding of some of the mechanisms of state formation. The same segmentary lineage structure that enables pastoralists to utilize precarious environments has also helped them develop larger political formations, including states and nations. Pastoral nomadic societies in the Middle East and other parts of the world have transformed families into politically cohesive states. Saudi Arabia coalesced from a society of pastoral nomads. Libya formed from segmentary lineages that came together to fight against colonization by a European power. Even today elements of a pastoral nomadic tribal organization can be seen in Libya's political structures and governmental administrative units.

Families based on patrilineal descent give every Hawazma individual both personal and group identity. Using kinship as an organizing principle enables the Hawazma not only to deploy small groups for better utilization of the environment, but also to have the strength of larger groups for common political action.

The selection of appropriate marriage partners is so important to the system that it is left to elders. Marriages to close cousins keep livestock within the same family in order to maintain herd viability and also to create and reinforce overlapping kinship relationships that strengthen obligations in a system in which success requires each person to be both independent from and dependent on a tight, cooperative group.

Although Hawazma women and men lead very separate lives, the intersection and interaction of their labor is equally significant to the success of the pastoral nomadic lifestyle. Hawazma men and women generate wealth for their families.

Disease in the herds and severe drought threaten to force the Hawazma out of their pastoral nomadic lifestyle, with consequences not only for family stability but also for family well-being. Conflicts at the interpersonal level, as well as at the state political level, mitigate against the continuity of families. Civil war in the Sudan is a prime example of contemporary conditions that not only make it difficult to herd animals, but also cause various disruptions of family life. Being caught between the lifestyles of pastoral nomadism and a modernizing world also affects Hawazma families and individuals.

The Hawazma are part of a modern nation-state that is unable to supply all the meat and milk products its citizens require without the help of pastoral nomads. An international need for wage laborers also is a means for Hawazma herdsmen to earn cash to purchase more cattle and to increase the productivity of their herds.

Many factors interact to make the Hawazma family system work within its physical, cultural, and political environment. It is well-adapted to deal with harsh conditions and the requirements of herds of domesticated animals. The family system is flexible enough to operate in small units to face environmental constraints and to come together in units large enough to deal with political contingencies. Marriage patterns serve to maintain wealth so that families can remain economically viable. Although the social and economic organization of Hawazma society is based on kinship relations, the actual content of those relations can be manipulated to serve other ends or needs, like political confederation. The flexibility of the family system has allowed the Hawazma to maintain their lifestyle while becoming more and more embedded in a nation-state. After all, it's all relative.

REFERENCES AND RECOMMENDED READINGS

Barfield, Thomas J.
1993 The Nomadic Alternative. New York: Simon and Schuster.
    In a readable overview of pastoral nomadism, Barfield considers such topics as animals, ecology, households, gender, honor, tribal organization, and sedentarization. He also describes selected groups of pastoralists in Africa, the Middle East, and Asia.

Barth, Fredrik
1964 Nomads of South Persia: The Basseri Tribe of the Khamseh Confederacy.
London: Allen and Unwin.
    A classic ethnography that focuses on political organization, it was one of the first to systematically consider processes of sedentarization.

Behnke, Roy H.
1980 The Herders of Cyrenaica: Ecology, Economy and Kinship Among the Bedouin of Eastern Libya. Chicago: University of Chicago Press.
This study uses an ecological perspective to consider how tribes and tribal sections are distributed across the landscape.

Chatty, Dawn
1996 Mobile Pastoralists: Development Planning and Social Change in Oman. New York: Columbia University Press.
An applied anthropologist considers the effects of change and development on Bedouin in Oman.

Cole, Donald
1975 Nomads of the Nomads: The al-Murrah Bedouin of the Empty Quarter. Arlington Heights, IL: AHM Publishing.
The al-Murrah are so dedicated to pastoralism that they are known as the ultimate nomads. Cole demonstrates the intricate symbiosis of people, animals, and environment and the structuring of the social relationships that support their existence.

Cunnison, Ian
1966 The Baggara Arabs: Power and Lineage in a Sudanese Nomad Tribe. Oxford: Clarendon Press.
A classic ethnography that focuses on kinship and political relationships among the Humr, another of the Baggara tribes.

Evans-Pritchard, E. E.
1940 The Nuer. Oxford: Oxford University Press.
This classic ethnography lays out what were new theories about the form of social organization known now as segmentary lineages and demonstrates how cattle are a focal aspect for all parts of the culture of these East African pastoralists.

Hobbs, Joseph J.
1989 Bedouin Life in the Egyptian Desert. Austin: University of Texas Press.
A description of the Ma'aza Bedouins that focuses on their relation to their land. The Ma'aza view themselves as caretakers of their harsh environment, and Hobbs suggests that desert development planners can learn from them. Includes an extensive glossary of Bedouin, Latin, and English plant and animal names.

Lancaster, William O.
1996 The Rwala Bedouin Today. 2nd edition. Prospect Heights, IL: Waveland Press.
An excellent discussion that thoroughly explains the principles of segmentation and how genealogies are manipulated to achieve social and cultural goals.

Michael, Barbara J., with Anne Kocherhans
1993 Nomads on the Savanna. Video. Pennsylvania State University Audio-Visual Services.
A visual ethnography of the Hawazma showing their rainy season activities.

Spaulding, Jay, and Stephanie Beswick, eds.
1999 White Nile, Black Blood: War, Leadership, and Ethnicity from Khartoum to Kanpala. Lawrenceville, NJ: Red Sea Press.
The best recent analysis of the protracted and complex conflict.

Young, William C.
1996 The Rashaayda Bedouin: Arab Pastoralists of Eastern Sudan. Fort Worth: Harcourt Brace Jovanovich.
An extremely readable and engaging discussion of the Rashaayda and the process of doing fieldwork in a pastoral nomadic society. It depicts family life and the use of space as well as a pastoral economy.

CHAPTER 5

THE CREATION OF SOCIAL HIERARCHY

C. RODERICK WILSON
AND JAMES A. YOST

PROBLEM 5 Why *do societies come to be characterized by social, economic, and political inequalities?*

INTRODUCTION
The New Amazons—From Equality to Dominance

In the world as we know it, there are rich and poor people, educated and uneducated people, black and white people, short and tall people, men and women, and children and adults. Before you read further, take another look at this list. Are these distinctions all of the same kind? Do they all involve inherent characteristics? Are all the characteristics important? Which involve power distinctions? Are the power distinctions inherent and natural, or are they created? If they are created, by whom and for whose benefit?

This chapter addresses these questions ethnographically by examining the Waorani, a small-scale society in Amazonian Ecuador. When the Waorani were first studied, they were extremely egalitarian, meaning that all members of the society were virtually equal. In recent decades, they have become more hierarchical, and some people now exercise power over others.

Traditionally the Waorani lived deep in the rain forest, near the small streams that cut through the steep, forested hills and ultimately flowed to the major rivers. They ate a few of the many kinds of fish inhabiting the streams, but their real interest was the forest where they hunted peccaries (much like pigs) with nine-foot wooden spears, and monkeys, toucans, and parrots with poison-tipped darts shot from blowguns. In season the jungle also provided foodstuffs like chonta palm nuts. More importantly, the Waorani made small clearings in the rain forest to grow crops, especially manioc and bananas.

Settlement was dispersed. The basic social unit, the **household**, typically included an older couple, unmarried sons, married daughters, the daughters' husbands, and their children. Quite commonly this unit was doubled, with the household formed by two extended families residing together. About the time the grandchildren became teenagers, their parents would likely set up a new household somewhere in the general neighborhood, producing loose clusters of **matrilineally** related households perhaps a half-hour's walk from each other. Each household maintained three or even four sets of gardens and houses, each a day's walk or more apart. As gardens in one location were depleted, those in another place would be coming into maturity. In a year or so, the family would move back to the first site. This cycle was partly to maintain a steady stream of food, since a new garden would always be coming into productivity; but more importantly it meant that a safe, provisioned refuge would be available if the community was raided.

A very few terms help clarify the basics of the Waorani social world. The first distinction is between people who are Waorani and *cowode*, outsiders, who are not. Among Waorani, the basic distinction is between *guirinani* to

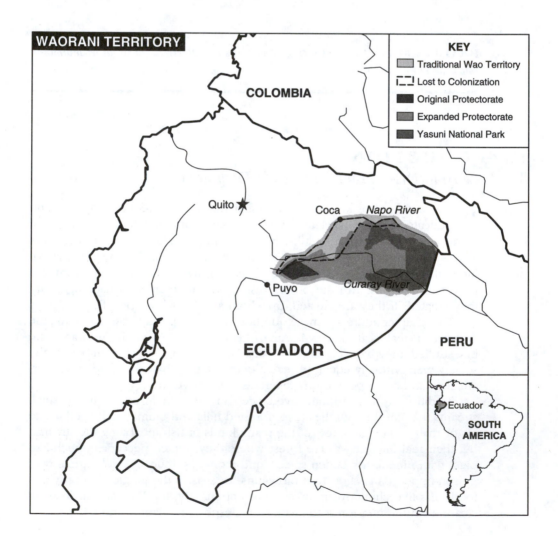

A traditional Waorani house that might be home to as many as 20 members of an extended family.
(Photograph by Jim Yost.)

whom one is related by known linkages and *warani*, other Waorani who are not related. For almost any of the 630 Waorani living in 1977, fewer than 20 would have been *warani*; the rest were related in known ways. Within the *guirinani*, there is a distinction between relatives like mothers, fathers, and sisters on the one hand, and relatives who are *qui*, meaning those whom it is permissible to marry. In anthropological parlance, *qui* are **cross cousins**, the children of one's mother's brother or father's sister.

The point of these distinctions is that they define much Waorani behavior. Since *cowode* were thought to be cannibals, the appropriate reaction was to kill them on sight, or at least to flee. On the other hand, for relatives like brothers or sisters, including **parallel cousins** (the children of one's mother's sister or father's brother), the system creates paired relationships with reciprocal rights and responsibilities, particularly involving the obligation to share. By restricting marriage to those who are *qui*, the system creates a tendency toward multiple bonds of relatedness and support.[1] A father-in-law might be the brother of the groom's mother, a person with whom there were prior obligations of respect and support even before the new mutual obligations of son-in-law and father-in-law are added. On the negative side, restricting marriage to those who are *qui* also makes it likely that some people will have difficulty finding a spouse at times, especially if their family has been involved in retaliatory spearing raids.

In traditional Waorani society, people were born into a network of relatives; marriage created additional ones. **Generalized reciprocity** was the rule; relatives were expected to share things without keeping track of who was ahead. Thus a man who failed to bring meat home any day would nonetheless find himself and his family enjoying fresh meat that evening. The forest provided the stuff of life—the wood for one's house or spear, the fiber for one's hammock or carrying bag, and the meat and vegetables for one's pot—and people transformed those materials into the things needed for life.

---

[1]This is much like the Hawazma Baggara in Chapter 4.

Kinship, marriage, and village life provided a social environment, a network of known people who repeatedly reaffirmed their responsibilities to each other through sharing.

Within this culture of sharing, the Waorani ethos emphasized individual accomplishment and personal autonomy. People were expected to provide for themselves. For instance, there was no item of technology used in the society that a person could not make for himself or herself. Some men could make exceptional blowguns, and some women were better potters than others; such a person might be asked to make a blowgun or a pot for a friend, usually with the expectation that the friend would somehow reciprocate in the future. Some women might be better gardeners than others, but all would be expected to grow food for their own families. No one would do for you what you could normally do for yourself.

The Waorani ethos was also emphatically pragmatic. Their technology was utilitarian. Things and people were decorated on occasion, but creating beauty was not the emphasis. What was important was to make something that worked. Similarly, the Waorani believed that people had souls and that there was an afterlife where life was much like the life they knew, but no one spent a lot of time worrying or talking about it. What mattered was to make this life work.

QUESTIONS

5.1. What is life like in a society without hierarchy?

5.2. How do egalitarian and hierarchical societies relate?

5.3. How can hierarchy get started?

5.4. What happens after hierarchy gets started?

5.5. How do formerly small-scale societies fit into hierarchical states?

QUESTION 5.1
What Is Life Like in a Society Without Hierarchy?

It is a virtual certainty that everyone reading this sentence and everyone likely to ever read it is a part of a hierarchical society—if for no other reason than because colleges are hierarchical institutions. Most people not only accept this fact but would also argue that colleges have to be hierarchical. We live in a series of embedded hierarchies in our workplaces, where we play, at worship, even in our homes. It is difficult to imagine that there might be another way of arranging things. Anthropologists who have studied societies that are not hierarchical in their structure find themselves worrying about their capacity to understand and to analyze them. For one thing, it is not clear that our vocabulary allows us to think about such things in an unbiased way.

Consider the heading of this section. Is it reasonable to define something by the absence of something else? Yet this kind of terminology is characteristic of much of the discourse in this field. When, for instance, we speak of acephalous (headless) leadership, what we really seem to be saying is that what we see these people doing is so different from what we do that we cannot even find a word that clearly describes it, only one that says it is not what we do. Nevertheless, it is important to attempt to understand societies that do not have hierarchy, in part to better understand our own society.

Situational Leadership

On hearing some teenage girls comment that a certain stream an hour's walk from the village has many fish, White-lipped Peccary, a middle-aged man, announced that he would fish there the next day. By early morning, he had dug up enough roots to stun fish in the stream and was joined by the two authors, two adult women with infants, two teenage girls, and three pre-adolescent boys. Other men, women, and children in the village decided not to participate. White-lipped Peccary led the way to the stream, carrying the roots in a string bag. Once there, he asked the girls where the best pools were, and after a short discussion, they agreed that we should proceed in a slightly different direction. The three men beat the roots into fibers while the others waited. White-lipped Peccary gathered the fibers and put them back into his carrying bag, and we proceeded to the pool the girls recommended. White-lipped Peccary swished the string bag through the waters. Stunned fish shortly began to appear at the surface, and several large fish were spotted attempting to swim upstream out of the pool. When someone called for help, the two girls took the scoop nets and ran there. Soon we were all working our way down the stream, more or less following the poison as it drifted along. We worked primarily as a loose aggregation of individuals, but small groups of shifting composition frequently formed. After about three hours, when the yield became minimal, we started back. White-lipped Peccary did not carry any fish; he had already eaten many of the small ones he caught raw (after thumbing out their stomachs), and most of the others were being carried by his daughter. We stopped when we got to the river, and all of us, including White-lipped Peccary, eviscerated the fish. On arriving at the village, each person went straight home with the fish he or she caught.

Another day, White-lipped Peccary decided to build a house in his village in order to induce one of the authors, Yost, to stay there more often. This was a fairly major undertaking involving obtaining logs to frame the structure, bamboo to be split for flooring, palm fronds to be woven into roofing, and other material from various locations in the forest; assembling the materials at the site as needed; and then actually constructing the house. He was assisted by his single and married sons, his daughters and sons-in-law, and his sister's sons and daughters. White-lipped Peccary assumed general supervision of the project and did more work than anyone else, but other individuals contributed directions as well as labor. Otter, an adult who was not well-connected socially and was not directly related to White-lipped Peccary, indicated that he would assist in the project. As construction continued and Otter did nothing, White-lipped Peccary made jokes about it. Otter finally worked on the house for several hours, but he chose a time when White-lipped Peccary and his close relatives were occupied elsewhere.

Tiger Heron announced that he was going to make a canoe trip to another village in several days. A half-dozen men decided to go along. Tiger Heron acted forcefully during the trip, making all decisions about the route and when and where to stop, and announcing his decisions in a loud, abrupt manner. When the travelers stopped overnight, he did not assume that the other competent, experienced adults would automatically go about making camp. Rather, he directed them and criticized the poor performance of some.

A different day, when Tiger Heron was visiting another home in his community, he asked his seven-year-old son to run home to get his shotgun, which needed repairs. The child replied, "No!" Tiger Heron waited a while and asked again. "No!" Tiger Heron commented to his host, "He says, 'No!'" After a while, he once again repeated the request. This time the child answered with the Waorani equivalent of a raspberry, whereupon Tiger Heron went for the gun himself.

These examples illustrate the nature of Waorani individual autonomy, which extends even to children to a remarkable extent (from our standpoint). People are free to participate or not in all activities. There may be social costs in not participating, as there are costs and benefits in any act, but one's right to choose to participate or not is never in question. Participating in certain activities creates temporary and very limited obligations to follow the initiator's lead, but the initiator's role as leader is clearly restricted to the specific situation.

The Waorani make a clear distinction between **status** and **role** that is quite different from ours. That is, there are many roles in Waorani society that people fill for shorter or longer periods of time. Waorani women, for instance, plant and weed gardens, while the men chop down the trees to clear a patch for the garden. Each sex has a distinct role, but neither sex is viewed as more important because of the role. In other words, they have distinct roles, but equal status. Complex tasks demand that someone take on the role of leader. But leadership is situational and ephemeral. In an egalitarian society, filling leadership roles, no matter how often or how well, does not confer enduring status. An individual's status remains that of an ordinary Waorani.

Shamanism

A **shaman** can be defined loosely as someone with special power to know and to heal. Waorani shamanism is an apparent exception to the generalizations we have just made, at least in the sense that the shaman has a role that continues through time and consequently has an enduring status.

Waorani practices in this regard differ substantially from those of their neighbors and are not classic shamanism. Two kinds of practitioners have shamanic qualities. A Jaguar Father is able, among other skills, to locate herds of peccaries by going into a drug-induced trance to summon his Jaguar "child," his spirit helper, who is also another hunter. Often the Jaguar Father is attended in his trance by the Jaguar Mother, who is his wife.

Unlike Jaguar Fathers, who are known people, there is never anyone in a village who admits to being an *ido*. There are people alleged to be *ido* in other villages who are able to use spirit helpers to cause serious illness, snakebite, or death. In theory an *ido* can cure illness as well as cause it, but Waorani believe that an *ido* can cure only an illness he or she caused. To admit to being an *ido* would be very dangerous. It is often suspected that Jaguar Fathers in other villages are also *ido*, but it is not necessary that they be so.

The level of shamanism among the Waorani is very low, in marked contrast to their neighbors. If Waorani shamans are exceptions to the Waorani rule of not recognizing status differentials, it is only in a very limited way. One reason not to see shamans as an exception is that they exercise their **power** through the use of threats, and threats are an intrinsic facet of Waorani individual autonomy. That is, in a society without specific institutionalized **authority** and with only physical power, social interaction normally tends to be characterized by mutual tolerance. However if an individual decides that he must have something that others could provide, the threat of physical violence may follow. The people being threatened must then decide on an appropriate response. This is also true for a shaman. Although the source of the shaman's power may be spiritual, the threat takes a physical form, and so may the response. If the shaman's threat is not believable, he may be ignored; if he is too threatening, he may be killed. Only in the narrow intermediate range will his threat produce dividends. Thus the shaman, like other threatening individuals, does not possess dominating power. In a society of autonomous individuals, an attempt to acquire that kind of power by threat would be dealt with quite directly. In the end, then, while a shaman does have an enduring role, it does not give him extraordinary authority.

Sexual Equality

There has been little in the discussion thus far to indicate that the Waorani differ from egalitarian societies in which equality is largely limited to men. However, their egalitarianism does include equality between the sexes. The equality of all Waorani and of women in particular is rooted in the arrangements of their economic system. A society that provides equal access to all goods and technology has little capacity for developing hierarchical relationships.

The forest provides plenty of protein and carbohydrates. It would be impossible for one person to exclude anyone who is part of a functioning family from full access to both types of food. Furthermore, Waorani traditional society did not have any technology or source of productive power that either individuals or groups could control in ways that would exclude others. In the absence of specialization or differential access to resources, neither could there be a market. The development of authority is severely inhibited in this context.

The relative ease with which game can be obtained and the frequency with which it is procured are not conducive to an overvaluation of meat and meat providers, as is the case in some Amazonian cultures. In normal circumstances, game is present in sufficient quantity for anyone with skill, inclination, and time to obtain it. This is not to say that all men are equally productive. Some men are better hunters than others; some are less inclined to exert themselves; some may have moved into an area more recently than others, and it takes about a year to develop consistently productive game trails. But whatever the variability between men, all can obtain adequate amounts of animal protein through their own efforts. Studies of hunting productivity among the Waorani have shown that a man could keep his family well supplied in animal protein by hunting a mere 4.5 days per month. The sharing of meat along kin lines after large kills adds to the sense that there is plenty of meat for all. Receiving gifts of meat from others is a recurring affirmation of an individual's equal place in the group.

Almost all women, including those who have not reached adulthood and the handicapped, can produce more than enough food for their families from their garden plots. Some women are more productive than others, but a more-than-adequate supply of garden produce is readily available.

Given the division of labor, a man and a woman are both necessary to provide basic sustenance for a household. It is not just that women provide produce and men provide meat; the complementarity is deeply embedded in the subsistence tasks themselves. The labor of men is seen as necessary in clearing trees for the garden plots, while the labor of women is necessary in bringing home larger game. Although the labor of women produces the greater volume of food and the women are generally responsible for food preparation, men and women seem to spend about the same amount of time in direct subsistence activities.

Traditionally, the one situation in which food was scarce was when people fled for their lives from a spearing raid and were unable to move to a location with producing gardens and game trails. Hunting in such situations was likely to be relatively unproductive, and it was almost certain to be nonproductive if they fled without weapons, but it was the lack of crops that was really serious. The Waorani definition of starvation is to be without their chief staple, manioc. Their expression for happiness literally means another bowl of *chicha*, which is a drink made from fermented, masticated manioc. While it may be true that prolonged conflict may in general tend to raise the status of men as warriors, the circumstances of Waorani raiding appear to have resulted in an emphasis on the economic value of women as providers.

Productive Activities. Although there is role assignment along sexual lines, the division is frequently fuzzy. In general it is men who hunt, but women often scout for peccary or tapir signs. After a successful hunt, the men may carry the

While carrying produce back to the village is exclusively the work of women (and girls), the collaborative labor of both men and women is necessary in successful gardening.
(Photograph by Jim Yost.)

game; they may ask the women to carry some of it; or the men and the woman may trade off. Weeding gardens is frequently pictured by the Waorani as women's work, and some women state emphatically that men never weed, laughing at the notion that they might. Some men, however, do weed gardens with their wives and children. The key factor seems to be whether the man was taught to weed by his mother. Other tasks seem unambiguously assigned to one sex; for example, women carry water and men fell large trees. The number of such tasks seems relatively restricted.

In some societies, taboos appear to be instruments of sexual oppression. The Waorani have relatively few taboos, and they appear to be applied in an egalitarian manner. For instance, a pregnant woman is restricted from eating some foods and engaging in some activities, but she is not regarded as unclean, and she can carry on almost all normal activities. The one productive activity from which a pregnant woman is barred is the preparation and application of any of the various poisons used in fishing. She can, however, participate fully in other aspects of fishing. Significantly, her husband is equally barred from the same activities, as well as from making the curare poison for blowgun darts. Not only is a *yaede waepo* (pregnant father) not supposed to touch poison, he is also to keep his "pregnant-causing penis" and his urine out of streams that will be fished.

Both women and men control the results of their labor. So strongly is this the case that, even in a **polygynous** household, each wife cooks the produce of her own garden over her own fire. In recent years, the Waorani have engaged in the sale of artifacts, and both men and women keep the proceeds from artifacts they have made and sold.

Decision-Making. Critical events such as marriage and divorce constitute a major test of egalitarianism. Among the Waorani, marriages are arranged by near kin. Men may decide to exchange their sisters or to have their children marry each other; more commonly, a brother and sister will decide that their children will marry. Traditionally, mothers take an active interest in the marriage of their children, particularly their daughters, and appear to be successful in stopping marriages they oppose. Moreover, there are numerous instances of marriages taking place after the fathers have objected and even after they have threatened to kill one or both of the parents of the prospective spouse or another member of the potential **affine's** family. The young people themselves also have a say, although primarily of a negative sort.

In one case, a young woman who had just reached puberty found herself at her own wedding. She kept saying, "No!" during the ceremony, did not allow her supposed husband to consummate the marriage, refused to serve him his drink the next day, and went back to her mother's house to sleep on the second night. A week later he left for another clearing. This young woman's second "marriage" had a similar history, and she avoided an attempted third marriage by fleeing. Ordinarily, young people do not object to the marriages arranged for them. If they do, divorce is not a problem in principle. The unusual behavior of this woman was motivated by her desire to marry a particular young man, to whom her brother objected violently.

The case illustrates a significant aspect of Waorani egalitarianism. In situations affecting several parties, such as marriage, individual autonomy is essentially negative. In other words, although a person may not be able to do what she or he wants to do, the person cannot be forced to do something she or he does not want to do. Women are not disadvantaged in this negative autonomy.

Not only do women exert control over their lives in key areas such as marriage, divorce, and location of residence; they also control numerous details of the daily routine. The adult male host offered a teenage girl a drink of *chicha* at a fiesta. She refused, saying, "I'm full." He became assertive, silently thrusting the bowl at her and glaring. In the face of her continued refusal, he gave the bowl to someone else. Ten minutes later he again offered her a bowl, was refused, and again became assertive. This time she reached into the bowl and scooped some *chicha* onto the ground, saying, "That's enough!" The host did not bother her again.

Cultural Valuation. Judging cultural valuation of the sexes is difficult, especially since the Waorani do not verbalize their valuations of categories of people or the tasks they perform. The indirect evidence is ambiguous.

Women might appear to be less highly valued than men in the following areas:

1. **Infanticide.** The victims of infanticide are predominantly female. In principle, all twins and illegitimate babies are not supposed to be allowed to live; in reality, male children appear more likely to be spared. In accounts we heard of family members arguing about a particular case, however, the sex of the child appears not to have been relevant.

2. **Workload.** Female children and unmarried teenagers clearly work harder than their male counterparts. Adult women sometimes help carry game back to the village. However, the Waorani do not devalue physically taxing labor or contrast it to recreational activity. Men may tote the meat themselves, and they are thought to already have worked very hard by the time they have shot the game.

3. **Shamanism** Although shamanism is devalued in general, the role of Jaguar Father is prominent and is exclusively male. On the other hand, he almost always functions with the Jaguar Mother, an exclusively female role.

4. **Derogatory comments.** From time to time, men make comments that may be seen as indicating a derogatory view of women. An anthropologist ineptly holding a blowgun may be compared to a woman attempting to use one. When asked if women ever chop down trees, men will laugh uproariously and say that women could not chop hard trees all day. But women make similar comments about the ineptitude of men, and one type of activity does not seem to be valued above another. The Waorani are bluntly honest in all matters, and many comments that might sound derogatory are no more than simple observations of fact that, like most aspects of life, are also sources of amusement.

Finally, while all spearing of people was done by Waorani males, Waorani victims were of both sexes and all ages. In Yost's accounts going back five generations, spearing accounted for 54 percent of male and 39 percent of female deaths. In this, as in all other aspects of life, the Waorani appear to have been thoroughly egalitarian.

QUESTION 5.2
How Do Egalitarian and Hierarchical Societies Relate?

Two answers to the question of how egalitarian and hierarchical societies relate to each other flow from the history of the Waorani. Prior to 1958, their relations with outsiders were unremittingly hostile; subsequently they have been peaceful.

Before 1958

It is tempting to think that the violence of the modern world was born only in the cycles of conquest, colonization, and exploitation initiated by the expansion of peoples and powers out of western Europe because that has been the case to a large extent. Certainly no other force has so shaped our modern world. But the idea and force of empire did not begin in Europe, and the Spanish were not the first outsiders who attempted and failed to incorporate the peoples of the western Amazon basin into their empire. The Inca, the last indigenous empire in the region, also attempted to do so. Others may have tried before the Inca.

It is not even clear that the propensity to conflict in the western Amazon began as an attempt to ward off the unwanted attentions of empire. The people who inhabited this area may already have been warlike when the would-be conquerors first arrived. There can be little doubt, however, that invasion did nothing to make the region pacifistic.

The Spanish were looking for gold when they first came to what is now eastern Ecuador in 1538. In 1599 local indigenous people rebelled against the Spanish invaders and, among their other successes, captured the governor of Macas. Telling him something like "You wanted gold; we'll give you gold," they forced his mouth open and filled it with the molten metal. The incident is striking both as history and metaphor. It speaks loudly to the rapacious colonial attitude of the Spanish and the equally deadly resistance of the locals. Indians remember the story as a symbol of hope, and national Ecuadorians recall it as a mistake that has not been fully rectified.

It is doubtful that ancestors of the Waorani participated in the revolt of 1599. We do know that the upper Amazon basin was inhabited by scores of groups with different languages and cultures, and that the vast majority no longer exist. Thousands upon thousands of people succumbed to diseases to which they had no resistance. The epidemic process was accelerated by the missions' policy of resettling the people in permanent settlements. The epidemics also decimated the Indians who were forced into slavery and serfdom and later a supposedly more civilized system of debt-peonage on the haciendas, or large estates. The haciendas also simply ran through a lot of people, some of them Waorani. To fill the need for more labor, the Spanish systematically raided groups like the Waorani to capture slaves.

The Waorani remember the rubber traders with more horror. In the mid-19th century, the demand of the industrialized West for rubber led to a great rubber boom in the Amazon. While great fortunes were made at the "civilized" end of the rubber trade, and rubber tires made life a little easier for many people, Waorani and others were captured as slaves and forced to work in unspeakable conditions. A few Waorani managed to escape and find their way back home, so people learned some of the specifics of the fate of loved ones. All Waorani can still name relatives who disappeared in the rubber trade.

With this history, it is no surprise that the Waorani considered *cowode* to be cannibals. *Cannibal* is an almost-universal metaphor for people who are supremely antisocial. The outsiders had shown themselves to be truly savage time after time. In the world of the Waorani, only known relatives are truly "the people," which is the literal meaning of *Waorani*, and it is prudent to be profoundly suspicious of those who are not "the people." What is unusual about the Waorani is not that they chose to reject interaction with people who had been aggressive and untrustworthy; it is that they included everyone, including indigenous neighbors, in their definition of those who were not human. Perhaps the ultimate irony is that in defending their lives and their lands against the cannibal *cowode*, the Waorani became generally known in Ecuador as *Auca*, savage, because people who trespassed on land the Waorani regarded as theirs invited death by spearing.

However just or unjust the term *Auca* is, it deterred most of those who had their own designs on the land and/or the people living between the Napo and Curaray Rivers. Although no one in the 20th century was as openly brutal as the rubber traders, the nature of the pressure on the Waorani had not really changed. Outsiders who had no respect for the Waorani still wanted what they had. In mid-20th century Ecuador, haciendas still depended on cheap Indian labor, and many were not above kidnapping the unwary or killing the intractable. Oil exploration began in 1937 and resulted in sporadic spearings by Waorani as crews penetrated into their territory over the next decade. As the century progressed, colonists from the desperately land-poor highlands increasingly became a problem for the Waorani and other Indians occupying the "underutilized" lands of Amazonian Ecuador.

Not all outsiders coming to the Amazon were physically predatory. Missions started establishing schools in the Oriente in the 1920s and were widely criticized for being pro-Indian. Both Roman Catholic and Protestant missions were reinvigorated in the years following World War II.

Almost unnoticed among these developments were five young Protestant missionaries from the United States who felt called by God to establish contact with the Waorani. They learned a few Waorani phrases from a young Waorani woman who had fled her homeland. Their plan was to establish contact by dropping gifts from an airplane, and then to land and meet the Waorani face to face. In 1956 they landed on a sand beach along the Curaray River. All five were speared. The events that followed from this spearing would forever change the Waorani world.

To this point, the Waorani had consistently and violently rejected all contact with the outside hierarchical world. Was their response rational? It may seem extreme, but was it really more violent than the actions of the Spanish and the rubber traders, among others? Can we who live inside hierarchy discern its external face?

We are not suggesting that the Waorani knew they were facing hierarchy. We are simply raising the possibility that they understood the nature of what they were facing better than we do.

Internal Correlates Before 1958

The previous section summarized the history of Waorani encounters with the external world prior to 1958 and the Waorani response—the virtually automatic spearing of all outsiders. This section examines some features of life in Waorani society that seem to relate to that response. In other words, what factors motivated the kind of sustained external violence characteristic of the Waorani before 1958?

All societies, egalitarian and hierarchical, have neighbors. One of the things that all societies must consciously or unconsciously do is develop a strategy for coping with their neighbors. All societies must also maintain internal order.

Hierarchical societies like ours have developed specialized institutions backed by force to handle problems of order. We have other institutions, like the family and all sorts of social groups, that also serve to help keep things going as we want them to. Egalitarian societies, on the other hand, have no formal mechanisms overtly designed to ensure order. Like all societies, they spend considerable effort socializing children to behave as they should. But unlike a hierarchical society, an egalitarian society must leave it to individuals or groups like families to decide whether to intervene when people behave badly. Anthropologists call such systems **self-help systems**.

A major risk in using a self-help legal system is that a **feud** may result. If someone in a self-help system intervenes to correct a wrong and everyone accepts the correction as valid, the problem has been solved. But if the one side does not accept the correction but instead see it as an offense to be corrected by further action, we have the beginning of a feud. Each side sees the other as being in the wrong, and each side believes that further correction is necessary.

No one knows with certainty how it got started, but Waorani society was involved in an all-encompassing feud for at least all of the 1900s prior to 1958. Men from one household group would stage a raid on another group to avenge past wrongs. If they were successful in killing members of the group, they would in turn be the objects of a raid to exact revenge. Such a feud has the potential to go on forever.

Some idea of the extent of the feud can be determined by statistics collected on cause of death. Going back five generations, more than 41 percent of all deaths were feud-based spearings. By way of context, 8 percent were caused by *cowode* and 9 percent by slavers. So even though the fear of outsiders was based in reality, the Waorani had more reason to fear other Waorani.

Parents in all societies raise their children to live in that society. They are probably not conscious of some of the ways in which they do this. Waorani parents still tell misbehaving toddlers, "Be good, or the *cowode* will get you." At an almost subliminal level, people sitting around a fire in the evening are conspicuously more relaxed in the full moon and more subdued in the dark of the moon when spearings were most likely to occur. The community moods surely transmit information, attitudes, and expectations to young people growing up in the community.

Boys as young as eight were taken on spearing raids. After someone was impaled, a boy would be given the spear to hold so he would learn what it was like to have someone die on the end of his spear. A mother calls out the name of one or another relative to her toddler as she rolls a ball across the

Campaede works on a spear as a grandchild looks on. Most education was through observation and participation.
(Photograph by Jim Yost.)

floor. The point of the game is to give the boy practice hitting moving targets with his toy spear and to make sure he learns at an early age which relatives he should attempt to kill on sight.[2]

As in most societies, gossip and direct commentary are major tools in shaping behavior that is encouraged and behavior that is discouraged. It is assumed that violence is a behavioral possibility on the part of the child and others, so violence is incorporated into the repertoire of potential actions; but it is also always assumed that the violence will be directed outside the group to *cowode* or to other groups of Waorani. In other words, violence is a part of life, but it is always projected externally. For instance, children are exhorted to be strong and competent so they will be able to defend themselves. Most children grow to adulthood fearing outsiders, but without ever having heard anger directed toward anyone in the family or having seen an act of violence within their group.

Violence is also linked to the strong sense of personal autonomy characteristic of the Waorani. They assume that they are in control of their lives, that no one can force them to do what they do not want to do, and that the world is theirs to use. Acts that thwart their will and that seem to them to be caused by someone else's will or by sorcery may well cause them to feel instant and almost uncontrollable rage. The death of a loved one, the rejection of a desired marriage, or any of a long list of acts can instantly transform a gentle and genial person into a murderer. Such a transformation would be sympathetically understood by another Waorani. It is simply the way their culture leads them to think.

---

[2]Remember that almost all Waorani are connected through known kinship links and that they do not kill brothers and sisters. For the most part, the people being killed belong to the groups one could marry into, one's actual or potential brothers-in-law.

Violence is possible if a society socializes its young into believing that it is normal. One of the prices to be paid is that the violence has both internal and external consequences. For some people, the price of violence is that life becomes unbearable. This was the case for a young woman named Dove whose family was systematically being hunted down by Black Hawk, a man who had taken the feud to psychopathic extremes. Dove decided that her life was so intolerable that it would be better to be eaten by the cannibals. So in 1947 she fled to unknown terrors on the outside, and she was eventually taken in at a hacienda.[3] There she learned a new way of life, married, and eventually taught a few Waorani phrases to one of the missionaries mentioned above.

After those missionaries were speared, the widow of one and the sister of another decided to continue in their places. They contacted Dove and stayed with her to learn the language. In the process, Dove, who was now a widow, decided to return home. She was thus able to introduce the two American women to her people and begin the first sustained peaceful contact between *cowode* and Waorani.

External Relations During the Next 20 Years

When Dove and the two women arrived, the Waorani totaled about 500 people occupying some 8100 square miles. They were divided into four groups, all of them mutually hostile. Seldom in history were a people as ready for change as the Waorani when the three women arrived and proclaimed that God loved them and wanted them to live in peace. Within an amazingly short time, members of the small group to which Dove had returned had accepted the message of peace and were actively attempting to share it with their fellow Waorani. They were soon joined by a group of 50. In 1968 a group of 108 came in. In 1969 the government established a protectorate of about 620 square miles. By the next year there were 300 people living there. Year by year, more came in, so that by the mid-1970s there were some 500 on the protectorate and only 100 off it.

One of the two missionaries who made the first contact with Dove left in 1961. The other lived with the Waorani almost continuously until her death in 1994. She was associated with the Summer Institute of Linguistics (SIL), an organization primarily interested in Bible translation. She was joined by a linguist in 1962, a nurse in 1969, a literacy specialist in 1972, and an anthropologist in 1974. The nature of the specialties says something about the goals of the organization. Most of the Waorani had already become Christian and had accepted the message of peace. SIL wanted them to become Biblically aware, to stay healthy (they were terribly vulnerable to outside diseases), to become literate in their own language and then in Spanish, and to be exposed to new things in culturally sensitive ways. They would inevitably become a functioning part of Ecuador, but on what terms—as literate, knowledgeable, and competent full participants, or as illiterate, ignorant, and marginal cast-offs?

In the early years, SIL clearly served as a gatekeeper, closely controlling access to the Waorani. The organization built an airstrip to facilitate importing goods and services, but controlled the traffic to a large extent. In terms of

---

[3]Dove's flight was an act of conspicuous bravery, but it was not really a rare event. Over the years, some 5 percent of the population had done likewise.

Waorani exposure to the outside, there were two main goals, which were largely met. One was to provide enough exposure to outsiders to allow the Waorani to gain confidence in dealing with them. The other was to give the Waorani time to develop the competencies needed to deal with the outside.

Some of the increased interaction can be said to have been due to SIL sensibilities. When polio struck in 1968, external personnel were brought in immediately. Although Waorani health was excellent in general, their teeth were among the worst in the world, so SIL brought in dentists from time to time. Vaccination clinics were also conducted by outsiders; the first volunteer Ecuadorian M.D. became involved in 1978. By the early 1970s, SIL was training some Waorani as health promoters who could provide simple Western medical procedures to their home communities.

Some of the increased interaction came from Waorani initiative. They had always been interested in the things possessed by outsiders. This proclivity was accentuated by Dove's experience on the outside. Dove had discovered the usefulness of aluminum pots and had experienced the denigration of being known as a naked *Auca*. She had learned that the Quichua, the dominant Indian group in the area, and others were prone to shoot naked Indians on sight. There was thus extreme pressure to arrange for ever-increasing access to outsider goods. As the Waorani gained confidence in their ability to interact with outsiders and learned what kinds of things they could sell to outsiders, they would increasingly walk to frontier towns to sell their wares and experience firsthand the pleasures of civilization.

Some of the increased interaction resulted from the initiative of external institutions. The national government had a major interest in establishing a presence, in part because of border disputes with Peru. Governments always seem interested in establishing the peace when encountering warrior societies, and they seem to think that machine-gun fire from helicopters is an appropriate way to do it. At the other end of the scale, all Waorani houses were mapped and numbered so that they could be drenched in DDT twice a year as part of the national malaria control program.

And, as always, there were oil companies that were eagerly seeking the next bonanza in an environment not given to much inspection or regulation. The Waorani were ambivalent about the industry's intentions. They feared what might happen, but they remained confident that they could, if necessary, simply kill the workers so that the companies would, once again, go away. In the meantime, they wanted what the companies could give them—exposure to *cowode* technology, *cowode* food, *cowode* ways, and eventually *cowode* jobs—and they wanted it fast. Prior to 1977 fewer than 10 Waorani men had ever worked for the oil companies. By the end of 1979 that number had grown to 73.

Tourism to Waorani villages had started by the early 1970s with the active cooperation of some Waorani. In a few years several hundred tourists arrived annually, putting at risk people who could die from exposure to a single cold.

Internal Correlates During the Next 20 Years

The advent of peace meant more than a cessation of killing. Soon after 1958 it also meant uniting groups who had been living in hostile isolation. It meant that siblings long-separated by surprise raids were reunited. It meant that there were now more *qui* available for marriage. It meant that the scale of things had increased; the Waorani were now part of a larger, more complex, more interactive community. Eventually the new Waorani community broke apart and smaller communities formed, but they remained in contact with each other with a different sense of what it meant to be Waorani.

A new institution was born to express what it meant to be at peace. It could be and was called a church, but it was not much like any other church. In some ways it was more like a New England town meeting, except that there were nursing mothers and naked kids wandering around. In some communities, it would meet every Sunday morning, but it would also meet whenever a nonresident showed up in the community. Both in terms of content and the timing of the meetings, it was clear that the central reiterated point was the reaffirmation of the message "We do not kill."

A soon-observable consequence of peace and exposure to Western medicine was an increasing population. In the late 1970s the rate of growth was calculated at 2.2 percent, high enough to produce dramatic increases.

As noted earlier, when Dove returned to her people in 1958 there was already a demand for outsider goods. Waorani expect their kin group to share meat and other necessities, but there are implications with regard to scarce and desirable goods like aluminum pots or dresses. If Dove has one dress, that is fine. But if she has two dresses, then a sister or another relative is entitled to demand a share. If Dove has ten sisters and only two dresses, then there is a tremendous demand to get more dresses, simply because they are a desirable prestige item. Since Dove had internalized Quichua notions of modesty and of the contemptible and dangerous state of being *Auca*, the need for more dresses and other externally produced goods grew even greater as she communicated her views to others.

The most obvious way to get more dresses, at least in the beginning, was from the missionaries. They were not particularly interested in providing dresses, but it was probably easy to rationalize giving the people something they wanted. So sewing machines and cloth were imported to make dresses for the women and shorts for the men. Eventually, the proverbial missionary barrels filled with an amazing assortment of mostly used North American clothing. Thus the Waorani became clothed. And they stopped wearing their balsa wood earplugs, which also marked them as wild Indians.

The first airstrip was built because SIL thought it advantageous. Now each Waorani village has one because the people saw airstrips as the best way to have quick access to goods from the outside. The significance the Waorani attach to the airstrips can be discerned by imagining the effort it takes people equipped with machetes, dibble sticks, baskets, and perhaps a few shovels to cut down enough 150-foot trees and to level enough land to serve as a strip for even light planes. It is also worth noting that the airstrips represent sustained cooperative effort on a scale far beyond anything before imagined.

The goods that first came in—clothing, pots, axes, blankets, rubber boots—were significant as symbols of change, but they did little to change the texture of life. Two items with a negative effect were dynamite and DDT, both used to kill fish. DDT has a superficial resemblance to the poisons traditionally used in fishing, but the new users were unaware of its environmental consequences. Dynamite is not only dangerous to the user; it also kills everything within the impact zone instead of just stunning the fish. The use of these two innovations transformed formerly productive streams within a few years. There was a limited exposure to and use of shotguns during this period. They were expensive and often unreliable, and the Waorani were still more expert in the use of their traditional hunting tools, but increasing utilization is likely.

We have noted that Dove was greatly influenced by Quichua culture while living outside Waorani territory. Several other Waorani women who had run away also returned after the killings stopped. These women all have well-established connections in neighboring Quichua communities, and they have all served as cultural brokers. All married into the Quichua communities themselves and/or married their children into them. Through them, many Waorani have established **fictive kinship** relationships with the Quichua. These arrangements give Waorani a place to stay and secure contacts in neighboring towns, and they give the Quichua access to Waorani hunting and fishing territory. By the end of the 1970s, tons of smoked fish and meat were being exported to game-deficient Quichua territory, and Quichua affines and fictive kin of Waorani were exerting claims to Waorani land, which was already much reduced by land-hungry settlers who were no longer intimidated by the threat of spearings.

Peaceful relations with outsiders created many changes in Waorani society. Some of these changes gave Waorani access to possibilities they did not have before; others presented risks to the society. Some of the changes did both.

QUESTION 5.3
How Can Hierarchy Get Started?

As we understand the world's prehistory and history, hierarchy has evolved out of nonhierarchy, not the other way around. Before 1958, the Waorani were so thoroughly and seamlessly egalitarian that it is hard to imagine how they might become hierarchical other than to be forced into it by a colonial regime. Nevertheless, they had changed sufficiently to allow the beginnings of hierarchy to be visible by the late 1970s.

A Different Model

When Dove and the other women who had fled to the *cowode* returned, they had a number of characteristics in common. The first thing was that they had been strongly **acculturated** into Quichua culture. They knew the Quichua language, and they had absorbed the way of life of a people who—while still jungle Indians, some of whom had recently moved into town—were more sophisticated and were the possessors of abundant goods.

The second thing they had in common was a strong devaluation of the *Auca* culture. This is not surprising given the long history of hostility between the two groups; the women were undoubtedly reviled when they first joined the Quichua. Dove's attitude toward Waorani culture is exemplified by her approach to literacy. Waorani literacy programs for children and adults were started by SIL, and these programs were taught in the Waorani language, used Waorani material, and attempted to be as culturally sensitive as possible. Dove rejected this approach and instituted a Spanish curriculum for the entirely monolingual children of her community. She hired a Quichua teacher who feared the Waorani and publicly disparaged all aspects of their culture, and she herself jumped up and down on Waorani literacy material, shouting, "The Waorani language is no good!" Given this attitude, it is no surprise that she and her fellow returnees dress like Quichua, live in Quichua-style houses, marry their children to Quichua, form reciprocal bonds with Quichua, and generally cultivate Quichua relationships and emulate Quichua behavior.

The third thing these women shared was knowledge of social institutions unknown to the Waorani but characteristic of the Quichua and of Latin America generally: the *compadrazgo,* the hacienda, and debt-peonage. The *compadrazgo* is a system of fictive kinship in which people not related to each other voluntarily enter into a relationship of mutual obligation and support much like the kin group among the Waorani. The hacienda is a class-based agricultural estate dominated by a patron who is served by various categories of lesser beings whose main function is to make the patron rich and comfortable. Debt-peonage is a system in which the buying and selling of goods is used to create indebtedness and thus to force debtors into a kind of perpetual servitude. These three institutions are all hierarchical in their nature.

The Application of the Model

Dove was particularly fortunate in the circumstances under which she returned to her homeland: she was the indispensable interpreter and assistant for one of the missionaries. She thus became the channel through which goods originating with the missionaries entered the society. This flow was never very substantial, but it was the primary source of new goods in the early years, and Dove was able to use traditional forms of reciprocity to parlay her advantages to considerable social and economic benefit.

In 1978, Dove and her husband were the dispensers and recipients of gifts, ostensibly in the traditional manner. In one case she gave medicine to a sick man. Two months later he gave her a blowgun. Within minutes she was boasting to her cronies that she could sell it for 1000 *sucres*. What the man did not realize is that this was a profit of 950 *sucres*. More significantly, as someone still part of the traditional culture, he would not have cared. Dove cared very much, and the profit allowed her to extend and deepen her ability to create social indebtedness through further gift giving.

Dove also traded for or purchased goods from villagers for later resale. Here her superior knowledge allowed her to mix traditional and commercial modes of exchange to her profit in both spheres. When a herd of peccary were sighted near the village, several of the local men had no spears, having sold them to her. She loaned them back. As traditionalists, they gave her about a third of each animal they speared. She then had far more meat than her household could consume, so she was able to distribute the surplus to those in her favor, thereby strengthening her hold on them. And she still had the spears to sell.

Dove also created what was in effect a cottage industry. Women who wished to benefit from her superior knowledge of the outside world and her commercial contacts would work under her supervision, for instance, to finish hammocks intended for sale. Dove would then market them for a substantial commission.

Several unmarried girls lived in her household, and she utilized their labor in exchange for caring for them and for providing various services to their families. Their labor increased the productivity of her household immensely, allowing her to be a hostess on a grand scale (increasing social indebtedness) and making it unnecessary for her to work in her own gardens.

Dove advertised on a local multilingual radio station for Quichua to come to her village if they wanted to fish Waorani streams. This arrangement allowed her to send out her favorites as guides, increasing their indebtedness to her, and it enabled her to receive a substantial share of the catch, a fee, or a return favor from the Quichua.

Dove and her husband have in effect started public works programs, organizing village labor to construct a school building and to clear two landing strips adjacent to the village. She has capitalized on the new circumstances to create a **public sphere** where none existed before. People in an egalitarian society can speak only for themselves; there are no public leaders. When government officials or agents for tourist enterprises come, they all assume that there is a public sphere with public leadership, just like there is back home. Dove has assumed that role. In so doing, she has lived up to the expectations of most Ecuadorians who read and heard about her in the national media as the most prominent of the "Auca Queens." Her assumption of the role was beyond the understanding of most Waorani. For those who were beginning to understand, the fact that she shared the benefits made it acceptable.

Comments

By 1978 the Waorani were becoming a **class** society. Through their superior knowledge and by controlling the major sources of desirable and locally unavailable goods, Dove and her husband had garnered sufficient power that they were able to act authoritatively on a continuous basis in their village, which at the time constituted 30 percent of the total tribal population. She and her family had more possessions and more kinds of possessions than anyone else did. She had a coterie of active supporters in her village, and the other Auca Queens were pursuing parallel courses in their villages.

Nevertheless, it is equally important to note that the society was in many ways still profoundly egalitarian and that the basis of the egalitarianism was still intact: no one could yet be denied subsistence needs. It is normal for a society to be a mix of the hierarchical and the egalitarian. Our own society, for example, which has been hierarchic from the beginning, also has strongly egalitarian features.

The fact that it is women who have gained power seems to be of no particular moment, since it is a product of idiosyncratic circumstances. Power is power, and women wield it the same way men would. Its primary significance is as further evidence that women are not socially disadvantaged in traditional society.

Finally, this ethnographic case confirms the principle that hierarchy can develop internally within an egalitarian society only by legitimate means—in this case through the use of traditional practices of reciprocity. Hierarchy resulted from exchanges that appear balanced when looked at in one light (I gave to you, and you gave to me) but that appear exploitative when looked at in another light (although I gave to you, I kept most of the value for myself).

QUESTION 5.4
What Happens After Hierarchy Gets Started?

What happens for most people after hierarchy gets started is that life goes on more or less as it was. There are still gardens to clear, and there are still children to feed. On the other hand, although structures change slowly, they do change; something new has been added, and the course of the society has been altered. Once established, hierarchy pervades all of life.

General Trends

Waorani life has gone on, but the society has experienced some changes in population, health, and the way food is obtained since the time hierarchy was introduced.

Population Growth and Health. With the cessation of spearing, not only do people live longer, but they also have more babies. This is in part because the Waorani accepted the message that God wanted them to stop practicing infanticide as well as to stop spearing. The annual rate of population increase has been 2.5 percent in recent years, which is quite high. Put another way, in 40 years the Waorani have grown from fewer than 500 to almost 1400.

The people now have better access to Western medicine, which does confer some benefits. However, they are still very vulnerable to Western infectious diseases. Recently there were a number of deaths from hepatitis. They are now more sedentary, which increases certain risks, like getting skin infections and intestinal parasites. Studies indicate that levels of ailments like hypertension are still very low.

Bottle-feeding has become popular, with very negative consequences because of the lack of sanitation, the use of river water, and the lowered nutrient level. There are also, for the first time, instances of child malnutrition, sexually transmitted diseases, and spousal abuse. These are related phenomena and are also related to hierarchy.

Hunting, Fishing, and Gardening. The Waorani are still unusually active and productive hunters, although less so than formerly. The shotgun has generally replaced both the blowgun and the spear. Dogs are now used, but they are regarded with ambivalence because they are not generally trained and they scare away monkeys. Traditional taboos have been relaxed so that deer, tapir, and caiman are now actively hunted. Because people are more sedentary, the areas close to villages have become relatively unproductive for hunting, and fishing is comparatively more important. Traditional poisons are still widely used in fishing, but so is dynamite. Some people have less time to hunt because of jobs, involvement in market activities, attendance in school, or involvement in political functions or soccer tournaments. Hunters may decide to take the results of a particularly good hunt to market, and this after-the-fact market hunting is usually the only kind of market hunting taking place.

Gardening continues to provide the greatest portion of the family diet. Much of it is still women's work, with men doing the heavy clearing and helping with weeding. In rank order, the dominant crops are manioc, bananas,

Women preparing surplus food for a fiesta. (Photograph by Jim Yost.)

corn, peanuts, and sweet potatoes. Gardens tend to be smaller nowadays, but they are worked for more years and left fallow for shorter periods of time. These changes are related to others. There is less fear of raids, so the alternate gardens are less important. There is more emphasis on education and participation in the market economy, and people buy some of their food. Younger people are less inclined to help. In the old days, some of the food was produced to host huge fiestas that had both political and social purposes; today political meetings feature outside food, often provided by the oil companies.

Increasing Hierarchy

This discussion of ostensibly general trends has drifted into explanations involving hierarchy. The philosophy and practice of hierarchy have penetrated all aspects of Waorani society, and there is no area of change that can be fully discussed without bringing in the notion of hierarchy.

Education. Education is not inherently hierarchical. When the Waorani were isolated, education was entirely informal and entirely devoted to the needs of the community. SIL subsequently provided Waorani education in ungraded classes, using Waorani material and language and attempting to be culturally sensitive. All that is now largely gone, and hierarchy permeates the present system.

Take, for instance, something as simple as the schoolhouse itself. According to the government model, the school must be constructed from sawn lumber. This feature alone sets it apart from every other building in some of the communities, as do the tin roof and concrete steps. Rather than being part of the community, arising out of the community, and serving the felt needs of the community, the school system is seen to be a thing of the government, imposed from the top down, with goals and curricula set by the government and with procedures mandated by the government. If there is congruence between government and community goals and aspirations, it is purely coincidental; the educational bureaucracy surely did not ask.

The Waorani initially embraced education with considerable enthusiasm, for they saw it as a means to acquire the things they wanted. There is currently a lot less enthusiasm and more ambivalence. A number of Waorani in their thirties and older who attended the old SIL schools express deep concern that their children are losing contact with traditional values and cultural knowledge in the latest version of the educational system.

As a typical hierarchical system, the school uses force to ensure conformity on the part of both students and parents. This attitude automatically generates resistance from people who are still essentially egalitarian and who assume that a six-year-old is an autonomous being with the right to make decisions. Nevertheless, substantial numbers of Waorani are getting an education; there are schools in about half the communities, and some 500 students are enrolled.

In her excellent study on Waorani education, Rival (1992) notes that the schools are major acculturative forces that emphasize the need to be modern, civilized, healthy, clean, a consumer of imported goods, and good Ecuadorians. They also promote sedentary living and the creation of political power by young, educated men, who are far more likely than women to complete an education.

Rival's language is much too civilized. The teachers, be they Quichua or Ecuadorian nationals, have, with a very few exceptions, nothing but contempt for the Waorani language and culture, and they denigrate it forcefully and continually. The educational process alienates youth from their parents and from their roots; many of them are openly contemptuous of their elders. A typical graduate knows less about the local ecology than does a child of eight who has not gone to school; neither is he or she likely to be well prepared for real jobs. A typical male teacher apparently defines his role to include impregnating all the girls he can, setting an example of abusing women, dispensing alcohol and drugs, and generally being a source of disruption. There is nothing much the community can do about any of this other than pull out of the official system.

That is exactly what some conservative communities have done. They are working with the woman who first started the Waorani literacy program more than 25 years ago, going back to educating children in their own language first. What a radical concept!

Oil Companies. By now some 90 percent of Waorani men have worked for the oil companies. Their work is basically labor—carrying heavy loads long distances or wielding machetes to clear seismic lines. It provides them with no new work skills. It does provide increased exposure to working with and for outsiders, new foods, and new ways of doing things. It also exposes them to the local jungle oil town, which almost anyone would deem a "hellhole." Three months of work will generate about $750. What will probably be brought home are a boom box, some clothes (for him), an alcohol habit, and a sexually transmitted disease. And these are the good times. The industry is moving from the exploration phase into the production phase, and the need for unskilled labor will virtually vanish.

Meanwhile, the wives back home are attempting to cope. A husband's absence probably means a major reduction in the amount of meat available. It also means substantially less produce from the garden because the husband is not there to do the heavy work.

In a 1999 study of Waorani subsistence, Lu recounts how one oil company attempted to ameliorate this problem by making helicopter drops of food to the families of employed men. Each kit contained two cans of tuna, five pounds of white rice, five pounds of white sugar, two kilograms of salt (the Waorani traditionally used no salt), a can of lard, and four packets of drink mix. Even if adequate quantities of this transparently deficient gift were given to the families, it would still represent much less protein, three times the fat, fewer carbohydrates, and one-seventh of the fiber they were accustomed to. Despite the public relations statements they make, none of the oil companies currently operating in Ecuador is serious about culturally relevant mitigation.

Colonists. For the Waorani, the problem with colonists is directly linked to oil company activity. In the mid-1980s, an oil company built a road into the heart of Waorani territory. A tidal wave of colonists from the overcrowded highlands swamped the region. There was some Waorani retaliation, so the government restricted colonization to a narrow band along the road. This action defused the tension somewhat, but the problem has certainly not been solved.

The 60 miles of road is not on territory recognized by the government as being Waorani land, but it is all in territory that was controlled by the Waorani for generations and that no one else used. They still think of it as their territory, and the thought of *cowode* living on it is almost more than some can bear.

The fact that the government attempted to contain the flood of colonists shows that the Waorani do have some political clout. But in a hierarchy, the biggest players get the most consideration; the oil companies and the rest of the nation will get more consideration than the Waorani.

Waorani Formal Political Structure. The terms Waorani and *formal political structure* once had nothing in common. But this is no longer true. The Waorani are now formally organized, confirming the maxim that bureaucracy begets bureaucracy.

The National Organization of Amazonian Ecuadorian Waorani (ONHAE) was born in 1990 at the instigation of very young graduates. It is a legal political entity with statutes approved by the government. Each village sends delegates to an annual congress, where the delegates discuss many matters and elect the officers of the organization. So far, this has been less democratic than it sounds. Only people who can read and write and who can speak Spanish have been allowed to vote. This rule effectively disenfranchises those who are older and the traditionalists. To date the prime function of ONHAE appears to be to present itself publicly as a formal entity interacting with the oil companies, to receive funds from the oil companies, and to disburse those funds.

There are countercurrents to the kind of hierarchical centralization represented by ONHAE. Some of the older and more traditional villages have declared themselves to be independent of ONHAE and to no longer be represented by it. A young and forceful missionary with roots in the community recently established a new centrally located village. The intention is to make the village both more traditional and more Christian than most present ones. It seems to have strong appeal. A church has been formed and legally incorporated.

The Cultural Brokers. The rejection of the SIL educational system and the substitution of a nationally directed one that emphasizes replacing the so-called inferior Waorani culture with a civilized, Spanish-based culture was done at the behest of the women who had lived among the Quichua. It is a clear expression of the values of these **cultural brokers**. To be fair, that schoolchildren now mock their parents is not entirely to be laid at their feet; respect for parents was never much of a virtue in fiercely autonomous Waorani culture. That parents are mocked for being Waorani is new.

Both Waorani society and Quichua society are kin-based, and both use marriage to forge alliances and create social and economic advantages. Quichua society also extends the notion of kinship by creating *compadres* who have the same obligations of mutual support as kin. In this context, patterns of marriage are critical. Dove married a Waorani, probably because she was the first returnee and had to demonstrate that she was still Waorani, but all of her children married Quichua. This is the pattern among the cultural brokers. There are currently 45 such marriages.

The marriages say something about attitudes. While Dove and people like her must maintain a local power base and thus must dispense some economic favors to their Waorani supporters, the marriages indicate that they see the Quichua as peers. The marriages also indicate that they believe that their major political opportunities are outside Waorani society, or perhaps it is more accurate to say that they believe their opportunities lie in incorporating Waorani society into Quichua society. What they can offer as inducement to prospective affines and *compadres,* besides relationship to the famous Auca Queens (which is not likely to be worth much to a Quichua), is access to Waorani land and resources. In land-poor Ecuador, this is a fabulous inducement.

Bringing Quichua affines into Waorani communities is not only a threat to Waorani resources in the long run; it also brings another source of acculturative influence into the community. Take, for instance, attitudes toward violence. Men in traditional Waorani culture might turn into raging killers, but the rage was normatively directed externally. In Quichua culture, verbal and physical abuse occurs in the home, and we are now seeing Waorani men striking their wives in emulation of their new neighbors.

It would not be fair to blame current Waorani involvement in the **market economy** on Quichua influence. From the first, Waorani people were very interested in obtaining outside goods through available markets. However, the Quichua focus on the importance of material acquisition, power relationships, and hierarchy expressed at all times by the cultural brokers is not congruent with traditional Waorani values. For instance, tourist visits to Waorani-land were probably inevitable. However, tourism did not have to develop the way it did. All arrangements are made by the Auca Queens, all moneys are received by them, all disbursements are made by them, and all power and much of the material benefit have accrued to them. That is not a Waorani model of interaction; it is a Quichua model heavily influenced by the hacienda model. It is also an example of the spread of hierarchy.

Much the same could be said about ONHAE. It is about power. There is no doubt that the Waorani need power in their interactions with government, the oil companies, and other outside agencies. ONHAE's potential is enormous. But for whose benefit will it operate? From the beginning, ONHAE was designed to keep the nonhierarchically oriented from even getting in the door. What the disbursement of benefits is about, especially in the absence of accountability, is the creation of power and hierarchy.

QUESTION 5.5
How Do Formerly Small-Scale Societies Fit into Hierarchical States?

Forty years ago, the Waorani existed as an independent, autonomous society. Ecuador and even Peru, at one time, drew lines on maps that incorporated the Waorani within their boundaries; but neither exerted any control or exercised any sovereignty over the Waorani. For their part, the Waorani did not know, could not guess, and had no reason to even imagine that such a thing as Ecuador or a government could exist.

By what logic, then, does the state of Ecuador now exercise authority over the Waorani? The answer is by the logic of hierarchy. This is the same logic of hierarchy that long ago allowed a pope who had never heard of the Waorani or any other South American people to draw a line on a globe and declare that Spain had the right to exercise authority in that part of the world. It let the colonial states of Europe get together to discuss the procedures by which they wished to control other people's land and to call those procedures international law. That is the world we and the Waorani live in.

Possibilities

There are several different ways that the Waorani can fit into the state of Ecuador. They include individualization, autonomy, and something in between.

Individualization. Individualization means that the Waorani would end up being treated as individuals who happen to live in the state named Ecuador, rather than as part of a separate corporate body representing all Waorani and acting on their behalf. Another way of saying this is that they would lose everything that speaks of any corporateness, of any peoplehood, of being Waorani in any sense beyond a vague, sentimental ethnicity that might comment, "My grandmother was *Auca*."

Of course, we would never hear it put that way. The language of hierarchy would express itself in the language of citizenship and democracy. It would comment that it is unthinkable in a democracy for all citizens not to be equal, for some citizens to have special rights not available to others. The language of hierarchy would assert that treating a group of Indians differently than all other citizens is particularly invidious, invoking images of South African apartheid-like horrors in the democratic New World.

The language of hierarchy never says what it means because it is the language of power and privilege. It seeks, under cover of the apparently egalitarian language of democracy, to incorporate people like the Waorani into the very lowest level of the established hierarchical order. Stripped of their undemocratic special privileges, they would sell their bodies as day laborers and prostitutes for their daily bread. But they would be "equal."

The individualization option would be a tragedy for the Waorani and the world. It is a tragedy that has been experienced by numberless others.

Autonomy. Allowing the Waorani autonomy means recognizing their right to exercise substantial sovereignty within a legally defined territory in Ecuador. Forty years ago, the Waorani occupied 8100 square miles. In 1968 a Waorani Protectorate of 620 square miles was established; the Waorani Ethnic Reserve was added in 1990, more than tripling the amount of land. While nowhere near as large as their former territory, the reserve is substantial and provides an already-existing legally defined land base from which to proceed. The fact that the eastern half of this territory is surrounded by the Yasuni National Park provides additional security.

Having an established land base is only the first step. The more fundamental questions relate to the division of powers. All would agree that defense and currency should remain with the state. However, all other powers could be accommodated in an autonomous region. Why not allow such a region to control its own education, legal system, health system, and legislation? Or, why not negotiate arrangements to share some of these functions? The point is that these are details; the real issue is that, for the most part, regional autonomy is never considered. We think it is a viable option. In such an arrangement, the Waorani would still find themselves within a hierarchically organized state. The advantage for them would be maximum flexibility and opportunity to work out institutional arrangements for doing the things that need to be done in a modern society in ways that are congruent with their own values and cultural traditions, not someone else's.

Most states seem to think that their survival depends on suppressing tribalism. We believe that more productive relations ensue when culture is celebrated and people are confirmed in their identity and allowed to develop their own institutions. From the state's point of view, a potential benefit would be the partnership with an internal dependent nation where things work because they are organized according to principles that express the character of the people. A state that evaluates this kind of relationship from the principles of hierarchy will see the loss of power and direct control as detrimental, and the people occupying high positions would suffer the loss of personal advantage.

Something in Between. There are other possibilities. The choices depend on how far decision makers are willing to stray from the established paths of hierarchy. Following are two examples that did not stray very far, but experienced very different results.

Canada's Northwest Territories were split in two in 1999, and the eastern portion was renamed Nunavut. It was widely heralded as Canada's first aboriginal territory since almost the only people living there are Inuit. It has a legislature elected, like any other, by the citizens resident in each electoral district, but the process is conspicuously different than in most places because it reflects Inuit values. There are no political parties, and candidates do not run campaigns because parties and campaigning violate Inuit sensibilities about appropriate behavior. In the legislature itself, the goal is consensus, not victory for one's party. These differences enhance the legislature's effectiveness because the people are able to take ownership of the institution.

The implications seem clear. As long as the boundaries of Waorani territory are maintained, considerable self-government could be granted. Ecuador, like Canada, is a federal state, so we think the model could be emulated.

A second in-between model is also taken from Canada, but this one had less-positive results. When reserves were set up in British Columbia about a century ago, they were created by a formula established elsewhere, and no attempt was made to include the bases of the people's livelihood, whether by fishing or hunting, in protected land. The reserves were then administered by rules established elsewhere, with no consideration for the local culture, by a bureaucracy largely contemptuous of the indigenous people being administered. To take but one example, the rules of hierarchy assumed patrilineal descent; these rules were followed even in administering the matrilineal people of the area. The result was cruel chaos. The people have survived, but it has not been easy. They are now faced with the task of undoing the results of a century of folly.

Again the implications for the Waorani case seem clear. We now have lengthy experience in attempting to incorporate egalitarian and nonegalitarian indigenous peoples into hierarchical states. We need not repeat the mistakes of the past.

Realities

Whatever one's ideals, whatever one's hopes for people like the Waorani, it is a given that decisions will be shaped by the "hard facts" as they are understood by the various involved parties. We cite two in particular: the importance of oil, and the sequence of choices the Waorani have already made. There are other realities as well, including the hunger of thousands of Ecuadorians for a piece of land of their own and the need for secure national boundaries.

Oil. It turns out that the Waorani homeland is floating on an ocean of oil. For the last 150 years or so, Ecuador has essentially been a single-export economy, and today the export is oil. Proven oil reserves are low. It is certain that the Waorani oil field will be developed with all possible speed—whatever the consequences to the Waorani.

Waorani Choices. The Waorani are not the people today that they were 40 or even 20 years ago. Choices have been made, decisions taken, options opened and closed. Some, but not all, have chosen the road of peace. Some have chosen to actively pursue power and profitability, while others prefer to live according to more traditional values.

In other words, there is more diversity within Waorani society than there was in the past. Traditionally, they had a lot of factionalism but not much diversity. In spite of the increased diversity and continued factionalism, there also seem to be signs of a reemergent sense of identity. ONHAE, which reinforces the corporate identity of the Waorani, is one illustration. Soccer is another example of a faction-spanning institution. It is not a given, however, that this reinvigorated sense of identity will go anywhere. As is no doubt clear, we are not sure that ONHAE is the right institution for the Waorani. But it is a start and a significant symbol of possibilities.

That is what we want for the Waorani and for all of us, that at the end of any particular day, we still have possibilities. Perhaps the main criticism of hierarchy is that it limits those possibilities.[4]

CONCLUSIONS

In many ways the Waorani are like us, or at least they are enough like us that we can see numerous points of similarity. They are born into families where they are cared for; they grow up to become competent adults who provide for their families; they live in communities with supportive and not-so-supportive neighbors. Unlike us, however, until very recently they lived in communities essentially without a social gradient, where no one had long-term authority over anyone else. People were free to make decisions for themselves to a remarkable extent. This personal autonomy seems to have been rooted in the ability of individual families to provide fully for themselves economically.

There is no single model of interaction between small-scale egalitarian societies and large hierarchical societies. Waorani history of the last century illustrates two extreme possibilities. The earlier period was characterized by virtually total rejection of even the possibility of peaceful contact with outsiders. This strategy was sustained by socialization processes that legitimized homicidal violence against anyone outside the local kin group. The more recent era has been characterized by increased openness to local, national, and international institutions, almost all of them hierarchical in nature. These new relationships have simultaneously opened new possibilities and created new risks.

For the Waorani, the development of indigenous hierarchical relationships began as the knowledge that relationships involving unequal exchange could lead to power, prestige, and wealth. Returning to Waorani society with knowledge of how exploitative relationships could work and with privileged access to external social and material resources, Dove and people like her began the internal transformation of Waorani society.

Few changes can be evaluated as simply good or bad. Most activities have both benefits and costs. Some recent changes that most people would judge to be beneficial (or at least potentially so) include lowered homicide rates, less fear, less time spent in defensive practices, access to Western medicine and education, cash incomes, new forms of recreation (and the very concept of recreation), and consumer goods. Unfortunately, these things come with a

---

[4]We have chosen to construct this analysis using *hierarchy* as the central concept. One reason is that the term is not often used, allowing the reader to evaluate what is said relatively free of prior conceptions. A more familiar concept that would cover much the same ground is *colonialism*. A second reason for using *hierarchy* is that it is a broader, more fundamental term.

price: a greatly reduced land area, high birth rates, new diseases, less-nutritious foods, cultural and personal denigration within the community, incorporation into the most marginal roles in the international economy, and loss of control over the socialization of children. It should be noted that some of these costs would likely be present regardless of whether or not the Waorani were themselves becoming hierarchical, and others are more directly a result of becoming hierarchical. In any case, the most consequential changes involve the internal reorganization of Waorani society and its incorporation into the local Quichua and national Ecuadorian society.

The economic, political, and social realities of contemporary Ecuador dictate that Waorani territory and people will be incorporated into the Ecuadorian state. It is not yet clear what form that incorporation will take. The history of other egalitarian societies incorporated into larger structures is not very encouraging. Nevertheless, options do exist. Perhaps we will yet learn from the past.

REFERENCES AND RECOMMENDED READINGS

Alfred, Taiaiake
1999 Peace, Power and Righteousness: An Indigenous Manifesto. Toronto: Oxford University Press.
> Authored by a Mohawk scholar, this book presents the argument that Native communities can and must return to their traditional values, including consensus-based governance, in order to recover from the effects of imposed colonialism.

Bodley, John H.
1999 Victims of Progress. 4th edition. Mountain View, CA: Mayfield Publishing.
> A comprehensive survey of the effect of development on indigenous peoples around the world.

Deloria, Vine, Jr., and R. M. Lytle
1984 The Nations Within: The Past and Future of American Indian Sovereignty. New York: Pantheon Books.
> A groundbreaking work by a noted Lakota scholar on how North American Natives can regain control of their lives by rethinking their traditional values.

Descola, Philippe
1994 In the Society of Nature: A Native Ecology in Amazonia. Cambridge: Cambridge University Press.
> A study of the Achuar, a neighboring group to the Waorani, who are quite similar in significant ways. The book focuses on the cultural construction of nature and, by the way, shows how their egalitarianism is rooted in that construction.

Elliot, Elizabeth
1961 The Savage My Kinsman. New York: Harper and Row.
> Written by one of the first two missionaries to live with the Waorani, this is a firsthand account of the early days of sustained peaceful contact with outsiders.

Kelly, Patricia M.
1988 Issues for Literacy Materials in a Monolingual Amazonian Culture: The Waorani of Ecuador. Master's thesis, University of British Columbia.
> Kelly has worked on educational and other issues with and for the Waorani since 1972.

Lu, Flora E-Shen
1999 Changes in Subsistence Patterns and Resource Use of the Huaorani Indians in the Ecuadorian Amazon. Ph.D. dissertation, Curriculum in Ecology, University of North Carolina.
> Up-to-date research on a key component of contemporary Waorani life.

Manuel, George, and Michael Posluns
1974 The Fourth World: An Indian Reality. Don Mills, ON: Collier-Macmillan.
> A Shuswap elder statesman uses personal narrative to develop an aboriginal political philosophy for the modern world.

Rival, L.
1992 Social Transformations and the Impact of Formal Schooling on the Huaorani of Eastern Ecuador. Ph.D. dissertation, London School of Economics, University of London.
> An analysis of one of the key components in the hierarchical transformation of Waorani society.

Robarchek, C. A., and C. J. Robarchek
1998 The Waorani: The Contexts of Violence and War. Orlando, FL: Harcourt Brace.
> The best single comprehensive overview of the Waorani.

Yost, James A.
1981a Twenty Years of Contact: The Mechanisms of Change in Wao (Auca) Culture. *In* Cultural Transformations and Ethnicity in Modern Ecuador. N. E. Whitten, ed. Pp. 677–704. Urbana: University of Illinois Press.
> A broad but detailed survey of the first two decades of postcontact change among the Waorani.

1981b People of the Forest: The Waorani. *In* Ecuador: In the Shadow of the Volcanoes. P. Gordon-Warren and S. Curl, eds. Pp. 95–115. Quito: Ediciones Libri Mundi.
> The best medium-length summary of traditional Waorani life.

CHAPTER 6

THE CULTURAL CONSTRUCTION OF VIOLENCE

R. LINCOLN KEISER

PROBLEM 6 *How do societies give meaning to and justify collective violence?*

INTRODUCTION
Falling in Love with Revenge

Watching television, reading newspapers, and going to see the latest summer blockbuster movies could lead to the conclusion that violence is endemic to the human condition. It would seem that people are born to be violent and that the proclivity to commit violence must have been hardwired into our very being through the course of human evolution. But although genetic makeup affects behavior, there is much about human violence that is not explained by genetics. Violence is not the same everywhere. Both the meanings and interpretations given to violence and the form violence takes vary across cultures and societies and through time.

Still, many Americans assume that violence is violence wherever it is found. For example, after reading a piece I wrote in *Natural History* about blood **feuding** in Thull (Keiser 1986), a Kohistani community located in the mountains near the border between Afghanistan and Pakistan, a woman asked me if it was safe to travel in that area. I had begun this particular piece with the following excerpt from my field diary:

FIELD DIARY: MAY 28, 1984
At eleven o'clock this morning Qai Afsal left after exchanging gossip and requesting medicine for his wife's illness. When he reached the road, rifle shots rang from the high mesa dominating the approach to my house. Even though the bullets hit close to his feet, Qai Afsal sauntered down the road with his usual swagger.

FIELD DIARY: JUNE 4, 1984

At seven fifteen this evening the sound of automatic fire from AK-47 assault rifles interrupted my supper. The shots came from Kallan where Qai Afsal lives. The fire fight lasted about thirty minutes. About eight o'clock a jeep arrived in front of my house with Qai Afsal lying on the back seat writhing in agony. Two bullets hit him, but fortunately both exited without damaging a vital organ or bone. After I bandaged his wounds my driver drove him to the hospital in Peshawar.

FIELD DIARY: JUNE 15, 1984

Qai Afsal returned from the hospital today vowing *badal,* "revenge." Though community leaders plan *jirgas,* "public councils," to encourage a peaceful end to the fighting, no one believes Qai Afsal will forego revenge.

FIELD DIARY: JUNE 20, 1984

On June 17th, while I was in Islamabad, another pitched battle erupted between Qai Afsal supported by his *ja* [literally meaning "brothers," but *ja* is commonly extended to include paternal cousins as well] and their enemies. Qai Afsal and his kinsmen successfully defended themselves because they possessed more automatic rifles than their attackers. The fight lasted about three hours. Tracers lit the sky and bullets flew in all directions from early evening until well after dark.

I had then gone on to say that you cannot live in Thull for even a day without becoming aware of the pervasiveness of organized violence. Men own specially made fighting knives, axes, clubs, walking sticks designed to double as stabbing spears, automatic pistols, revolvers, bolt-action rifles, updated versions of 19th century British cavalry carbines, and Kalashnikov AK-47 assault rifles. One even finds bolt-action versions of the AK-47 designed and produced by the local arms industry. The sounds of Thull reflect its weaponry; rifle shots fill the air day and night. Religious authorities almost succeeded in stamping out singing and drumming; gunfire became the music of Thull in their place.

Unfortunately, the woman who called concluded that the people of Thull have a penchant for chaotic violence and must be bloodthirsty beasts. But such attitudes are a mistake. Kohistanis interpret violence differently than we do, and this interpretation affects how violence is played out in their communities. Americans traveling in the mountains of Kohistan have nothing to fear from Kohistani blood feuding (although they have a lot to fear from Kohistanis' belief that Christians, Jews, and any other kind of non-Muslims are fundamentally selfish, untrustworthy, evil people). Differences in the way Americans and Kohistanis interpret violence are rooted in history and in culture, not in genetics.

Thull is a community of roughly 6000 Muslims located in the uppermost reaches of the Panjkora Valley. A traveler cannot find a more remote community in Dir Kohistan. Dir District, of which Dir Kohistan is a part, is a section of Pakistan's Northwest Frontier Province. Chitral borders it to the north, Swat to the east, Afghanistan and Bajour to the west, and Malakand to the south. The community lies along some 40 kilometers of river valley. It includes a core village, 15 satellite districts, and 28 summer pastures areas.

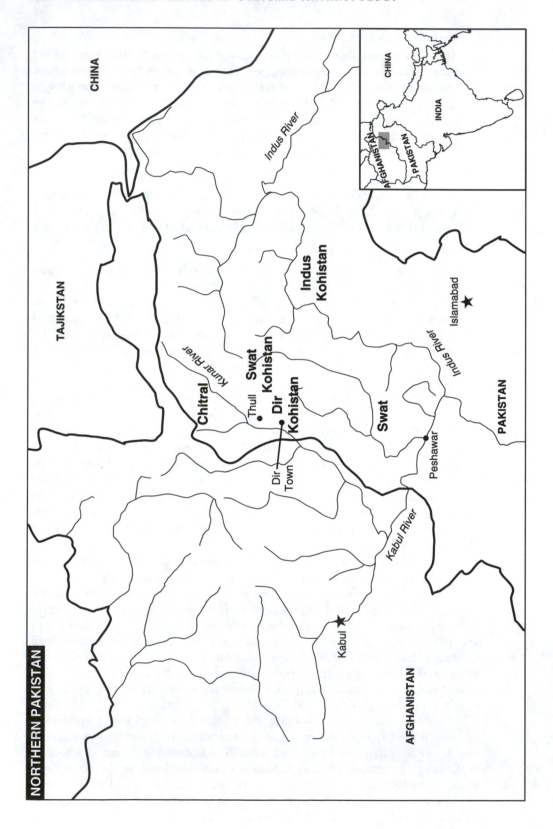

Getting to Thull is not easy. The road leads across the Indus River to the foot of the Hindu-Kush Mountains, then climbs the switchbacks of Malakand Pass to Chakdarra. Near here a small contingent of British soldiers (including the young Winston Churchill) fought 6000 native tribesmen in the Yusufzai uprising of 1901. From Chakdarra the road winds up the Panjkora Valley to Dir Town, the market and administrative center for Dir Kohistan. The road is paved to Dir Town, but Thull lies some 40 miles beyond, at the end of a dirt road that is impassable in bad weather. The main settlement lies at approximately 7000 feet. The community owns roughly 40 kilometers of territory along the upper reaches of the Panjkora Valley, including land for fields and summer pastures.

Those hazarding the trip to Thull find a bleak, but nonetheless beautiful, landscape at journey's end. Houses cluster at the foot of towering peaks that reach as high as 15,000 feet, and others are scattered here and there on lonely outcrops and hidden plateaus. Crags brood over land littered with smashed boulders, severed by swift-running streams, and periodically shattered by the growing pains of mountains whose convulsions occasionally approach the top of the Richter scale. Throughout the valleys and mountains, humans cultivate thin, sandy-colored soil where the terrain permits, and they pasture their herds on fairway-smooth meadows bordering the Panjkora's edge and strewn high among mammoth evergreen forests.

The Panjkora Valley widens within the confines of Thull's boundaries, thus permitting the cultivation of land adjacent to the river's edge without a complex system of stone terrace walls and irrigation channels. Most fields, however, are located away from the river on mountain slopes, where the ter-

Bolt-action version of the AK-47 made by local gunsmiths. (Photograph by Lincoln Keiser.)

rain requires extensive terracing. The builders carefully fit stones together to construct most terrace walls. According to local traditions, the walls date back some 300 years to pagan times.

Thull enjoys relatively plentiful rain and snow. Snow sometimes accumulates to six feet at the valley floor, and at much greater depths in the mountains. Runoff from melting snow provides a major source of the Panjkora's water. The high mountain peaks wring moisture from the air throughout the early spring, and so much precipitation falls in some years that the Panjkora ravages the land with spring floods that destroy fields and wash away houses, livestock, and even people. In late summer, monsoon rains provide an additional source of moisture, drenching the land. Nature provides so little rainfall from May to mid-August that crops growing in fields away from the Panjkora require periodic watering from irrigation channels.

The people of Thull make their living by farming and herding. Traditionally, women took primary responsibility for cultivating corn and other crops in fields located near permanent settlements, while men herded goats, cattle, water buffalo, and sheep. The herdsmen of Thull practice vertical **transhumance**: the animals are pastured on land near the permanent settlements during winter and are taken to the high mountain pastures for summer. When potatoes were introduced as a cash crop some 20 to 30 years ago, the **division of labor** changed, and men took on the primary responsibility for organizing the cultivation of that crop. Men now dominate the agricultural dimension of **subsistence** as well.

QUESTIONS

6.1. Do violent people always have a history of violence?

6.2. How do ideas and values give meaning to violence?

6.3. How do ecological relations affect violence?

6.4. How do political forces contribute to violence?

6.5. How did honor come to play such an important part in instituting organized violence in Thull?

QUESTION 6.1
Do Violent People Always Have a History of Violence?

The ethnographic literature on mountain communities in Pakistan and Afghanistan poses intriguing questions about blood-feud violence. Among the tribes of Indus Kohistan, a region bordering the Indus River to the east of Swat Kohistan, intracommunity political relationships are organized around institutionalized revenge and highly complex notions of personal honor. In contrast, the value of maintaining communal harmony is generally unquestioned among many of the tribal communities located in the higher valleys to the west of the Indus, and such harmony is a potent force in organizing politics within those communities.

Initially, I planned to focus my research on these differences by studying a community that forbade blood feuding. Thull looked like a good field site because earlier reports indicated that the people who lived there generally settled their internal disputes without bloodshed. I was really surprised to find organized vengeance (*mar dushmani,* or death enmity) entrenched in Thull. Further research revealed that the obsession with death enmity that warps contemporary social relations in Thull developed in the last few decades. Before then, most fights had been between **descent groups**, whose members share common descent from a named ancestor, and had not involved deadly weapons. Death enmity between descent groups was seen as having the potential to ultimately destroy the community, so village leaders worked to settle disputes peacefully and punished those who seriously threatened village peace. Now, in contrast, most fights are between individuals or between adversaries supported by various kinds of allies. Enemies attempt to kill one another to avenge personal injury, and no rules limit the use of weapons.

I could find no statistics on the number of murders committed in the community in recent years, although the leader of Thull's small contingent of police told me that revenge killings averaged two per month during his tenure. Shaking his head, he declared that the people of Kohistan were among the most lawless in Pakistan—and that the men of Thull were the most lawless in all of Kohistan.

This change poses interesting questions. How can we account for the appearance of *dushmani*[1] such a short time ago? Part of the answer lies in the relationship between Islamic ideology and men's sense of their personal integrity. However, organized violence must be understood as a process in time with a contemporary structure that resulted from a history of social and cultural transformations. The story begins 400 years ago.

Based on what we know of contemporary non-Muslim tribes in the area, social organization during the pre-Islamic period probably focused on independent communities consisting of a core village surrounded by a few satellite settlements.[2] Each community was divided into groups of people tracing descent from a common ancestor through the male line only. These descent groups were **exogamous**, meaning that men within each descent group married women from different descent groups. Looking at it from a male point of view, this is an exchange of women between **patrilineal** descent groups. Such exchanges organized intergroup relationships. Community political organization centered on relationships among descent groups. Political decisions were made in councils of descent group representatives, and membership in descent groups provided individuals with their primary source of political support.

Women did not seclude themselves, as they do now, and relationships between men and women were relatively free and open. The sexual purity of women was not a basis for judging a man's honor. This is not to say that disputes over women were not politically volatile. Wife stealing was probably a major source of internal political conflict, as accounts of contemporary non-Muslim tribes show. Nevertheless, even though wife stealing was an attack on a husband's rights, it did not involve his personal integrity. Consequently, men could peacefully settle such cases, more often than not, by paying fines and

[1]This term refers to enmity in general. It includes both death enmity and less intense forms of enmity leading to nonlethal violence. The same social changes have led to an increase in both forms of enmity.

[2]The best information we can get about what the people of Thull were *probably* like in the pre-Islamic period is obtained by studying similar people in the region who continue to be non-Muslims.

compensation. Moreover, because wife stealing took place between descent groups, it struck at important political alliances built on ties of marriage. Paternal relatives of both opponents in such disputes generally pressed for their peaceful settlement in order to maintain these alliances.

Leadership institutions and political values in the pre-Islamic period probably reflected the general insecurity in the region. Communities drew their leaders from descent group elders chosen ad hoc for the specific problem at hand. These leaders considered maintaining village peace through the nonviolent resolution of internal disputes to be one of their most important duties. Had the disputes not been settled, factionalism would have dangerously weakened the community's ability to deal effectively with external threats.

Village peace was an important political value in many pagan societies in the eastern Hindu-Kush. Among the Kom tribe in Afghanistan near the Pakistan border, for example, people so valued village harmony that elders forced disputants to settle their differences peacefully. The Kom recognized that uncontrolled violence posed a serious threat to their continued existence. Hence, community leaders expelled murderers and confiscated their property (Robertson 1896:439–442). No rules precluded immediate vengeance, but those who chose to accept compensation instead of exacting revenge received high praise from their fellows. Barth (1956) reported that similar customs were followed in the Kohistani communities east of Dir in the Swat District, making it probable that Kohistani communities in Dir treated murder and revenge in a similar manner during the pre-Islamic period. Even today in Thull, *lamo aman,* village peace, is a respected value, and to be called *aman pasand,* peace lover, is a compliment. Descent-group elders still negotiate dispute settlements, although their efforts in murder cases often fail.

The members of non-Muslim tribes recognized the legitimacy of some retaliatory vengeance murders. Among the Kom, for example, men directed retaliatory vengeance at members of surrounding tribes. For example, Kom tribesmen raided neighboring communities belonging to the Pathan ethnic group in retaliation for their allegedly killing members of the Kom tribe (Strand, personal communication, 1975).

Today, there is sometimes *dushmani* between Kohistani communities as well as between individuals. The Kohistani villages of Kalkot and Birikot, which are located on the Panjkora River just west of Thull, have a relationship of enmity going back 15 years. Because of it, 15 men have lost their lives.

In all probability, organized vengeance formed a part of the social order in pre-Islamic Kohistan, although it was not related to honor based on the sexual purity of women and it was limited to intercommunity relations. Intracommunity peace was critical for survival in an environment where force often decided political differences between tribal settlements. Networks of alliance and hostility among communities provided a degree of order in an otherwise anarchical situation.

Conversion to Islam

The cultural values, concepts, and ideas basic to organized vengeance in contemporary Thull were probably introduced at the same time Muslim missionaries converted the Kohistanis to Islam in the 16th century. They set processes of change in motion that ultimately resulted in a new and unique Kohistani sociocultural system. This system is neither logically consistent nor tightly structured. It could not be, since it is the product of multiple and contradictory forces interacting in complex ways through time.

It appears likely that the core of Kohistani social organization and culture remained generally unchanged immediately after conversion of the Kohistanis to Islam. As late as 1954, according to Barth, seclusion did not organize women's lives in the Kohistani communities in Swat east of Thull, and both men and women enjoyed free and open relationships (1956:66). Similarly, informants in Thull stated that the rules of strict *purdah* (the stringent seclusion of women) now in force are recent innovations that appeared only in the last few decades.

Barth's male informants stated no preference for marrying any category of women, and in particular expressed no preference for marriage with close paternal cousins (1956:66). This differs considerably from the current assertion that marriage to paternal cousins is not merely a preference, but that it is strictly adhered to. It also unquestionably represents a change from strictures against marrying within descent groups in force during the pre-Islamic period.

Initially, politics within Kohistani communities probably remained unchanged as well. In the unstable conditions that continued after the Kohistanis converted to Islam, the political unity of communities remained crucial to survival. Consequently, organized vengeance within communities was too threatening to be permitted. Nevertheless, forces of social and cultural change set in motion by contact with nearby Pathan communities (the dominant ethnic group in the Northwest Frontier Province) and conversion to Islam increasingly affected patterns of organized vengeance in Kohistan, just as events in the outside world continued to modify the political milieu in which Kohistani communities existed.

Thull Under the Nawabs

India became a crown colony of the British Empire in the mid-1800s. As Britian secured control of India, Russia advanced into central Asia, incorporating many formerly independent states into the Russian Empire. Tension between the British and Russians soon developed. The British government saw the Russians as a threat to their control of India, and much British colonial policy in India in the last half of the 19th century was designed to halt the Russian advance. In particular, the British saw controlling the state of Chitral, located in the far northwest corner of India, as critical in stopping the Russian threat. Troops and supplies had to go through the state of Dir to get to Chitral.

A Pathan chief in southern Dir conquered Dir Kohistan in 1888, and his successors, known as nawabs, succeeded in subjecting Thull and her Kohistani neighbors to the vagaries of their rule. Throughout the days of British rule, maintaining a friendly government in Dir strong enough to protect the road to Chitral was a cornerstone of British colonial policy in the Northwest Frontier. As long as the nawabs protected the road and allowed the British Army to use it, the British government was satisfied. Consequently, the British provided the nawabs with arms, subsidies, specially arranged meetings with the British Viceroy, and carte blanche to rule as they saw fit.

The rulers of Dir built their political policy on twin pillars: loyalty to British rule, and a tenacious adherence to *pakhtunwali*, the traditional code of the Pathans, which includes honor, revenge, hospitality, and giving protection to all who ask (even sworn enemies). Unlike the rulers of neighboring Swat who pursued a policy of social and economic development, the nawabs of Dir strove to maintain Dir as a patrimonial state. They neither adopted nor developed any kind of formal legal code to regularize their rule, instead governing by arbitrary decrees. They constructed few roads. The highway linking Dir to Chitral was the only notable exception, since the British insisted that they build it. Consequently, most Kohistani communities in Dir remained physically isolated and at least partially quarantined from political, ideological, and economic developments outside the district. Finally, in order to weaken potential opposition, the nawabs actively encouraged local strife. At the same time, they suppressed armed conflicts between the communities of Dir and Chitral at the demand of their British patrons.

The nawabs' policies effected particular cultural changes in Thull. In order to promote contention within communities, the nawabs encouraged blood vengeance by levying light fines for murder while at the same time advocating the idea that injured parties retaliate rather than accept compensation. They instituted this policy under the guise of promoting *badal,* revenge, which was a key idea in *pakhtunwali.*

Nevertheless, institutionalized vengeance did not become an important element in Kohistani social relations, though Kohistanis came to recognize *badal* as an important value. There are several reasons for this. Most importantly, *badal* contradicted *aman pasand,* the indigenous Kohistani value of village peace. It also contradicted the way prestige and leadership operated. Leadership in Thull depended on possessing *aizzat,* prestige, which, among other things, required a man to have good relationships with other men in the community. Peacefully settling one's disputes helped maintain good relations. If a man continually refused to settle disputes peacefully, troubled relations often resulted, lessening his prestige and weakening his ability to lead. Members of descent groups chose leaders who would represent their interests, and they suspected that a man who was generally unwilling to forego personal revenge might further his own ends at the expense of the group. Hence, countervailing forces compelling men to make peace tempered the power of *badal.* Though vengeance became an accepted value in Kohistani culture, it was only one of many often-contradictory forces, which partially explains why it did not result in widespread *dushmani.*

QUESTION 6.2
How Do Ideas and Values Give Meaning to Violence?

Honor is an important part of religious belief in Kohistan and is thus imbued with religious sanctity. The people of Thull are Muslims, and their religious faith is central to their sense of self. Visitors to Thull see mosques (Muslim places of worship) everywhere they look; I counted 18 and was never certain I had found them all. The mosques range from simple wooden platforms along the road and next to the river to ornately decorated buildings situated at the center of settlement clusters. Unlike villagers who live in the plains beneath Malakand Pass, who construct concrete mosques, men in Kohistan build mosques primarily of wood and stone. The roof of the community's central mosque located in the core settlement rests on gigantic wood columns covered with carved geometric figures.

Near the central mosque is the large, low, one-story house of one of the most influential religious leaders in Thull, a learned Muslim scholar who teaches Islamic faith in the local primary school. He wields considerable power in community affairs because of his reputation for religious learning and piety. The building's large, flat roof, called *torwalo shan* (Torwal's roof) after its original builder, provides a site for town meetings and serves as a constant reminder of the political vigor of Islam. Indeed, Islam lies over, under, in front of, behind, around, and beyond society and culture in Thull; nothing escapes its sway.

Everywhere and in all eras, people have creatively adapted religious teachings to fit their particular cultural circumstances. Thull's version of Islamic ideology does not determine what its people do in any mechanical fashion. Instead, it possesses the power to help shape action. In many instances Islam culturally defines meaningful options. Sometimes it weights options differentially so that people pay prices and/or obtain rewards for choosing to act in particular ways. It also corners people, severely limiting their options to the extent that their behavior appears almost predetermined. No matter how people act in Thull, Islam always affects the consequence of their choices. Finally, Islamic beliefs play a crucial role in how men conceptualize their own personal integrity and thus create and release powerful emotions that propel people toward courses of actions despite personal costs.

I once asked a Kohistani friend to name the most important parts of Islam. He answered, "The *Kalima*,[3] prayer, fasting, and faith." These four features make up the heart of Islam in Thull, although other characteristics are also meaningful to Kohistanis.

God in Thull does not resemble a distant father who sees his children only on Sunday mornings, Christmas, and Easter. In Thull, God is part of everyday reality, and his name, Allah, is a regular part of formal greetings, casual conversations, and even most arguments. His relevance is overwhelmingly clear to everyone. Allah does not take the appearance of a loving parent, but instead appears as an imperious ruler who demands that his subjects unconditionally submit to his will. Fundamentally, Islam means submission as well as peace, with the implication that one achieves peace by submitting to God's will.

Submitting to God's will involves embracing *iman*, Islamic faith, which includes belief in angels, God's omnipotence and oneness, and a day of judgment. Muslims believe that God sent a series of prophets to spread his message on earth, and that Mohammed was the last one because he brought the perfect truth to mankind.

Kohistanis understand that their Muslim faith is a particular kind of gift from God. God gives *ghrairat* (honor in the sense of personal integrity) to all Muslim men at birth. No one can gain it by his actions, but anyone can lose *ghrairat* by failing to protect it. With few exceptions, protecting *ghrairat* requires taking revenge. Kohistanis believe that Muslims must protect God's gift by taking vengeance at appropriate times, or they are not meeting their

[3]The Kohistani term for the Muslim affirmation of faith, "There is no God but Allah, and Mohammed is his prophet."

obligations to him. Kohistani notions of *iman* thus inject vengeance into constructions of Muslim identity and help create social and cultural contexts that incubate death enmity.

For example, keeping the fast during the month of *Ramazon* (called Ramadan in the western Muslim world) is an important part of religious faith according to Muslim preachers, and no one admits publicly to breaking it. Accordingly, accusing anyone of failing to fast constitutes a serious charge that can lead to fighting, bloodshed, and even murder. *Ramazon* should be a time of prayer and a time for contemplating one's obligations as a Muslim. The pace of life changes dramatically. A kind of tense stillness hovers in the air. Men's speech and movements become slow, studied, and controlled, and a faint threat of violence continually lurks beneath the surface. Hunger and thirst create volatile tempers, and contemplating one's faith involves embracing one's obligations for vengeance. Everyone in Thull knows that *Ramazon* is the season for revenge.

Islam in Thull differs from the more orthodox fundamentalism found in other parts of the Muslim world as a result of a special set of accretions. These elements of Islamic ideology focus on death enmity and mold it in specific ways. Kohistanis have competed with their politically powerful Pathan neighbors for centuries. Accordingly, the peculiar nature of Pathan Islam made a deep and lasting impression on Kohistani culture. As stated earlier, Pathans differentiate themselves from surrounding people by strictly adhering to a tribal code of conduct called *pakhtunwali*. At its core lie four obligations: to commit vengeance, to provide hospitality, to give refuge to anyone asking for it (even a mortal enemy), and to treat a fallen adversary who sues for peace with generosity. *Pakhtunwali* and Islam interconnect in Pathan culture in an ambiguous way. Most Pathans claim that their common ancestor converted to Islam at an early date, allegedly becoming one of the first of Mohammed's converts. Consequently, most Pathans see themselves as archetypical Muslims, believing their way of life to be fundamentally and profoundly Islamic. At the same time, Pathans set themselves above other Muslims by strictly adhering to their distinctive code of conduct. Some Pathans will occasionally admit that *pakhtunwali* ostensibly makes them poor Muslims because orthodox Islamic teaching does not recognize it. Nonetheless, they declare everything Pathan to be Islamic almost by definition. An educated Pathan graduate student attending a major American university argued for the Islamic quality of Pathan culture, saying in the same breath, "No. Of course *pakhtunwali* is not Islamic. But yes, it is Islamic."

Kohistanis borrowed the essential features of *pakhtunwali* over the last 300 years of contact with the Yusufzai, the dominant Pathan tribe in Dir. Taking revenge, providing hospitality, giving refuge, and being generous to a fallen enemy became accepted rules of behavior in Thull. No Kohistani ever claimed to follow *pakhtunwali,* for one must be Pathan to do that. Nevertheless, Kohistanis accepted the rules of *pakhtunwali* as integral to Islam because they accepted the Pathan claims to be archetypal Muslims. Friends unhesitatingly told me that because the Koran (the holy book of God) and the Hadith (the holy prophet's sayings) prominently displayed these rules (which, of course, they do not), following them demonstrated Muslim piety. Revenge, consequently, became a defining characteristic of their Muslim identity.

Preachers in Thull also admonish men to control their women. The way women act directly affects *ghrairat,* men's gift of personal integrity from God. A woman must never walk outside her husband's (or father's) house without a proper escort, preachers proclaim. A woman must never speak to an unrelated man. No man's direct gaze should fall on another man's wife or daughter. Women (men, too, but especially women) must not sing or dance, particularly at weddings. Finally, women should always comport themselves with modesty to protect their *sharam* (shame), hiding, controlling, minimizing, and completely denying their sexuality if possible. Men who allow their women freedom become *baghraitman* (men without integrity). So do those who refuse to retaliate violently against anyone purposely threatening their women's shame.

Which particular women's shame puts a man's integrity at risk varies with the situation. This factor alone intensifies death enmity in the community. Wives, daughters, and sisters always posses the power to endanger men's integrity. A man's vulnerability can extend to other women under a variety of situations. For example, the men who owned the house where I lived always guarded my research assistant's wife with their rifles whenever she left our compound. They knew she needed little protection, since only a minimal threat to her physical safety existed. But because she lived in their house, any attack on her shame by men outside the household, even a simple stare, threatened their integrity. By guarding her, they guarded themselves.

Men's vulnerability to attacks on women's shame can stretch beyond the household. Once I asked a friend to arrange a visit to a Kohistani house in the neighboring Swat valley for a group of American teachers traveling through Pakistan under the auspices of the Fulbright program. After we finished our obligatory tea and left the house, a woman in the group asked one of the Kohistani men to have his picture taken with her. Unfortunately, Kohistanis interpret such actions as explicit sexual invitations, and the man attempted to embrace her. Visibly shaken, she asked me to tell my friend, but I refused, knowing the potential for deadly violence. Three days later, after we returned to Thull, I did tell my friend. He immediately demanded to know the name of the culprit. He had arranged the visit, so he was responsible for the women in the group; his personal integrity was at risk. "Why didn't you tell me this immediately? I should have given the man an instant gift of bullets! Tell me who he is now, so I can kill him! He has made my *ghrairat* bad." Fortunately, I did not know the man's name.

QUESTION 6.3
How Do Ecological Relations Affect Violence?

Configurations of moral values were not the only forces inhibiting the development of *dushmani* during the nawabs' reign. Ecological relationships as well as the nawabs' refusal to build roads were also relevant factors. During the nawabs' rule, alpine herding and agriculture formed the basis for subsistence in Kohistan. In the winter, herd owners kept goats and cattle in special quarters in or near permanent settlements, while in the summer they took their animals into the mountains to graze on the rich grass found in high alpine meadows. Men generally did the herding, while women cultivated maize in the fields surrounding the permanent settlements. While subsistence necessitated both herding and cultivation, herding also provided cash income. Men walked to surrounding market centers in order to sell the cheese and *ghee* (butter) produced in the mountains.

Herding was a chancy operation at best. Disease, accidents, and sudden changes in weather common in high mountains often decimated the herds. In the past, Kohistanis raided herds in Chitral to recoup animal losses. After the nawabs incorporated Thull into Dir, however, raiding Chitral became uneconomical because the nawabs harshly punished raiders at the insistence of the British. Consequently, conflicts within the community significantly increased. Disputes over stray animals and arguments about animal theft became common, and strife turned inward.

Increased conflict did not lead to *dushmani*. The reason lies partly in the nature of descent group organization and the rules distributing rights to pasture. The people of Thull divide into three large patrilineal descent groups, each of which splits into various subgroups. The larger groups owned important ceremonial functions, which no longer take place, and often opposed one another politically during the era of the nawabs. When disputes erupted between subgroups of different larger groups, other subgroups often became involved through ties of common patrilineal descent.[4] Hence, the potential existed for disputes between subgroups to grow until large numbers of people were involved. On occasion, fights involved most of the men in the community.

Rules allocating pastures, however, reduced the acrimony of conflicts. Summer pastures in Thull are divided into distinct units, each with a particular name and well-defined boundaries. Thull allocates these units to herding groups for a one-year period. Each herding group is composed of subgroups whose members come from all three descent groups. Thus, the people who herded together—who had common rights to pastures and common interests in protecting these rights—were often the same people who opposed one another in descent group disputes.

This created a classic system of crosscutting allegiances. Resolving conflicts in loyalties through settling disputes dovetailed with the value of maintaining village peace. Despite the increase in intracommunity contention, dispute settlement mechanisms operated successfully because moral values and political and economic interests favored settling conflicts.

The nawabs' failure to build an extensive road system had two consequences for inhibiting the growth of *dushmani*. First, it physically isolated the Kohistani communities. Thull and her neighbors inhabit a high mountain valley that was connected to the rest of Dir only by narrow, treacherous footpaths during the time of the nawabs. People found communicating with distant settlements difficult in the best of weather and impossible when snow or mudslides blocked the mountain tracks. As a result, the nawabs' representatives could not visit Kohistan much of the time, which left power in the institutions of the indigenous political system. Public assemblies continued to make political decisions, and lineage leaders continued to mediate disputes on the basis of local custom and morality. Thus, the institutions for dispute settlement remained largely intact even though Thull was part of Dir.

---

[4] A Sudanese parallel is discussed in Chapter 4.

Even more important, the lack of roads limited economic **development**, which in turn limited the amount of cash individuals could accumulate. Consequently, few Kohistanis could purchase rifles. Clubs, knives, stabbing spears, and slings were the most common weapons in Kohistan during the era of the nawabs. Using these weapons required men to get close to an intended victim, making it difficult to kill him. Consequently, disputes that escalated to violence did not usually result in murder. Opponents could peacefully settle such disputes because they did not arouse the same violent emotions as murder cases. Even in murder cases, men were often (although not always) willing to accept compensation because they found retaliatory killing so difficult to carry out successfully.

QUESTION 6.4
How Do Political Forces Contribute to Violence?

Following the breakup of British India into the independent countries of India and Pakistan in 1947, Pakistani officials assumed administrative duties in the Northwest Frontier Province. At first the nawab maintained control over internal affairs in Dir. But when tension developed between the nawab and Pakistani officials over his opposition to social and economic development, the government forcibly deposed him and assumed direct administration of the district in 1965. A new era marked by far-reaching change began.

The Pakistani government immediately embarked on an ambitious program of social and economic development. Government agencies built a large, modern hospital complex in Timargara, Dir's administrative center. They constructed schools, administrative offices, medical clinics, and police posts throughout the district, even in the most remote mountain regions. Government construction crews began work on an extensive network of roads to link hitherto isolated villages with the rest of the country. A bus company initiated service to Kohistan after workers completed an unpaved road connecting Thull to Dir Town, and travel outside Thull became comparatively easy. Rural electrification and the establishment of a national television channel made it possible for Kohistanis to watch reruns of *Kojak* and *Trapper John, M.D.* in hotels in Dir Town. Crews strung telephone lines in many parts of the district. And *mar dushmani* swept through the network of social relationships in Thull like the flu in January.

Why did *dushmani* become focally important in Thull social relations at the same time the government integrated the community into a modern state, implemented an educational system, and instituted programs of economic development? The answer lies in understanding how *dushmani* evolved in the context of changing external political conditions.

The most important external change was the construction of a transportation system linking Thull with the rest of Pakistan. During the nawabs' reign, subsistence in Thull had depended on a balance between alpine herding and agriculture. The road changed that. The rapid and inexpensive trucking of produce to market centers throughout Pakistan made potatoes an economically viable cash crop. It permitted farmers to cultivate more land by letting them import artificial fertilizer. Manure from animals had previously been the sole source of fertilizer, so the number of livestock in the community had limited the amount of land farmers could cultivate. Accordingly, the economic base in Thull shifted from a system balanced between herding and cultivation to one weighted in favor of the cultivation of potatoes as a cash crop, a transition manifested by several changes. First, the proportion of men actively engaged in herding significantly decreased after the road was built. Herding was no longer the primary source of cash income for many families, although they continued to keep four or five goats and a few head of cattle. A significant minority of men now own only a few goats, although everyone owns more than enough land for subsistence requirements. An increased proportion of land came under cultivation as herding decreased in economic importance. Farmers converted privately owned early spring pastures to more financially lucrative potato fields when they became less dependent on natural fertilizer. Few of the adult men who continued to maintain large numbers of animals remained personally active in summer herding, preferring instead to hire shepherds from other communities.

These changes nurtured *dushmani* in two ways. First, crosscutting ties weakened when the proportion of men actively involved in herding diminished. Maintaining good relations with members of one's herding unit became less important for the many men no longer involved in herding activities, even though the system of allocating pastures remained virtually unchanged. As crosscutting ties lost their potency in maintaining peaceful relations, *dushmani* began to flourish. Second, the change to an economic system based on cultivating potatoes as a cash crop coupled with an increased number of fields significantly increased the amount of money in the community. The money supply expanded even more as a result of large-scale timber exploitation, which was the main reason the government built the road in the first place. Not only did timber contractors hire local men as wage laborers, but the government also paid royalties on the timber to the community as a whole.

Thull village. (Photograph by Lincoln Keiser.)

With increases in wealth, the number of firearms owned by members of the community increased as well; even poor men could buy rifles. "Such a lot of guns around town and so few brains," as Humphrey Bogart's character quipped in the movie *The Big Sleep*. Although this comment is perhaps a bit ethnocentric when applied to Thull, it seems appropriate nevertheless. Timber royalties and potato earnings made purchasing guns easy, and men acting out emotions framed by *ghrairat* and sanctified by *iman* turned their newly purchased rifles on neighbors in a gluttony of death enmity.

QUESTION 6.5
How Did Honor Come to Play Such an Important Part in Instituting Organized Violence in Thull?

The construction of the road to Thull and the establishment of regular bus service led to more than economic change. Changes in cultural values were crucial in instituting organized violence in the network of social relationships in the community. After bus service to the outside world became available, an ever-increasing number of Thull's religious leaders traveled to Mardan and Peshawar to study with noted Pathan scholars and teachers in centers of Islamic learning. These religious leaders brought back new concepts of honor and different notions about women that helped trigger the eruption of *dushmani*. Innovative ideas regarding the concept of *iman* acted as the catalyst.

Iman has two distinct but related meanings: faith, and gift or blessing from God. *Iman* as faith distinguishes Muslims from Kafirs—people who have shown defiant ingratitude by their refusal to accept God's word and become Muslims. Kafirs are by definition cruel, immoral human beings. *Iman* as God's gift saves Muslims from being Kafirs and thus from a life of evil and depravity. What constitutes *iman* is subject to interpretation. All Muslims interpret *iman* to include the oneness of God and his omnipotence, the existence of special messengers who have brought God's word to mankind at various times, the existence of angels, and the belief in a day of judgment.

For many Muslims, *iman* also includes belief in the sanctity of saintly individuals and their power to mediate between God and man. Saint cults were an important part of Islamic beliefs and practices in Thull before the road to Kohistan was built. The belief in saints became heresy, however, following the indoctrination of Kohistani religious leaders in fundamentalist schools of Islamic theology that denied the existence of humans with special access to God. Religious scholars returned to their communities armed with fundamentalist theology to campaign against the belief in saints and to purify Kohistani Islam. Today there are no shrines to saints in Thull, and Kohistanis believe that *mushriks* (believers in saints) are little better than Kafirs.

Religious leaders also opposed music and dancing, especially at weddings, and preached that secluding women was necessary to maintain men's *ghrairat*. This became especially important for *dushmani* because it personalized the connection between male honor and the sexual purity of women. Situations demanding deadly retaliation increased.

Once the road linked Thull to Islamic centers of learning, *ghrairat* soon replaced the belief in saints as part of Islamic faith. Today, Kohistanis consider it a critical aspect of *iman*. Defining *ghrairat* as crucial to *iman* made taking vengeance a serious religious obligation, thus creating a fertile environment for *dushmani*.

The concept of *ghrairat* is closely related to *badal* (revenge), and when the *ghrairat* code became intertwined with faith, revenge became fundamental to a Muslim man's identity and self-respect. English speakers often translate both *ghrairat* and *aizzat* as honor, but these concepts have distinct meanings in Kohistani thinking. *Ghrairat* is perhaps best understood as honor in the sense of personal worth, integrity, or character. It is natural, a part of *iman,* and, therefore, a gift from God (in fact, God's most valuable gift). Every Muslim man is born with *ghrairat;* a man can lose it only by failing to protect it. Other people can pollute a man's *ghrairat* in the same way that stepping in manure pollutes one's shoe.

Protecting *ghrairat* depends on following a clearly defined code of conduct. A man must provide his wives and daughters with appropriate food and clothing to the degree his wealth allows. He must never permit his wives and daughters to speak with men who are not closely related. He must never eat or exchange friendly conversation with the enemy of a close paternal kinsman, and he must always attack anyone who sullies his *ghrairat*. A husband's or father's *ghrairat* is sullied if another man stares at his wife or daughter, reflects light from a snuff box mirror on his wife or daughter, proposes intimacy with his wife or daughter, looks through a camera at his wife or daughter, flees or attempts to flee the community with his wife or daughter, or has illicit sexual relations with his wife or daughter. The murder of a close paternal kinsman (father, brother, son, father's brother, or father's brother's son), verbal abuse, theft, and assault also pollute a man's *ghrairat* and require vengeance.

Aizzat is best translated as honor in the sense of prestige. In contrast to *ghrairat, aizzat* is artificial since the community rather than God awards it. *Aizzat* depends on personal accomplishments and defines the men of worth in the community; it fluctuates with an individual's fortune. One measures *aizzat* by the *adab* (respect) accorded by others. Wealth, education, piety, and elected position all merit respect and thus confer *aizzat*. Although a *baghrairatman* (one without *ghrairat*) would not be given the respect necessary for *aizzat,* losing *aizzat* does not affect *ghrairat*. If a man loses his elected position or his wealth, he loses *aizzat,* but his *ghrairat* is unchanged.

Political honor contrasts with moral honor in Thull. *Aizzat* is political and thus primarily involves politicians actively competing for power. Hence, it is vital to self only for men with political or social ambitions. *Ghrairat,* in contrast, is moral, a quality definitive of Muslim identity for all men, and it is relevant, potentially at least, to most male social relations. The pollution of *ghrairat* calls for revenge, so revenge too is potentially relevant to most male relationships.

Kohistani self-respect has been rooted in Islam for centuries. Consequently, men often cast aspersions on opponents in terms of the Muslim–Kafir distinction, each accusing the other of *kafirano kar karant* (acting like a Kafir). Such accusations often lead to violence and even murder. Any act considered an attack on *ghrairat* arouses particularly strong passions which are usually expressed through violent retaliatory actions because it strikes at the core of a man's self respect, his identity as a Muslim.

Ghrairat requires men to always be wary and ready to kill in order to protect their integrity. Men who may have inadvertently or deliberately acted in ways that can be interpreted as polluting another man's *ghrairat* must be constantly vigilant to stay alive. Hence, *ghrairat* creates a sea of potential enemies and places each man squarely in the middle. That tension is pervasive in male social relationships and acid indigestion a common medical complaint should surprise no one.

Ghrairat not only encouraged *dushmani,* but the rules defining attacks on *ghrairat* also created linked sequences of reciprocal murders. If, for example, a man killed another man for shining a light on his wife, then that murder cleansed his *ghrairat*. But the killing polluted the *ghrairat* of the murdered man's close paternal kin, requiring them to kill in return. Consequently, men developed relationships of *dushmani* both easily and often. Once developed, these relationships were difficult to end. The blood feud had come to Thull in full force.

CONCLUSIONS

Genetic explanations do not work well in explaining blood feud violence in Thull. Blood feuding developed only recently in that community, and it developed within a historical context shaped not by the genetic makeup of the inhabitants, but rather by economic change and political **modernization**. It can best be understood as the result of two interrelated developments: the transition to an ideological system in which honor became critically important, and the transition from a subsistence system based on herding and cultivation to an economic system built on timbering and cash-crop agriculture. Linking honor to Muslim faith injected revenge into religion and made taking revenge critical to men's self-respect, while economic development made the spread of modern firearms possible. Together they encouraged and perhaps even required organized vengeance within the community. The people of Thull give meaning to and justify violence through the interaction of historical, cultural, ecological, and political variables, which are systematically interrelated. They are all parts of the same puzzle.

REFERENCES AND RECOMMENDED READINGS

Ahmed, Akbar S.
1983 Religion and Politics in Muslim Society. Cambridge: Cambridge University Press. A study of Islam, honor, and politics among the Waziris, a Pathan tribe located in the Northwest Frontier Province of Pakistan.

Barth, Fredrik
1956 Indus and Swat Kohistan. Oslo: Forenede Trykkerier. The classic study of Kohistani social organization and culture in the Indus and Swat valleys.

Biddulph, John

1971 [1880] Tribes of the Hindoo Koosh. Graz, Austria: Akademische, Druck-u. Verlagsanstalt.

> An early account of Hindu-Kush tribal communities, including Thull, by a colonel in the British Army.

Edwards, David B.

1996 Heroes of the Age. Berkeley: University of California Press.

> Contains an excellent account of honor and blood-feud violence among the Safis, a Pathan tribe located in Afghanistan across the border from the Northwest Frontier Province of Pakistan.

Jettmar, Karl

1961 Ethnological Research in Dardistan. Proceedings of the American Philosophical Society 105(1):28.

> A useful summary of ethnographic research in Dir, Swat, and Indus Kohistan prior to 1961.

Keay, John

1979 The Gilgit Game. Hamden, CT: Archon Books.

> A historical account of British explorers in the Hindu-Kush Mountains during the 19th century.

Keiser, Lincoln

1986 Foul Shots and Rifle Fire. Natural History 95(9):8–14.

> An account of Kohistani pickup basketball as shaped by Kohistani cultural values and economic change.

1991 Friend by Day, Enemy by Night. Fort Worth: Holt, Rinehart and Winston.

> A study of blood-feud violence in the Kohistani community of Thull.

Additional Reference Cited

Robertson, Sir George Scott

1896 Kafirs of the Hindu-Kush. London: Lawrence and Bullen, Ltd.

CHAPTER 7

THE CULTURAL CONSTRUCTION OF POVERTY

ANN MILES AND
CHRISTINA SONNEVILLE

PROBLEM 7 *How can we understand the lives of the working poor in the United States?*

INTRODUCTION
America's Invisible Harvest

Every spring and summer, some 2 or 3 million Americans take to the open roads and move from state to state, often for months at a time. They are not families on vacation, college students on a road trip, or carefree retirees checking out national parks. Rather, these travelers are migrant farmworkers who constitute the backbone of America's agricultural labor force. Moving steadily northward with the ripening crops, migrant workers contribute the hand labor necessary for the successful cultivation and harvesting of 85 percent of U.S. fruits and vegetables. But despite their crucial contributions to the multi-billion-dollar agricultural industry, migrant workers themselves earn annual incomes well below the federal poverty level of $9000. They are almost invisible in the communities where they work and in the American consciousness.

The living conditions of migrant workers vary across the country. Many live in substandard and overcrowded housing comparable to that of a Third World country. They often work for low wages in unsanitary and dangerous conditions, and they receive few of the benefits and securities afforded other U.S. workers. When the U.S. economy was growing at an unprecedented rate, migrant workers' real wages (wages adjusted to the cost of living) fell. Indeed, many migrant workers today earn only the equivalent of what they earned in the 1960s. Yet their contributions to the U.S. economy are indispensable, and all Americans have benefited from their labor, usually in very direct ways. The fruits and vegetables we have come to expect to be readily available have more than likely been cultivated, harvested, and processed by migrant workers.

This chapter explores migrant farm labor in the United States with a focus on southwest Michigan, where an estimated 9000 migrant workers labor every year. Michigan is one of the northernmost destinations for many migrant workers. The growing season typically begins in late April with asparagus, peaks in July with the cucumber crop,[1] and diminishes in late September with the apple harvest. Some workers remain in the area into the winter to work in nurseries or on Christmas tree farms. Most migrant workers in Michigan are Mexican or Mexican-American, and they will be the focus of this chapter.

Migrant labor is a fact of life throughout the world. Not only do resources and products move across political and national boundaries to be manufactured, assembled, and sold, but the producers themselves are also often a part of this transnational process. Ecuadorian manual laborers toil in Spain; Turkish workers live in Germany; and, as noted in Chapter 1, Tongans provide essential labor in New Zealand. Most often, the movement of workers is from developing countries with a surplus of labor to more developed regions with labor shortages, especially at the lower end of the economy.

In the last decade or so, anthropologists have become increasingly interested in the processes of **globalization**, including both domestic and transnational labor migrations. Anthropologists are concerned with a variety of topics, such as the ways in which labor migrations affect the ethnic, cultural, and/or national identities of workers and of those they leave behind, how the demands and benefits of migrant labor affect workers and their families and communities, and how gender roles are altered by multinational factories' preferring to hire women, who are often perceived as dexterous and docile. Aiwha Ong (1987), for example, has examined how rural Muslim girls and women attempt to comply with some of the demands placed on them by laboring in multinational urban factories in Malaysia, while resisting other demands, and has shown how the combination of Islamic models of feminine propriety and capitalist practices of production have created nearly impossible conditions for them. What lies behind much of the anthropological interest in issues of labor migration is the desire to understand the complex relationship between workers and the socioeconomic systems they enter, leave, and often return to. In most cases, migrant workers are vital to the economic systems in which they are working, yet they often must negotiate in social fields that ultimately relegate them to the margins.

QUESTIONS

7.1. Who are migrant farmworkers?

7.2. Why is farm labor performed by migrant workers?

7.3. What factors contribute to the perpetuation of poverty among migrant farmworkers?

7.4. What are the particular hardships of migrant farmworker life?

7.5. How have migrant farmworkers organized to improve their lives?

---

[1]The cucumbers in question are destined to become pickled and are referred to by people in the industry as pickles.

QUESTION 7.1
Who Are Migrant Farmworkers?

I've been in the U.S. now 14 years. When I came it was an adventure; I didn't know anybody. I didn't speak English. I didn't have anything. Back then there weren't very many Mexicans there [in upstate New York]; no one spoke Spanish. I like working in the countryside because life is more tranquil here . . . but the work, you know, can be very hard. We get up early at four in the morning, make our lunch, and we don't get home until eight or so at night. We have time only to make something to eat, take a shower, and go to sleep. We do this seven days a week including weekends. When we leave here, we go to New York to pick apples. I've worked for the same rancher there for ten years. Then we go to Florida to pick citrus fruits. There it is really hard. You have to find an apartment and it costs $800 or $900 for small place and you have to pay for lights and heat. The work is very difficult there.

CARLOS, AN UNDOCUMENTED IMMIGRANT FARMWORKER

We come from the Valley [the Rio Grande Valley of Texas] and I like it here because it is pretty; it's very green and peaceful. We come here from July through October. We've been vagabonds really. If things don't go well in one place we try someplace else where we have family or someone we know. The way it works is that for some people things work out well and for others it does-n't. Unfortunately for us it almost always works out badly. When one comes from far away you come with the idea that you will earn and prosper. Here we are working to live and eat and nothing else. We'll go back to Texas in October and rest. We'll be able to collect unemployment—there are no jobs in the Valley. My dream is to have a little house with furniture and to have my husband go off to work in the morning and come back at night.

LUCIA, A SECOND-GENERATION MIGRANT WORKER

We've lived all over. The worst job we've had is in the poultry factory—that was really awful and we didn't stay there long. We also lived in Chicago but for me the city just doesn't work! I didn't like it there. I like to be in the countryside. It's not very enjoyable to migrate but the time passes.

SOFÍA, A MEXICAN-AMERICAN FROM THE RIO GRANDE VALLEY

Migrant workers are a diverse group. Some are American by birth; some are naturalized citizens; some are invited guest workers from other countries; and some are undocumented immigrants without papers legalizing their presence in the United States. Migrant farmworkers who were born in the United States come from a variety of ethnic backgrounds and include African Americans, whites, Latinos, and Native Americans. Increasingly, migrant labor needs are filled by immigrant labor. In fact, about 70 percent of migrant workers are foreign born, and 94 percent of these are of Mexican origin. More than 50 percent of foreign-born migrant workers are undocumented, even though it is illegal for farmers to hire them.

There are West Coast, East Coast, and Midwest streams of migrant workers. In theory, each stream originates in a southern region, such as California, Texas, or Mexico (West), Florida (East), and Texas or Mexico (Midwest), and moves steadily northward as the growing season progresses. For a variety of historical and geographical reasons, each stream is characterized by some differences in the ethnic groups that participate. For example, the East Coast stream generally contains more African American and Caribbean workers than the other two. Migrants often travel in nuclear and even extended family groups, although recent immigration guest-worker programs have been favoring single men over families.

Although most workers move from south to north within a stream, individuals have a great deal of flexibility in their work itineraries, and travel plans often change suddenly. Word of mouth about working conditions plays a major role in determining where a migrant chooses to work, and workers can move from one state to another if they hear that conditions are better there. Individual migrant workers may also move in and out of the migrant stream over the course of their lives, perhaps settling in one place for a while and then returning to migrant labor.

Because of the diversity of the migrant farm laborer population, it is impossible to talk about a typical migrant worker. Each stream is composed of people from a variety of ethnic backgrounds, but even those of the same ethnicity are different from one another. While the majority of migrant workers in southwest Michigan are Mexican Americans who make their homes in Texas or Florida, a significant number are Mexican, some of whom work illegally while others hold valid work visas. Some of the recent immigrants from Mexico came from small rural communities, while others were from the teeming metropolis of Mexico City. Similarly, where workers go after they leave Michigan varies considerably. Some workers return to Mexico to work or rest in the off-season; some find nonagricultural employment or collect unemployment insurance in Texas; and many others go to Florida to harvest citrus fruits. In other words, just as it is almost impossible to speak of the typical American, we cannot really describe the average migrant farmworker.

Farming practices and the organization of seasonal farm labor vary considerably by region. This variation is due to a number of factors. Patterns of land ownership are one cause of variation; large farms managed by a major corporation are organized differently than small family-run farms. Climate and/or soil conditions may favor one crop over another and thus necessitate different labor requirements. The history of labor management, the presence of state or federal services, and the enforcement of state and federal regulations governing such things as housing, sanitation, and education also play a role. Together these factors influence whether workers find acceptable living and working conditions, how long workers will be needed in the area, how much money they can make, how difficult the work is, and whether there are educational opportunities such as Head Start and summer-school programs for the children. Head Start programs provide developmentally appropriate care for children younger than five as well as a host of comprehensive health and social services.

In southwest Michigan, a number of factors combine to create a very great need for short-term seasonal migrant labor and also the inability to successfully compete with other regions for these workers. In contrast to many areas of the country where large farms predominate, southwest Michigan is still characterized by small family-owned and -operated farms, many of which produce diverse crops, including fruit crops like strawberries, cherries, blueberries, and apples, and vegetable crops like cucumbers and tomatoes. These crops are often picked by hand and need to be processed quickly after harvesting. The typical farmer frequently needs a significant number of workers, but often for only a very short time—perhaps a month or six weeks. Larger producers who work for large food companies can generally pay more than these smaller farmers.

Migrant workers in Michigan form various types of relationships with farmers depending on the type of farm and/or the attitude and practices of the farmer. In some cases, the same migrant family returns repeatedly to the same farmer and stays the entire season doing a number of different tasks. In increasingly rare instances, the workers almost become members of the farmer's family for that period of time. Others work with different farmers from season to season, depending on local labor needs.

Farmers and migrant workers commonly have little contact with one another, and all of the negotiations between workers and farmers are conducted by contractors or crew leaders. Before the growing season begins, farmers tell the labor contractors what their labor requirements will likely be for the upcoming year. The contractors are then responsible for recruiting workers and negotiating pay rates with them. Contractors organize daily work routines and manage payrolls, and they usually live in the labor camps with the workers. Even though most contractors are Mexican American and often come from the communities in which the migrants live in the off-season, they are paid by the farmers and are often viewed as representatives of the farmers by the workers. There are good and bad contractors. Some work very hard to see that their workers get a fair deal, while others may purposely recruit undocumented workers who will be unable to contest oppressive conditions.

QUESTION 7.2
Why Is Farm Labor Performed by Migrant Workers?

My family settled in the Valley [in the mid 1940s] because my father and older brothers had been working there some years before—probably during the Bracero program. They worked citrus and irrigation. Most of that work in the Valley is gone now. When my family first came up [in the 1950s], it was with a troquero *[truck driver/contractor]. The* troquero *was a person who recruited people from the neighborhood [in the Valley]. The families would come in his huge truck, maybe three or four families. There would be 10 to 20 people in the truck—men, women, and children. I'm thinking our trek to Michigan then took about three days. We would sleep in the truck and had to do what we needed to do when the truck stopped. The* troquero *wasn't one to stop often—he wanted to get us here as quickly as possible. It's funny, I was probably about five or six and I remember my mother carried boiled eggs with us. I remember eating egg sandwiches in the truck.*

MARCO ANTONIO, COMMUNITY ACTIVIST AND FORMER MIGRANT

Many of us that work the fields are undocumented. All of us are hoping one day for an amnesty. Only once, about four or five years ago, were there problems with immigration. They came to a field one afternoon. They caught 24 people that day while the rest of us took off running. We hid in the fields and bushes until they were gone. That's the only trouble we've ever had.

CARLOS

Amerian farmers depend on migrant labor for complex reasons with deep historical roots. American immigration and farming policies and practices and Mexican agrarian and social reforms have long affected and informed one other, and both are part of global economic, social, and political processes. Social processes on both sides of the border are linked to European colonization of the New World, American involvement in World War II and the Korean conflict, and international agreements like the North American Free Trade Agreement (NAFTA).

Why Do Laborers Leave Mexico?

Around the 1550s, in the early colonial period in Mexico, the king of Spain often awarded Spaniards rights over the labor of Indians in a system known as the *encomienda*. The result was a social system similar to slavery in which Indians were forced to work for the Spanish without remuneration. Over time, the *encomienda* gave way to the hacienda system where land, not people, was owned. The result was the same: the best agricultural lands were in the hands of a few, and poor peasants either worked as peons for the wealthy or independently scratched out a living on infertile land.

When Mexico gained its independence in 1821, there was little improvement in the living conditions of rural peasants, and land was increasingly consolidated in the hands of a few wealthy *hacendados* (ranchers) over the next century. By 1900, an astonishing 97 percent of the land was owned by only 1 percent of the population. Peasants worked the land for ranchers, often in sharecropping arrangements, and they were rarely able to move out of debt. During this time, large farmers were also afforded benefits by the state, such as obtaining loans at favorable rates for irrigation and other technological improvements, that were not shared with smaller producers, making it even more impossible for the small farmers to compete.

Such massive inequality could not stand uncontested, and by 1910 popular discontent had reached the boiling point. Five million landless peasants took up arms in the Mexican Revolution. The primary goal of the conflict, which cost 2 million lives, was to institute land reform by breaking up the large haciendas and redistributing land to poor communities. Unfortunately, the revolution did not accomplish the extensive land reform it sought. While some lands were redistributed, a large rural population still had little or no access to productive agricultural lands.

Today, many of the people who emigrate from Mexico to work as migrant laborers do so because of economic hardship and the unequal distribution of land and wealth in Mexico. In the 1980s and 1990s, rural poverty increased because of economic policies aimed at reducing public-sector spending in order to increase the repayment of international loans. Also, the free-trade arrangement between the United States, Canada, and Mexico known as NAFTA favors large agribusinesses over smaller producers, and it has increased Mexican rural out-migration.

U.S. Needs for Farm Labor

On the other side of the border, U.S. farming has also undergone radical shifts in the last century and a half. By the middle of the 19th century, the United States began making the shift from family farms to large farms, increasing the need for temporary agricultural workers. This was especially true in California where new lands were coming under cultivation and sharecropping arrangements had never taken hold. Rothenberg (1998) notes that the majority of immigrant workers in California were initially recruited from China and that 75 percent of California's farmworkers were Chinese at one point. As their numbers increased and they began to organize, anti-Chinese sentiments mounted, and fear caused most of the Chinese to move to urban centers. Anti-Chinese immigration policies (including the Chinese Exclusion Act) followed, severely limiting the number of Chinese immigrants. Japanese immigrants soon suffered a similar fate, and by the early 20th century, the Japanese had been driven out of farm work and were replaced by Mexicans. By 1910 there were 20,000 Mexican workers on American farms.

Contributing to the growing needs for seasonal, rather than permanent, farm labor were major changes in farming technology in the 20th century. Planting became increasingly mechanized. In the 1930s, the development of inexpensive tractors further reduced the need for permanent farmworkers. However, cultivation and harvesting still often required human labor, creating a need for temporary workers. During the Great Depression, this need was largely filled by white Americans displaced by the Dust Bowl, a severe drought that devastated Midwest agriculture in the 1920s. As dust storms raged across the Great Plains, migrant labor camps were set up throughout California to provide work exclusively to these displaced American farmers. In fact, many Mexican workers were encouraged and sometimes forced to repatriate to Mexico during this period to preserve jobs for Americans.

In the early 1940s, these American workers shifted to factory work or joined the American forces fighting in World War II. Once again, organized efforts were made to recruit foreign workers.[2] In 1942 the United States began a guest worker program that encouraged Mexican workers to legally enter the country to work, especially in agriculture. That program, later known as the *Bracero* (hired hand) program, was renegotiated many times between 1942 and 1964. At its peak, from 1951 to 1959, 2.5 million Mexican workers were admitted into the United States. Many of the migrant workers in southwest Michigan today can trace their family's entry into the United States to the *Bracero* program.

One reason that it has been difficult to hire Americans for farm labor since the 1930s is that farm laborers have been systematically excluded from many of the labor reforms and privileges enjoyed by America's industrial workers. President Roosevelt's New Deal program in the 1930s created many of the standard labor practices and workers rights that are taken for granted today: it restricted child labor, established minimum wage policies, provided for overtime pay, and instituted retirement benefits in the form of Social Security. However, farmworkers were excluded from these basic labor provisions, thus creating a second-class workforce. Throughout the 20th century, seasonal farmworkers in the United States have earned only a quarter to a half of what factory workers made. It was not until the civil rights movement of the 1960s and the organizational work of labor leaders like Cesar Chavez that America's farmworkers were granted even the basic rights of other American workers, like being paid a minimum wage.

[2]The labor shortage created by World War II continued in the early 1950s as a result of the Korean conflict. It set the stage for the greatest effort by an American government to recruit foreign laborers.

QUESTION 7.3
What Factors Contribute to the Perpetuation of Poverty Among Migrant Farmworkers?

We come here to earn a better life, and I'm grateful to the U.S. because I've been able to make some money and become something in life. But, we have to save money or we'll be nothing in the end. We're not always going to be able to work the fields and we're not always going to be young. We have to have something for our old age. If we don't save our money, coming here would have been for no purpose at all. Sometimes I think I'd like to return to Mexico and build a nice house but I want to make a better future for my children.

CARLOS

A few years ago I hurt my lower back and really couldn't work anymore in the fields. I was happy working in the fields. Before I never had an education— and now I do. I started as a cook in the day care center and now I am study-ing for a CDA (Child Development Associate Degree). This, after so many years of having no options because I had no education—until I hurt myself. [Sofía's daughter also works in the day care center, while her son-in-law is an agri-cultural worker.]

SOFÍA

Right now we're hoping that this will be a good year [for apples]. So far it's bet-ter than last year. Last year after the expenses of getting the car fixed to get back to Texas we had nothing left. It looks like it will be better but because there are so many people here there won't be work for very long. Last year we worked until the end of October because there were fewer workers here. It's really some-thing to worry about. So far we've been here three or four months and we haven't done anything yet [in terms of saving money].

LUCIA

My father is 69 years old. He's old, and his bones hurt, but he's still working. That's all he knows how to do. It's hard work. It affects his back and his arthri-tis. He limps, but somebody's got to do it. Sometimes I say, "We are feeding the world!" That's one thing I like, but then again, it's hard.

ALMA

Despite federal and state regulations concerning wages, housing, and safe-ty, migrants often lead precarious lives. Because of this, it can be difficult for migrant workers to save money and/or educate themselves, goals they clearly identify as necessary for economic advancement. Thus the cycle of poverty is difficult to break.

One of the major themes that emerges from conversations with Mexican American migrant workers is that life is unpredictable and insecure. The best-laid plans can be overturned by events that seem impossible to plan for. From one season to the next, from one crop to the next, wages can vary dramati-cally. Working conditions literally change overnight. Even the most experi-enced English-speaking migrants have little control over work schedules, wages, and living conditions. As a woman who spent most of her adult life as a migrant worker explained, "We have traveled to so many places in search of a good life, but we have yet to find it."

What is particularly troubling to many of the migrant workers we spoke with is that planning for the future, even in the short term, is difficult. It is impossible to save money while earning the minimum wage, especially when transportation costs, car repairs, and other expenses are figured in. Some want to save enough to buy a house and settle out of the migrant stream, while others worry about the time when they will no longer be able do the hard physical labor of agricultural work.

Many migrant workers live in extended families that include mothers, in-laws, and even cousins. In the insecure conditions of migrant work, these extended family groups provide emotional and financial support. Often both parents in a young family will work very long hours. Work may begin at 6 A.M. and can last until 8 or 9 in the evening. A nonworking mother or a mother-in-law can stay at home during the day to cook meals, wash clothes, and care for children. However, even with several incomes and shared expenses, migrants still find it difficult to save.

Some migrant workers dream of "settling out" of the migrant stream, finding steady employment, and providing for the education of their children. To them, success means no longer being a migrant farmworker. Others enjoy agricultural labor and speak of the peace of country living and their enjoyment of their way of life. Many migrants like to spend summers away from the heat of Texas in the relative cool of the Michigan countryside. What those who wish to leave migrant life and those who do not have in common is the desire to be treated fairly and to make a steady and secure living. Both are usually frustrated in their attempts, and most workers earn only enough to meet their day-to-day expenses. Many of the insecurities of migrant-worker life are a result of the nature of agricultural production, while others can be attributed to social conditions.

The Unpredictability of Agriculture

We went to Minnesota once, but it didn't work out. There was no place to rent. It was in April, and we didn't really know what the climate was like there. We ran out of money because we needed someplace to stay. We stayed in a motel but we were only able to work at most for half a day and for the minimum at that.

SOFÍA

Sometimes people come here too early and there isn't enough work for them. They will have to wait for the season to arrive. They might spend 8 to 15 days in their cars with no work. Bad contractors who don't care about their people sometimes try to let people go—and then they are on their own.

CARLOS

Things are bad right now. Because of the rain we haven't been able to work. I'm not making any money and there's nothing to do. I'm really hoping we can get to work tomorrow.

MARTA, CARLOS' NIECE, IN HER FIRST SEASON UP FROM MEXICO

Timing is everything in agriculture. The farmer must time planting to maximize the growing season, a difficult task when dealing with uncontrollable variables such as rainfall and temperature. For migrant laborers, timing arrival and departure often determines whether a season will be a success. Contractors who are in close contact with their farmers may have an idea of when labor will be required, but crops are rarely that predictable. Unscrupulous contractors may let workers go if there is not enough work, often forcing workers to live in their cars, possibly for several weeks, until work is available.

Independent workers, who rely on reports from previous years when conditions may have been different, must take their chances. If warm weather is late in coming, migrants may find themselves without enough work to pay even basic bills. In such cases, they face no-win decisions: should they stay and hope to recoup the cost of getting there and supporting themselves, or should they move on in the hope of finding immediate employment? Either option includes the considerable expense of paying for lodgings or the discomfort of sleeping in the car.

The 1999 growing season in southwest Michigan was typically unpredictable. Summer heat began early, and the corn, blueberry, and cucumber crops ripened at the same time, several weeks early. Many of the expected workers were still detasseling seed corn (removing the cob's tassel to promote the growth of seeds) in Indiana. Detasseling is hard work, but it pays a steady hourly wage. By mid-July most of the workers had arrived in Michigan, but there were still not enough of them to harvest all the berries and cucumbers at the same time. Blueberry farmers reported labor shortages throughout the summer, and many were later fined for employing underage children. Ironically, there often was not enough work for those picking cucumbers.

Cucumbers are an erratic crop, and labor needs fluctuate on a daily, or even hourly, basis. The most valuable cucumber crop for Michigan farmers is the type that makes small gherkin pickles. Cucumbers can reach the correct size overnight, so farmers must have a readily available labor supply. Workers

When "pickles" mature, they need to be harvested swiftly. Farmworkers frequently put in 12- to 14-hour days during peak periods. (Reprinted courtesy of the Kalamazoo Gazette. Photograph by Mark Bugnaski.)

can be called into the field at any time to harvest or tend the cucumbers. They are hesitant to move to a different farmer's blueberries, and sometimes contractors or farmers do not allow them to move, anticipating that they will be needed in the cucumber fields. Since harvesting cucumbers usually pays more than blueberry picking, in part because it requires back-breaking stooping, workers will often wait out the cucumber harvest. Because of poor growing conditions for cucumbers in 1999, many of these workers found themselves out of work for days at a time and making very little money.

Timing also caused problems for workers who were hoping to make decent money on the apple harvest. Michigan apples usually ripen in mid-September, when many of the cucumber workers have already moved on. But in 1999 a bumper crop of apples began ripening in mid-August, when the cucumber workers and blueberry pickers, some of whom had not earned what they were hoping for, were still around. Therefore, there was abundant labor for the apple harvest, and—following the laws of supply and demand— wages were lower and individual workers were more dispensable. Hector, Sofía's son-in-law, told this story:

> One day last week I was sent home because I took a break for lunch. The farmer wanted me to finish one section before lunch. He thought it would take less than an hour but I knew it was much more work than that, maybe two hours or even more. When I left to go to lunch before I finished the section, he told me that if I left I couldn't come back that afternoon.

The Organization of Work

This farmer pays really badly. The only thing we get is unemployment [for the winter]. You have to work very, very hard to make the minimum. You just can't earn enough to save for the winter, unemployment is what gets us through to the next season. We only get the unemployment if we stay for the whole season. Sometimes I get really tired from picking apples; because I'm pregnant [about 7 months] it's difficult going up and down the ladders and bending way down low.

LUCIA

He [the farmer] pays us less all the way through the season but if we agree to stay here until the end of the season we get our bonus of $300. He is such a cheap guy. Even though he has millions we saw him walking along the roads picking up bottles and cans to recycle.

MONICA, SOFÍA'S DAUGHTER

Adding to the unpredictability of wages is the fact that migrant farmworkers are most often paid by the piece, not by the hour. Piecework means that a worker is paid for each bucket, bushel, or box of produce harvested. According to federal law, workers must be paid at least the minimum wage of $5.15 an hour. However, workers reported to us over and over again that they were not, in fact, paid the minimum wage. Under piecework, a worker can work an eight-hour day in bad conditions and come home with only a few dollars.

While some workers are aware that the law requires them to be paid a minimum wage, most are afraid to report employers who violate the law. "If we report him, we're afraid we'll lose our jobs," said one worker. Another explained that workers who get reputations as complainers may find themselves without any work.

Many employers are able to attract and keep workers because of other incentives, such as an end-of-season bonus or off-season unemployment. Farmers who offer an end-of-season bonus do so to assure themselves an ample supply of workers for as long as they need them; the bonus is paid only to those who stay for the whole season. Some workers see this arrangement as manipulative: "We can't get up and leave. We're stuck here or we lose our bonus. I don't like that. I wish he would just pay us what we earn, what he owes us, and we would be free to go when we wanted to!"

While some workers have a good relationship with a farmer and return season after season, the relationship between many workers and farmers is filled with mistrust. "This guy is cheap," said one worker. "He is so rich, yet he pays his workers next to nothing." "Everyone wants quality and production," said another woman, "but they want it at very low wages." Many workers have heard stories of generous farmers, and they hope to find a good *patron* (boss) or *ranchero* (rancher) who will pay them a fair wage and respect their work. "All I really want is for the farmer to honor and value my labor," said one woman. "To say 'thank you' at the beginning of the season for coming and at the end of the season when we leave. To recognize when we are good workers and give us a raise the next season when we come back. Both of us would have a little more security and I would feel that he understood my worth." The most unfortunate aspect of the distrust between farmers and workers is that, with the exception of a few wealthy large producers, family farmers in southwest Michigan are often under financial constraints themselves.

Living and Housing Arrangements

We've had lots of problems with housing. Some farmers won't give you housing or they make you pay rent and security deposits. There aren't refrigerators, stoves, or heaters. It's really difficult. The houses in Michigan are horrible. It's better when you can rent housing, but in Michigan most people have to take what the farmer gives them. When you go to the countryside camps you'll see they don't clean them and there's garbage everywhere. There's a lot of disorganization. There's a lot of single men and bathrooms are outside and they catcall the young girls. That's why we rent here [a public housing development].

SOFÍA

One of the most important factors for attracting migrant workers is the availability and quality of the housing. Migrants, especially families with children, are much more likely to come to and stay in a location with clean, comfortable housing. According to Griffith and Kissam (1995), Michigan has very poor housing, a fact corroborated, sometimes emphatically, by our informants. One woman called Michigan housing "horrible," and another said that although it was inexpensive, it was also the worst she had seen.

Most migrant workers in Michigan live in housing provided by the farmers, although some may live in independent apartments, some of which are federally subsidized. Housing provided by a farmer may consist of cabins with outside communal showers and toilets or, more commonly, furnished mobile homes. Some mobile homes are equipped with toilets, but others are not, and residents must use portable privies outside. Mobile homes are often poorly insulated, becoming very warm when it is hot and quite cold when tempera-

After a long day's work, camp residents relax with friends and neighbors. Camps are usually without cable or local television, so residents may share access to satellite disks.
(Reprinted courtesy of the Kalamazoo Gazette. Photograph by Mark Bugnaski.)

tures fall. There is little privacy within camps; homes are usually placed so close to one another that sound from radios and televisions easily penetrates the thin walls. Furthermore, while farmers usually supply the housing free of charge, there are frequently additional fees assessed for electricity, garbage collection, cleaning, and maintenance of the grounds.

While extended family groups may live in the same camp or even in the same trailer for a season, many workers have only a passing acquaintance with the people who live only a few feet away and with whom they share showers, toilets, and washing machines, often for several months. This can create problems, especially for those with young families who do not know and may not trust their temporary neighbors. "I would never let my daughters go out at night to the bathrooms," reported Sofía, who now lives in a subsidized apartment complex rather than in a camp.

Camps range in size from just a few homes to several dozen, and in quality from brand new units to, more commonly, well-worn older models. Some camps are known for having well-maintained units, while others are in regular violation of housing laws. Despite strict state housing regulations governing such things as the minimum square footage allowable per person, and despite yearly preseason inspections, some camps have difficulty maintaining sanitary conditions throughout the season. Farmers place camps in areas that are not suitable for crops, which means they may be found on wet grounds, near major roads, or, in some cases, far from roads that are accessible to garbage trucks. Griffith and Kissam report that a lack of inspectors and a number of legal loopholes combine to make the laws difficult to enforce.

Out of fear of reprisals, most workers do not report even obvious housing violations. Their fears are justified. They can easily be replaced by others who are even poorer and are more willing to work under difficult conditions. For example, because state regulations mandate 100 square feet of living space per resident, including children, many farmers are increasingly interested in attracting single males, usually from Mexico, rather than families. The H2A immigration program, which began in Michigan two years ago and which allows farmers to recruit guest workers from Mexico, also has legal restrictions and requirements.[3] A single mobile home, for example, will be able to house four to six workers rather than two workers and three dependents, thus reducing a farmer's costs. It is also thought that single men need fewer services and are less particular about their living conditions than are families.

As immigration programs like H2A take hold in Michigan, the face of migrant labor may change significantly over time. This may not be completely advantageous to farmers. While there may indeed be an economic advantage in bringing in single men, it may turn out to be a short-term advantage if the camps are less stable as a result of the absence of women and children.

QUESTION 7.4
What Are the Particular Hardships of Migrant Farmworker Life?

Just last year I went into a store and I was paying for my groceries and the clerk didn't think I spoke English. She was out of plastic bags so she said to the bagger, "Just go ahead and put it in paper bags, they don't care," as if I didn't know what she was saying. So I said, "But I do care. I like it in plastic better." I think because we're Hispanic and they know we do field work, and we're new in the area, they think less of us. We're human and we work hard. Maybe we don't work in a store, but we're picking apples for them to sell in the store. You have to do what a migrant does to really know.

ALMA

Such hardships as the inability to control housing options, attend good schools, and obtain good health care are compounded by other problems. The population's transience makes it difficult for migrants to know about their options and rights. Most institutions in American society, like schools and health clinics, are not equipped to successfully integrate a population that moves from state to state over the course of a year. Racism and prejudice can marginalize Mexican farmworker families in rural communities that are primarily white and not always welcoming.

Families, Children, and Education

It [migrant life] is most difficult for the children. My son here who is nine—in Texas he gets really good grades. Here [in Michigan] his grades have fallen way too much. I don't understand what could be the problem. But here, he's gone as far down as one can get. In Texas he has made the honor roll since kindergarten—pure 100s and 90s. Here he needs help in math, in reading. I don't know how this can be. And in Texas school is very different and more advanced than here. The school in Texas is very difficult—they are one or two grades ahead of the schools here. As a mother I would prefer to let him finish his year in one school, but we are obligated [if they are to receive unemployment] to come up here in April.

SOFÍA

We had butterflies in our stomachs every time we started a new school.

MONICA, SOFÍA'S ADULT DAUGHTER

[3]The H2A program gets its name from the kind of visa number type that is issued.

I love migrant farm work. I like doing it and I've been doing it a long time. It's outside and when we're picking, all of the family is together. You can share ideas with them and you're together with them. Being close to your family— that's the one thing a migrant has. You have a close relationship with your kids. The only bad thing was being teased by the kids at school. They would pick on me and say, "Here comes the onion girl." It still makes me cry when I think of it.

ALMA

Many of Michigan's migrant farmworkers travel with their families. Earlier we discussed some of the advantages of traveling as an extended family. But families also have concerns about raising children on the migrant circuit. While the brunt of the physical work falls on adults, the disruption of children's lives and education when they move from place to place is often considered to be a far greater problem.

Parents in most migrant families must both work just to make ends meet. Families that cannot bring an older adult to care for the children must make other arrangements. Child-care options vary considerably in quality, cost, and reliability. Some parents leave their children with another migrant worker who provides baby-sitting services in the camp. Federally subsidized Head Start programs are an option for children of five years or under. They provide developmentally appropriate care as well as a host of comprehensive health and social services that are highly valued by clients (another way of saying that there are long waiting lists to get in). A major drawback is that they run from 7 A.M. until only 4 P.M. This is a problem for people who work until at least 5 or 6 in the evening. Ad hoc arrangements, many of them deemed unsatisfactory, have to be made. Mothers complain that they have to leave their children with strangers.

School-age children can attend free summer school programs, stay in the camp with or without supervision, or accompany their parents into the fields. Although it is illegal for children under the age of 12 to work, young children are frequently found working alongside their parents, especially in less physically challenging harvests such as blueberries. Children 12 and 13 years old may work legally with the written consent of their parents.

While it may seem that child labor is exploitative and illegal and therefore should not be allowed to continue, an exploration of why children are in the fields reveals that the issue is not quite that simple. A family may need the wages and may have few child-care options. Summer school is a valuable experience for children, but it often ends in early August, three weeks before regular school starts again. If children are in the fields, their parents know exactly what they are doing. Also, strong cultural values of family loyalty, responsibility, and unity mean that having parents and children together, with everyone helping and working with one another, is important. Individual achievement is secondary to family cooperation.

Cultures that value group orientations can be called **sociocentric**, while North American society, which rewards individual achievement, is labeled **egocentric**. In egocentric societies, it is thought that individuals ought to act independently and that they can and should transcend their pasts. Conversely, sociocentric cultures place a higher value on how an individual contributes to the maintenance and success of the group, in this case the family. In sociocentric societies individual aspirations are de-emphasized, while group aspirations take precedence.

The value of emphasizing group solidarity rather than individual achievement within migrant families is openly debated among Latinos who have settled out of the migrant stream and understand what it takes to succeed in North American society. Some of those who have settled out of the migrant stream argue that a sociocentric orientation ill prepares children because it teaches a value system that is not rewarded in American society. Others contend that the personal and emotional dimensions of having strong family support outweigh the disadvantages. Family can provide a sense of belonging, love, and support to the individual. Alma, who settled out and has a small child of her own, fondly recalls the time when she learned the value of hard work and was able to spend her days with her parents. Although she does not wish her child to work in the fields, she worries about how she can communicate the values of hard work and family responsibility in an American context.

> We were a family unit. There was no problem that we couldn't deal with together. We learned so much: responsibility, the value of money, the value of family, who we were, and where we came from. I'm not saying that all farmworkers like the work, but there was a lot of togetherness for us. We were there, next to our mother, all day long. That made me the person I am today. I know I can do the job and I know I can survive. I know I can make it.

Despite the fact that children may be working during the summer, the families we spoke with all saw education as key to their children's future success. Because many workers arrive in Michigan in April or May, children often must leave their schools in Texas or Florida and finish the academic year in Michigan. Migrants generally stay in Michigan through September and October, so children must begin school in Michigan in August, only to transfer to another school later. A typical child might attend a Michigan school for two months in the fall, return to Texas for five months, and then complete the remaining two months in a different classroom or school in Michigan in the spring. The lack of continuity is difficult: young people make and lose friends; readjust to new curricula, books, and teachers; and try to meet the graduation requirements of two or more school systems.

Schoolchildren experience multiple stresses that range from concerns about social and academic integration to administrative battles over transferring credits from one state to another. Different school programs are often structured in incompatible ways. Some systems have six-week courses, while others have semester-long courses. Schools with longer terms are often loath to accept credits from schools with shorter terms. Students must sometimes pass an exam in order to enter into a particular grade. So as not to lose time waiting for the exam to be given, they often start a new school at a lower grade. "Credits don't transfer easily between Michigan and Texas," said one young man. "You get backed up in school and have to go to night school or do a GED [take a high school equivalency exam]."

Often high school students and their parents are torn between the sometimes-conflicting goals of providing for the children's education and of keeping the family economically solvent. According to one migrant, because transferring credits can be problematic, high school students often get discouraged and "lose track of their education" in April when they come to Michigan. Rather than going to school, they begin working and "helping their families."

School grades can decline when children transfer because students are unfamiliar with the new material and the new teacher's style and expectations. Also, they must cope with less tangible issues such as the emotional stress of being the new kid who may not speak English fluently and whose poor background is readily known. Migrants believe that consistency is important to doing well in school, but there is often not much they can do to ensure it. Additionally, parents think that teachers do not put much effort into getting to know their children and helping them learn. "The migrant kids always have their desks at the back of the classroom," noted one mother. "The back row is all Mexican kids." Compounding these issues is the fact that parents are often unfamiliar with the school system and/or may not speak English and therefore do not seek out teachers to report special needs or concerns.

Racism and prejudice also figure heavily in the migrant child's experiences in Michigan. Many of the migrant farmworkers we spoke with told stories of their children being teased or ostracized by "whites." Even when children are with their families in restaurants or stores, they are made to feel unwelcome. Mexicans and Mexican Americans are usually in the minority in schools, and they are further marginalized because of their temporary status. One young man sensed that attempts were made to keep the Mexicans separate from the other students. For example, on school buses the drivers separated the Mexican students from the others. If there were any problems on the bus, the drivers would "always go with white or black kids. . . . They have it against the Mexicans," he elaborated; "when I was in school I stuck with the Mexicans . . . there's a lot of racism in Michigan."

The racism this young man points to also occurs in other segments of the community. Local residents in southwest Michigan have vigorously contested a variety of federally funded migrant service efforts, including migrant Head Start programs and rest stops at which arriving workers could obtain housing and legal information. Indeed, one of the obstacles to expanding migrant Head Start programs in Michigan is the difficulty of finding a community willing to host a facility.

The children of migrants often face the task of bridging the Spanish-speaking world of their parents, which may be centered on agriculture and family solidarity, and the world of the broader American society that values these characteristics very differently. This can be particularly difficult for young people whose parents do not have a high school education and are unable to provide the support the children need to finish school.

A study released by the Government Information Sharing Project (1998) indicates that only 12 percent and 22 percent of the Latino population of two rural southwest Michigan counties had completed any schooling beyond high school in 1990, as compared with 35 percent and 37 percent of the general population. Similarly, the per capita income of Latino workers in the same two counties was $8142 in 1989, significantly lower than the $12,731 figure for white workers. Forty percent of the Latino residents were living in poverty in 1989 compared with only 13 percent of the white residents. Clearly, the disadvantages faced by Latino children in schools contribute to a pattern of disadvantage faced by Latino workers in the region.

Mobility, Poverty, and Health

Migrants usually still pick even when they are sick. They say, "We're coming from far away and we need to pick." I know, because that's how my Dad is. He says, "Well, I'll have time to go to the doctor later, but now I have to pick." And also there's the fear of the farmer, the fear that if I go to the doctor the farmer will get mad because we need to be picking.

ALMA

I know whenever we were sick my mother would make an herbal tea for us. Whatever the problem, she had a remedy. My father, well, he just didn't get sick.

MARCO ANTONIO

One of the central concerns for migrant workers is keeping themselves and family members healthy enough to continue working. While compiling accurate statistics on the state of their health is difficult because of the transience of the population and because many workers do not or cannot access health services, the data we have show significantly lower health levels than for the general population. For example, the infant mortality rate for migrants is 125 percent higher than the national average; life expectancy is 49 years, compared to 75 years for Americans in general; and the rate of parasitic infection is 11 to 59 percent higher among migrants than in the general population (National Center for Farm-Worker Health, 1987). Nationwide, there are not enough clinics to serve all of the migrant farmworkers and their families; in fact, it is estimated that clinics are able to provide services to only about 20 percent of this population. Many clinics that serve migrant workers are overburdened and often are able to offer only short-term solutions for long-term problems.

Some of the health concerns of migrant workers are directly related to their participation in or proximity to agricultural work, and others are linked to or exacerbated by poverty, a transient lifestyle, and a lack of continuity in health care. Among the specific health concerns linked to agricultural work are high rates of accidental injury and death and an increased incidence of toxic chemical exposure. Farm equipment is dangerous, and accident rates are high for both migrant and permanent workers. As a group, farmworkers suffer the highest rates of toxic chemical injuries in the United States. The toxic chemical injuries documented by health workers probably represent only a small fraction of the actual cases. Many workers never seek out care, and even when they do, diagnosing chemical exposure is often difficult and may require special blood tests and exams that are not available. The effects of toxic chemical exposure are frequently experienced weeks, months, or even years after the encounter, so it is difficult to link disease with exposure. Many health workers are not adequately trained in the recognition and diagnosis of chemical exposure, and many cases go undocumented. The risks of chemical exposure extend beyond the workers to include family members who are in or near sprayed fields. Mothers express particular concern for small children who often play in close proximity to newly sprayed fields.

Other work-related health problems include high rates of urinary tract infections (often the result of urinary retention because of a lack of toilet facilities) and high rates of heat stress and dehydration. By law, toilets and running water for hand-washing are supposed to be located within a quarter of a mile of workers in the field. This law is sometimes violated. Even when facilities are nearby, workers feel that they cannot or should not lose the time it takes to reach the facilities and return to their place in the fields or the processing line.

Many of the other health problems of migrant workers resemble those of other poor populations both in the United States and internationally. Diseases of poverty are often linked to poor diet, substandard living and sanitation conditions, inadequate medical care, and social stress. Among the most common acute problems afflicting migrant workers are high rates of infection, including gastrointestinal infections, which are no doubt related to crowded and unsanitary living and working conditions.

The most common chronic conditions among migrant workers are high rates of diabetes, hypertension, and alcoholism. There is evidence of a genetic component among people of Native American heritage for these conditions, but we also know that they are exacerbated by social conditions such as poverty and poor access to health care and culturally appropriate health education. Controlling diabetes and hypertension usually requires dietary changes that may be difficult to achieve when grocery stores are far away and food budgets are severely limited. Unfortunately, health workers and nutritionists are not always aware that cost, cultural preferences, and other variables affect food choices, and they prescribe diets originally designed for white, middle-class, urban Americans. It is almost impossible for a poor migrant worker to comply with such recommendations. Furthermore, diabetes and hypertension may also require strict drug regimens that may be difficult to maintain because of expense and problems in filling prescriptions across state and international borders.

These and other conditions are exacerbated by the transience and instability of migrant life, which make monitoring and follow-up, especially of chronic conditions, difficult. Often workers are in an area for only a few months at a time, and they rarely bring their medical records with them. The lack of continuity in care may also be a contributing factor to the high rates of infant mortality among migrant workers. For example, a woman may forego early prenatal care because she is planning to move, then begin to receive care later, only to deliver in another state—without medical records in hand. Inconsistent or late prenatal care is linked to higher infant mortality rates, as is poor nutrition, low education level of the mother, and other markers of poverty.

Perhaps because of cultural preferences, inability to reach overcrowded clinics, or fear of entering the "system," many migrant workers rely on family members, traditional healers, or medical hucksters who peddle pharmaceuticals bought over the counter in Mexico. While family members and traditional healers usually do no harm, especially if the condition is minor or self-limiting, self-medicating with pharmaceuticals can be extremely dangerous, and the unregulated use of antibiotics contributes to the increasing resistance of microbes to standard antibiotics.

QUESTION 7.5
How Have Migrant Farmworkers Organized to Improve Their Lives?

I remember when I started to become aware of my heritage of who I was, I was in high school. Over the summer I changed my name back to Marco Antonio [after years of being called Willy in school]. I was an activist—I was involved in all sorts of things like the Brown Berets [a radical student group]. You never know what kind of change you make . . . you never know who you affect, sometimes until years later. A friend of mine who was two years behind me in school started telling someone the other day how much he looked up to me in high school because I would go and talk to the principal and the teachers.

MARCO ANTONIO

Farmworkers lack the basic benefits and working conditions enjoyed by most U.S. workers. Sick time, worker's compensation, paid holidays, medical insurance, and overtime pay are generally unavailable to migrant workers. The relatively few protections required by law, such as the guarantee of a minimum hourly wage, are difficult to enforce. Migrant farmworkers are trying to change these situations. Many factors frustrate their efforts.

It does not help that this population seems to be invisible to most Americans. Very few have any idea that most of the fruits and vegetables on their tables were harvested by migrant workers living a life of Third World poverty in the United States. What awareness exists is usually characterized more by assumptions and stereotypes than by facts or firsthand knowledge.

Community empowerment, according to Baldemar Velásquez (1999), who is a migrant union organizer, refers to the ability of people to participate in the decisions that affect their lives and their communities. Examples of empowerment include making a choice about where to seek health care, moving to a new neighborhood to escape environmental contamination, volunteering to work in a community organization, and joining a student group. Literacy, educational level, income, language skills, life experiences, political knowledge and access, and health status all may affect levels of empowerment. People who do not speak the language of the dominant group in the society, for example, have a difficult time accessing services and participating in decision making. A person who is unfamiliar with the political system or feels alienated from it may not know how to protest injustice. People without power are subject to the influences and the decisions of those around them and lack opportunities to participate in the process for change. For lasting change to occur, members of a disadvantaged group must be able to identify their own resources and methods for addressing oppressive conditions and then must be able to implement the solutions they identify.

Migrant farmworkers have historically lacked power and have been one of the most easily exploited workforces in the U.S. economy. Many lack the education, language skills, and cultural knowledge they need to be able to address the inequities and injustices they experience. In Michigan these include housing and sanitation violations, fair-wage infringements, and the use of the illegal bonus system. Since most workers in southwest Michigan lack the advocacy of a national labor union, they must advocate for themselves in an economic and political system that is largely unfamiliar to them.

The transience of the workforce adds to the difficulties of developing long-term organized strategies for addressing economic and social issues. Migrant workers rarely live in a community long enough to complete the succession of legal and political steps that must be taken to even investigate an unjust situation. Constant movement from community to community and from state to state and the lack of telephones and mailing addresses compound the difficulties of organizing this dispersed and fluid group. Sometimes crew leaders, who have a vested interest in the maintenance of the system, try to prevent visitors from entering a camp, despite the fact that doing so is illegal.

Attitudes among some migrant farmworkers may further limit their ability to get help that could potentially empower the community. Many migrant farmworkers distrust farmers, and this feeling may extend to agencies that offer services to farmworkers. Workers may believe that agency staff members are collaborating with the farmers. "I don't trust anyone here" said one young man when we asked why he did not report his employer for underpaying him. "They all know each other and protect each other."

There has never been an accurate analysis of migrant living and working conditions on a national or even regional level. Something as elementary as a census of the population, which would provide quantifiable data on size, location, and age distribution, has proven elusive because of the transience and invisibility of the population. How do you count a population that lives in unidentified camps in rural areas and that is constantly moving? Undocumented migrant workers avoid being counted or identified whenever possible. Most of the population figures assigned to the migrant population are estimates and probably underestimate the number of migrants. Without reliable data, it is not easy to get government officials to listen and act.

The conditions in which migrant workers live and work are just as fluid as the population. It is often difficult to identify or correct problems because they can change faster than bureaucracies can respond. State officials called in to investigate illegal or dangerous working conditions, for example, may discover that the workers have since moved on to another field or job. Investigators can probe a problem only if a complaint is filed. So officials can be called in to investigate a sanitation problem in field A only to find that field A is no longer being worked when they arrive. They may observe violations in field B on the same farm, but they are not allowed to investigate unless a complaint has been received about field B. Agencies in Michigan lack the resources and the public mandate to persistently monitor conditions.

Without the connection to political, legal, or social systems or even to the greater farmworker community, an individual worker who wishes to take a stand about working or living conditions may need to be willing to take a personal risk. Therefore, it is not surprising that migrant farmworkers rarely openly contest living and working conditions. They believe that they are faced with a large, complex, and organized system in which everyone protects everyone else while exploiting the worker, who stands alone. The farmers, the packers, the processors, and the food conglomerates that purchase the crops all have more power than the migrant farmworker. They are connected to the larger society through shared culture and citizenship and to the political system through lobbying groups that advocate for their interests on the state and national levels.

Since the late 1990s, many growers have been lobbying in favor of revising the legislation that makes it possible to bring foreign guest workers into the United States. A revised H2A program could allow farmers to request a certain number of workers for a specified period of time, thus freeing them from having to actively recruit workers. Although details of H2A proposals vary, farmers argue that such programs would ease the seasonal labor shortage they claim to be experiencing. Opponents point out that if wages and other working conditions were adequate, there would be no labor shortage, and they fear that H2A workers would be easily exploited. Importing temporary workers under a government plan would undermine migrant farmworkers' movement toward empowerment.

The small independent farmers who constitute the majority of growers in southwest Michigan share some of the economic powerlessness of migrant farmworkers. Corporate farms have been producing an increasing percentage of this country's agricultural products during the last 30 years, and they are steadily replacing small independent growers. Throughout the country, small farmers are struggling financially, often earning less for their products than they must spend to run their farms. Rothenberg (1998) notes that the majority of U.S. farms are so small that their owners are unable to derive a living from farming and that they seek additional employment to make ends meet. These farmers have to cut costs just to stay in business, and they are hard-pressed to offer more equitable compensation or improved living accommodations to their workers. It appears that the independent farmer, who could possibly identify with the farmworker's plight, is too consumed with his own vulnerability in a farming system that increasingly favors large corporate farms.

Despite these obstacles, however, migrant farmworkers have attempted to make economic, social, and political improvements in their lives. They have creatively sought ways to empower themselves and their communities. On a personal level, individuals try to increase skills that will allow them greater participation in American society. One important skill is learning English. "With English you can open doors on both sides—Mexico and the U.S.," explained one man; "without English in this country you are nothing, no one." Others try to enter job training programs. Most migrant workers make personal sacrifices so that their children can receive an education.

Leaders on the local, regional, and national levels have become models and perhaps spokespersons for the community's concerns. In southwest Michigan, one of these local leaders was Eugenio Aleman, a well-respected member of the migrant community who settled out but continued to work tirelessly for migrant rights during his lifetime. He participated in marches to protest the use of pesticides and worked diligently to make sure that mechanisms were in place to provide food and shelter to migrant workers coming to Michigan. Individuals like Mr. Aleman provide hope and encouragement for members of the migrant community.

National leaders have emerged from migrant farmworker unions. The United Farm Workers Union (UFW) was organized by Cesar Chavez in California in the 1950s. It was a social force during the civil rights movement of the 1960s, and, Chavez, who died in 1993, is revered as a hero by many Latinos in the United States. Baldemar Velásquez organizes Midwest workers through the Farm Labor Organizing Committee (FLOC) and speaks of the plight of migrant workers at universities and in other forums. In general, farmworkers' unions attempt to negotiate wages and benefits for their workers, particularly those working on large corporate farms.

Efforts to organize farmworkers have been largely unsuccessful because of the large pool of available labor; resistance by farmers, crew leaders, and corporations; and the inherent difficulties of organizing such a large, diverse, and transient population. There have been pockets of success, notably in California, where agriculture is comprised primarily of huge corporate farms, and in areas of the Midwest, where agreements between farmers, workers, and food corporations have been negotiated. Because of regional differences, organizing efforts have had to address regional and local conditions in order to achieve success. There is currently no organized farmworkers' movement in southwest Michigan, a situation that some of our informants regretted. "We need to have a leader here like Chavez," said one man. "Our problem is that we don't know how to organize as a group. We have too much distrust—even of each other. We need someone to help us organize."

Labor contracts would significantly improve the quality of migrant farmworkers' lives by increasing their overall income level and empowering them with a sense of pride and control. The economic gain would positively affect other aspects of their lives, such as health and education. In addition to negotiating salaries and working conditions, unions can be advocates for health care and can help workers file grievances and address civil rights violations.

Social services can empower people or keep them powerless. Services that foster a dependence on resources and knowledge outside of the community or that do not allow recipients to participate in the decision-making process are perceived as a handout. In the end, such services do not contribute to the community's self-sufficiency. Services that are empowering equip individuals and communities to participate in problem solving and in implementation of solutions. For example, the Camp Health Aide Program in Monroe, Michigan, attempts to empower the migrant community by delivering services at the same time it equips community members with real skills. The program hires and trains community members to act as intermediaries between the migrant camps and the local clinic. The aides look for creative ways to educate their neighbors about common health problems. As members of the migrant community, Camp Health Aides understand the limitations and concerns of the people they work with, and they are able to address them in a direct and meaningful way. The information they relay is culturally relevant and accessible.

CONCLUSIONS

Even though the work of migrant workers touches every American in a very personal way as we shop for, prepare, and eat the products of their labor, the workers themselves are essentially invisible. We have tried to show who these people are. There are three migrant streams in the United States, and the Midwest stream is composed primarily of Mexicans and Mexican Americans. It is difficult to generalize about the routes that any individual may take during the annual migration. Flexibility is key to survival, and individuals may move in and out of streams for personal or work-related reasons. There is also tremendous variability in the circumstances of migrant workers once in Michigan, with undocumented Mexican workers often working and living in the most difficult conditions.

Both the United States and Mexico have long had economic policies that have undermined small agricultural producers and promoted industrial production over agricultural production. In Mexico, this has resulted in a surplus of peasant laborers who could not be absorbed into the floundering manufacturing economy, while in the United States agricultural workers have historically been treated as second-class workers. Only rarely, such as during the Dust Bowl in the 1920s, were there enough American workers to fill these low-wage, no-benefit jobs.

The insecurities of farm labor have contributed to the perpetuation of poverty because of the inability of workers to both save money and provide for their needs, and because the farm labor system often exploits vulnerable workers. Wages are always dependent on the crops picked; if the crops are poor, so are the wages. Often there is no way to predict a bad season until after workers have arrived and agreed to work. Financially strapped small farmers are often so desperate for labor that they will make illegal bargains with workers to keep them working through a poor season; such bargains rarely benefit the workers. Many workers, especially undocumented ones, feel they cannot complain about unfair working conditions. After they meet living and travel expenses, migrant workers often have little money to take home at the end of the season. Poverty becomes entrenched.

Multiple school systems make fulfilling graduation requirements difficult, and health care systems are not equipped to deal with a mobile population with significant health risks. Less obvious to outsiders is the racism that Mexicans and Mexican Americans repeatedly report they experience in Michigan schools, stores, and public services, often provoking them to abandon school or to avoid seeking care or assistance. While the sociocentric family provides daily financial and emotional support for most migrant workers, real structural reform that addresses the problems of migrant life is decidedly more complicated.

REFERENCES AND RECOMMENDED READINGS

Barger, W. K., and Ernesto M. Reza
1994 The Farm Labor Movement in the Midwest: Social Change and Adaptation Among Migrant Farmworkers. Austin: University of Texas Press.
   This book documents the history of the Farm Labor Organizing Committee, the only active farmworker's union in the Midwest. Using a systems approach for studying social change, the authors identify the social forces that have contributed to the union's successes. They examine how both internal and external forces have influenced the process of social change.

Buss, Fran Leper, ed.
1993 Forged Under the Sun/Forjado Bajo del Sol. Ann Arbor: University of Michigan Press.
   This book is the autobiography of Maria Elena Lucas, a Chicana farmworker and labor organizer. In a very personal voice, Lucas describes the challenges, oppression, and discrimination she faced as a result of her ethnicity, gender, economic status, and occupation. The book offers important insights into the manner in which the different aspects of poverty and oppression intersect and reinforce each other.

Fletcher, Peri L.
1999 La Casa de Mis Suenos: Dreams of Home in a Transnational Mexican Community. Boulder, CO: Westview Press.

> Globalization brings widespread changes and adaptation on the local, national, and cross-national levels. This study documents the complex effects that ongoing migration patterns to the United States have had on the social and economic life of a Mexican community, especially its social networks, household organization, land distribution and use, and household economies.

Hondahneu-Sotelo, Pierrette
1994 Gendered Transitions: Mexican Experiences of Immigration. Berkeley: University of California Press.

> A concise and useful history of Mexican immigration to the United States and an examination of how that migration has been affected by both micro- and macro-level variables, especially gender ideologies and roles.

Kushner, Sam
1975 Long Road to Delano. New York: International Publishers.

> Reviewing the century-long struggle of farm laborers in California, this text provides detailed coverage of the nine-year United Farm Worker's Union strike as well an analysis of its historical significance. It offers an important perspective on the work of the UFW, the leading farmworkers' union in the United States.

Richardson, Chad
1999 Batos, Bolillos, Pochos and Pelados: Class and Culture on the South Texas Border. Austin: University of Texas Press.

> Using the voices and stories of Mexicans, Mexican Americans, and others, this sensitive and readable book examines the subcultures of the Rio Grande Valley. The title refers to slang terms indicating in-group solidarity and out-group identity and exemplifies the complex interrelations between the various groups that meet and live on the borderlands.

Valdes, Dennis Nodin
1991 Al Norte: Agricultural Workers in the Great Lakes Region: 1917–1970. Austin: University of Texas Press.

> A social history of the work and world of Latino agricultural workers in the Midwest with a special focus on the class struggle between employers and farmworkers, this book also emphasizes the role of agricultural innovations and transitions.

Valle, Isabel
1994 Fields of Toil: A Migrant Family's Journey. Pullman: Washington State University Press.

> This book records a year in a migrant family's life, beginning at home in Texas and following them north to Washington. The author accompanied the family for the entire year and wrote this account to provide an insider's view of the challenges of migrant life.

Government Information Sharing Project
1998 USA Counties 1998. Electronic document, http://govinfo.library.orst.edu.

Griffith, Davis, and Ed Kissam
1995 Working Poor: Farmworkers in the United States. Philadelphia: Temple University Press, 1995.

National Center for Farm-Worker Health
1987 White Paper on Nutrition. Electronic document, http://www.ncfh.org.

Ong, Aihwa
1987 Spirits of Resistance and Capitalist Discipline: Factory Women in Malaysia. Albany: State University of New York Press.

Rothenberg, Daniel
1998 With These Hands: The Hidden World of Migrant Farmworkers Today. New York: Harcourt, Brace and Co.

Velásquez, Baldemar
1999 Speech delivered at Western Michigan University, August 1999.

CHAPTER 8

BEYOND "DILBERT": THE CULTURAL CONSTRUCTION OF WORK ORGANIZATIONS IN THE UNITED STATES

MARIETTA L. BABA

PROBLEM 8 *Why do such large-scale organizations as corporations and government agencies develop their own distinctive cultures, and how do these cultures affect human behavior and organizational performance?*

INTRODUCTION
Organizational Culture—Does It Matter?

The United States is one of the last frontiers for American anthropologists. Because cultural insiders have difficulty detecting subtle patterns of behavior and thought that are familiar and taken for granted, there was a widespread belief that anthropologists born and raised in the United States should seek foreign field sites from which they could view culture more clearly as outsiders. In recent years, however, this conventional wisdom has been called into question. Political and economic constraints have made foreign field sites more difficult to access, and the choice for many researchers has become either doing anthropology at home or not doing it at all. As scarcity forces more American anthropologists to repatriate their craft, some have been surprised to discover that many seemingly ordinary American venues are every bit as exotic as those situated overseas. Some of the most puzzling cultural practices in the United States can be found inside large-scale work organizations.

As anthropologists have discovered their own backyards, they have also "rediscovered" that many problems in modern corporations can be approached through the same basic conceptual and methodological means used to study traditional societies. This means that anthropology is beginning to find a place inside the world of corporations and other large-scale work organizations, and may be able to play a key role in reshaping organizations during the 21st century.

The hugely popular comic strip "Dilbert" exaggerates the observer's sense of witnessing something absurd in order to satirize common organizational practices. Readers encounter bosses who fly in and out of departments too quickly to learn anything about them, canine and feline consultants who earn large sums of money for dispensing advice that is obvious, or obviously flawed, and members of warring employee subcultures who terrorize and torture one another. A funny thing about "Dilbert" is that these absurd scenarios do not seem that improbable to people who have experienced life inside large-scale organizations. According to Scott Adams, the creator of "Dilbert":

> Most of the themes in my comic strip "Dilbert" involve workplace situations. I routinely include bizarre and unworldly elements such as sadistic talking animals, troll-like accountants, and employees turning into dishrags after the life-force has been drained from their bodies. And yet the comment I hear most often is: "That's just like my company." No matter how absurd I try to make the comic strip I can't stay ahead of what people are experiencing in their own workplaces. . . . Thousands of people have told me workplace stories (mostly through e-mail) that are even more absurd than the examples given above. [1996:1–2]

How is it that corporations and other types of large-scale work organizations encourage what appears to be managerial incompetence, rely on self-serving advisors, and tolerate open internal warfare, especially since they claim to use rational methods of planning and control to achieve serious economic and social objectives?

The scenarios portrayed in "Dilbert" represent recognizable cultural patterns—that is, shared ways of organizational life that are distinctly American and can be understood in terms of concepts and methods that anthropologists employ in more traditional settings. Anthropologists do not claim to have all of the answers to the mysteries of organizational life, but they bring a fresh perspective that takes seriously the apparently illogical or nonsensical practices that "Dilbert" lampoons. To an anthropologist, the practices found in

DILBERT reprinted by permission of United Features Syndicate, Inc.

"Dilbert," while funny, also invite social analysis, for they represent human social traditions that have as much cultural authenticity as the pyramids and the potlatch, and can also have troubling consequences for millions of people in this country and around the world.

Organizations are a significant feature of life in the United States. Large private and public organizations touch virtually everything we do—the newspapers we read in the morning, the food we eat, the clothing we wear, our jobs, our schooling, our forms of entertainment. Corporations decide which products and services will be available for purchase, and governmental agencies monitor their production and marketing. Private corporations and public agencies provide millions of jobs and thus influence the way many people spend the better part of their waking day.

The influence of large-scale corporations and government is so pervasive that most of us take it for granted; big organizations are the "way we do things around here." While we cannot help but recognize the effect of corporate policy and practice in the marketplace, we may not be fully conscious of the ways in which companies and agencies invade our private lives. Yet our novels, movies, television programs, cartoons, and jokes are permeated by such mundane yet stressful matters as landing a job, managing the boss, schmoozing with coworkers, making sense of workplace politics, juggling work and family obligations, and trying to "get a life" despite all of the interference. Just as the lives of people in traditional societies are shaped by family and kinship patterns, our lives are profoundly structured and patterned by the ways of big corporations and other types of bureaucratic organizations. In the United States, traditional cultural forms such as the family have relatively less influence over people's lives than they do anyplace else in the world. Ours is a culture of organizations.

We may define specific things that originate from organizational sources, such as environmental pollution, downsizing, and job stress, as problems, but we typically do not define the general fact of organizational influence in our lives as a problem. We accept the influence as the price of economic growth. Nevertheless, the problems of big organizations create problems for all of us. When large corporations and public bureaucracies encourage or tolerate practices that waste scarce resources and human potential, we are all impoverished.

Disciplines such as economics, engineering, and industrial and organizational psychology attempt to explain what is going on (or what should go on) inside large-scale organizations in order to improve industrial efficiency and effectiveness. Such functional and rationalist perspectives provide guidance to managers, but they often fail to capture underlying patterns of organizational life that are nonfunctional and nonrational in nature. Many of the seemingly irrational or inexplicable Dilbertesque practices of managers and employees, including those that detract from an organization's capacity to meet its larger social and economic goals, make sense only when viewed through a cultural lens. The anthropological perspective can help find the roots of these practices and can identify their implications for organizational performance.

To understand the cultural nature of organizations and their influence in American life, this chapter explores the concept of organizational **culture** and the ways in which it shapes human behavior and performance in the workplace, drawing on organizational ethnography to illustrate key points. It also examines the origins and developmental processes of organizational cultures, the multicultural complexity that exists within large-scale organizations, and the concepts and methods anthropologists use to study the cultures of organizations. Throughout this discussion, the term organization refers to the formal organization, which is an organization created for a specific purpose.

QUESTIONS

8.1. What is organizational culture, and how does it affect human behavior in the workplace?

8.2. How does culture develop in an organization?

8.3. What roles do occupational and professional cultures play within the overall culture of a large-scale organization?

8.4. How does organizational culture affect human performance and social control?

8.5. How do anthropologists study culture in organizations, and what ethical issues are involved?

QUESTION 8.1
What Is Organizational Culture, and How Does It Affect Human Behavior in the Workplace?

Prior to the 1930s, the behavior of people working in large organizations was thought to be determined largely by the technology and physical environment of the workplace and by the purposes and commands of management. In the early decades of the 20th century, an industrial engineer named Frederick Winslow Taylor helped to develop the first theory of management by explaining how managers and other employees should behave to ensure high productivity.[1] According to Taylor, it was management's responsibility to conceptualize and command the work system, and workers were to execute managers' commands. This is fundamentally a military model. The term *management* is derived in part from the French *manege*, which means "to put a horse through its paces"; in other words, management means command and control of the workhorses. In keeping with this analogy, Taylor believed that management could precisely specify the body motions of each worker to achieve greatest productivity. Based on time-and-motion studies conducted by industrial engineers, each worker would be told how to walk, bend, lift, and manipulate tools. The behavior of the workforce thus would grow out of managerial intent and technological requirements.

Despite their time-and-motion studies, managers failed to improve the productivity of American industry, especially during the 1930s and 1940s when productivity improvements were urgently needed to help the nation recover from the Great Depression and to support participation in World War II. Productivity growth was sluggish, even though managers in many indus-

---

[1] *Productivity* is the amount of goods produced divided by the labor hours required for production.

tries utilized incentive pay systems to encourage employees to work faster. In the incentive system, each employee receives a standard base pay in exchange for a standard amount of work, plus a bonus determined by the amount produced above and beyond the standard. In many companies, this incentive system failed to induce employees to produce more than the standard, even though industrial engineers demonstrated that it would be relatively easy to do the extra work and earn a bonus. Managers believed that people behave in accordance with economic self-interest,[2] and they could not understand why individual employees would fail to respond to the incentive system. Some assumed that employees—many of whom were recent immigrants and could not speak English well (or at all)—lacked the education or intelligence to comprehend the workings of an incentive system. Such negative stereotypes prevented some managers from questioning whether there might be other reasons for the ineffectiveness of incentives.

In the late 1920s, at the same time Taylor's approach to management was being implemented, an important experiment conducted under the auspices of Harvard University and the Western Electric Company[3] shed new light on human behavior in organizations. The study was initially designed to identify factors that contributed to productivity, and it was conducted using actual workers doing real work at Western Electric's Hawthorne Plant in Chicago. Elton Mayo, a Harvard psychologist, believed that the physical conditions of work were causing worker fatigue, thereby preventing employees from delivering higher rates of production. He systematically tested his hypothesis by modifying physical features of the workplace to reduce fatigue and by measuring the output of various work groups.

In one of the most famous experiments, Mayo and his colleagues provided a number of different amenities to a group of women employees while measuring the number of components they assembled. These amenities, which included extra rest breaks, special snacks, recognition of birthdays, and health checkups, were intended to reduce fatigue. Throughout the experiment, production increased each time new amenities were provided. This was not unexpected. What puzzled Mayo was that productivity continued to increase as he withdrew the amenities. In fact, productivity climbed throughout the experiment, regardless of whether amenities were provided or taken away.

Today we recognize this result as an artifact of the experimental situation; it is called the **Hawthorne effect**, and it occurs when special attention is focused on a group of employees, regardless of experimental conditions. At this point, however, Mayo assumed that the continual increase in production resulted from some unknown human relations factor. The work group had been taken off the production floor and placed in an observation room with observers who doubled as supervisors. Perhaps, he reasoned, the group had developed improved relationships with supervisors, informal group leadership, higher group cohesion, and/or higher morale.

To investigate the mysterious human relations factor, Mayo called on Harvard anthropologist W. Lloyd Warner, who had just completed fieldwork in Australia. Mayo told Warner that he wanted to observe employees under actual conditions of work, with minimal intrusion by the scientists, so that he

[2]This is an "**economic man**" theory of behavior.
[3]Western Electric later became part of AT&T and then of Lucent Technologies.

could understand how the relationships among the employees might contribute to their rate of production. Warner designed the next phase of the research based on anthropological concepts and methods. A replica of the shop floor was set up in a special observation room, and an intact group of employees was instructed to work as usual inside this room. Observers were trained to record details of the employees' behavior while remaining as unobtrusive as possible. This experiment was run during 1931 and 1932.

What was discovered in this first ethnography of American work organizations forever changed our understanding of human behavior in such settings. Observers found that employees were indeed able to speed up their rate of production at will, and often did so at the beginning of a shift when everyone was more likely to be rested and fresh. Later in the shift, however, production would be slowed considerably, so that an overall average rate per day was maintained with only minor variation. The average rate of production was just enough to justify the standard base pay provided by the company. Employees rarely exceeded this average, even though they could easily produce more and obtain higher pay.

Fatigue was not the source of the employees' reluctance to produce more. Rather, it was based on employees' distrust of management. Employees believed that once they established a higher rate of production, management would increase the standard amount of work required to earn the base pay, and they would have to work faster for the same pay. There was an informal understanding among employees that a "fair day's work" should be given for a "fair day's pay"—doing more could harm the group and was therefore severely discouraged. An employee who violated this understanding by working at a faster pace was disciplined by coworkers. Discipline included "pinging" the offender (placing the thumb over the middle finger and snapping the middle finger against the victim's arm), threatening worse, and finally completely ostracizing an overachiever who still failed to conform to the group's norms.

The Hawthorne researchers also discovered that shared work practices were supported by an **informal social system** on the shop floor (an *informal organization,* as it was called at the time). This miniature social system had its own informal leaders and was organized around friendship networks, or cliques, that were defined by patterns of association and interaction among the workers. Each clique had a distinctive work style, and some produced more work on average, although no more than "a fair day's work." Workers who did not comply with work groups' norms were isolated outside the friendship circles. To protect this social system from the prying eyes of managers and industrial engineers, the workers had established signals to alert coworkers to the arrival of those who might discover their manipulation of production rates. Supervisors on the shop floor were aware of these practices and basically cooperated in their maintenance and continuation.

The Hawthorne study revealed the basic nature of **organizational culture** and the reason it is considered an important influence on human behavior in organizations. Groups of coworkers who share common work tasks and methods create shared patterns of meaning and practice that emerge over time from specific conditions inside and outside the organization. Today, these patterns are recognized as manifestations of work-group culture, or occupational culture. They are not consciously planned or formally controlled but arise spontaneously as a work group attempts to do the work and also achieve its own goals. In some cases, the shared understandings and practices of work groups run counter to the goals of management, and they may prove resistant to business strategies and tactics that managers believe are necessary for a firm's survival and growth, especially if workers view such strategies as harmful to themselves.

There are many different work groups in a large-scale organization, and each has unique patterns of thought and action. In the Hawthorne study, for example, the greatest differences were found to exist between management groups and workers' groups. Each type has a distinctive work-group culture. Conflicting worldviews and practices among work groups are key reasons for the organizational conflict depicted in the "Dilbert" cartoons. The interaction among all of the work-group cultures in an organization gives rise to an organizational culture. At the Hawthorne plant, the interaction between management and the work group in the observation room was characterized by distrust and a lack of mutual understanding, which in turn prevented the company from achieving its productivity goals. Organizational cultures do not always work against company goals. There are a number of empirically documented cases in which the culture of an organization has been found to enhance corporate performance.

There are important differences between **classical cultures** such as national and ethnic cultures and organizational cultures. One significant difference is the influence of formal mission and structure in an organization. A large-scale work organization has a formal or official purpose or an end (it is rational), while classical cultures generally have no formal mission per se but simply exist (they are nonrational, or natural). Organizations vary greatly in terms of how seriously and effectively managers and employees pursue the formally stated goals, and this variation has a profound effect on thinking and behavior inside the organization. The formal aspect of the organization may have a stronger influence on work-group culture in an organization where dedication to the formally stated mission is taken very seriously, such as a Fortune 500 company, than in an organization where employees are encouraged to pursue individual goals, such as a large research-oriented university. Regardless, there will be a state of tension between the formal and the informal parts of the organization. The informal and formal can never be fully separated, as seen in the Hawthorne case, which creates a huge challenge for anyone who wants to study or manage an organization. Both the formal and the informal sides, as well as the complex interactions between the two, must be understood and accounted for, and the informal side will never be completely under management's control.

Another important difference between organizational culture and classical culture is the nature of members' involvement. In a classical culture, people are born into membership and typically have little choice in the matter, although they may choose to become expatriates later on. **Primary enculturation**, the process by which an individual learns his or her culture, takes place inside a classical culture, meaning that its members are influenced by the culture during infancy and early childhood, when such influences are most effective. In an organizational culture, on the other hand, people enter as adults and can choose whether to join and remain. Often, the choice is made on the basis of the "fit" between the culture of the organization and the individual's personality and primary enculturation. Organizations tend to hire only small numbers of people who are different in some way from their more typical employees, so their memberships may be less heterogeneous than one would expect from examining the larger external population. Also, an organization's **socialization** process creates beliefs that are not as deeply rooted as the primary enculturation experienced as an infant or small child, meaning that people in the organization may be better able to resist the influence of an organizational culture. These paradoxical tendencies—one that creates a certain "fit" between the individual and the organizational culture, and the other that enables a degree of cultural resistance—are present simultaneously, creating a sense of ambivalence or ambiguity in members' alignment with stated formal goals.

QUESTION 8.2
How Does Culture Develop in an Organization?

Americans became interested in the idea that an organization can be understood as a culture when Western corporations were assaulted by competition from their counterparts in the East during the 1980s. Companies based in Asia, most notably in Japan, South Korea, and Taiwan, were strikingly different from those based in the United States, Canada, and Western Europe. Eastern firms were well coordinated and highly focused, and they captured market share in many industries. However, they did not acknowledge, much less adhere to, many of the assumed "truths" of Western management science and economic theory. For example, they did not pursue the maximization of short-term profits; they did not rely primarily on major capital investment as a foundation for productivity improvement; and they did not promote people on the basis of individual achievement.

Instead, Eastern firms operate under rules derived in part from the cultural environments in which they are grounded and from historical processes that shaped their cultures. The Japanese concept of the family as an *ie*, a household, rather than as a blood lineage, for instance, allows the incorporation of members who are not kin into the family unit, and ultimately permits the family to serve as a model for extended economic enterprise. Many centuries of irrigation agriculture in Japan required cooperation among families in farming villages, promoting the notion of trust-based collaboration beyond the basic family unit. Another major cultural influence in the East is Confucianism, which conceives of society as an organic whole composed of mutually supportive parts that exists continuously through time. This cultural concept emphasizes duty to ancestors and descendants as a key moral principle; people owe their own lives and culture to their ancestors and are responsible for handing down their heritage to their children. These forces helped shape societies that were group-oriented, cohesive, and connected by bonds of mutual responsibility and obligation. The firms that grew from such ancient collectivist roots measured time in centuries rather than years, based productivity improvements on workers' ideas for continuous incremental improvement, and developed reward systems that idealized the ability to preserve group cohesion and harmony.

The success of the Eastern firms drove home the point that companies can have different cultures and different habitual practices. It led to a permanent shift in Western thinking about all business enterprises, not just those in the East. From the 1980s on, enterprises were not viewed only as technical mechanisms crafted to achieve rational business goals, but also as places where different kinds of cultures can be expressed and, more importantly, can critically affect business results.

One of the most salient influences on organizational culture and behavior is the national or regional culture in which an organization develops and is headquartered. Ethnographic research has demonstrated that many of an organization's key features, such as formal strategy and structure, decision-making style, and communication processes, are shaped by the **ambient national culture**. For example, in an American firm, employees are encouraged to bring new ideas and proposals to the boss and to try to "sell" the boss on the ideas. This pattern reflects the egalitarianism and relatively informal nature of authority relations in the United States, as well as the high value placed on individual initiative and creativity. Employees may even disagree or argue with the boss, and it is not unheard of for an employee to win the debate. In French companies, however, employees may be quite uncomfortable with the idea of trying to "lead" the boss, and instead expect to wait patiently for the boss to provide instructions. Authority roles and relationships in France are more formal and distant than they are in the United States, reflecting the French history of centralized government and clearly defined, generally exclusive social classes. Many major corporations in France are government-owned, and formally defined bureaucratic processes are the norm in business. Employees are trained to follow the rules and the formal chain of command. Japanese companies display yet a third decision-making pattern. The chief of a unit is vested with authority to make any and all decisions, but employees expect the chief to submit some decisions to the group for discussion and possible disagreement. Likewise, a middle manager who develops a proposal generally must circulate it broadly and obtain input from managers of a wide variety of other groups throughout the company. A consensual style of decision-making is the norm, reflecting the networks of mutual trust, obligation, and reciprocity that bind individuals into social collectives within Japanese society.

Ethnographic studies of foreign firms, such as Thomas Rohlen's (1974) classic ethnography of a medium-sized Japanese bank, illustrate the complex and subtle influence of national culture on organizations. Rohlen conducted participant observation, entering the company as a new recruit and attending the bank's training institute with a cohort of new employees. At the institute, Rohlen observed many ritual practices that mirrored aspects of Japanese culture. One unique ritual found in many Japanese firms but not in their Western counterparts is spiritual education. This involves structured exercises aimed at shaping the character of new employees in ways that create more complete respect for the social requirements of the institution. In an exercise called *roto*, new recruits dressed in white uniforms were sent to a nearby market town where they were required to go door-to-door asking residents to assign simple household chores that they could do without pay. Each employee had to do this alone, not as part of a group, and employees could not return to the institute until they had succeeded in working for someone free of charge. This was especially embarrassing and awkward because Japanese people tend to be uncomfortable asking strangers for favors or bestowing favors on them; getting or granting a favor establishes an obligation that a stranger finds difficult or impossible to fulfill, so strangers generally ignore one another. After being rejected by town residents once or twice, most trainees were relieved and happy to find someone who would allow them to do the most menial labor; even cleaning an outhouse was welcome work. Rohlen explained the point of this spiritual education as follows:

> When the group had all returned, a general discussion was held. Each squad was told to discuss the relevance of the roto experience to the question, "What is the meaning of work?" As usual, a variety of opinions emerged. Some had such an interesting and pleasant time that it had not occurred to them to think of their tasks as work. When this was noticed, it was generally observed that enjoyment of work had less to do with the kind of work performed than with the attitude the person has toward it. The bank's reasons for utilizing roto centered on establishing precisely this lesson. . . . Because it must assign rather dull and methodical tasks to many, management finds this lesson of obvious value. [1974:204–205]

Roto and other forms of spiritual education are rituals that build individual acceptance of conformity to group requirements and help align individual values and attitudes with group norms and practices. In exchange for conformity, male employees in larger Japanese organizations typically had employment security, and a corporate welfare system took care of everything from housing to vacations. While global competition is creating pressure for change in this system, the job-mobility rate across firms in Japan is still among the lowest in the world, reflecting high levels of loyalty between an organization and its employees. Such loyalty allowed Japanese companies to invest heavily in employee education (since employees are not likely to take their training and go to elsewhere), creating one of the world's best-trained workforces.

Businesses operate differently in other parts of the world. In the 1990s in Silicon Valley, for example, individuals typically gained new knowledge by switching employers every two years, on average. The fast pace of change in the computer industry forced people to keep up-to-date or risk losing their competitive edge. Because of the high concentration of technology-based firms in the Valley, an individual who was not learning quickly enough at one firm could easily switch to another firm in the same locale. People frequently jumped ship to work on new technical projects at other firms or to help start new companies. They also shared technical and business information across firms, even with competitors. All of this helped everyone learn more and learn faster, thereby fueling the pace of change.

So many people flowed so quickly across so many different companies in Silicon Valley that the region was characterized as one vast organizational network with a pooled labor supply. The rapid flow of people and information gave Silicon Valley very high rates of job mobility and new business generation. In this environment, shared values and norms gave high priority to entrepreneurship and technological innovation, both of which were encouraged by placing the needs of individual entrepreneurs, inventors, and venture capitalists over those of existing businesses. American society as a whole is characterized by high rates of technical invention and economic entrepreneurship, both of which are promoted by strongly individualistic inventors and entrepreneurs. Our society encourages such individuals and allows them to be well rewarded for their success, in part through legal structures that protect private property (including intellectual property) and in part through tax rates that are among the lowest in the industrialized world. These larger American patterns had a unique regional twist in Silicon Valley, where the computer industry both created and responded to a breakneck pace of technological change. The culture of Silicon Valley was unmistakably American, but it was also unique.

Whether an organization is based in Japan, Silicon Valley, or elsewhere, its culture is in part a reflection of the society in which it is located. However, there are cultural variations across firms in the same nation or region that derive from the unique historical learning experiences of each company. For example, General Motors and Ford are both large automobile manufacturers based in the Detroit area. Both firms are heavily invested in engineering activity, and both employ thousands of workers who belong to the United Automobile Workers (UAW). It might seem on the surface that the two firms are much the same and that their organizational cultures must be similar as well. A closer look reveals a different picture.

General Motors was formed in the early years of the 20th century when an entrepreneur named Billy Durant raised funds from a group of investors to purchase a number of independent engineering and manufacturing firms around the Detroit area. His idea was to create a powerful automobile manufacturing confederation. Durant was not a strong manager, and when the new company foundered, the investment group hired Alfred Sloan. Sloan was a brilliant executive who invented a new way to manage what became the world's first multidivisional company. Each division of General Motors had formerly been a separate firm, and each was allowed to run itself as a quasi-autonomous entity. Divisions with stronger financial performance were supplied with an increasing amount of investment dollars and thus were able to do more and grow. Internal competition for investment among GM's divisions stimulated improvements in operations and financial returns, making GM one of the most successful companies in history and, at one point, the largest company in the world, with approximately a million employees.

The multidivisional structure of General Motors had profound cultural consequences. Since the divisions were rewarded for their independent performance, each learned to create strategy and make decisions that would maximize its own success, even if it meant that one division's actions would harm another division. It was no secret that the Chevrolet, Pontiac, Buick, Oldsmobile, and Cadillac divisions competed with each other, perhaps even more than they competed with external rivals such as Ford. Divisional autonomy and an internal competitive focus became hallmarks of GM's culture during its growth years in the middle of the 20th century. Unable to assess clearly or take seriously any competition beyond its own boundaries, GM failed to recognize the threat from Asian automakers, and this blind spot eventually cost GM half of its domestic market share. Even worse, the different divisions of GM appeared to find it difficult to cooperate with one another to reduce costs and improve quality, steps that were prerequisites to economic survival in the 1980s and 1990s. Executives in different divisions continued to make decisions based on divisional interests, rather than on GM's interests overall, still believing that what was good for their division was in the best interest of the company.

The situation at Ford, American's number-two automaker, was different. Ford was founded and managed for many years by a single entrepreneur, Henry Ford, who invented the moving assembly line. Henry Ford was known to be a strong-willed and autocratic leader who ruled his company with an iron fist, even going so far as to use physical force against employees who defied him, such as those who attempted to organize a labor union. After he retired, the company continued to be led by members of the family, as it is today. Even though Ford stock is now publicly traded, family members have been in top leadership positions for more than 70 years. A unity of command issuing from the top of the company countered tendencies toward divisional autonomy, while Ford's relatively smaller size (about one-third that of GM) also enabled stronger management discipline across the firm. The alignment of units within Ford was reinforced in the early 1980s when the company faced the very real possibility of bankruptcy. This chilling experience, made all the more real by the actual bankruptcy and government bailout of America's third automaker, Chrysler, struck a note of fear in the hearts of executives and employees alike and encouraged them to find new ways to work together, especially in the manufacturing plants. As a result, Ford's labor-management relationships improved significantly and are acknowledged to be among the best in the American automobile industry. Meanwhile, labor relations at GM have become increasingly antagonistic, leading to bitter strikes with ruinous financial consequences. Significantly, GM never faced bankruptcy, largely because its huge size and vast financial reserves provided an ample cushion that carried it through the worst years.

Historical differences between GM and Ford mean that each company has had different learning experiences, so they have developed different cultural patterns. Today, one company continues to struggle with management discipline and labor-management conflict, while the other is able to devote its energy to an enormous restructuring effort aimed at improving the efficiency of global design and manufacturing processes and the effectiveness of brand recognition. The conditions under which a company is founded and its situation during early growth years are highly influential in shaping deeply ingrained patterns of understanding and practice that persist over long periods of time. This is particularly the case when an organization has been successful for many decades, as was GM through the 1960s. In such cases, new employees are enculturated by their peers and managers to accept and adopt longstanding ways of thinking and behaving, and the culture thus is passed on to new generations even as the environment around the company is changing. When an organization stands on the brink of disaster, on the other hand, there is an opportunity for new learning that can lead to change.

Organizational anthropologists debate whether national or regional culture is more important than historically grounded local culture in explaining the behavior of people in an organization. An organization becomes imprinted with ambient cultural patterns because most of the people who found and grow it have been enculturated during childhood to accept and adopt the cultural patterns of the society in which they were born. When an organization is founded, its leaders unconsciously draw on these ambient cultural patterns to create the organizational culture, much as Sloan designed GM around the concept of internal competition among individual divisions. As the organization grows, it brings in managers from the surrounding society who also are marked by the same ambient culture as the founders. Thus, in its early years, an organization is imprinted with the mark of its founding society, and it continuously reinforces this imprinting by importing people of influence who also carry the same cultural patterns.

While an organization's workforce may be diverse and multicultural, the influential management cultures often are much less so, in part because of educational systems that align managers around a common set of business principles, and in part because managers born and raised in many different nations often are educated in the United States or Europe. In understanding organizational culture, it is therefore always necessary to begin by understanding the ambient cultures of the geographical area in which the firm is based and the major cultures from which the firm derives its managers and employees. The way these influences are expressed depends on the firm's historical learning experience. Other critical cultural influences, as seen in the Silicon Valley and automobile examples, are the nature of the industry and markets in which the firm competes, the technologies that dominate the organization's products, and the historical time period during which the organization was founded.

QUESTION 8.3
What Roles Do Occupational and Professional Cultures Play Within the Overall Culture of a Large-scale Organization?

Large-scale organizations do not have a single monolithic culture. Instead, they reflect the dynamic interactions of multiple cultures or subcultures that cut across the company and link it to various external constituencies. Especially important are the interactions of various occupational and professional cultures, such as the cultures of management, scientists, skilled craftspeople, and assembly-line workers. Each of these cultures or **subcultures** has its own distinctive way of understanding and acting within the larger organization. The cultures cooperate, collaborate, compete, and conflict with each other in complex ways, creating an overall pattern of culture that is different in each organization. Occupational and professional cultures also cut across different organizations and tie them together through occupational and professional networks.

According to Van Maanen and Barley (1984), occupational and professional groups can be considered cultural communities when four characteristics are present. First, individuals identify themselves as members of a special occupational or professional group whose boundaries are defined by agreed-upon criteria, such as a particular educational background and a certain type of work. Second, members of the group derive their valued identity or self-image from their occupational or professional role. For example, when asked, "Who are you?" or "What do you do?" they are likely to answer by naming their profession or occupation. A third feature of such communities is that their members serve as one another's point of reference for beliefs, values, norms, and interpretations associated with the workplace. This tendency leads to the creation of shared patterns of thinking and behaving. Electrical engineers, for example, share a keen interest in keeping their technical skills honed, and they form networks of colleagues who help each other find jobs that maximize their opportunity for learning. Finally, there is often a blurring of the distinction between work and leisure in these occupational communities; members not only work together, they often socialize and play together as well.

At times, an occupational or professional group may evolve to become a **community of practice**—an occupational or professional network that shares a worldview and a group identity, engages in interpretive sense-making, and develops shared adaptive responses to environmental challenges. Such communities typically work together on common tasks and collaborate in solving task-related problems. Information needed to solve problems is communicated openly within the network. Knowledge is readily available to insiders, particularly to newcomers who assume the role of apprentices. Individual learning in the network is contingent on group learning; the individual learns as the group learns, and vice versa.

Xerox Corporation's Palo Alto Research Center (Xerox PARC) is a well-known community of practice. Xerox Corporation employs a large cadre of repair technicians who perform client services in the field to keep the company's photocopy machines in good working order. The repair technicians receive formal technical training focused on the mechanical aspects of the equipment, and they also learn diagnostic procedures that allow them to troubleshoot and repair machines. It is generally acknowledged that their training is not sufficient to allow them any substantial knowledge of how a photocopier actually works.

Although the technicians competently handled the vast majority of repair calls, Xerox management was worried, and the company created an information system of "directive documentation" that supposedly would enable faster resolution of problems in the field. The documentation includes set-up and repair procedures, simplified schematic diagrams, and diagnostic methods with a decision tree that describes a series of actions in considerable detail. This diagnostic methodology was cumbersome to use, and it did not enhance the technician's learning because it did not provide a rationale for the actions described in the decision tree. Technicians were uncomfortable with it, primarily because it did not allow them to provide customers with a clear explanation of how a problem was solved. Thus, while technicians might refer to the documentation during the course of a repair call, they often put it aside and proceeded with diagnosis on their own.

Wondering how the technicians managed to be so successful in machine repair despite ignoring the documentation, Xerox deployed anthropologist Julian Orr (1990) to travel with them. Orr soon discovered their secret. When technicians ran into machine failures that could not be resolved with standard diagnostic procedures, they relied on tools that the company knew nothing about. The most potent was a form of storytelling in which technicians shared "war stories" about past machine failures and heroic saves. They swapped these war stories at lunch, on coffee breaks, in training sessions, and during off-duty socializing. They liked to tell stories about their problem-solving heroics because they gained status on the basis of technical prowess. The more difficult the problem, the more status gained by telling a story about solving it. The stories also helped other technicians learn how the machines operate, thus enhancing the technicians' knowledge base. The tendency to share problem-solving information freely within the group is a key characteristic of a community of practice. It is an important way in which communities of practice contribute to an organization's knowledge assets.

Once Xerox found out how technicians solved difficult machine problems, they decided to facilitate and enhance this grassroots approach by equipping technicians with mobile radio phones that would enable them to call each other in the field and contact a roving "tiger team" of highly skilled troubleshooters. Technicians willingly adopted the radio phones, not only because they were compatible with their preferred practices, but also because the phones provided greater opportunity to connect personally with other people while on the job, frequently on job-related matters. This example illustrates one of the primary reasons an occupational culture adopts or rejects a new technology.

By their very nature, occupational and professional cultures tend to orient their members inward, toward the shared understandings and practices of the group. These understandings and practices are defined by the type of work the members do and the developmental processes within the occupation or profession. The understandings and practices of different occupations and professions are often very different, and they may conflict with one another. Frank Dubinskas (1988) used the term **Janus organizations** to describe genetic engineering companies with two conflicting professional faces. Laboratory scientists with backgrounds in academic research and entrepreneurial executives with backgrounds in management and finance had to collaborate closely in order to make their companies successful despite their lack of knowledge about one another's profession. Specifically, they needed to work together to plan and deliver marketable products that would make good on large venture capital investments before their investors and creditors pulled the rug out from under them.

The laboratory scientists and the executives often did not see eye-to-eye on matters critical to effective project planning. Differences in the two professions' conceptions of time were especially problematic. Executives were driven by relatively short-term time horizons, especially their need to provide quarterly financial reports to investors. Investors wanted to know what the stages of the work were and when each stage was expected to be completed. They also wanted explanations when a goal was not met, and they needed to be convinced that future goals were realistic. The executives said they had no time for long-range planning. Scientists, on the other hand, said they could see distant and indistinct goals. They believed that an open-ended temporal frame was appropriate for science, which cannot unravel the puzzles of nature in a planned time sequence. From their point of view, there was no fixed end in view; science is an endless horizon. The scientists devalued the quest for commercial success and monetary gain, and they believed that the managers were shortsighted. As a result of these differences, the executives and scientists had difficulty understanding one another and experienced conflict when trying to develop business plans. Such conflicts are often at the root of failure in start-up firms.

Not all occupations and professions conflict with one another because they have different points of view. Occupational and professional communities sometimes develop cooperative relationships that contribute to mutual goals. For example, managers in large automobile manufacturing corporations may develop close **exchange relationships** with design engineers who work for smaller companies that supply materials or parts. In such cases, each professional group has something that the other needs; the managers have work contracts that provide income to the smaller firm, while the smaller companies' engineers have technical expertise that the managers need to obtain high-quality components. Relationships like these involve high levels of trust that enable professionals in the two firms to cooperate beyond the exact letter of the contract that binds their companies. For example, engineers in the small firm may provide free consultation about equipment or other material purchases. In some cases, the firms may even exchange people; when managers retire from the larger company, the smaller company can hire them to help maintain the ongoing relationship. Just as in traditional societies, economic exchange in organizations is embedded in social relationships of cooperation and trust, and it is difficult to determine where the social ends and the economic begins.

Individual members of an occupational or professional community often switch their orientation from one culture to another and back again, thereby providing a mechanism for integration across the organization. For example, a Japanese American engineering manager named Hiro holds membership in two professional communities (engineering and management) and one ethnic community (Japanese American), and he can orient his behavior toward any one culture at specific times and places based on contextual factors and individual choice. Thus, he may behave more as a manager in a meeting convened to pressure engineers to make cost reductions in their component designs. At a lecture at the research laboratories, however, Hiro may sound more like an engineer when he asks technical questions. Later that evening, he may again shift his orientation by speaking Japanese at a traditional dinner hosted by a Japanese American professional network in his company.

Hiro's different cultural hats may create headaches for him at times, as when his managerial role requires him to give a negative performance evaluation to a Japanese American engineer in his work group. They can also help him reduce tensions in the company. His engineering identity helps him understand why the engineers in his group disagree with decisions made by higher-levels managers, and his managerial identity lets him help other Japanese Americans in the firm to improve their career opportunities.

All of us are multicultural to a greater or lesser extent. The capacity to **code switch**—to shift cultural perspective and use different sets of symbols to communicate-is one of the ways integration is achieved in large-scale organizations. Individuals with diverse cultural identities can facilitate cooperation among different occupational, professional, and other types of cultural groups through their ability to understand, translate, and negotiate across divergent cultural worldviews.

The "Dilbert" cartoon that shows a manager being "bungeed" into Dilbert's department depicts a common point of tension between higher-level managers on the one hand and lower-level managers and employees on the other. The occupational culture of managers strongly values upward mobility

DILBERT reprinted by permission of United Features Syndicate, Inc.

within an organization. Managers are rewarded by being promoted to higher levels, and staying too long in one place is taken as a negative signal. In other words, failure to be promoted means failure. Managers who are being groomed for top positions are often moved very quickly from one assignment to another, both to expose them to different parts of the company and to signal that they are on the fast track to higher responsibility. This practice enables managers to believe that they know about the entire organization. It also facilitates retention of top talent, since a manager on the way up is unlikely to look for another job.

In American organizations, however, the fast track is at odds with the tendency of managers to "make their mark" by ordering significant changes in their departments or divisions. This reflects the American emphasis on rewarding individual achievement. A manager who wants to be noticed and rewarded must stand out from the crowd, and one way to do this is to make big changes. A fast-track manager may spend only a few months in a unit and thus not really know enough to make sound changes or not be around long enough to experience the consequences. Workers, on the other hand, may spend their much of their working lives in one part of the organization, so they may know much more about it than does the fast-track manager. They also have to live with the consequences of changes ordered by the bungee boss. The manager may not consult the workers prior to making changes since managers are supposed to know more than workers. This dynamic sets up a conflict between the bungee boss and the workers, and the workers expect the manager's effect to be temporary and probably negative.

QUESTION 8.4
How Does Organizational Culture Affect Human Performance and Social Control?

Cultural patterns and processes can influence the functioning and long-term well-being of a social group. Culture shapes people's interactions with one another and with the environment, and such interaction is critical to any group's capacity to sustain itself. The shared patterns of understanding and practice in a company influence employee motivation and morale, interactions with suppliers and customers, internal cooperation across units, and the ability of the organization to adapt and change in response to environmental shifts. As a result, organizational culture is a critical dimension of business performance that managers cannot ignore.

The U.S. business community was introduced to the idea that organizational culture can have a powerful effect on a company's success in *In Search of Excellence* (Peters and Waterman 1982) and a number of other best-selling management books written by business consultants. These books theorized that there was an ideal type of culture that consistently produced increases in sales and profits beyond what other firms in the same industry were earning. Deal and Kennedy (1982) claimed, for example, that companies with the "right" culture could expect one to two additional hours of productive work from employees every day.

One influential idea that emerged from these books was the notion that strong corporate cultures have the ability to generate superior business performance. *Strong culture* was defined as consensual and voluntary conformity to a system of shared behaviors and values, so that employees work toward common goals. The reasoning behind this idea was that voluntary conformity to shared goals would make a stifling formal bureaucracy of control unnecessary. Also, it was reasoned, a strong culture contributes to employee motivation. Employees who share goals are better able to see themselves as members of an exclusive club, and people tend to work harder for something they are a part of.

The notion of a strong corporate culture is a modern expression of the old sociological idea of **normative control**. Normative control is a subtle and often invisible means of influencing an individual's behavior that can be more effective than overt economic incentives or punitive sanctions. The idea is that an individual internalizes the social group's norms and values and enforces them through self-discipline. Self-discipline works all the time, not only when a supervisor is watching. Harnessing the "zone of discretion" enjoyed by all human beings—that part of our life where we are unobserved and uncontrolled—is thus thought to become an opportunity for pursuit of the organization's best interests, thereby supposedly yielding results superior to those achieved by an alienated workforce that has to be monitored and policed constantly. Those who support the use of normative control as a management tool see it as a way to reduce **anomie** (normlessness) and contribute to the development of human potential; the individual whose interests merge with those of the group finds opportunity and support for self-actualization. Others fear that normative control is a more subtle and thus more dangerous form of tyranny in which people are controlled not in body, but in mind and soul. The debate over normative control has intensified with increased interest in organizational culture.

Gideon Kunda (1992) explored the nature of normative control in his ethnography of the engineering division of a high-technology company that he called Tech. The engineers at Tech were legendary for their obsessive dedication to work. Many worked late into the night and on weekends for months or even years at a time. These engineers claimed to love their work so much that they were grateful for the opportunity to dedicate themselves to new technology development and volunteered to work overtime. Some worked so hard that they burned out, became alcoholics who could no longer cope with the pressure, and had to take less cutting-edge roles or leave the company. These engineers were viewed as people who had sacrificed themselves for Tech, another sign of voluntary commitment.

What surprised Kunda was the apparent lack of overt control. On the surface, the workplace appeared disorganized and chaotic. An accurate organizational chart was virtually impossible to find because the organizational structure constantly changed as engineers moved from one work group to another in support of new technology projects. Engineers had a great deal of autonomy to come and go as they pleased and to take their careers in various directions depending on individual ability and interest. One manager told Kunda:

> The guys up here are independent and ambitious. They are working on state-of-the-art stuff—really neat things. Everyone, including the president, has a finger in the pot. The group is potentially a revenue generator. That they are committed there is no doubt. But they are unmanageable. . . . Power plays don't work. You can't make 'em do anything. They have to want to. So you have to work through the culture. The idea is to educate them without them ever knowing it. Have the religion and not know how they ever got it. [1992:4–5]

According to Tech's managers, the company's culture was the primary means by which engineers' talents were harnessed for the corporate good. Virtually all of the managers had been practicing engineers in the past, and they were convinced that they had created a culture that engineers could embrace. Embracing the culture meant enmeshing individual interests with the interests of the corporation. In fact, the culture was a managerially constructed definition of the engineer's role in the company, and it included guidance on appropriate ways to behave, to think, and, most importantly, to feel. Management spent considerable time developing, articulating, and disseminating it through an explicit organizational ideology that portrayed Tech as morally sound, honest, people-oriented, humane, and in the business of making a contribution to society through the development of advanced technology. These ideological principles were embodied in specific policies and practices that aimed at normative, rather than bureaucratic, control. For example, everyone was supposed to behave in a manner that reduced hierarchy, meaning in part that engineers were supposed to be able to walk into the offices of higher-level managers to talk about problems. The ideology thus signaled that Tech was a good company worthy of an engineer's loyalty and devotion.

Formal statements about the culture were ubiquitous in the Tech environment; e-mail messages, newsletters, posters, videos, and training sessions continuously reinforced the ideology. For example, video monitors frequently replayed an image of Tech's chief executive officer delivering the "We Are One" speech in which he elaborated on the theme that the individual and the corporation were inseparable. Managers also frequently invoked the ideology in meetings, and engineers were subtly pressured to use emotion-laden words such as *pride, loyalty, excitement, fun,* and *ownership* to describe their feelings about being a Tech engineer. Public displays of deviance, for example, from a burned-out engineer, were countered with silence or ridicule. When sanctioned behaviors like dedicating one's free time to work resulted in success, the engineers were rewarded with salary increases, promotions, and greater authority. The higher an engineer advanced on the career ladder, the more he was expected to openly and genuinely endorse the culture and to forego displays of autonomy or cultural criticism that were permitted among lower-level engineers. That such critical displays were permitted at all was pointed to by managers as evidence of the culture's benign nature.

Kunda concluded that, over time, engineers were submerged in an environment dominated by an engineered culture of normative control. Eventually, the individual engineer's life was monopolized by the corporation, and establishing an independent life became increasing difficult, if not impossible. Although the engineers of Tech enjoyed the fruits of capitalism, the price was a loss of autonomy and a diminished life outside the corporate sphere. Kunda worried that people in this kind of situation would also be diminished as citizens and as human beings.

While Kunda's ethnography is a chilling vision of human experience inside a modern American corporation, it is not without limitations. Kunda focused attention on the managers' self-proclaimed cultural engineering practices, and he did not delve too deeply into the collective lives of the practicing engineers. In effect, Kunda described the culture of engineering management at Tech, not the culture of engineering per se. Managerial culture is all about control, so it is no surprise that engineering managers believed they were controlling the engineers through a culture that the managers themselves engineered. We would expect that the engineers had created and maintained their own professional engineering culture and enjoyed some degree of autonomy despite managerial intentions. Dedication to work is a characteristic of many professional cultures. That Tech was able to provide a work environment that sustained the engineers' pursuit of their technological passion does not need to be interpreted solely as a manipulative form of normative control. Tech managers had been engineers at one point in their careers, and they created an environment engineers could be passionate about. This is not necessarily a bad thing.

Quantitative research on strong culture ultimately revealed that conformity to collective values, norms, and behavior cannot in and of itself guarantee superior financial performance (see Kotter and Heskett 1992). The organization's ability to adapt to environmental change has been found to be even more significant. An environmental shift, such as a change in customer preferences, may mean that people in a strong culture are all marching in the wrong direction. Sometimes it turns out that the very individuals who deviate from the confines of normative control are the ones who point the way to a new future.

QUESTION 8.5
How Do Anthropologists Study Culture in Organizations, and What Ethical Issues Are Involved?

To study culture in organizations, anthropologists modify the concepts and methods of cultural anthropology to work within an organizational context. These concepts and methods distinguish the anthropological approach and represent the value added to the study of organizations by anthropology.

Direct Observation in a Field Setting

Anthropology is a natural science like biology or astronomy in the sense that it seeks to directly observe subjects in their natural environment, rather than in a laboratory or an anthropology office. This is what is meant by **naturalistic inquiry**. Anthropologists want to observe and record what is really going on, rather than take someone else's word for it or rely on written reports. Data from other sources suffer from biases introduced by an artificial environment; only observation enables comprehension of actual behavior under real-life conditions.

Anthropologists nearly always spend considerable time in the field. In the case of organizational anthropology, this means spending time on the site of the company they are studying. The amount of time an anthropologist can spend in the field is determined by the nature of the study and its objectives. Organizations are often reluctant to allow researchers to distract employees for long periods of time, particularly if the researchers are not working on a problem of direct interest to the organization. The budget for a study may not be sufficient to permit long periods of direct observation, and the anthropologist may need to use "rapid sounding" techniques to efficiently capture relevant data in a few weeks or even days (see van Willigen and Finan 1991). In some cases, organizations may permit anthropologists to spend several months or even a year or more inside their facilities, especially if the study pertains directly to resolution of organizational problems.

Focus on Operations-level Activities and People

Anthropologists generally are most interested in what is happening on the "ground floor" of an organization. Instead of spending most of their research time talking with high-level managers and experts, anthropologists generally spend most of their time in operations, often talking to entry-level or other nonmanagerial employees. There are two reasons for this anthropological bias. One is that anthropologists are interested in documenting in detail how an organization actually functions. They want to know in concrete terms how employees get things done, what resources they use, how they interact with others, and what barriers they encounter. This can only be done by a detailed mapping of work activity, which requires a focus on work operations rather than the executive suite.

Secondly, managers and executives frequently have a distorted or incomplete view of what is happening "on the ground." They may rarely go to the places where work gets done, and they often rely on other people's reports. Generally, only the people at the operational sites really understand how work gets done in the organization, and this is what the anthropologist wants to find out. Anthropologists may draw work-process maps, take photographs, and even make videos to capture detailed workflow information. Such data are used to understand the nature of an organization's culture, since routine work practices embed shared understandings and relationships, and to understand the sources of problems in an organization.

Local Knowledge and the Insider's Point of View

Anthropologists not only focus on the operational details of an organization; they also value the knowledge held by working people within these operations. From classical studies of culture in traditional societies, anthropologists have come to realize that people in a local area often possess specialized knowledge about plants, animals, natural resources, and their own or others' cultures that can be quite valuable from a scientific or commercial standpoint. Ethnopharmacology, for instance, applies some of the knowledge indigenous peoples have about the medicinal uses of plants in order to create medicines commercially available to all. Likewise, anthropologists studying organizations have discovered that members of work groups possess informal, undocumented, and unspoken knowledge of how to make equipment or processes operate more efficiently, how to solve problems, and how to get things done. "Native theories" that explain certain issues or problems from the standpoint of the people working inside an operational area have proven to be useful in the resolution of problems and improvement of operations; indeed, Japanese quality improvement methods are based on obtaining input from workers.

Local knowledge pertaining to operations develops over long periods of time within occupational communities that need to get work done despite many kinds of obstacles and resource constraints. The Xerox repair technicians discussed earlier are an example. Members of these communities create localized knowledge by trial and error, exchange knowledge with their coworkers, and pass it on to newcomers. Management may know nothing of these activities. Recently, management scholars and practitioners have become interested in this type of local knowledge, which is now being viewed as an organizational asset, and in the possibility of formalizing and appropriating it for use elsewhere in the organization. This interest has created new opportunities for anthropologists to conduct research inside organizations.

Historic, Holistic, and Comparative Perspectives

Other important hallmarks of anthropological research in organizations are the historical analysis of organizations, a **holistic** approach to human behavior, and cross-cultural comparison. Since the cultures of an organization emerge from its historical experience, understanding the organization's history can provide many insights into cultural patterns that might otherwise remain invisible or inexplicable. This was seen in the comparison of the cultures of General Motors and Ford earlier in the chapter. Anthropologists often access archival material or oral histories to identify critical events in an organization's past and to obtain clues about how past events were interpreted and used to guide actions.

Anthropologists also tend to expand their field of study beyond the narrow confines of a research question or problem to encompass multiple dimensions of people's lives. Examples include the special language or jargon of the workplace, the influence of work on home life, and the influence of external communities on places of employment. In his Yankee City studies, for example, W. Lloyd Warner showed that it was necessary to take economic and technological changes and the reaction of the community to those changes into account in order to understand an unusually long and bitter strike at a shoe-making factory (Warner and Low 1946). Casting a wide net to gather and analyze data often turns up hidden factors that influence behavior on the job.

Cross-cultural comparisons are also of high utility. Anthropologists may compare and contrast organizational behaviors across national cultures, across industries, across organizations in the same industry, or across sub-units in the same organization. Comparison helps illustrate the wide range of possible ways to organize virtually anything in an organization, and it also helps to illuminate the influence of otherwise intangible forces such as national culture.

Gaining Access

One of the most difficult aspects of conducting anthropological studies in organizations is the problem of access. Anthropologists need to get inside to do their work, but most organizations are very reluctant to let in outsiders who could distract employees' attention, reduce productivity, and possibly leak proprietary or damaging information to competitors or the public. Refusal to grant access to researchers has been an important barrier to advances in our knowledge of organizations.

Generally speaking, an anthropologist who is working on a problem of critical importance to the organization has a much better chance of gaining access. Whether such problem-oriented research is supported by a public agency such as the National Science Foundation or by the company itself through a consulting contract, corporations may be eager to have anthropologists investigate problems that are affecting their profitability. Such research often involves exploring the cultural dimensions of strategic issues—such as developing better relations with customers and suppliers, improving performance after a merger or acquisition, recruiting and retaining top technical talent, or implementing major new information technologies. Anthropologists must often work in collaboration with managers, and possibly with employees, to support the implementation of significant changes in policies, structures, processes, and skills. Successful implementation requires an understanding of existing cultures and their role in strategic initiatives. The anthropologist may also be asked to make recommendations about how the company can be more successful in implementing its strategy given current cultural realities.

The fact that anthropologists may have to engage in useful problem-oriented research in order to gain access does not mean that they cannot explore fundamental disciplinary questions. Frequently, plans for an investigation will call for basic research in areas where little is known or has been published. For example, globally distributed teams are new in corporate experience, so if a company wanted to find out how to make its teams more effective, it would be necessary to do basic research on how such teams are structured, how they operate, and how organizational cultures evolves when people of many different national cultures work together. This is especially true for research projects that are funded by such public agencies as the National Science Foundation. When this is the case, anthropologists may be able to publish all or part of their findings after ensuring that identities are protected and after the organization reviews a draft manuscript and requests modification to protect sensitive information. It might be necessary, for example, to disguise additional details such as the industry in which the work was conducted, or to omit proprietary or confidential information.

Ethical Considerations

Some anthropologists worry that research in organizations can create ethical dilemmas, especially if the research is focused on specific problems and/or is supported by the organization though an employment or consulting contract. Of particular concern is the possibility that the organization's management or others could pressure the anthropologist to divulge confidential information learned in observations or interviews that could damage individuals or work groups.

These concerns must be taken seriously. The American Anthropological Association's code of professional conduct provides guidelines for ethical decision-making in organizational research (available at http://www.ameran-thassn.org). The code clearly states that subjects must be protected through the confidentiality of data. All anthropologists working in organizations are expected to review this stipulation with organizational representatives prior to beginning fieldwork and to obtain guarantees that:

1. All employee participation in the research will be voluntary.
2. The anthropologist will own all of the data collected.
3. Data will be stored off-site.
4. No data that reveal individual identities will be divulged.
5. No secret or covert research will be conducted.

Anthropologists must also obtain the informed consent of participants, which means that they are required to provide organizational members with sufficient information about the research to enable each individual to make an informed decision about participation. Organizational managers nearly always understand the logic behind anthropological ethics, and they also realize that they must respect the ethical codes of professionals working in their organizations. In the great majority of cases, anthropologists' ethical obligations are not challenged.

A few anthropologists are so concerned about the potential for ethical difficulties that they choose to forego the knowledge and benefits that could be obtained from organizational research. This point of view fails to acknowledge that all anthropological research involves ethical challenges. All anthropologists elicit knowledge from people and use it to enhance their professional careers. If they do not exchange something of value to the people being studied for this appropriated knowledge, there may be the perception or actual danger of exploitation. Many anthropologists believe that such exploitation is just as serious an ethical issue as confidentiality or intervention.

Anthropologists working in organizations have found that they can exchange the knowledge they appropriate for something of value to the people being studied. For example, employees can give anthropologists permission to transmit information to managers who might otherwise never have an opportunity to hear employee voices. Anthropologists can explain problems from the employees' point of view and can promote solutions proposed by employees. The knowledge gained through anthropological inquiry thus can be harnessed to improve the quality of working life inside the organization, which may also contribute to improvements in organizational products and services.

When anthropologists gain key insights that lead to advances in organizational theory, they are contributing to the future design and operation of all organizations, thereby having a positive effect on society as a whole. Most organizational anthropologists believe that the value they can bring to an organization and its people outweighs the potential risks. The greater risk, both to the organizations in question and to anthropology, would be to ignore the millions of people and the cultures they create inside organizations.

CONCLUSIONS

Large-scale organizations are important features of the modern cultural landscape and shape much of what we do. There is ample evidence that many large organizations are plagued by seemingly irrational practices that waste human potential and other valuable resources. Anthropologists have found that such practices reflect cultural patterns that can be studied and understood using concepts and methods employed in ethnographic investigation of more remote societies.

The existence of organizational culture was first discovered through the application of anthropological concepts and ethnographic methods in the Hawthorne study during the early 1930s. Workers in the Hawthorne plant were found to share a distinctive set of ideas and practices that led them to withhold the extra production that management desired. Managers did not understand the reasons behind workers' reluctance to produce more, and instead saw the workers as poorly educated and incapable of economic rationality. The workers and managers were members of distinctive occupational cultures that reflected differing and conflicting interests and perspectives. Such organizational cultures arise spontaneously through their members' efforts to achieve individual and social goals.

The national culture in which a firm is grounded shapes the patterns of behavior and thought found within that organization. Ethnographic research in a Japanese bank revealed the ways in which Japanese culture is reflected in the bank's educational practices. These practices can be contrasted with those of Silicon Valley firms, which reflect American culture. Despite the importance of national culture in shaping organizational behavior, the organizations based in any country also display cultural variability among themselves. This results from differences in organizational learning experiences as well as differences in industry structure, technology, and the historical period in which a firm was founded.

Occupational and professional cultures also have a profound influence on human behavior in organizations. Members of an occupational culture share a common identity that defines their self-image, and they accept other members of their group as reference points for beliefs, values, and behaviors. At times, an occupational culture may evolve to become a community of practice in which members share knowledge and collaborate in problem-solving activity. Ethnographic research at Xerox demonstrated the importance of collective knowledge-sharing and problem-solving within the community of repair technicians. Members of different occupational communities may compete and contend with one another, causing difficulties in achieving organizational goals, or they may cooperate and collaborate on the basis of mutual interest. The fact that many individuals belong to more than one occupational community within an organization and can switch their orientation from one community to another at will serves as a means of organizational integration.

The influence of organizational culture on business performance has been of keen interest to organizational theorists and practitioners. One hypothesis suggests that strong culture, in which there is a high degree of conformity to corporate values, norms, and behaviors, is a critical ingredient in high performance. This hypothesis draws on the sociological notion of normative control—that people can internalize the beliefs, values, and norms of a social group and enforce them through self-discipline. Such internal control is more effective in aligning individuals around group goals than external forms of control such as incentives or supervision, since internal control is more consistently enforced and less costly. The dangers of normative control include the potential for exploitation, burnout, and loss of autonomy, as illustrated by ethnographic research on a high-technology firm known for its strong culture. Quantitative research on culture and performance suggests that strong normative control is not sufficient to ensure high performance. Rather, the ability to adapt to environmental change, which often requires some degree of independence from group thinking, has been shown to be more critical to success over the long term.

Some of the hallmarks of organizational ethnography include direct observation in a field setting, a focus on operations-level activities and people, a search for local knowledge and the insider's point of view, and historic, holistic, and comparative perspectives. Two key issues involved in studying organizations are the problems of gaining access and dealing with ethical dilemmas. Access often is very difficult to arrange unless the anthropologist is willing to offer something of value in exchange, such as work addressing organizational problems. Regardless of whether the anthropologist is doing strictly academic research or problem-oriented research, it is imperative to review guidelines for the ethical conduct of research with organizational sponsors or clients and to get their acceptance. Anthropologists must put safeguards in place to protect the identity of informants and the confidentiality of data, to ensure informed consent by all participants, and to return something of value to the people involved in a study.

REFERENCES AND RECOMMENDED READINGS

Applebaum, Herbert
1981 Royal Blue: The Culture of Construction Workers. New York: Holt, Rinehart, and Winston.
>   A classic ethnography of an occupational community in the "anthropology of work" tradition.

Baba, Marietta
1995 The Cultural Ecology of the Corporation. Journal of Applied Behavioral Science 31(2):202–233.
>   An exploration of cultural diversity in a large manufacturing organization, with an emphasis on different occupational cultures and their interactions during strategic change.

Briody, Elizabeth, and Marietta Baba
1991 Explaining Differences in Repatriation Experiences: The Discovery of Coupled and Decoupled Systems. American Anthropologist 93:322–344.
> A study of management culture in a large corporation that focuses on conflict of managers in different divisions of the company and the effects of this conflict on professionals' taking overseas assignments.

Britan, G., and R. Cohen
1980 Hierarchy and Society: Anthropological Perspectives on Bureaucracy. Philadelphia: Philadelphia Institute for the Study of Human Issues.
> A reader examining the culture of organizational bureaucracies inside in the United States, China, Ethiopia, and Nigeria.

Frost, Peter, L. F. Moore, M. R. Louis, C. C. Lundberg, and J. Martin
1991 Reframing Organizational Culture. Newbury Park: Sage Publications.
> A reader covering key theoretical and methodological issues in the study of organizational culture.

Gregory, Kathleen
1983 Native-view Paradigms: Multiple Cultures and Culture Conflict in Organizations. Administrative Science Quarterly 28:359–376.
> Multiple cultures and their interactions in Silicon Valley firms.

Hamada, Tomoko
1995 Inventing Cultural Others in Organizations: A Case of Anthropological Reflexivity in a Multinational Firm. Journal of Applied Behavioral Science 31(2):162–185.
> Shifting identities and cultural orientations in a Japanese-owned plant based in the United States.

Hofstede, Geert
1984 Culture's Consequences: International Differences in Work Related Values. Beverly Hills, CA: Sage Publications.
> A study of differences in work culture and values across 40 nations, utilizing survey data gathered in a large global corporation.

Schein, E. H.
1991 Organizational Culture and Leadership: A Dynamic View. 2nd ed. San Francisco: Jossey-Bass.
> A now-classic work on the role of organizational founders in creating cultural patterns in organizations, written by a leading organizational psychologist.

Smirchich, Linda
1983 Concepts of Culture and Organizational Analysis. Administrative Science Quarterly 28:339–358.
> A theoretical paper that distinguishes between concepts of culture developed in anthropology and those utilized by management scholars and business practitioners.

Additional References Cited

Adams, Scott
1996 The Dilbert Principle. New York: Harper Business.

Deal, Terrence E., and Allen A. Kennedy
1982 Corporate Culture: Rites and Rituals of Corporate Life. Reading, MA: Addison-Wesley.

Dubinskas, Frank
1988 Ethnographies of High Technology Organizations. Philadelphia: Temple University Press.

Kotter, John P., and James L. Heskett
1992 Corporate Culture and Performance. New York: Free Press.

Kunda, Gideon.
1992 Engineering Culture: Control and Commitment in a High-tech Corporation. Philadelphia: Temple University Press.

Orr, Julian
1990 Sharing Knowledge, Celebrating Identity: War Stories and Community Memory Among Service Technicians. *In* Collective Remembering: Memory in Society. D. S. Middleton and D. Edwards, eds. London: Sage Publications, Ltd.

Peters, Thomas J., and Robert H. Waterman
1982 In Search of Excellence: Lessons from America's Best Run Companies. New York: Harper and Row.

Rohlen, Thomas
1974 For Harmony and Strength: Japanese White Collar Organization in Anthropological Perspective. Berkeley: University of California Press.

Van Maanen, J., and S. Barley
1984 Occupational Communities: Culture and Control in Organizations. *In* Research in Organizational Behavior. B. M. Straw and L. L. Cummings, eds. Greenwich, CT: JAI Press.

Van Willigen, John, and Timothy Finan, eds.
1991 Soundings: Rapid and Reliable Research Methods for Practicing Anthropologists. Washington, DC: American Anthropological Association.

Warner, W. Lloyd, and J. O. Low
1946 The Factory in the Community. *In* Industry and Society. William Foote Whyte, ed. Pp. 21–45. New York: McGraw-Hill.

CHAPTER 9

THE ORAL LITERATURES
OF
SMALL NATIONS

DONALD M. BAHR

PROBLEM 9 *Why do peoples put and not put things in their oral literatures?*

INTRODUCTION
The Pima-Papago and Their Oral Literature

The Pima-Papago live in the desert of southern Arizona and Sonora, Mexico. They call themselves *O'odham,* meaning true humans or true people. The word *Pima* comes from a phrase in their language, *Pi iñ-ma:c*,[1] which means "I do not know." The old-timers say this is how their ancestors answered questions asked by the first Spaniards who arrived 400 years ago, and the Spaniards took that response to be the tribe's name.

The Pima-Papago divide themselves into *Akimel* (river) and *Tohono* (desert) people. *Papago* comes from the expression *Babawi O'odham* (tepary-bean people), which is what the Pima *O'odham* who lived along rivers called those who lived in the drier desert where only the tepary bean would grow. Actually, all the Pima-Papago lived in a desert, and they were all sophisticated agriculturalists as well as hunters and gatherers. They grew crops on the basis of a short season of summer thunderstorms, but those near a river did so with more confidence and could stay in their villages through the year. The desert or bean *O'odham* tended to move to high rocky areas with water springs in the winter. Conventionally, the river people have been called the Pima and the desert people the Papago, but they shared a culture and a language, with only local dialect variations, so I call them all Pima-Papago.

---

[1]The colon in this word indicates a lengthened vowel.

This chapter concerns what the Pima-Papago said and preserved in their language about themselves and the universe. Because their method of preservation was memory, they could not keep very much—more than we memorize, but much less than is in the books in a small-town library. What they kept was their literature. Literature is both more and less than what one says in speech; it is what one says and keeps, either in writing or in memory that is the "more." It is less because one knows and says far more than one keeps in memory or in writing. Literature kept in memory is **oral literature**, and that is the only literature the old *O'odham* had. In that regard they were like thousands of other **small nations** (tribes or bands) of a few thousand souls with no writing and no central government, who for most of human history were the only people there were and who, incidentally, were anthropology's first subject matter.

The desert home of the Pima-Papago is along the line where Arizona and Mexico meet and is nearly identical with the range of the giant green candelabra-shaped saguaro cactus. Between 1600 and 1853, the land belonged to Spain and Mexico. Spain and Mexico made settlements on what had been Pima-Papago land in today's state of Sonora, Mexico, but the area in Arizona occupied by today's Pima-Papago was not settled. Arizona was the frontier; it was too far from the heartland of New Spain and Mexico. It was *Ningun Parte en el Desierto* (nowhere in the desert) as far as Spain and Mexico were concerned. The Pima-Papago were left alone.

The Pima-Papago were generally friendly with the Spanish and Mexicans (unlike some of their neighbors, such as the Apache and Yavapai). They worked for them in Sonora and in California, which was not settled by Spain until the 1770s. But Spain and later Mexico could not offer them much materially nor demand much from them, nor could they demand much from Spain and Mexico. From what we can tell from archaeology and the scant written records, their housing, cooking, and family life did not change much during this period.

The Pima-Papago learned of Christianity. They sought baptism and got Spanish names. The result, to outsiders, looked like something new—a form of folk Catholicism called Sonoran Catholicism, with every household having its own shrine—and the continuation of what seems to be something very old—the traditional songs, stories, and ceremonies of the people. To them, it was all one thing, an example of what anthropologists call **syncretism**, the blending of cultures.

One reason that this fusing of ideas and practice took place with apparent ease is that, like colonial Spanish culture, Pima-Papago culture and literature were not secular. Both peoples understood causation in spiritual terms. Crops grew to maturity because people conducted ceremonies and the rains came. Human beings were not seen as a product of biological evolution, but rather as the product of the action of God or gods. In the language of anthropology, which itself possesses a secular perspective, both the Pima-Papago and the Spanish had a **sacred worldview**, in contrast to the **secular worldview** characteristic of Western civilization and academia in general. *Secular* means using naturalistic mechanisms for explanations rather than using God or other spiritual entities. It is not that anthropologists or others with a secular worldview cannot dream, or use their traditions, or believe in God, but that they do not use these as explanatory principles.

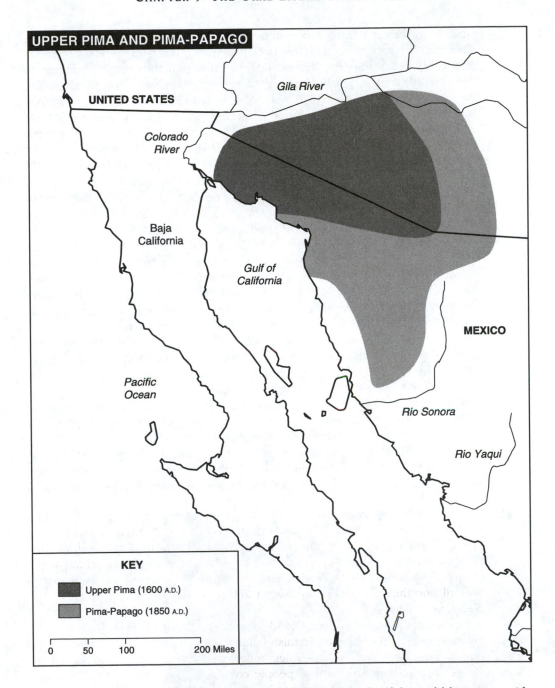

The Pima-Papago have by now replaced much of their old literature with American forms, but the replacements are no closer to secularism than were the old-timers' texts. Now the people buy and play tapes and videos, but the American things they memorize and perform are mainly Spanish and English hymns, some of which have been translated into *O'odham*, and all kinds of popular music, especially rock, country and western, Tex-Mex, and reggae. Stressing God and miracles on the one hand, and luck, destiny, and magical power on the other, these are not very secular.

We do not know with certainty about Pima-Papago intellectual and spiritual life in the early historic period because, from the scientific point of view, there are not good records. They had their own records in the form of songs and other oral traditions, but we do not know whether those traditions of 1900, which are the oldest documented, were the same as those of, say, 1600, which were undocumented in writing. It is reasonable to assume that they always had the same kinds of oral literature (prose, oratory, and song), and that the purposes and compositional principles of those forms remained the same, but the details probably changed as new ideas came along.

By contrast, the Anglo-Americanization of the land that began in 1853 transformed their material life and ultimately drew the Pima-Papago into new ways of thought. The United States brought peace to the region, which meant that the wars and raiding between the Pima-Papago and their Yavapai and Apache neighbors had ended by about 1880. The United States also brought windmills and well drilling, so the desert peoples' villages could be lived in year round and all Pima-Papago could use mud as a building material (formerly they did not, seemingly because water was too precious). The *O'odham* promptly built adobe houses, churches, and feast houses where on feast days or for Protestant revivals (in recent decades) they served free Mexican-style dinners to all who came: white yeast bread, chili con carne, bone-and-vegetable soup, beans, salad, coffee or tea, and dessert. Thus their architecture and village and festival life were not so much Americanized as Mexicanized, but by their choice and made possible by the U.S.-imposed peace. During much of this time, their oral literary life and their sense of who they were remained strongly *O'odham*. They had Spanish prayers and knowledge of the saints, God, and the Devil, but they ran their own folk Catholic churches and kept up with their old Native, non-Christian religious life.

By the 1940s their children attended schools, mainly taking the school bus in the morning and coming home on it in the afternoon. By the 1960s nearly everyone had cars or trucks, and good roads reached every village. By the 1970s

A painting by Michael Chiago showing a traditional Tohono O'odham ceremony.
(Photograph by courtesy of Donald Bahr.)

nearly all had electricity and clean water piped into their houses. And during this time the oral literature and non-Christian religion lost much of its force.

Why did this happen? The Protestant missionaries preached against the oral literature and all traditional practices; the Catholics did not like them; and the schools had no use for them.[2] Of course none of those institutions knew the literature or practices intimately. The Euro-American teachers and preachers thought they were bad, or unnecessary, or both. I suppose those American attitudes and the appeal of the new are why the old practices weakened. The young took up new forms, and the old forms, which needed fresh talent and fresh ideas, faded in importance.

In explaining the changes of the last 150 years among the Pima-Papago, we could look at the social, economic, political, and religious changes themselves, at how the practices of life changed. Alternatively, I concentrate on their literature, both oral and written. I do so because it is literature that people turn to when they want to justify—explain, make sense of, give a reason for—life. That is the power and importance of literature. We want to see how it worked out and how the old literature stopped for the Pima-Papago as a small nation.

Here is an example of how the old literature and the language itself did not keep up with the times. Although Spain brought carts, clocks, and navigational instruments with wheels to the Americas, the *O'odham* did not involve themselves with wheels until the 1900s. To this day, there is no standard word for *wheel* in *O'odham*, much less an oral literature about wheels. Some people call wheels *shoes* (a vehicle touches the ground with them), some call them *legs* (what connects vehicles to the ground; these people use *shoes* for *tires*), and some people call them *circularities* (thinking that the other names miss the essence of wheels).

The naming of European things was not always delayed. The *O'odham* quickly adopted the Spanish words for horse, saddle, cross, and money, for example. Yet they did not pick up *rueda,* the Spanish word for wheel. The reason, I suggest, is that they did not get their own wheels until the 20th century, and people usually do not have words for things they do not use or imagine using. Americans make much real and metaphorical use of wheels. We have the expressions "big wheel" and "wheel of fortune," and we have a myriad of "real" wheels. The *O'odham* know all those expressions, but they know them in English, which is now their main language for keeping up with the world. They had stopped trying to keep up in the *O'odham* language before wheels became part of their culture.

QUESTIONS

9.1. What is literature, and what role does it play?

9.2. What are small nations, and what unifies them?

9.3. What is memorized, and how?

9.4. What is anonymity, and why?

9.5. What is ethnography, and why?

---

[2]The schools and the churches relented in the 1970s, but the decline, from this and from other causes, was already far along.

QUESTION 9.1
What Is Literature, and What Role Does It Play?

It was not the language's responsibility to bring *wheel* into the *O'odham* culture; it was the mythology's responsibility. Mythology was a key part of *O'odham* literature and culture.

Literature is kept stretches of language: told and retold, read and reread, heard and reheard, thought and rethought. In other words, literature is language that is judged to be valuable and worth keeping. A string of numbers would be literature if it was kept and used. In fact, numbers and tallies were among the first things to be written, probably because people could not trust memory when numbers representing property were at stake. Writing makes an external record, and the information cannot then be remembered differently.

Strings of numbers are not prominent in oral literature. Stories in words dominate. The most important stories tell about the ancient past of a people. They are not about somebody's traceable ancestor. Rather, they are about a past so ancient that no one can trace an exact genealogical line to the characters. Together, they form **mythologies** and are the shared ancientness of a whole people, a mutuality of story stemming from the time of **creation** and providing a charter for their existence. Some of the stories may be kept secret from some people, such as children or members of a different clan, but they are still things of "our" past, which brought "all of us" to where we are now.

Whereas the first written tallies were made to guarantee agreement over exactly what was said or counted, a small nation's mythologies tend to be the same even though no one guarantees agreement. The mythologies of small nations are amazing in this respect. There is no official version. The mythologies are too long to be told all at one time. They are told in a normal, quiet voice, so they are too "soft" to be heard by an assembled mass of people. They are told in the home, usually at night and ideally, in the case of the Pima-Papago, over the longest four nights of the winter. It is amazing that all of these private mythologies are so similar. They are not perfectly identical, but their main characters and episodes are very widely shared, or so I have found among the *O'odham*. It is as though they all secluded themselves in their houses where they could not be watched, and all told the same story in unison for 48 hours.

These stories are about creations and origins: the first humans; the earth, sun, moon, and stars; plants and animals; death and marriage; cooking; and coming-of-age ceremonies. Their content often is not limited to the pre-Columbian world. The Pima-Papago tell of the creation of white people, horses, the rotation of the earth, Jesus, smallpox, and other things conventionally thought to be unknown prior to European contact. What is accounted for in origin stories varies from group to group.

The subject of marriage is explicit in several stories in a people's mythology, but the mythology as a whole, from beginning to end, actually refers to a time before human procreation and marriage were firmly established. The many narrated acts of creation involve a fully human-looking person of one sex and an unusual or abnormal representative of the opposite sex: a man makes humans from mud (which is female and is the mythic substitute for a normal woman); a woman is impregnated by a rolling ball, a falling feather, or rain from a cloud (male substitutes); a man ejaculates the first deer from his mouth (auto-creation by mouth). Thus one way of seeing a small nation's mythology is as a long recitation of just such creative premarital events that the Bible confines to the time before the expulsion from Eden, which ushered in the time of normal human procreation and marriage. The mythologies of small nations are long equivalents to Eden.

Compared to them, the Bible's Eden is short, just the first three chapters of Genesis. The Native Edens make a small book when told completely with all of the stories of ancientness in the order in which the narrator thinks they should be told. We will have bits and pieces from Pima-Papago versions below, but I will not give an outline of the whole. One can find the whole in a book I participated in (Bahr et al. 1994).

The Pima-Papago, like most of the world's small nations, have been aware of Europeans and Christianity for centuries. The Pima-Papago knew about and used some European things, including horses, iron, factory-made cloth, money (called *lial* from the Spanish *real*), holy water, and coffee, for the last 400 years. Some of those things are included in the mythology, but always in terms of their origination, never as histories of use. In short, they are "written into" Eden, and that is all. Although white people are considered to have been made in the ancient Pima-Papago land, then sent away, there is no history of relations between the Pima-Papago and the Spanish, Mexicans, or North Americans. It is as though the mythology stopped the night before the Euro-Americans returned from where they had been sent. This is one reason why the old literature became less important. People became ever more involved with the American world, but the mythology ignored this, except for stating some origins.

Many people think that Native American mythologies are like the Gospel parables in that they give guidance to and provide models for today's life. I respect this idea, but Pima-Papago mythology does not seem to me—and was not taken by the old-timers I knew—to be a model of how people should live. Rather, the stories are what was remembered of what was said about how life was first lived. The things that are remembered are far from normal or ideal by old-timers' standards. I believe that Native mythologies are more like the story of the garden of Eden than like Jesus' parables.

Why did the Pima-Papago have this particular form of literature? One response is to note that all small nations have or had something like it. Another is to note that we can assume that whatever is saved is saved for a reason. We can also suppose that the different kinds of things a people save, combined with their different ways of saving in memory, make a kind of house of oral literature in which each kind or genre is a specialized room. Anthropology and comparative literature have barely begun to learn what these houses of literature are. It is a rare small nation language that has one good dictionary and grammar written for it; and although the nations all had their languages and literatures, their people did not tally, analyze, or critique them.

Anthropologists and ethnographers should tally, analyze, and critique their languages and literatures, using our analytical mode of writing. It will not hurt literatures. In fact, I believe that literatures may like to be studied this way, just as cats like to be rubbed, with appreciative attention. We should do this first, and only then ask why they were saved.

Here is a song that I take as a metaphor. It is said to have been sung by and Apache who had been captured in war by the Pima. They were about to kill him, and he sang:

Not knowable land, on it take me,
Not knowable land, on it take me.
Great flowery land, on it take me,
On there I'll stay. [Sung by Paul Manuel, not previously published]

For us the land (literatures) is knowable because no one will kill us. We should, however, get well acquainted before attempting explanation.

QUESTION 9.2
What Are Small Nations, and What Unifies Them?

Small nations are peoples without political centralization and with a distinct sense of their own ancientness, which they memorize and tell in mythologies. The members of a small nation speak one language. Each small nation typically gives itself a name that means "the [true] humans" in that language. Small nations usually number from 5000 to 10,000 people.

Small nations were the only nations prior to writing. Writing did not cause larger nations. Large nations created writing, especially at the beginning for the making of tallies. Large nations already had mythologies in oral memory. They soon began to write them to promulgate official state cults.

The large nations were **states** (centralized, hierarchically organized societies employing coercive power). Once they formed, they affected their smaller neighbors, mainly by absorbing them and by implanting their written mythology and stone monuments among them. They evangelized, or conquered, or merely attracted. When left to themselves, the small nations overtly ignored their neighbors, mythologically speaking, and they would never convert a neighbor to their sense of the past. Covertly, however, they were attentive to their large- and small-nation neighbors. Neighboring nations took care to be different from and yet resonant with each other. They had to be different in order to maintain their distinct sense of peoplehood. But they did not want to be, or could not imagine themselves as being, very different from each other. Thus they imitated each other by performing variations of each other's stories, a process that the great anthropologist and student of myth, Claude Lévi-Strauss (1983–1990), called **transformation**.

This process is exemplified by comparing some myths of the Pima-Papago and their neighbors, the Maricopa and Yavapai tribes. By the 1850s the Pima-Papago, or at least many of them, told of the related but distinct careers of two man-gods, Earth Medicine-Man and Elder-Brother Medicine-Man. Each created a group of Pima-Papago speakers. The group made by Earth Medicine-Man had to flee the world because of a flood and go to the underworld. Then Elder-Brother created a second group who eventually killed him. He revived and recruited the first group from the underworld to kill his killers. Pima-Papago mythologies generally say that Earth Medicine-Man got angry with Elder-Brother and went to the underworld to join his people who had gone there earlier. He and his people waited there until Elder-Brother arrived, ashamed and chagrined after his death and resurrection. Nothing is said in those versions about Earth Medicine-Man's dying, only that he went to the underworld and stayed there. There is one version, however, in which Earth Medicine-Man dies in precisely the same way one of the two key man-gods of the Maricopa mythology dies—from a wasting sickness caused by his daughter. On his deathbed the Pima god, like the Maricopa one, institutes farming and a calendar of moon-months. After dying, Earth Medicine-Man, like the Maricopa god, is cremated (Benedict, n.d.). Most Pima-Papago mythologies have quite different accounts of the origin of farming, and while the Maricopa god's cremation is taken as the origin of that people's death observances, the Pima-Papago did not cremate their dead. They buried them.

Did this one Pima-Papago narrator or his predecessor "steal" the Maricopa episode? I think so, and I think he wanted to add this version to his own people's past because he knew it was as important to the Maricopa's sense of the past as Elder-Brother's death and resurrection were to his own people. I also believe that most other Pima-Papago and Maricopa, if they heard this version, would know that the narrator has taken the Maricopa version, since the main lines of both peoples' mythologies had been agreed on and this Pima appropriation of an episode stands out like a sore thumb.

Another example of transformation is the prose myths on the origin of white people from the Pima (river people) and two neighboring tribes, the Maricopa and Yavapai. The neighbors do not contradict each other absolutely since, for all the tellers know, there were several distinct creations of white people, but they do indicate different and distinct origins for the same kind of thing.

Pima. The known local Native American tribes—the first Pima-Papago, Maricopa, Yavapai, and others—were made from mud by the man-god Earth Medicine-Man. Sometime later an eagle began to kidnap the people made by Elder-Brother Medicine-Man. The eagle stored them dead on a cliff where he lived. Elder-Brother Medicine-Man climbed the cliff, killed the eagle, and brought the dead back to life. Some had been dead for so long that they had turned white. Those became the whites, and Elder-Brother gave them feather pens to write with. The eagle also had a pet dog who had pups. These Elder-Brother turned into Africans. [Bahr et al. 1994:166–169]

Maricopa. Two man-gods rode together on a log in a flood at the beginning of time. The water subsided, land appeared, and the two made humans from mud. They made the people who became the local tribes and also the whites, who were crybabies. (The Pima-Papago have a similar scene, but in their version the flood came after the first creation of people.) [Based on Spier 1933:394–347]

Yavapai. Nothing is said about the origin of the tribal ancestors, which is unusual in Native America, but at different points in the mythology the origins of the Pima (enemies to the Yavapai) and whites are explained. The whites came from the bones of male Yavapai-speaking humans who were killed by a bear that had formerly been the victims' human sister. A surviving brother killed this bear-sister. Then he made a brush house, put the bones inside, and sat quietly outside for four nights. The bones began to rustle and talk, and finally whites came out with their cursing, complexion, horses, metal, and characteristic clothing. They went away but eventually came back. [Based on Gifford 1933:377–381]

That "everyone around here" derives from ancient events that took place "right here" is typical, even required, of small nations' mythologies, as is the neighborly disagreement over particulars. If the derivation of blacks seems unkind, I would point out that some Pima-Papago also derive a portion of themselves from a female dog. These stories were told in private, not in public, and there was no official public version. They were offered as something the teller had been told was true, but could not prove.

Of course, these peoples had mythologies long before they met whites and blacks. They updated or changed their mythologies over time. We cannot know with certainty what their mythologies were like before the whites and blacks came because oral traditions change without anyone's saying so. Thus, we know them scientifically only as far back in time as there were writers to document them.

Thus, what they had were stories about Eden. Why was this? I think it is essential for humanity to state in stories how humanity came to be. The reason the tribes in a region did not agree on one story is that the question did not arise; what needed explaining is what was, a world of small societies. If someone had suggested that there should be agreement on one story, it would have been seen as nonsense. They could not imagine a unified world. They had very little unity or centralization in their politics, and even after some of them developed centralization (in what anthropologists call **chiefdoms**), they still had no official, socially sanctioned mythology. Each clan still had its particular story. Moreover, it is my opinion that the small nations all thought of the universe as young and of their own way of life as ephemeral. It could all change tomorrow. Thus, the proper question is not why neighboring tribes did not tell the same story, but why all the versions internal to a tribe were so similar. They were similar, I believe, because the mythologies made the tribes; they gave the members of a tribe a conviction of oneness.

Nearly every Pima-Papago says that the old oral literature is dying. I have seen it decline over 40 years as old-time traditional tellers and dream singers have died and have been replaced by new country gospel singers and school teachers.[3] The retelling of old native language oral texts has lagged, and the introduction of new ones (by dreaming them, for example) has almost stopped. The pruning, flexing, and retelling of old texts appear to have ended. Those actions are necessary if the texts are to stay vital in the home communities. We cannot see into peoples' memories and cannot hear what they say when we are not there, so we do not know how healthy the old texts really are. We can be sure that their health will improve if they are honored, spoken, and read in the community schools, especially if community members do the speaking, reading, and writing without outside help. This is happening, and at the least it instills pride and identity. There are a thousand former small nation communities, and I cannot say how general or great the decline is. I hope it is small, but fear it is not.

If small nations were unified by their mythologies and not by any central ideological authority, what unifies them now when their mythologies are in decline? Specifically, what unifies the Pima-Papago now? The answer is: something smaller than originally, and something larger.

The smaller thing is a set of four miniature republics of a few thousand citizens with constitutional governments composed of legislative, executive, and judicial branches, and with executive branch departments of health, education, land and water, roads, library, fire department, elder affairs, tribal farm, and casino. The four republics, each on its own reservation, are the Salt River Pima-Maricopa Indian Community, Gila River Pima-Maricopa Indian Community (both are binational entities; the Maricopa are a distinct people), Ak Chin Indian Community, and Tohono O'odham Nation (formerly called the

---

[3]But there is still more of it left than I will ever know.

Papago tribe). These republics were created in the 1930s, but they did not become important until the 1970s when the U.S. Bureau of Indian Affairs and the Public Health Service began to transfer their services to tribal control. Then, happily, the tribes began to acquire some wealth from casinos in the 1990s. No one knows how long the Native American casino industry will thrive, but at present one republic has one casino and the other three each have two. Together the republics hold about a third of the U.S. land held by the Pima-Papago 150 years ago. The lost land is mainly in the hands of the Bureau of Land Management, the National Park Service, and the Department of Defense, but the large cities of Phoenix and Tucson lie on the edge of their old territory, and several large farming towns were built in a wide railroad concession that crosses their former land.

The larger unity the Pima-Papago now participate in is the same as the sum of the smaller ones, but it includes more peoples. It is the culture or sub-culture of all U.S. Indian reservations, nations, tribes, or republics. These are more similar than different: the same yellow school buses make their rounds from 7:00 to 8:30 A.M. and 3:00 to 4:30 P.M.; the same black leather executive chairs stand in the governing council chamber of the legislative branch; the same Housing-and-Urban-Development-approved, Tribal-Housing-Department-contracted modest suburban tract developments provide housing; the same grid plan of roads originally laid out by the U.S. Geological Survey connect people; the same practice of leasing lands to non-Indian farmers and businesses passively benefits the tribe or individual Native landholders; the same economy is timed by checks that come once every two weeks for jobholders, once a month for welfare and pension recipients, and two or four times a year for leases; and people follow the same cycle of Monday through Friday for school and work, and weekends for family, fun, and religion.

QUESTION 9.3
What Is Memorized, and How?

In oral societies, there is a tradeoff between the amount of story that can be memorized and the level of language at which memory operates. Corresponding to the levels, there is a difference in mode of oral delivery. One can memorize the most story at the linguistic level of plot outline. At this level one knows what happened, but one tells it in slightly different words each time. The performance mode for this kind of memorization is what I call **oral prose**. Prose texts are spoken in a normal voice at the same volume and pitch as ordinary speech. The small nation texts we call **myths**[4] are mostly of this performance mode and this level of memorization. Prose myths are always paraphrased, so the narrators can make their delivery lively. The stories of origins presented in the previous section were prose myths.

[4]Whether a story should be called myth or history seems to me to depend on the attitude of the hearer or reader. If the hearer or reader believes the story to be true, it is history for that hearer. If the hearer does not, it is myth. The teller must believe the story in either case. If neither the teller nor the hearer believes the story, it is fiction. If the teller does not believe it and the hearer does, it is a (successful) lie. I call the Pima-Papago stories myths because the tellers believe them and I do not. That is, I do not believe they tell things that happened exactly as they say they did.

Pima-Papago Orations

There is also a level of sentence memorization. At this level, the stories are shorter and are usually more stereotyped than those told in prose. Such texts are generally called *orations*, *chants*, or *prayers*. They are typically about ten minutes long, in contrast to a prose story, which can take an hour or two. They are generally performed out of doors in a loud voice, while the prose stories are quieter and are told indoors. Orations and prayers are commonly considered to be the words of the gods and are commonly connected to events told in the prose mythology.

Pima-Papago orations tend to tell the story of one person's journeying and to follow a formula:

I set out,
I travel,
I arrive somewhere,
I do something.

The "doing" part of an oration may be quite elaborate, and characters other than the hero may go traveling at points in the speech, but the plot formula constrains the kind of story that can be told. It must tell of an "I's" brief encounters with a series of other things. It dwells more on the "I" than on the things and tells much about the means of travel. The narrators of Pima-Papago oratory—and also of songs—are ancient gods or modern spirits.

The following oration, which was part of ceremonies for war, is attributed to the man-god Elder-Brother Medicine-Man who, according to the mythology, came back to life after being killed by the Pima-Papago-speaking people he had created. He arose, traveled east (described in part in this excerpt), came to the place where the sun rises, arose like the sun, crossed the sky, and descended into the underworld to gather an army of other Pima-Papago, whom he took to the world's surface to destroy the people who had killed him:

[Preface]
Thus I did, Elder-Brother Medicine-Man, on open ground laid himself down, on it lying, on it four days completed, on it really pressed and arose, around himself looked and tried to see.

Land got put, distantly lay.

Mountains stood [formerly by somebody], now rottenly stood.

Trees stood, now [as] firewood toppled, and that I tried to see.

There to the east he caused to run his white winds, by means of which his heart got moistened and finished.

[This preface, which sets the stage, continues through three more moistening winds. It is followed by the first part of this six-part oration, which is organized on the journey formula.]

[Part 1]
[I] set out,

Stepped,

And someplace sat the talker man [of the people who had killed him]. I neared him, on him really stepped, again stepped.

And someplace sat the medicine man. I neared him, on him really
   stepped, again stepped.

And someplace sat the warrior man. I neared him, on him really
   stepped, again stepped.

And someplace sat the knowing women, good gatherers, good storers.
   On them I really stepped.

[Part 2]
And there [I] sank, then eastwards thinly myself buried,

Reached the rich mountains.

At their bases they seeped, with water plants were covered,

In that I entered, my heart got moistened.

Reached the feathered house.

In that lay various possessions,

In that I entered, my heart got vitalized. [Underhill et al. 1979:116-119]

This next bit of oratory, which was also prominent in ceremonies for war,
is narrated by an unknown god whose place in the chronicle of ancientness
is no longer known. It is not the only one like that; in fact, only a minority of
the orations are clearly tied to the mythology. This was not a fault. The
mythology does not tell everything, and the oratory has its own purposes, one
being to tell of an ancient creative Eden-before-marriage, the other to tell of
fantastic (but believed) journeys by a medicine man or **shaman**:

[Preface]
Yes, who did it?

It was I, earth put down and finished,
On top, mountains stood up and finished,
On top, trees stood up and finished,
On top, spring waters laid and finished,
On top, people made and finished.

I for a long time will watch it, I thought.

Then after a while there moved at the base of the west the bitter wind.

From there it ran and standing trees uprooted to use for killing, along it
   went and was doing and away off it stopped.

It turned itself and looked.

Nowhere a tree stood, nowhere a person moved.

[Part 1]
The land on the other side felt fine,

And on it I came out,
My white shoes took and came out,
My shoulder blades flowered and came out,
Below my forehead wrapped and came out,
Bent bow took and came out,

A portrait taken in the 1980s of an excellent Tohono O'odham singer who was the author's good friend. (Photograph by Donald Bahr.)

Arrow took and came out,
My rolled up shield took and came out,
Headed stick took and came out,
All windy and came out,
All cloudy and came out,
My face zigzag painted and came out.

The land on the other side felt fine.

Then they reached me, the many birds, and crowded me and hooted.

And I feared them and cried and turned,

Soon reached home again

And because of that felt very strongly. [Underhill et al. 1979:132-136]

[This is the entire first part; there are nine more parts.]

Pima-Papago Songs

Finally, there is memorization at the level of the individual metered sound. Such texts are songs, or actually song-poetry. They have fixed underlying beats and a range and regularity of pitch that mark them as distinct from prose speech and from oratory, prayer, and chant. Songs typically last about a minute but are repeated several times when danced to, which is common. They are often performed in series, as stanzas of sung verse. Like oratory, prayer, and chant, they are often connected to events of the prose mythology.

One can easily recognize the words of oratory; it is more difficult with songs. The original singer of the song was usually a spirit, and most songs originated in dreams. Songs commonly, but not always, have the following three-part structure:

1. There is something (a mountain standing, songs starting, etc.).
2. Something else (I, he, she, or it) travels toward or acts at a distance from the something.
3. And I do something.

The following five songs illustrate this structure. They also illustrate the point that the Pima-Papago language lacks a specific word for wheel, but is able in its poetry to discuss wheels. The first three examples are songs used for pleasure or social dancing. I heard the first two during the 1980s; they were dreamed from swallow birds and are understood to be swallows' gifts to human culture. The first is about a swallow circling like a buzzard:

> And I circling go,
> And I like a buzzard do.
> To the sky's front I attach,
> This, my heart, awakens. [Bahr 1986: 180]

The second is about a fish who imparts circling to the swallow's brother:

> Great painted fish arrives,
> Medicine man's house sees and circles.
> Poor my little brother, will you circle,
> Medicine man's house, see and circle? [Bahr 1986:181].

The third is a song dreamed from bats. Like the swallow songs, it is used for social dancing.

> Bent Mountain,
> Bent Mountain,
> There beside it iron circling goes,
> With the wind circling goes.
> Here below us lying water iron circling goes,
> With the wind circling goes. [Sung by Carlos Santos, not previously
>   published]

The song is a riddle whose answer is windmill. The Pima-Papago word for windmill is *papalo:di,* from the Mexican Spanish *papalote.* The windmill's "wheel" is surely a wheel. The song makes us "see" this once the riddle is solved, even though the word *wheel* is not used.

The next two songs are about the circularity of the earth, one on its shape, the other on its motion. They are not dreamed dance songs; rather, they are mythology songs used in telling the history of the world. They are from two slightly different renderings of Pima-Papago mythology, one recorded in 1902 and the other in 1935. The tellers believed that the characters of ancient times sometimes burst into song, and certain of the songs have been passed down word for word. The first text describes a moment in which the man-god Earth Medicine-Man made the earth from skin he had rubbed from his chest. There were no people at this time, so it is not known how the song was heard; perhaps it came from a later person's dream about those ancient times.

> Earth Medicine-Man earth makes, come and see what he does!
> Round makes, come and see what he does!
> Earth Medicine-Man mountains makes, come and see what he says!
> Smooth makes, come and see what he says! [Russel 1908:272]

The second text is from a time after a Noah-like flood when Elder-Brother Medicine-Man created a new race to people the world. The subject, as in the swallow songs above, is the dizziness caused by spinning—this time by the spinning of the earth. This song was translated by a Pima into a more colloquial English than was used for translating the other songs.

> The earth is spinning around
> The earth is spinning around
> And my people are spinning around with the earth.
> The earth is spinning faster
> The earth is spinning faster
> And my people are spinning faster with the earth. [Bahr et al. 1994:80]

These translated texts look more like prose than do the Pima originals. This is not just because the pitches and rhythm are not indicated. Also missing is allowance for the fact that Pima-Papago song language has more syllables per word than does Pima-Papago prose. The difference is something like that between plain English and the pig Latin that children used to speak. ("Can you talk pig Latin?" becomes "Ankay ouyay alktay igpay atinlay?") The purpose is different, however. Pig Latin is meant to disguise English by taking off a word's initial consonant, moving it to the end, and adding "ay." Pima-Papago song language is not meant to disguise anything. It is used to make prose language melodious, that is, to form speech into melody. The same word can behave differently with different melodies.

Here is what the first song translated above looks like when the English syllables are multiplied to correspond to their Pima-Papago song counterparts:

> And I-i ci-ir-cling go-o-o,
> And I-i li-i-ike a buzzard do-o-o.
> To the sky's fro-o-ont I attach,
> Thi-i-is, my he-eart, awakens.

The original is about as easy to understand as that, although some Pima-Papago songs are harder to understand.

QUESTION 9.4
What Is Anonymity, and Why?

Writing began with people already in possession of memory-kept mythologies like that of the Pima-Papago. People with writing centralized their mythologies and made them official. This process has never been described by live observers, but Herbert Butterfield (1981) did an excellent study of how it may have occurred in the Old World. Two crucial parts of the process were the acknowledgement of live authors as producers of texts, and the development of the recent, as opposed to the ancient, past as a subject for literature.

Anonymous means having no known author. The prose parts of all mythologies were anonymous. Oral prose is paraphrased anew on each telling; therefore, no one person can lay claim to a stretch of it. But Pima-Papago mythologies also included songs and orations. These fixed mythological texts do have named authors, but the authors are ancient characters, not the current speakers. Pima-Papago songs and speeches without a place in the mythology also have authors, but these are spirits heard in dreams, not living people.

In general then, the live human singer or orator is not the author, but only the repeater of a text. Earth Medicine-Man was an author in the Pima-Papago view, and he is as real to and believed in by them as George Washington is by modern Americans. But Earth Medicine-Man was an ancient author, and what the Pima-Papago lacked were contemporary authors. The tribe did not have people who said, "I made that song. It's mine. I am the author." They lacked the thing that makes our literary world go round: living authors, the most successful of whom become celebrities. What they had were dreamers and repeaters of spirit and godly voices. They lacked mortal hero authors in the present and also in their sense of the past. They had Earth Medicine-Man, an ancient author-god whose songs were repeated, but they did not have texts by mere observers of Earth Medicine-Man, observers equivalent to the journalists and diarists who wrote about George Washington. They did not have texts from witnesses who look, listen, and describe, but generally do not enter into, the action and who therefore do not change what happens, but only tell about it.

In their songs and orations, they and the other small nations believe they have the exact words of ancient speakers. The Pima-Papago do not know how their ancient songs and orations were preserved. For example, they do not know how the creation song quoted above was heard when there were no people to hear it, or how an oration was heard when no one today even knows who the god was. They have songs and orations that were passed through uncounted generations of mortal singers and orators.

The Pima-Papago get many songs from dreams. A present-day *O'odham* can dream back to mythic time, or at least dream of being present with the spirit of an ancient mythic person. Here, for example, is a song dreamed from Jesus about his departure from this world and ascension:

> Ah, ah, ah,
> Nowhere will you find me to call to,
> Wandering on this world with
> Nowhere to stretch your heart. [Bahr 1987:216]

And here is one from Mary, also about stretching, this time about stretching a flower in relation to Joseph:

> Do you think you're my husband?
> Do you think you're my husband because I go with you?
> Do you think you're my husband,
> A flower stretches between us? [Bahr 1987:214]

These songs, which originated around 1900, did not replace the Gospels for the Pima-Papago, but they did provide a powerful and persuasive supplement to them: a dreaming Pima-Papago heard of Jesus and Mary and then went to heaven to hear them in person. With their traditional mythology, the Pima-Papago also had the ability to supplement the old, accepted oral prose texts with dreamed revelations, but these revelations lacked the anchor of written witness texts like the Gospels.

Why is there an absence of witness authoring in small nations? A true and simple answer is that it had not been thought of yet; it was an invention of the future. Also true, but not as simple, is that oral societies had more important things to memorize than the "news" of contemporary authors. They had their identity-giving mythologies to look after, their ceremonial oratory, curing, and social-dancing songs. A small nation had to economize on its oral literature, and perhaps members could not waste memory on contemporary events. Finally, there was a social force against witness authorship. In effect, being a living author was taboo; it was felt to be dangerous.

The Pima-Papago have a word, *e-shemacud,* which they often think, but rarely say. According to the dictionary of their language, it means "to act boldly or meanly without regard to possible punishment" (Saxton, Saxton, and Enos 1983:53). In short, it means "to act heedlessly tough." The word is almost never addressed to a person. Rather it is said, and then only rarely, about someone to someone else. Although not at all obscene, the word is like a curse, for it accuses someone of a serious breach. Today, the word is mainly used about young people who act like "gang kids." But the word also applies to adults who step forward too much, who act like they think they are better than anyone else.

Being a witness author, a producer of current societal news—in other words a producer of gossip—would be to act in a bold and mean manner without regard to possible punishment. Punishment might be a beating, or perhaps a stabbing or shooting for a young person. For adults it is **sorcery** or **witchcraft**, the intentional harming of humans by humans with magic. In small nations, where no one is specifically authorized to act as a kind of police in the name of public law and order,[5] there is generally a concept like the Pima-Papago's *e-shemacud* that minimizes what we would call self-assertion. And a widespread mechanism for accomplishing this is by the fear—not necessarily the detectable practice—of sorcery.

Among the Pima-Papago peoples, there also was no idea of natural sickness or death. In Western societies, death that is not caused by killing, accident, suicide, or war is considered natural death. In small nations, all death falls into the category we would call "unnatural." Much of this unnatural killing was understood as magical. Sorcery was considered to be common.

Among the old-time Pima-Papago, magical attacks by animals for transgressions against their "ways" were given more attention than sorcery as a cause of human pain and suffering.[6] When people were seriously ill, a medicine man (or, more rarely, a woman) worked over them all night to learn the cause of the trouble. Almost always, the first thing the medicine man found was sorcery. This was attended to at once by seeking small, bullet-sized things in the patient's body or around the house. Later in the night came a search for sicknesses, which were always in the patient's body. There was often more than one sickness, and the medicine man would deal immediately with some aspects of each, but the final cure required night-long cures by other specialists who sang dreamed songs for the "way" of each kind of sickness the medicine man had found. The "way-sent" sicknesses were more prominent than

---

[5]There are tribal police and tribal courts today, but there is still a deep reluctance to interject oneself into the affairs of others.

[6]This was still the case in the 1960s.

sorcery in that they were the last and the more elaborately treated. Sorcery, by comparison, was routine; it happened all the time and was not *necessarily* fatal.

Why do I link witness authoring with sorcery? The link is speculation since the argument is that this kind of writing *does not* occur because sorcery *does*. It is hard to prove the cause of something that does not occur (all the harder when the sorcery does not really happen either in the opinion of science). I make the link because I think Pima-Papago feel it. In the end, self-promotion simply goes against the grain of Pima-Papago culture.

Today there are Native poets, novelists, and journalists. Nearly every large reservation has a newspaper. Those poets and novelists published by commercial publishers are famous. It is significant that they write fiction. They do not write history, and when Natives do write history it is usually about the times before 1940, not more recent decades. As far as *e-shemacud* is concerned, fiction is safer than history, and 60-year-old history is safer than last year's.

The Pima-Papago have no published novelists, but they do have a poet. Ofelia Zepeda has authored two books of poetry (1982, 1995), coauthored another with Larry Evers (1995), and published a grammar of her language (1983). Anna Moore Shaw has published a book of myth stories of ancient times (1968) and an autobiography (1974). George Webb (1959) and Nathan Allen (1995) have published essay-like memoirs. I have coauthored books and articles with about 15 different Pima-Papagos; sometimes I took the lead in composing the text, and sometimes they did. Some of these are cited at the end of this chapter. I hope more such works will be produced, especially by others. I especially wish that more ethnographers would "go Native" this way, learning a Native language and its oral literature well enough to fill the gap between ethnography and Native literature with coauthored pieces.

What, then, of the Native journalists? They are celebrities, especially when they write about people living their everyday lives. However, the way the newspapers are, there is not much call for such writing. There are acts of government and feasts and powwows to report: things that were public when they were done, not the everyday private things that would be made public by publishing them. For better or worse, writing about private life is what ethnography does.

QUESTION 9.5
What Is Ethnography, and Why?

Up to this point I have said that the old-time Pima-Papago did not have witness authoring. Now I will say that they did not have the kind of text produced by witness authors. In particular, they did not write ethnography.

As a folklorist, I define an ethnography as a witness-authored text, based on observation and conversation, that describes the full span of a people's culture. The description (the "what") must be limited to what waking eyes can see, and the explanation (the "why") must be secular and causal.

The Pima-Papago in their old literature and old habits of life did not make ethnographies. They effectively tabooed witness authors; moreover, their habit of explanation was not secular, but sacred, magical, and traditional ("This is what the old-timers said, and so we do it"). Furthermore, ethnography traditionally has concentrated on peoples other that those of the author. While the Pima-Papago were attentive to their neighbors, they were more concerned with forming transformations of each other's stories than with giving a full and fair representation of a different people's culture.

This reluctance of the Pima-Papago to be ethnographers came as a personal disappointment to me. "As an anthropologist," I had thought, "I would like to describe their culture in the form of an ethnography, and yet I don't like to intrude on the people. Perhaps I can get an ethnography from them in the form of their oral literature." The disappointment was in learning that what anthropologists make in their ethnographies is not what the Pima-Papago make in their oral literature. Thus, wonderful though their traditional literature is—and I hope you find it wonderful—it is not, and would not be, and would not want to be anthropology or ethnography. Nor, to make a slightly different point, would the Pima-Papago want to be anthropologists or ethnographers.

In the world at large, once writing started, the making of texts that could be kept became easier. The economic inhibition against witness authors fell away. Still, it was not until modern times, say until the 1700s, that anything like ethnography got started. There were other factors, like international travel and colonialism, but my emphasis is that ethnography grew hand in hand with print journalism. Both are popular at heart (in the sense of being for the general public), and both hope for mass readership. Early ethnographic writers were not widely read, but some more recent ones, such as Margaret Mead, were. More recently, however, I would say that journalists have surpassed anthropologists in telling the world important things about culture. Although anthropologists have recently discovered American culture (see Chapters 7 and 8), in my opinion ethnographies on American culture have been overshadowed by the nonfiction books of Truman Capote, Frances Fitzgerald, and Norman Mailer. Even in the area of ethnography's historic strength of telling the world about Native cultures, I would note especially Heather Robertson's (1970) and Peter Matthiessen's (1992) books on Native Americans as examples of excellent and provocative journalism.

Anthropology has the beautiful idea of ethnography as an eyewitness portrait of a culture, especially the culture of a small nation. Each portrait gives much cultural information, but no portrait can tell everything, and all ethnographies have a focus. Only in "memory ethnography" was something close to completeness attempted. These ethnographies were made by interviewing the old about the culture of their youth. Most Native American ethnography, such as Frank Russel's (1908) book on the Pima, is of this nature. These were not accounts of culture as witnessed by anthropologists. Neither, however, were they a Native form of literature. They were an anthropological form, dependent on Native testimony. What they told was what the anthropologists knew to ask about and what the Natives were willing to respond to, usually in private and even in secret (because being a witness to a witness author carried its own risks).

Let me explain why I think journalism has surpassed anthropology in telling the world about Native cultures. First, the classic ethnographies on Native Americans described the peoples as traditional, autonomous small nations. Those peoples have now stopped being like that. They have become materially and culturally incorporated into the larger modern world. Second, life in traditional small nations centered on families. Just as the mythologies dwelled on what they understood as creative, ancient pre-families, so people's real lives were organized mainly by, and enacted mainly within, family relations. Third, these people's family lives did not stop with their incorporation into the modern world, but they did change, and firsthand "culture portrait" descriptions of their family life surely *did* stop. Anthropologists took up observing and writing about Natives in more public settings, such as schools, clinics, and job sites. Such studies were thought to be of practical value, while studying home life was seen as intrusive. I regret this change because family life is still interesting and is still a major part of who they are, and I really cannot say that the journalism of Robertson and Matthiesen has said much about it either. Their emphasis is on politics, not on the intimacy and routine of daily life.

The best way to learn about this topic is by reading the fiction of Native authors, some of which are noted in the references. And yet, being invention, their fiction is not the same as the real thing.

CONCLUSIONS

The problem around which this chapter is organized is the question of why peoples put or do not put things in their literature. The starting point is the basic observation that the essence of literature is that it is kept stretches of language and that the fundamental characteristic of literature for most of human history has been that that literature was oral. People keep only those things that are useful, and literature is thus language that is both kept and useful. What all people have found especially important to keep are stories that tell of the nation's ancientness. Those stories are history to those who believe them and myths to those who do not. In small nations, they are stories of the gods and heroes who made today be today.

Small nations is the term I use for what anthropologists have generally called *bands* and *tribes*. They are defined by the shared ancientness, expressed in their stories. Record keeping, writing, and reading were invented by large nations and have served to help shape their character, including their tendency to reshape the small nations in and around them. The Pima-Papago, for instance, still have much of their old stories, but these no longer define the people as they once did. They are now defined by their separate reservation bureaucracies and by the national bureaucratic and popular subculture of being Indian in the United States. There is an emergent Indian written literature, but it is in English, in forms that are not traditional to the Pima-Papago, and it is not really distinctive to them.

The Pima-Papago song is memorized to the individual metered syllable. At the other extreme is plot memorization, in which the wording and elaboration of episodes is left to the narrator. Each form has its own characteristic structural features. Most scholars of oral literature put less stress on memorization than I do, and I admit my approach excludes absolutely spontaneous, original performances of oral verbal art. Other scholars tend to see small nations as lovers of spontaneity, and I see them as preservers of texts. Both are true, but we need to know more about how and under what circumstances each is more true. I hold that oral traditions are mainly memorized and that a small nation's literary specialists are more repeaters than authors of texts, notwithstanding that their repetition of oral prose involves considerable improvisation, and their repetition of oratory, prayer, and chant also involves some spontaneity.

The Pima-Papago did not have witness authors in our modern sense. Some of the authors of their texts were the ancients. Other texts were dreamed, and the authors were understood to be various spirit beings. Being the kind of person who might engage in witness authorship was inconsistent with Pima-Papago values. The self-promotion inherent in authorship was the kind of behavior that might well be discouraged by the fear of sorcery.

This chapter's lesson on the difference between ethnography and oral literature should not come as a surprise, but as I said, it took me a while to understand it. Nor is the lesson entirely disappointing. That small nations do not write their own ethnographies gives anthropologists something to do for and with them. And while ethnographies are science, they are also art. Their construction is a creative act not easily mastered and best shared with Native colleagues. While the best ethnographies are both beautiful and useful, they can never replace what the old-timers had in their wonderful literature.

REFERENCES AND RECOMMENDED READINGS

Cook-Lynn, Elizabeth
1991 The Power of Horses and Other Stories. New York: Arcade.
     Native-authored short story fiction about present-day Native American life.

Joseph, A., with R. Spicer and J. Chesky
1949 The Desert People: A Study of the Papago Indians of Southern Arizona.
Chicago: University of Chicago Press.
     One of the last comprehensive eyewitness ethnographies written about Native Americans, and one of the founding studies of American applied anthropology.

Kaplan, David, and Robert Manners
1972 Culture Theory. Englewood Cliffs, NJ: Prentice-Hall.
     Scratch any anthropologist, and you'll find this theory of culture.

Lewis, Oscar
1961 The Children of Sanchez: Autobiography of a Mexican Family. New York:
Random House.
     A classic study of a poor Mexican urban family of Native heritage, written in the translated words of family members. It is a splendid Native-made witness history.

Matthiessen, Peter
1992 In the Spirit of Crazy Horse. New York: Penguin.
     Journalism/history on the controversial search for, arrest, and conviction of American Indian Movement activist Leonard Peltier for the murder of two FBI agents at Wounded Knee.

1992 [1987] Indian Country. New York: Penguin.
     Journalism/history on the encroachment by whites into Native American lands and culture.

Ong, Walter

1967 The Presence of the Word. New Haven: Yale University Press.

A seminal although controversial work on the nature of oral tradition, especially as it contrasts with literate traditions.

Robertson, Heather

1970 Reservations Are for Indians. Toronto: James Lorimer.

Journalism/history of Canadian Native reserves and their surroundings. The writer has a keen eye for symbolism.

Russel, Frank

1908 The Pima Indians. *In* 26th Annual Report of the Bureau of American Ethnology. Pp. 3–389. Washington, DC: Smithsonian Institution.

A comprehensive ethnography achieved by interviewing the old Pima in 1902 about what they remembered from their young adulthood.

Spicer, E.

1962 Cycles of Conquest: The Impact of Spain, Mexico, and the United States on the Indians of the Southwest, 1533–1960. Tucson: University of Arizona Press.

A history of the Pima-Papago and 20-odd other neighboring tribes. It is basically a history of policies, that is, of initiatives taken by the three large nations toward the small ones.

Welch, James

1987 Fools Crow. New York: Penguin.

Native fiction set on the night before the Americans came—that is, at the point the old-timers' mythology usually stopped. Foretells the end of the old way of life.

Wilson, Edmund

1998 Consilience. New York: Random House.

A call for a unified, secular, but deistic science of everything from physics to ethics.

Zolbrod, Paul

1995 Reading the Voice: Native American Oral Poetry on the Written Page. Salt Lake City: University of Utah Press.

A commentary on the oralness and sacredness of traditional Native American literatures.

Additional References Cited

Allen, Nathan

1995 Keeper of the House. Wicazo sa Review 9(2):50–51.

Bahr, Donald

1986 Pima Swallow Songs. Cultural Anthropology 1(2):171–187.

1987 Pima Heaven Songs. *In* Recovering the Word: Essays in Native American Literature. B. Swann and A. Krupat, eds. Pp. 198-246. Berkeley: University of California Press.

Bahr, D., with J. Smith, W. Allison, and J. Hayden

1994 The Short Swift Time of Gods on Earth. Berkeley: University of California Press.

Benedict, Ruth

n.d.   Pima Texts. Special Collections Department, Vassar College Library.

Butterfield, Herbert
1981 The Origins of History. New York: Basic Books.

Capote, Truman
1965 In Cold Blood. New York: Random House.

Evers, Larry, and Ofelia Zepeda
1995 Home Places: Contemporary Native American Writing from Sun Tracks. Tucson: University of Arizona Press.

Fitzgerald, Frances
1987 Cities on a Hill. New York: Simon and Schuster.

Gifford, E.
1933 Northeastern and Western Yavapai Myths. Journal of American Folklore 46:347–415.

Lévi-Strauss, C.
1983–1990 Introduction to a Science of Mythology, vols. 1–4. John Weightman and Doreen Weightman, trans. Chicago: University of Chicago Press.

Mailer, Norman
1979 The Executioner's Song. Boston: Little, Brown.

Saxton, D., with L. Saxton and S. Enos
1983 Dictionary: Pima/Papago-English, English-Pima/Papago. Tucson: University of Arizona Press.

Shaw, Anna (Moore)
1968 Pima Indian Legends. Tucson: University of Arizona Press.

1974 A Pima Past. Tucson: University of Arizona Press.

Spier, Leslie
1933 Yuman Tribes of the Gila River. Chicago: University of Chicago Press.

Underhill, R., with D. Bahr, B. Lopez, J. Pancho, and D. Lopez
1979 Rainhouse and Ocean: Speeches for the Papago Year. Flagstaff: Museum of Northern Arizona Press.

Webb, George
1959 A Pima Remembers. Tucson: University of Arizona Press.

Zepeda, Ofelia
1982 When It Rains, Pima and Papago Poetry. Tucson: University of Arizona Press.

1983 A Papago Grammar. Tucson: University of Arizona Press.

1995 Ocean Power: Poems from the Desert. Tucson: University of Arizona Press.

CHAPTER 10

THE CULTURAL RESPONSE TO DEATH

SHARON HEPBURN

PROBLEM 10 *How do people deal with the fact that they die?*

INTRODUCTION
Death, the Final Frontier—
To Boldly Go Where All People Have Gone Before

Cultures differ, but all people die, and people in all cultures have to do something about it. A corpse does not go unnoticed; the death of a loved one often brings on strong emotions that cannot be ignored; and a social group has to accommodate the loss of a member in order to go on. Somehow people have to account for the fact that although they are living and breathing today, one day they will stop doing so. What happens then? Does a person have a soul that continues after death? Does that soul remain linked to the living? The purpose of this chapter is to consider some of the questions that the inescapable fact of death raises and to consider some of the answers given by people in Tana Toraja, Indonesia, and in contemporary London, England.

Although I was born and grew up in London, I have never been to Tana Toraja. So I should say from the outset that, unlike the other authors in this volume, I have not conducted anthropological fieldwork in the cultures I am writing about in this chapter. I became interested in studying death during three-and-a-half years of fieldwork in Nepal. Sometimes my research came close to death, for example, when I was doing research on how people understood the causes of infant and childhood mortality. But what was striking and inescapable in Nepal was the visibility of death: chanting kinsmen carry a corpse wrapped in a white cloth through the street; a mother wails as she watches her child burn in a public cremation; people walk by as a man who is bone thin from hunger and shaking with fever lies dying in the street. To me this was something of a shock. Until then I had always lived in urban centers of what is often referred to as a death-denying culture.

Death in the Western world has not always been hidden and denied. Starting this chapter with an account of British death practices over the past two centuries helps us appreciate all the more the Torajan inclination to be, as the Torajans themselves sometimes say, death-obsessed. Although people in the West take death practices for granted, most of us do not know enough of our own cultural history to know how or why we got where we are now.

This chapter presents a comparison of Western and Torajan death rites. In this I am guided by the work of Robert Hertz, whose "A Contribution to the Study of the Collective Representations of Death" (1960) has been highly influential in the study of death over the past century. By **representations** Hertz meant the ideas, beliefs, and sentiments shared by members of a society. He was interested in the relationship between ideas and social organization. He suggested studying mortuary rites by tracing the trajectories of the soul of the deceased, the corpse, and the community of grievers. In this chapter, I implicitly follow these three aspects of mortuary rites and make an explicit comparison of Western and Torajan death beliefs and practices.

The British Way of Death

Around the turn of the 18th century, there were no funeral parlors in Britain.[1] A funeral took place over a few days and was totally controlled by the family and the immediate community of the deceased. Most people had close family ties and usually died at home, within the family. In conditions of overcrowding, there may have been few alternatives. There were no hospitals or hospices as we now know them.

Ideally, a person remained conscious and sociable until actual death. After death occurred, relatives of the deceased would lay out the corpse with the help of local female specialists, the midwives who also helped with births. The women washed the body and plugged its orifices, combed the hair, and straightened the limbs. They folded the arms across the chest and wrapped the corpse snugly in a sheet, much like they swaddled a baby. The dead body was "watched" by family members, was the center of a lively wake, was visited and seen, and was eventually carried from the home to the graveyard to be buried—in a coffin if the family could afford the carpenter's services. Many of these practices continued in parts of Britain until the 1930s.

There were variations. The very poor might have been dumped into a communal grave at the edge of ever-more-crowded cemeteries. Wealthy families would have lavish ceremonies with elaborate hospitality and ornate grave markers. Whether they were perfunctory or pompous, the rites marked the transition of the dead to "the other side" and marked the time of grief as a time apart. The wake kept a potentially angry or lonely spirit away. Clocks were sometimes stopped to mark the hour of death; mirrors turned so that one could no longer see into them; and fires, the source of warmth and light, not lit for a time. Well into the 1960s, when my own father died in London, curtains were drawn to cut out the light and to let the neighbors know that the members of that household were in actual as well as emotional darkness.

[1]This account of British practices draws heavily on Bradbury (1999).

All these practices mark what Van Gennep (1960) called the **liminal** phase of a **rite of passage** that marks the transition of a person from one social status to another. In this case, the deceased is liminal between being a living and present member of society and being, as we say, dead and buried. The mourners too are liminal; they are separate for a time from normal social life and have not yet been reintegrated as, perhaps, a widow or widower or an orphan.

Two things led people in the West to our common contemporary inclination to "keep a stiff upper lip" and "let the dead bury their own dead" as we try to "soldier on" and "get back to normal" as soon as possible. These influences were the gradual growth of modern medical practice and the social mobility of the Victorian era. With improved medicine and sanitation, people lived longer and the time of death became more predictable. A person with money could be attended by a doctor who might supply opiates to reduce pain. Disease and death had previously been seen as events that God controlled and man accepted. Increasingly, disease came to be seen as the cause of death, and doctors who intervened in the course of a disease came to be seen as controlling death. The dying person is now a patient. Previously a priest was the mediator at the time of death; now the priest generally presides after the doctors have given up hope or have written DNR (do not resuscitate) on the patient's chart.

At the start of the Victorian era, only the elite could afford elaborate funerals in which the coffin rode in a carriage pulled by black horses. In the funeral of a less-affluent person, family, friends, and neighbors carried the coffin on their shoulders. Only the elite could afford the conspicuous display of yards of black crepe and silk and could afford to withdraw for a time from the wider rounds of social life and the business of making a living. But within a few decades, the growing middle class came to emulate the elite. Significantly, women of upwardly mobile families withdrew into deep mourning for up to a year. They withdrew from their previous role in laying out the corpse, at first leaving this work to the lower-class "deathwives." Eventually funerals became more complicated, and male specialists took over. The roles of the carpenter who made the coffin and the livery man who rented out the horses joined to give rise to the specialized funeral professional, the undertaker. Tending the dead moved out of the control of the family circle.

Although elaborate funerals became the norm early in the 20th century for people who could afford them, the massive slaughter of World War I made extensive rites impractical. So many young men died that society would have been unable to function if large portions of the population engaged in formal mourning. People were unable to display and enact grief repeatedly, let alone to pay for consecutive expensive funerals, and this established a trend toward more limited practices that persisted after the war. The bloodbath that was World War II and the necessity for the British to "make-do" and "get on with it" while the nation was at war completed the transition from conspicuous grieving to the display of forbearance. People were expected to show a "brave face." This culturally sanctioned reaction to death and the professionalization of the tending of the dead prepared the cultural stage for the death-denying culture that came to be seen as normal by the middle of the 20th century.

Even though death is denied to some degree and hidden to a large degree, British cultural practices surrounding death are very complex. The

newly bereaved must negotiate bureaucracies and go shopping. When someone dies, the sheet is pulled up over the face, and the nearest and dearest are
often ushered away from the deathbed by hospital staff and must begin to
process forms. A signed death certificate must be collected, and the death
must be registered. The bereaved sign for plastic bags that hold no-longer-
needed bedroom slippers, pajamas, and toiletries. They travel to the city reg-
istrar's offices where they sit and wait alongside people registering marriages
and births. They then quickly find and visit a funeral director, who will "take
care of the details in your time of need." Cremation or burial? Which plot?
Which coffin? Which lining? What will "the person" wear? Flowers? How much
to spend, to save both dignity and the bank account? How many limousines?
To view or not to view the corpse? Then there is the service itself: secular or
religious? Can the funeral director find a "tame" priest who will not dwell on
God too much? The ceremony must be kept short—usually 20 to 25 minutes—because there is likely to be a group booked in the next time slot at a
busy crematorium or funeral home chapel. Through all this, the bereaved are
starting to receive and entertain people who come to offer condolences.

Meanwhile, the corpse has taken a different journey. After the bereaved
have left the deathbed, the corpse may simply be certified as dead, but it may
also be the object of a postmortem (an autopsy). The organs may be "harvested" for transplantation, or the entire body may be "given to research," in
which case it may be kept breathing for quite some time. Once the body is
released by medical professionals, it is in the hands of the professionals whose
job is to keep the bereaved from the unpleasantness of a rapidly decomposing body. The laying out was previously done by women, and the corpse
remained in the home until carried by the family to the grave, but now these
functions are carried out far from the sight of the bereaved. The undertaker
transports the corpse in a nondescript vehicle from the hospital morgue to the
back entrance of the funeral home. The corpse is usually embalmed (though
this is not legally required), and its abdominal cavity is partially emptied
(through a vacuum tube), as is the lower colon. The rigor mortis is broken so
that the limbs can be arranged; makeup is applied, nails manicured, and hair
arranged. The mouth is sewn shut, and the eyes are covered with plastic forms
to maintain their shape and then sewn shut. When the preparation is finished
and the corpse looks as close as possible to the cultural ideal of sleeping in
peace, it begins its progression in a coffin to the front rooms of the funeral
home where, at an appointed time (the clocks cannot be stopped here), the
family and friends come to view their loved one and pay their last respects.

In a reversal of past practice in which the bereaved entertained guests who
came to see the deceased at home, the bereaved are now the guests of the
funeral director and come to view their loved one in his or her temporary home.
The corpse then travels out the front door to its former home, where the friends
and family are picked up in limousines and carried by professionals to a church,
a crematorium, and/or a graveyard. Depending on how busy the crematorium
or graveyard is, the actual cremation or burial can be delayed until days, weeks,
or if the ground is frozen, even months after the funeral. Often the family does
not know exactly when the cremation takes place: the journeys of the dead and
the still living have parted ways in time and space. After the deceased is cremated, there is often a second rite in which the ashes (the "cremains") are dispersed; sometimes families leave it to the funeral home or crematorium to scat-

In Great Britain, as in North America, graves serve as a focus for an important funerary practice—the rites of visitation and remembrance.
(Photograph by Sharon Hepburn.)

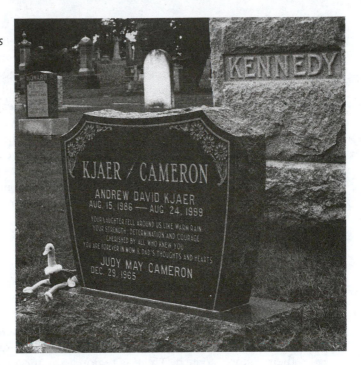

ter the ashes in a garden of remembrance. The final stages of the death rites are an increasingly elaborate and expensive process of memorialization, whether with a gravestone, an urn, a bench, or some other object; the point is to have a place where the dead can be visited and remembered.

In a Christian marriage, the couple is wed "until death do us part"; in secular Western culture, a marriage is no longer binding when the partner dies, and the surviving partner is free to remarry. Western people have relatives "in law" and relatives "in blood." In the terminology of anthropology, most relatives in-law are **affines** (relatives by marriage), and all relatives in blood are **cognates** (physically related). After the death of a spouse, relationships with affines often become weaker over time. In saying "till death do us part," we acknowledge that death breaks ties by marriage.

People biologically related to the deceased still remain related to each other to the same degree. After death, the property of the deceased is distributed according to a legal process that involves more professionals and more bureaucracies and often involves a written will. The will is intended to determine the distribution of property among family members and people who are not relatives. There is a widely shared sentiment that the wishes of the dead should be respected. Sometimes, however, family members are still contesting the terms of the will and distribution of property long after the death. Bitter fights sometimes ensue, leading to the division of families. Relatives may never speak to each other again, and they take their grudges to the grave— their own but also, perhaps, the grave of the deceased, which they may visit on occasion. If there is no will, distribution of property is directed by the state and/or legal professionals, and the process is often slow.

We have not even touched on ideas about the soul or afterlife: both these aspects of death are generally vaguely conceived by people in Western culture, more so than in almost any other culture. We have not asked why we fix up a corpse the way we do, or why most people want the corpse out of the house as soon as possible. And we have not asked how, why, and whether people find these rituals and practices meaningful. Nor have we considered variations in death practices outside Britain, or even in different parts of Britain. But this account does show us how death rites and ideas, or social representations of death, are highly integrated with other aspects of Western culture. Death is not something set apart, even though it is largely hidden; it is understood and dealt with within a complex web of institutions and beliefs. People everywhere must deal with death, but we must understand what bereaved people do in the same way that they make sense of their actions; we must understand death in terms of the larger vision of society and life in which it takes place.

The Tana Torajan Way of Death

The vision of life and death of the people of Tana Toraja in Indonesia leads them to devote considerable energy and resources to death rites. These rites often take place over a year or two. Just as Western rites must be understood **holistically**—that is, in terms of the other beliefs and social institutions in which they are embedded—so too must Torajan death rites be understood in their cultural context. There is regional variation in all aspects of Torajan life, including beliefs and ritual. What follows is gleaned from reports of research based in different parts of Tana Toraja, notably by Adams (1993, 1997), Hollan (1998), Hollan and Wellenkamp (1994, 1996), Volkman (1984, 1985, 1990), and Wellancamp (1988, 1991). When I write "sometimes" a Torajan will do this or "often" a Torajan will do that, this is a signal that all Torajans are not the same. This account focuses on traditional practices that have declined or been transformed over the past 40 years or so but do still persist. The last section of the chapter deals with the nature of the changes. When I write of "the past" I mean the time before many reliable ethnographic accounts were written, that is, before the 1970s.

The Toraja live in the highlands of Sulawesi (formerly called Celebes) in Indonesia. The Sa'dan River cuts through the Torajan heartland at an elevation of about 800 meters, and the valley is overshadowed by peaks that average 1300 to 1600 meters; some peaks of craggy basalt reach 2000 meters. Sulawesi rests where two large continental shelves meet, and the entire area is geologically active with earthquakes and erupting volcanoes. Most of the 350,000 people who live in the 3000 square kilometers that make up Tana Toraja farm and subsist through growing rice and keeping small gardens of sweet potatoes, cassava, vegetables, and sometimes coconuts and bananas. They also grow coffee and cloves to sell for cash. Water buffalo, pigs, and chickens are raised to be used in rituals and eaten afterwards.

Most Torajans live in small villages and hamlets, many of which are perched on the top of ridges and hillsides and staggered in layers. As you walk up and down the trail, you pass successive clusters of houses—sometimes a few, sometime several. Surrounded by lush, towering stands of bamboo and red-leafed cordyline (palm-lily) and sandalwood trees, the houses

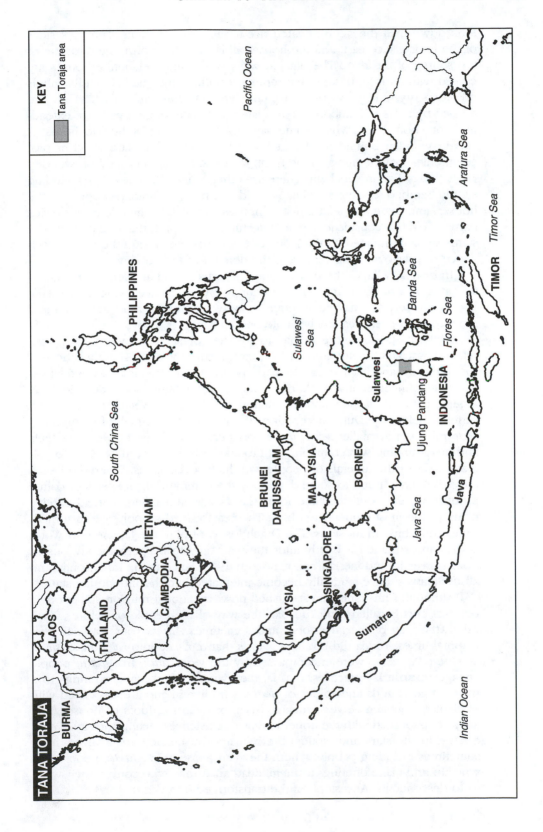

look down over the steep irrigated rice terraces and gardens. The right sides of the houses face east, and the houses all look to the north, the direction of the source of the river. The outside walls of the more elaborate houses are carved with intricate designs that represent buffalo, insects, rice, and symbols of prosperity, and they may be painted red, yellow, and black. They are topped by roofs of bamboo or corrugated iron with long curved arcs extending from both ends, which some say look like a boat or buffalo horns. A carved wooden buffalo head and horns from buffaloes slaughtered at past ceremonies may be hung on the front. Many houses are elevated on wooden posts two to five meters high. There are other styles of houses, too, including simple bamboo structures. Torajans build rice barns or granaries opposite the houses, and these face south. Just as houses vary in their grandeur, so do rice barns. Wealth is conspicuous in architecture. In the past, this visual display of status was accentuated by the kinds of trees growing around the houses, evidence of previous rituals that were the domain of the nobility.

In or near villages these days, you will usually find an elementary school and at least a rudimentary Christian church. More advanced schools, bazaars, and health services may be an hour or so away, and the most advanced and most complete services are available only in towns.

In the past, even more so than today, the Toraja were diverse. Language, religion, social structure, and agricultural practices varied. Although the surrounding lowland Islamic kingdoms of the Bugis and Makassar were relatively unified under central authorities, the Toraja retained considerable local independence until the colonial Dutch asserted their power in the early 20th century. Before the Dutch occupation, Torajan nobles competed for control of territories. On a smaller scale, there was periodic fighting between villages, and head-hunting was common, both to take revenge for a death and to collect heads for the funerals of people with high social status. When the Dutch arrived in 1906, lured to some degree by the commercial prospects of coffee production, they outlawed the local slave trade and killed or held captive many of the most influential nobles. They established schools, Western medicine, and Christian missions. The Dutch lost control to the Japanese in World War II and regained it briefly after the war, only to be permanently ousted from power by Indonesian nationalists in 1945. Since then, Tana Toraja and all of Sulawesi have gradually become integrated into the Indonesian state.

Although Christianity is established now, traditional religion still strongly persists. This is called *Aluk To Dolo* (the way of the people of before), *Aluk Nene* (the way of the ancestors), and sometimes *Alukta* (our way). In precolonial times, Toraja did not have words that translate into *religion, custom,* or *ritual*. All these were encompassed by the word *aluk*. In *Alukta*, people engage in **animist** practices; that is, they worship and make offerings to a wide range of gods and spirits, or *deata,* who live in and are associated with particular mountains, rivers, snakes, trees, or even the roofs of houses, and are also associated with the upper realms of existence, such as the sky. *Deata* can be in the stars and clouds, the rain and mist. They are in everything, sometimes including people, whom they can possess. In *Alukta,* people also worship and make offerings to *nene,* dead ancestors, who convey their wishes to descendents. Ancestors can be transformed into *deata*.

Torajans perform many rites and **rituals** and observe taboos, of which there are thousands. All *aluk* ritual involves slaughtering animals and making offerings of rice and meat to the *deata* and ancestors. The smoke of burning incense or the odor of offerings is, they say, like the smell of good coffee; it attracts and pleases the gods, who do what people want them do in return. This is the heart of *aluk* belief and practice, and it is referred to as feeding the ancestors.

The point of many of the rituals is to separate the east or smoke-ascending parts of the world from the west or smoke-descending parts of the world. "Parts of the world" refers not just to the physical world, but also to the forces that influence people's lives even though they cannot see them—the parts we might call supernatural. The smoke-ascending realm includes the *deata* and involves rituals aimed at health, vitality, fertility, successful house-building, wealth, and the rising sun in the east. Smoke-ascending rituals offer thanks and clean the cosmic slate if prohibitions have not been observed. The smoke-descending realm, on the other hand, includes the *nene* (ancestors), the souls of *bombo* (people who have recently died), the setting sun in the west, and death rituals, which are at the heart of it. To please the gods, these two realms must be kept separate.

Torajan society was and is **hierarchical**, though less so today than in the past. **Status** depended largely on whom a person was born to. One might be a noble, a commoner, or a dependent slave.[2] A person's status is inherited from parents **bilaterally**—from both parents—and although there are three overall grades, there are many fine gradations. A person's status can change by gaining or losing significant wealth, but this was relatively rare in the past. A noble was still noble even if he lost his wealth, but his social and political influence declined considerably. Over generations, fractions of mixed blood may be forgotten, especially if it is low-status blood; likewise, fractions can be remembered, particularly if it is high-status blood. This is one way the system provides for social mobility. It is generally hard to determine the real correlation between status and wealth because boasting of wealth or anything else is disapproved of. Nobles tended to have the largest, most elaborate houses. In the past, before slavery was abolished, slaves tended to have the smallest shacks, which were set around the noble houses.

A magnificent *tongkonan* (ancestral house) is not just a physical structure; it is the very heart of Torajan social organization and of how people think about what and who they are. When a woman is asked who she is, she may say, "I have a house over there." She is saying that she is related to all the people and ancestors linked to that house. She may not actually live in that house; she may cook, eat, and sleep elsewhere. But she is linked to the house by kinship ties; a parent or a grandparent, or possibly her husband's grandparent, came from there. People are related to each other through many different social groups that form and become significant in different contexts. Sharing ancestors and sharing social bonds are expressed in terms of sharing "blood bones." The ideal is for such people to be one word, one breath. People use the imagery of the plant world to express this unity. The woman

---

[2]This is no longer the case because slavery has been abolished. Nevertheless, its social residue remains, affecting the status of those whose ancestors included slaves.

might say that her nuclear family (she and her husband and children) is like a single branch of the rice plant. She might also compare all the people she is linked to through a common ancestor at the house over there to a dense patch of bamboo or a grove of coconut trees, all close together as if growing from a common root.

As is the case in most of the world, preparing meals and eating together is a way of creating and maintaining social bonds. So strong is this sentiment in Toraja that sharing food is symbolic of social bonds. The hearth is at the center of the house. To marry is to plant a hearth. To lose a spouse through death is to become half a hearth. To divorce is to divide a hearth. To be buried is to go to the house without smoke, that is, the house without a hearth. Meat divided up in public at a ritual is given to the hearth.

People like to be part of and participate in the life of as many houses as possible. The woman who has a house over there could probably point out up to five houses in which she can be actively involved. She can claim to be part of both of the houses her parents came from and all of the houses her grandparents came from, as long as the the relationship is maintained through activity. A woman who has children is part of her husband's ancestral houses, and he can claim to be part of hers; the members of all these houses are now joined through the children. The mere fact of blood relationship is not sufficient to keep this woman in active relationship to all the houses she is related to; she must participate in the rituals of the house, including giving and receiving meat. She confirms the ideal of enduring unity and maintains its reality by giving animals, rice, or money to the *tongkonan*. If she did not attend the rituals and give, the ties would be weakened or even broken.

Because the society is organized by bilateral descent, all Torajans feel equally related to both maternal and paternal kin, including dead ancestors. The emphasis is not on which side of the family someone is, but in which generation they are. Torajans use what is known as **Hawaiian** (or generational) kinship terminology. That is, they use kinship terms that draw attention away from distinctions within generations. For example, all people who would be called aunts and uncles in Western culture are simply called mother and father.[3] The kin terms draw attention to differences between generations; there are different terms for different generations up to the level of great-great-grandparents. Beyond that, the term *nene,* the ancestors, applies to people still living and to people who are dead. Even a child who dies is thereafter called a *nene.*

The Torajan woman may also point out where her umbilical cord was buried. Houses are sometimes referred to as places where umbilical cords are buried. In the past, before women gave birth in hospitals and clinics, the umbilical cord was wrapped in a little woven pouch on the day after the birth, and it was buried in a carefully marked spot on the east (smoke-rising) side of the house, the side of fertility and wealth, which children represent. The spot is protected with rocks, and thereafter the members of the house are the guardians of the umbilical cord. Just as the ancestral house is the focus for relations through the generations and after death, so too is it the repository of the evidence that future ancestors (babies) are being produced.

[3]This does not mean that the uncles become fathers, but that rather that they are thought of as something like "male relative of my father's generation."

QUESTIONS ───────────────────────────────────

10.1. How can you tell that a person is dead?

10.2. How is grieving done?

10.3. What happens to a person's soul after death?

10.4. How do people deal with the social disruption that a death causes?

10.5. Can death practices change?

QUESTION 10.1
How Can You Tell That a Person Is Dead?

In the West, we generally think that a person is dead when vital signs (breathing, heartbeat) cease. But exactly when death takes place can be tricky to determine. For example, advanced life-support technology allows a body to breath when there is no brain activity and keeps the heart beating long after there is any chance of resuscitation. Is a person who is warm and appears to be alive actually dead? King Hussein of Jordan died in the United States in 1999 and was kept "alive" so that the burial could take place in Jordan within the 24 hours of death required by Islamic custom.

This biological definition of death is simply one of the ways people can decide whether someone is dead; often the social or religious recognition of death is quite another matter. In central Africa, for example, the Lugbara people recognize that a man's death has occurred when his heir, usually a son, begins to sing the personal chant of his father. This signals the beginning of the sequence of funeral rites. The son begins chanting after he and his father have had their final words and he has left his father's hut. Sometimes a father recovers after his son begins chanting. But it is too late. Even with a complete recovery, he is dead and has no claim on the property or status that he had when alive. Similarly, if a member of the Dogon people of West Africa was missing and presumed dead, had rites performed for him, and later reappeared, people would treat their former kinsman or neighbor as dead and would act as if they did not recognize him; he would spend the rest of his life as a nameless, homeless beggar. Hindu ascetics on the verge of entering a life of renunciation perform their own funeral rites. Thereafter they are considered to be dead, and they would be treated as unwelcome ghosts if they tried to return to normal life. Later, when their vital signs do cease, there are no funerals. In East Arnhem in Australia, it is believed that people can be killed by supernatural attacks. When a supernatural cause of death has been determined, all aid is withdrawn and the death songs begin, even when the victim is still alive. The ill person often does die shortly thereafter—perhaps from dehydration or the power of suggestion. In some cases, sick people returning home by plane have been greeted at the airport by relatives already well-advanced in the cycle of death songs and waiting for the "dead" person to arrive and participate in the proceedings.

In Tara Toraja, by contrast, a person is usually not pronounced dead until at least a week after he or she has stopped breathing, and often not for much longer. For the Toraja, death is not a narrowly defined event but is instead a gradual process that takes place over time. Weeks, months, or even years might pass between the time breathing and heartbeat stop and the end of the funeral. The amount of time depends on the preparations that have to be made and on the establishment of an auspicious date.

Torajans recognize approaching death by a number of signs. Delirious speech is taken to mean that the soon-to-be dead is talking with the souls of the already dead. Other signs include the inability to identify people who are present and the request for luxury food items such as chicken, palm wine, and buffalo milk. The wandering of the soul or *bombo* (ghost) can also be a sign that death is imminent because the soul is already separating from the body. Only a few people are said to be able to see these wandering *bombos*, but they are also reluctant to tell anyone because seeing these signs of death would put them next in line to die.

When signs indicate that the individual's thread of life has reached its predetermined end, close relatives are called to keep the dying person company. The eventual cessation of vital signs is recognized. Because lying down is a tabooed way to die, the person is cradled as an infant child might be and then propped up into a sitting position. The person is not declared dead at this point, however, and is not referred to as a dead person. Nor is a death announcement made. Instead the deceased is referred as a person with a fever, the hot one, the one whose breath is no more, or simply as a sleeping person. It is important for people to know that there is a person with a fever because all smoke-ascending rituals are now forbidden so as to keep them separate from smoke-descending rituals related to death. So it is announced in the surrounding settlements that a leaf has fallen in the village. When close relatives or friends are notified, they may be told even more indirectly; the "straight news" is thought to be too strong, so they may first be told that someone is ill. Then, when they are traveling from the settlements to the house, they may be told that the person has a fever.

Soon after breathing has stopped, the corpse is washed and dressed in fine clothes and ornaments. People go to great lengths to view the remains, and they say that they want to be viewed properly and extensively when they themselves die. If possible, Torajans take photographs of the corpse and send copies to relatives who were not able to see the actual corpse. If there is no body to view (as may happen, for example, in the case of drowning), an effigy is made out of fabric and vegetation, and a photo of the deceased is placed where the face should be. This effigy is treated like a real corpse: it is wailed over, wrapped, and buried.

A corpse may be partially embalmed with formalin, and it is wrapped in cloth. A thin cloth is wrapped around the chin to close the mouth. The person with a fever is then put to sleep along the south wall of the house, with the head facing west, the direction associated with the smoke-descending realm. Sometimes the corpse is put under reed mats, and sometimes it is put in a wooden coffin. Often it will remain there, decomposing, for months or even years in a very extended liminal period, as the family engages in the activities of its own liminal period. The family begins to notify all of the people related to the ancestral house(s), begins preparations for the funeral rites, and begins to consider its financial situation. The person with a fever will not be pronounced dead until the funeral rites begin. He or she is offered food and drink, told of the activities of people in the house, and greeted cordially, as any living person ought to be. Meanwhile, the *bombo* hovers close by, more of a bother than a menace.

QUESTION 10.2
How Is Grieving Done?

People in different cultures do not react to death in the same way, and they certainly do not express emotion in the same way. The expression and even the experience of grief follow social patterns. In the case of British death rites, the elite display of sometimes-hysterical formal grieving was supplanted by emotional restraint in the face of death. Though today many British people may not cry at funerals, their somber appearance and expression let everyone know that appropriate grieving is being done in an appropriate place, that is, in private.

Although hysterical wailing might seem like an extreme expression of grief at a funeral, in fact it is comparatively tame behavior. Accounts of Warramunga funerals in Australia at the turn of the 20th century described howling, wailing, and moaning men who lay on top of the body or pierced their heads with sharp sticks so that blood streamed down. Other howling men slashed their own thighs with knives, severing the muscles so they were unable to stand. And this was before the body actually became a corpse. Once the dying person stopped breathing, the wailing and self-mutilation began again, this time louder, with more vigor, and accompanied by violence toward others. This continued for an hour. Then the corpse was carried to a tree and left in its branches. Sometimes the mourning was so ferocious that it added to the death toll, and the sequence began again.

We must be careful to distinguish between what people are doing and what they may actually be feeling. Many people acting in appropriate ways at a Western funeral are not actually grieving. Similarly, I once watched a woman wail in the middle of field on the border of Tibet and Nepal; she was a picture of grief and despair at the appointed time in the rites following the death of a relative. In her kitchen that evening, however, she complained to me about how much time participation took and said that the deceased used to beat his wife, so, essentially, good riddance to him. What is seen as the emotional response of people after death and particularly at the funeral is never random. It falls within a pattern particular to a culture and is understood in terms of how people are supposed to act.

In everyday life in Tana Toraja, people are supposed to act in a way that furthers community calmness, cooperation, and the overall smoothness of life. People are expected to display emotional restraint and equanimity almost all the time. In general, Torajans avoid showing, or even experiencing, strong emotions of any kind, particularly negative and potentially disruptive emotions. Anger, fear, and sadness are things you are expected to keep to yourself in Torajan society. This not because being utterly self-contained and, like the British, keeping a stiff upper lip are admirable character traits. People are expected to ward off and hide these emotions because they are bad for their mental and physical health, because they make cooperative, smooth human relationships difficult, and because it is in bad taste to seem visibly upset. People are expected to accept partings from both people and things with calmness.

Death, however, is a different parting. It is one of the few contexts in which Torajans think it is not only good but also necessary to show intense emotions; wailing and crying are expected. Like the cases described elsewhere, however, the expression of grief is not random; it follows a pattern closely tied to the funeral rites as they unfold. Torajans can show grief, but only at particular times and in particular ways.

All funerals facilitate the movement of the corpse from inside the house to the funeral ground and then to the burial site. Funerals are the major smoke-descending ritual, and the movement of the corpse is the movement of the *bombo* of the deceased to the next world, the world of the ancestors. Rites are extensive, and only close kin of the dead go to all the events of a funeral. Torajans joke that the kin themselves are half-dead from the effort by the end of the rites. People tend to come and go, sometimes repeatedly visiting a number of funerals if the funeral season is a busy one.[4] Attendance involves a lot of waiting and socializing between high points.

Not all Torajan funerals are the same. Children and people of poor or low status have simple rites; the older, richer nobles have more elaborate ones. There are variations by region and also according to the wishes of the deceased. There are cases, for example, in which people have not wanted to be buried with others for fear that the substance of other decaying bodies would seep onto their bodies. People comply with wishes to be buried separately, not just because it is what the deceased would have wanted, as we say in the West, but because they fear what a displeased ancestor might do to retaliate.

Wailing and crying is permitted right after the person is declared to have a fever. Grievers usually cry in a subdued way and punctuate their sobbing by calling out to the dead. Wailing, on the other hand, is loud and intense. Everyone is permitted to wail, and people can do so not just out of grief for the dead, but also out of sympathy for the bereaved. This is thought to be consoling to the bereaved because it reminds them that everyone has suffered losses and understands how they are feeling. To wail, a person has to be near the person with a fever or near a representation such as an effigy. Wailers often cover their face with a cloth and touch the corpse.

Wailing must stop while the body is kept in the house for as long as it takes to arrange and begin the funeral. This is a difficult time, and many find it burdensome. There is the smell, for one thing. Although the body has been wrapped and perhaps injected with formalin, the odor is sometimes intense. Because the *bombo* of the deceased is hovering near the body, people do not complain for fear of offending it and risking retribution. The body is a constant reminder of the loss that people are suffering. They are endlessly reminded that the person with a fever can no longer respond to them. They are expected to show calmness as usual during this time. Lack of appetite,

[4]There is no season when funerals must occur, but the scheduling of a funeral is complex. Factors involved in scheduling a funeral include completing the main harvesting and having sufficient resources in hand. Funerals thus tend to be clustered in the months following the rice harvest.

lack of interest in daily life, and a sense of disorientation are all expected and tolerated by other people. People occasionally feel suicidal. They do not, however, report feeling anger or aggression. This may be because the emotion is strongly disapproved, or it may be because deaths are generally taken to be predestined, so there is no cause for anger. However, a person who does not seem to feel strong emotion at the death of a close family member is likely to be despised. It is a delicate emotional balancing act.

What makes people feel worse is the prospect of arranging and paying for a funeral. Once finances have been reckoned and preparations have been made, the death is socially recognized and the funeral proper begins. The death is first announced by striking a gong, preparing those in the area for the death drumbeat that will begin in the afternoon. Once the drumbeat begins, relatives (members of the ancestral house) who have now finally assembled go inside to see the transformation of the person who has a fever into a dead person. This might involve the sacrifice of a chicken and a rite called suicide of the cat, which mark the beginning of formal mourning. A cat is thrown from the window and told, "Kill yourself, cat; your master is dead." In fact, Torajans love their cats, and a cat may merely be held up to the window. As the day progresses, the sacrificial stakes get larger, and, as in the earlier rites, the sacrifice of a pig and buffalo calves represents the death of the self or the body of the deceased. Close family members cannot eat the meat of these animals. The corpse is moved to the west wall (the smoke-descending realm), with its head to the south (the direction it will travel to the afterlife). It is now the dead one.

Torajans can participate in formal mourning by wearing black clothes and by abstaining from particular foods to various degrees. Many see the practices as strenuous and demanding; many do not even try to participate because they fear the results of breaking the rules, which include blindness, illness, or even insanity. A surviving spouse is now required to go into mourning by removing normal clothes and putting on a large, loose cloth. It is the spouse's duty to watch over the corpse while always facing away from the sun and to observe rigorous taboos about what can and cannot be eaten. For example, rice, the central food of life, cannot be consumed until all the ceremonies are over, often ten days later, sometimes even longer. With the start of the funeral and official mourning, people are once again permitted to wail or cry openly, in the same style as before the vital signs ceased.

On the second day, the one who wraps (the undertaker) arrives. The undertaker wraps the corpse in many layers of cloth into the shape of a long cylinder. He also makes a bamboo two-dimensional effigy on which the clothes and jewelry of the dead are hung. Pigs are sacrificed for an offering: 64 pigs are killed through the course of the funeral to mark various phases of the process in a constant stream of offerings to *deata* and *bombo*. The undertaker and *aluk* priest carry on their ceremonies, and the relatives pay very little attention. Especially during the early days when there is little meat to divide, people come and go, help out, gossip, and talk about the events to come. Nights always draw more people who come to chant and to partake of the funereal ambiance even if they were fairly indifferent to the deceased. Young people enjoy the larger-than-usual gathering and become rowdy. The strongest turnout is usually older people, who chant.

Women may sit with the mourners next to the corpse, singing dirges and telling lewd jokes. Outside, men sing laments for the dead and/or dance in unison around a fire where yet another pig is eventually cut and divided among all present. The life story of the deceased is told in the first of a number of recitations through the course of the funeral. The story begins with the birth of the dead and continues through adulthood, death, and the funeral to the coming journey to *Puya,* the land of the ancestors. Women eventually head outside to sing their own chants, which blend with the men's chants in one breath, as befits the ideal of the solidarity of the larger kin group. The sounds carry across the valleys, letting all know that a funeral is in progress. These evening pleasantries continue for a week or so.

The action starts to build when the day to bring the corpse down to the rice granary arrives. After noon, a buffalo is brought into the yard and tied to a very tall bamboo stake that is decorated with the horns of buffalo sacrificed in the past. The priest prepares the animal with prayers for its later task of transporting the *bombo* to *Puya.* It is led away until the ritual moment that will end its life. The stake is cut down and reassembled as part of a long string of bamboo sections representing the string or thread of the deceased's life. This very large necklace is then draped on the east side of the yard, becoming a physical link to the life of the deceased. The story of that life is told a few more times. Every telling further prepares the *bombo* to move along the road to *Puya.* As the tale is told for the last time, the undertaker offers the *bombo* some meat and palm wine to see him on his way. The death beat sounds on a drum, and a procession leaves the house. Some people carry plates, pots, an umbrella, and other provisions for the deceased's journey, and some carry the corpse itself. It is put under the granary for the night while the priest continues to chant.

The next day, an effigy of the deceased is made in front of the granary. The frame is generally bamboo, although a carved wooden effigy is made for a person of very high status. The effigy is draped with fine clothing, often a combination of batik and Western garments, and with heirloom swords. Male effigies wear a magnificent headdress of buffalo horns, silver coins, and bright bird feathers. Both male and female effigies have bright red cloth faces with white paper or wooden eyes. When everything is done, the priest turns the effigy around three times to awaken it and offers it some pork and a bit of wine. Relatives now come forward offering betel nuts and tobacco and ask for blessings and to live to old age.

Now the corpse is moved a little closer to burial, and this time the *bombo* travels alongside the effigy. They are carried to the ritual field in a lively procession and installed on a tall platform together with spears and other decorations. The corpse and effigy are left to look out together from the platform for two days, after which time the final separation of the corpse and *bombo* takes place. The buffalo that was prepared to be the guardian of the effigy is sacrificed and its meat distributed. The corpse is carried away to be buried in a limestone cliff; the effigy is quickly stripped; and that is more or less the end of it. If a wooden effigy was made, it is installed alongside effigies from previous funerals on a balcony built into the cliff. The corpse has gone to its house without smoke (the grave), and its *bombo,* now a full-fledged *nene* (ancestor), has headed south on its journey to *Puya.*

Everyone goes home. There are a few more minor sacrifices during the next few days; mourning taboos are lifted; rites are performed to ask for blessings from the *deata;* and people gradually get back to normal. Grief often lessens considerably once the body is buried. People say they are relieved, but they also feel sad because the deceased has left the house for the last time and has become truly dead.

QUESTION 10.3
What Happens to a Person's Soul After Death?

If you were a Torajan and were about to die, your soul would have become a *bombo* and may have started to wander from your body. A few people might have seen your *bombo,* but they would not have told anyone. Once you stopped breathing, your *bombo* would have become able to move around without being attached to your body. You would truly be liminal, no longer the breathing human you were before, but not yet the *nene* you will become. As a *bombo,* you would linger around your ancestral house as people made arrangements for a funeral that would transport you to *Puya.* You would wait and watch because you want to see how people are acting, and you want to make sure they are making proper preparations for your funeral. You have, or will soon have, the power to give blessings or trouble depending on how they behave.

Your soul would progress through the funeral rites until it was carried to *Puya* by the guardian buffalo. If you are a male *bombo,* you would be glad that you had inflicted painful burn wounds on your upper arms when you were about eight; the scars are required to get into *Puya.* If you had committed suicide, had been a leper, had been a very young child, or had been marginal to or opposed to social life and norms in any other way, you would not be allowed in.

Your life in *Puya* will be remarkably like life before you stopped breathing. You would keep the same social status, and you would be as wealthy or poor as you were before. There would be buffalo. You would be a *nene,* and you would watch to see whether the living were honoring and respecting you as they should. If they made you angry, you could harm them; if they pleased you, you could help them.

What you would really want your descendents to do is to finish off the business of death and do the rituals to turn you into a *deata.* As a *bombo* and *nene,* you are in the smoke-descending realm. As a *deata,* you would be in the smoke-ascending realm. This reversal requires your descendents to build a tower about seven meters high made of lengths of green bamboo and to tie sacred clothes to it. This is an inversion of the structure built for your funeral. This time, however, you would watch the tower being put into the earth in the direction the bamboo naturally grows, representing growth and renewal, and you would see it topped with lush red cordyline (palm-lily), which is associated with the *deata* you are on your way to joining. All members of your *tongkonan* (ancestral house, or "blood bones") would give whatever antique clothes they had. These clothes are considered to be gifts of the ancestors, and there are many prohibitions related to their use and storage. So putting them all together in the tower is a way to concentrate power that is otherwise spread out among kin. You would likely enjoy yourself as ritual specialists gather in the main room of the house to retell myths and chant the genealogies of the assembled kin for a few days. They would also entreat the *deata* to give their blessings to all present and draw the spirits into the "family bamboo clump" to see how many kinsmen have come to honor them. Everyone would eventually go outside to a large field, and you would watch the ritual leaders call on the *deata* to come closer. They do, to the point of possessing people who then dance wildly with hair flying and jump on drums and sharp objects (if all goes well, they will not bleed). The tower and the whole area are said to be aflame with the power of the forces set into play for your benefit. The spirits eventually leave, and after the tower cools it is carried to the house to be stored in the rafters. This concludes the ritual.

In this rite, your corpse is not significant. It may have been buried long before. Your soul interacts with the community you once lived in and is transformed by the unified ancestral powers of your kin, living and dead, over the generations. You would now be a *deata* and would have left with the other spirits to enjoy your life with the trees, the mist, and the sky, which are associated with the east. You would still be in contact with and watchful over your respectful descendants and kin. They are glad to be associated with another *deata,* and they aim to keep you happy by observing prohibitions and offering up meat (your sustenance) on future occasions.

QUESTION 10.4
How Do People Deal With the Social Disruption That a Death Causes?

Deaths disrupt social life. In Tana Toraja, such disruption must be understood in terms of the continuities between the living and the dead. Relationships do not so much end as change, and the barrier between the living and the dead is not closed. When grieving or the official time for expressing grief is over, people are encouraged to get over sad feelings. In accordance with Torajan views about emotions, they are advised to try not to think about their loss because thinking about it might make them sick. They are also counseled to think about the different ways in which their relationship with the dead continues. We have seen that the dead are believed to watch and influence social life. When people dream about a dead person, they believe that they are communicating with an ancestor.

Even after the extensive funeral ceremonies are over, people visit the dead in the ritual of *ma'nene,* which takes place at least every few years. This is thought to be a happy reunion with the deceased ancestors after the rice harvest and before the funeral season begins. *Ma'nene* is another occasion for the living to show their ever-watchful ancestors how much they respect and care for them. Offerings are made, coffins are repaired, and what is left of remains is rewrapped.

The naming of Torajans symbolically expresses relationships between the living and the ancestors, although it is not thought to involve an actual crossing over from the grave. Ancestors' names circulate through the generations by the practice of **teknonymy**, in which people are named according to their relations to kin. A child is usually named for an ancestor, say, Sam. The parent is then called by the firstborn child's name (mother of Sam) and later after the first grandchild (grandmother of Jane). If her own mother was also called Jane, a woman might spend her last years with her mother's name. Her own name possibly originated from another ancestor and may come into circulation again in the next or a later generation. In this way, the ancestral names circulate through the "blood bones" (the ancestral house) and remind people of the continuities and progression of people from life to death and back, through names, into life again.

The social disruption of a death is sometimes most profound for a surviving spouse. Western culture is strongly oriented toward couples, and a widow or widower may experience more loss by being slowly dropped from social circles. The Torajans have practices that smooth the way to social reintegration and perhaps also alleviate feelings of loss to some degree. When a spouse dies, the survivor must continue to observe the mourning taboos even after everyone else is free to return to normal life. Finally, a very minor ceremony takes place in which the surviving spouse is married to another person whose spouse has died. After the ceremony, the newlyweds are considered purified of the pollution of death and spend a few days and nights together. It is up to them to decide whether they want to have sex and stay married, or if they want a simple divorce so they can marry someone else.

The continuities between the living and the dead lessen the disruption of a death because Torajan society is larger than the totality of living people; it also includes the dead. The remarriage tradition mends some of the disruption for the surviving spouse. The fact of death and the funeral and its sequels provide occasions for society as a whole to reaffirm its alliances and its order. For example, people who want to reaffirm their membership in the *tongkonan* must participate in the festival in which the ancestor becomes a *deata*, or at the very least send meat and/or rice. Another rite that lasts over a year might follow; in it all the ancestral power that was condensed into one place is transformed into fertilizing power for crops, livestock, and descendents of the members of the house. Funerals and subsequent rites, then, draw remaining members together and reaffirm that they are still one word, one breath.

The close family of the deceased must assert their status in the funeral process, and all others jockey for position in the shame and honor stakes of social life. The two days during which the corpse and its effigy stand in the ritual field are the social climax of the funeral. The are called "the big day" or "the guest day," and they sometimes draw thousands of people if the deceased was wealthy and of high status. As the soul and the corpse remain stationary, the community of grievers asserts the current structure of society. Most of the expense of hospitality falls to the immediate family of the deceased, but others are expected to donate meat, particularly buffalo and pigs, sometimes in large amounts. These slaughtered animals are the medium through which people extend and maintain alliances and membership in ancestral houses. The complex tallying of debt and repayment may go back for generations, and new donations of meat begin new cycles of debt and repayment. These animals are offered up to the ancestors, maintaining relationships with them.

Pigs are brought for the feast in preparation for the part of the funeral celebration known as guest day.
(Photograph by Ferne Kvill.)

They are also divided in a highly formalized way, and people understand what it means to receive meat of a certain cut, quantity, and type. People watch the live drama of donation and distribution with great interest, and the subtle calculations of meat donation and receipt are calculations of honor and shame, that is, of gradations of status. After the big day, people talk about the politics of meat.

There is social disruption if we see death as an absolute barrier. In Torajan terms, however, death changes the nature of the relationship between the living and now dead, but it is not a barrier that severs the bond. On the other hand, the funeral and subsequent rites that require slaughtering animals are a forum in which the high stakes of social status can be fought over and defended, in which debts and obligations can be acquired or released. At funerals, people demonstrate their status and wealth and redefine their relationships to one another. On the guest day, the corpse and soul have actually halted in their journeys. In a sense, the dead person is waiting for the broadly defined community of grievers to assert their current rankings and allegiances. The no-longer-living kinsman watches as society declares that it will go on despite the disruption of the death.

QUESTION 10.5
Can Death Practices Change?

Death is a constant. Being born comes with a death penalty. But although death remains the same in that we will all stop breathing one day, ideas and practices surrounding death are specific to particular cultural contexts. British death rites changed over the course of a century in response to internal changes and external forces. Such was also the case in Tana Toraja. Despite the rise of Christianity, the outward migration of many young people, and increased exposure to tourists and to such institutions of a modernizing state as schools, hospitals, and an expanding cash economy, funerals have flourished in Tana Toraja. For many people, however, their meaning has changed.

Dutch colonials were accompanied by missionaries who had great success in converting Torajans, and by 1923 a council composed of missionaries, teachers, and Torajan elders was firmly established to direct Christianity in the region. The council's particular concern was the relationship between *aluk* and Christianity. As indicated earlier, *aluk* is not just a matter of beliefs; it is integral to social organization too. The council's most influential move was to define *aluk* as religion and to use the term *adat* (custom) for practices that would no longer be considered part of the religion. *Aluk* was forbidden, but *adat* was tolerated. Christians could engage in the customs of attending funerals, killing animals, and sharing meat, but they could not offer meat to the spirits. The very heart of *aluk* was forbidden.

By 1942, 10 percent of Torajans were Christian. There was widescale conversion in the 1950s, and today at least 70 percent are Christian. Yet traditional funerals still flourish. Many people no longer believe in the underlying premise of the ritual, but these same people still sacrifice large quantities of meat at funerals. In the past, the division of meat at a funeral was a vehicle to confirm one's status in society and to confirm that status was the natural basis of society. The funerals are now used to challenge this understanding of society or at least to facilitate the rapid rise in status of people who would have had low status before.

The children of former slaves and commoners increasingly leave Tara Toraja to obtain an education or work elsewhere in the modernizing Indonesian state. They sometimes return to host and finance elaborate funerals for their relatives, involving the slaughter of many buffalo and the offering of many pigs so as to push debt and obligation on others. Many of these returning children no longer believe or care to engage in *aluk*. They do, however, use *adat,* custom, to achieve unprecedented social mobility. The wealth they earned in an expanding cash economy is translated into social status back in the village. Others, including some high-status nobles, have not moved with the times, and because they cannot compete in terms of wealth, they lose their place in society.

Some Torajans have come to view Christianity as a way to avoid the expense and expenditure of energy required by *aluk* rituals of all kinds, especially funerals, and have opted out of the system. In doing so, they break social bonds or recast the terms in which social bonds are established and thought about.

Despite the prohibition of offerings to ancestors, some aspects of *aluk* persist among Torajan Christians. In the description of Western death rites at the start of this chapter, I pointed out that Western concepts of a soul or afterlife are vague. Even Christians who believe in heaven and hell often admit that their ideas about the nature of those realms are vague. Torajans notice this too, and even devout Torajan Christians integrate *aluk* beliefs into their conceptions of life and death. Although the *adat* funeral with slaughter has become void of *aluk* for many, the Christian funeral without slaughter incorporates aspects of *aluk* in other people's minds, if not in the explicit ritual.

CONCLUSIONS

This chapter has considered some of the questions that the inescapable fact of death raises and has considered the diversity of answers given by different cultures, in particular by people in Tana Toraja, Indonesia, and in London, England. Although the cessation of vital signs is universally recognized as a profound change of state, the social and cultural recognition of death can be considerably more complex. In the West it defines death; in Tana Toraja, a person is not declared dead until the funeral begins after a long period of preparation.

The expression of grief is patterned to take place on defined occasions. In Britain, the expression of grief is private, and public expressions are subdued and do not extend too long after the death. In Tana Toraja, there are opportunities for wailing and crying at different points in extended rites, and people are expected to adhere to general Torajan ideals of emotional restraint at other times.

People everywhere notice that a person no longer looks the same soon after he or she stops breathing. Survivors sense that something has left the body. Cultures give different accounts of what happens to that something after it has left. Western culture has an extremely unelaborated vision of the soul and afterlife, and even primary religious texts such as the Bible do not provide much guidance. Torajans, on the other hand, have a very distinct idea about the soul's journey to the afterlife, and they perform rites to facilitate its safe passage. The soul becomes an ancestor and lives with other ancestors in a social life much like the one before death. The soul continues to interact with the living and, in some cases, may be transformed into a *deata* spirit.

In Western culture, the primary focus is on the legal distribution of property. In a complex society, many of the rends in the social fabric—such as when a person no longer shows up to work on the factory line or a customer no longer comes to the bank counter—are quickly restored because they are not part of interdependent personal social networks. In many contexts, individuals are interchangeable. In Tana Toraja, where most social life and subsistence centers around extended kin groups, a series of rites serves to maintain continuity between the dead and living kin. Funerals are forums for the negotiation and expression of the present state of society that continues onward; the social fabric is mended by the continued weaving of alliances through the exchange of meat at funerals.

British rites changed over a few centuries as a result of changes in medical science, hygiene, and the social mobility of the middle classes. In Tana Toraja, death rites have changed in response to missionaries, schools, and opportunities for wage labor. Some people still take part in *aluk* funerals and offer up meat to ancestors and *deata*. Others, including many who are Christian, also take part but do not offer up the meat. They contribute primarily to raise their social status through the politics of meat. Still others reject *aluk* rituals altogether, preferring Christian funerals, sometimes to avoid the expense. Some Torajan Christians continue to turn to *aluk* to provide a more satisfying vision of the afterlife than Christianity provides.

The introduction to this chapter presented some of Robert Hertz's (1960) ideas about the interrelationship between social organization and death rites.

Hertz proposed studying death rites by following the trajectories of the soul of the deceased, the corpse, and the community of grievers. I have followed his model in this chapter. Although British and Torajan societies are dealing with the same questions that death poses, they offer very different answers. In one case the soul is peripheral to the rites; in the other the soul is always present and potentially interactive, even long after the funeral. In the British case, the corpse is made to look as if the person is sleeping; it is viewed by a few close friends and relatives; and it is disposed of quickly and away from the family. In the Torajan case, the corpse undergoes many procedures on its way to the grave and even after; it is primarily in the hands of the close family; and it is viewed by many people. In Britain, the community of grievers joins together in a brief rite that is in itself a minor interruption of social life, and mourners try to go on with life as soon as possible. In Tana Toraja, the community of grievers is large, meets on many occasions, and engages in the funeral as a central rite of the wider society.

Hertz wrote in 1907, when anthropological fieldwork was not practiced as it is today. His sources were primarily the accounts of travelers, missionaries, and colonial agents. At that time, anthropologists were trying to pool available information to document the diversity of cultural life around the world and to look for possible commonalties. This came to be known as the comparative method, and these anthropologists were later described, usually with derision, to have been engaging in armchair anthropology. As well as borrowing Hertz's basic but fruitful analytic strategy, I have also borrowed his method to some degree; I have compared two cultures on the basis of material I learned from the comfort of an armchair, not from the rigors of field research. Times and the discipline have changed, however, and today we have access to the fruits of decades of thorough, long-term fieldwork. The sources I used to paint this picture of the overall shape of Torajan society and practices are all written by well-trained anthropologists committed to rigorous field methods and analysis. There is not a missionary, tourist, or colonial agent among them. I am not advocating a "back to the armchair" movement.

Hertz and his contemporaries read the sources they had because they had big questions about society and the world. You may have been inspired to take this anthropology course because of questions that you have—the questions addressed in this book or equally compelling and important questions. Clifford Geertz, a prominent contemporary anthropologist, tells us that the point of anthropology is "not to answer our deepest questions." Rather, its purpose is "to make available to us answers that others, guarding other sheep in other valleys, have given, and thus to include them in the consultable record of what man has said" (Geertz 1973:30). The consultable record is vast, and it is yours to enjoy and think about. Welcome to anthropology!

REFERENCES AND RECOMMENDED READINGS

Bloch, M., and J. Parry, eds.
1982 Death and the Regeneration of Life. Cambridge: Cambridge University Press.
The ethnographic essays in this important book are based on fieldwork in a wide range of cultures. They focus on the symbolism of rebirth in death rites.

Bradbury, Mary
1999 Representations of Death: A Social Psychological Approach. London: Routledge.
>   An excellent ethnographic study of late 20th-century death beliefs and practices in London, England.

Chidester, D.
1990 Patterns of Transcendence: Religion, Death, and Dying. Belmont, CA: Wadsworth.
>   This book explores a great diversity of approaches to death based on ethnographic, archeological, and textual sources. There is extensive coverage of world religions.

Counts, D. A., and D. R. Counts, eds.
1991 Coping with the Final Tragedy: Cultural Variations in Dying and Grieving. Amityville, NY: Baywood.
>   As well as describing diverse death practices, the articles in this book are usefully grouped and cross-referenced to help comparison and understanding of variation.

Davies, J. D.
1997 Death, Ritual and Belief: The Rhetoric of Funerary Rites. London: Cassell.
>   A theologian discusses how a wide range of cultures cope with death, in particular through the potent weapon of words.

Field, David, Jenney Hockey, and Neil Small, eds.
1997 Death, Gender, and Ethnicity. London: Routledge.
>   A series of articles examining the ways in which gender and ethnicity shape the experiences of death and dying in contemporary Britain. The topics covered include parental bereavement, palliative care, and media treatment of violent deaths.

Gorer, Geoffery
1965 Death, Grief and Mourning. New York: Doubleday.
>   A classic study of the transformations in British death rites until the mid-20th century.

Hollan, Douglas W., and Jane C. Wellenkamp
1994 Contentment and Suffering: Culture and Experience in Toraja. New York: Columbia University Press.
>   An ethnographic account of Torajan emotion, cognition, motivation, identity, and ideas of the self and how they relate to Torajan culture and society.

1996 The Thread of Life: Toraja Reflections on the Life Cycle. Honolulu: University of Hawaii Press.
>   Two anthropologists chart the entire life cycle of Torajans, using extensive quotations from Torajans describing their own lives.

Metcalf, P., and R. Huntington
1991 [1979] Celebrations of Death: The Anthropology of Mortuary Ritual. Cambridge: Cambridge University Press.
>   A thorough introduction to the ways anthropologists have thought about death, drawing on the wide-ranging and often classic ethnographies of the past century as well as historical examples.

Volkman, Toby
1985 Feasts of Honor: Ritual and Change in the Toraja Highlands. Urbana: University of Illinois Press.
>   A description of Torajan funeral rites in their cultural context and of the way in which they have been central to transformations in social life.

Additional References Cited

Adams, Kathleen

1993 The Discourse of Souls in Tana Toraja (Indonesia): Indigenous Notions and Christian Conceptions. Ethnology 32:55–68.

1997 "Ethnic Tourism" and the Renegotiation of Tradition in Tana Toraja. Ethnology 36:309–320.

Geertz, Clifford

1973 The Interpretation of Cultures. New York: Basic Books.

Hertz, Robert

1960 [1905–1906]   A Contribution to the Study of the Collective Representation of Death. *In* Death and the Right Hand. R. Needham and C. Needham, trans. Pp. 27–86. Glencoe, IL: The Free Press.

Hollan, Douglas W.

1998 Staying "Cool" in Toraja: Informal Strategies for the Management of Anger and Hostility in a Nonviolent Society. Ethos 16:52–72.

van Gennep, Arnold

1960 [1908]   The Rites of Passage. Monika B. Vizedom and Gabrielle L. Caffee, trans. Chicago: University of Chicago Press.

Volkman, Toby

1984 Great Performances: Toraja Cultural Identity in the 1970s. American Ethnologist 11:152–169.

1985 Feasts of Honor: Ritual and Change in the Toraja Highlands. Urbana: University of Illinois Press.

1990 Visions and Revisions: Toraja Culture and the Tourist Gaze. American Ethnologist 17:91–110.

Wellencamp, Jane C.

1988 Notions of Grief and Catharsis Among the Toraja. American Ethnologist 15:486–500.

1991 Fallen Leaves: Death and Grieving in Toraja. *In* Coping with the Final Tragedy: Cultural Variation in Dying and Grieving. D. R. Counts and D. A. Counts, eds. Amityville, NY: Baywood.

acculturation The process of learning a second, or subsequent, **culture**.

affine Someone to whom a person is related by marriage.

agriculture Food production by means of permanently farmed fields and the use of nonhuman labor and complex techniques.

ambient culture The national or regional **culture** that is the background on which an **organizational culture** is developed.

ambilineal descent Descent reckoned through either male or female links.

animism The belief that spirits exist widely in nature—in trees, rivers, etc.

anomie Normlessness; the state of feeling that life has no rules, that there are no longer any certainties.

assimilation The process whereby an individual or a group no longer identifies with the primary **culture** and becomes part of another social group.

authority The **power** to influence others through means recognized within the society as legitimate.

band The basic social unit among people who practice **hunting and gathering**, often consisting of fewer than 100 people.

bilateral kinship A system in which people are equally related to both their father's and their mother's families; **descent groups** are absent in such a system.

bilocal residence Residence of a married couple with or near the family of either the wife or the husband.

bridewealth (bride price) A gift from the groom and/or his kin to the bride's kin as part of the marriage arrangement.

chiefdom The form of sociopolitical organization intermediate between the **tribe** and the **state**; it is kin based, has differential access to resources, and has a permanent political structure.

civilization A complex society with a formal government and classes. The term derives from the Latin word for city and is essentially synonymous with **state**.

clan A kin group whose members believe themselves to be descended from a common ancestor so distant in time that not all the connecting links can be specified.

class (1) A category of people with roughly equivalent opportunity to gain wealth, **power**, and prestige. (2) A society characterized by groups with unequal access to resources, power, and prestige.

classical culture A "natural" culture, such as a national or ethnic culture, as opposed to an **organizational culture**.

code switching Shifting from one language or other set of **symbols** and one cultural perspective to another.

cognate Someone to whom a person is biologically and socially related; a person colloquially referred to as a blood relative.

cognatic groups Formed by the operation of rules in which descent is reckoned through both male and female links, most commonly in the form of either **bilateral** or **ambilineal descent**.

community empowerment People creating for themselves the ability to participate in the decisions that affect their lives and their communities.

community of practice An occupational or professional network that shares a **worldview** and a group identity, engages in interpretive sense-making, and develops shared adaptive responses to environmental challenges.

consanguine A formal equivalent of the colloquial term *blood relative*.

corporate A term used to describe social structures that have an identity, that have functions that involve collective action, and that continue through time.

cosmology A "map" of the social and natural world for a **culture** that explains what kinds of beings there are, where they are, and how they interact.

creation myths Stories unique to each society that account for the origins of that society and the natural and social world it inhabits.

cross cousins Children of siblings of the opposite sex—mother's brother's children or father's sister's children.

cultural broker Someone who acts as an intermediary between members of two **cultures**, usually helping members of a subordinate culture learn to operate in a dominant culture.

culture The set of learned behaviors, beliefs, **values**, and attitudes characteristic of a social group.

descent group A group made up of individuals who trace their descent from a common ancestor.

development The process of a society's increasing its economic output as measured by market sales, so named because of the assumption that better living conditions for all will result.

dibble stick A gardening tool consisting of a wooden stick, usually with a sharpened and fire-hardened end.

division of labor The practice of dividing economic activity according to what group customarily does it. All societies divide labor according to sex and age; some also have other specializations.

economic man The idea that human behavior can be explained by economic self-interest.

egocentric society A society that emphasizes the well-being of the individual over that of the group.

enculturation The process of learning one's primary **culture**.

endogamy Marriage within a specified social group, such as a **clan**, caste, or community.

ethnocentrism The attitude that the behaviors of people in other **cultures** can be judged or evaluated by the standards of one's own culture.

ethnography (1) The fieldwork method of cultural anthropology in which a specific group is studied intensively through participation in their daily lives. (2) A published study reporting the results of such fieldwork.

ethnology (1) The theoretical method of cultural anthropology; the study of human behavior, generally through cross-cultural comparisons. (2) A published study reporting the results of such an analysis.

ethos (1) An attitude or **value** ascribed generally to a group, as in "The members of the group have an ethos of sharing." (2) An abstract construction of all the values of a **culture**.

exchange relationships Interpersonal relationships characterized by **reciprocity**.

exogamy Marriage normatively being outside of one's own group.

extended family A social group consisting of near relatives in addition to the central conjugal unit and their offspring; sometimes defined as consisting of at least three generations.

feud A state of ongoing hostility between two groups in which each side feels obligated to "get even" with the other group.

fictive kinship The practice of treating some people who are not kin as if they are kin.

generalized reciprocity Gift giving within a social unit without keeping track of who is ahead.

globalization The process by which **states** are increasingly linked into one interdependent system of commerce, communication, and **power**.

Hawaiian kinship system A system of kinship terms that emphasizes the generation to which participants belong.

Hawthorne effect Changes in behavior that occur because a group is being studied or is otherwise being paid attention to.

hierarchy A social structure characterized by the presence of "vertical" as well as "horizontal" relationships—that is, in which some people have power over other people.

holism The idea that human behaviors and institutions must be understood contextually, in terms of the beliefs, practices, and conditions in which they are embedded.

horticulture Food production from temporary fields using human labor and relatively simple tools.

household The social group living together as a domestic unit.

hunting and gathering Refers to **subsistence** by means of hunting and fishing and by collecting more-or-less naturally occurring vegetal material; also called foraging.

indigenous knowledge The knowledge that a people native to a particular place have of that place and how to live in it successfully; also known as local knowledge and traditional knowledge.

informal social system In contrast to the formal organizational chart, an intentional system that develops "on the ground" through patterns of association and interaction.

Janus organization A company with two conflicting professional faces or **organizational cultures**.

liminality The critical in-between stage or marginal phase of a **rite of passage**.

lineage A set of kin whose members trace descent from a common ancestor through known links.

literature Language that is judged to be valuable and worth keeping.

magic The use of **ritual** to compel spiritual beings to act in specific ways.

market economy A system of exchange in which goods are moved through the mechanism of buying and selling them for money.

matrilineal Pertaining to descent traced through the female line; children of both sexes are assigned membership in the kin group of their mother.

matrilocal Residence of a married couple with the family of the wife's mother.

modernization The process by which a society becomes "modern," which is commonly taken to include such features as being educated, secular, more urban, and involved in the cash economy and in non-kin-based social groups.

monogamy Marriage between one woman and one man only.

myth Narrative story about supernatural forces or events.

naturalistic inquiry A characterization of anthropologic fieldwork emphasizing that it is usually not conducted in a laboratory, but rather in a setting natural to the phenomena under study.

negative reciprocity Exchanging gifts in a way that advantages oneself.

nomadic Having no permanent settlement; most commonly found among **hunter-gatherers** and **pastoralists**.

norm That which is normative, meaning either that which is statistically common, or that which should be.

normative control The idea that people's behavior is largely a consequence of the **norms** they have internalized, and therefore that employees' behavior can be managed by manipulation of their norms.

nuclear family The basic family unit, consisting of a mother, father, and their unmarried children.

oral literature Most simply, **literature** that is not written. Implicit in the term is the idea that oral literature has the same kind of qualities as other forms of literature.

organizational culture The shared system of meanings and practice developed within an organization through time.

pagan An adherent of a nonmonotheistic religious system.

parallel cousins The children of siblings of the same sex—mother's sister's children or father's brother's children.

participant observation Learning by doing; the primary method of cultural anthropology, wherein living within an ongoing community provides the primary means for discovering how the community lives.

pastoralism A form of **subsistence** in which food is obtained largely by keeping domesticated animals; requires being **nomadic** in many environments.

patrilineal Descent through the male line; children belong to the father's kin group.

patrilocal A couple living with or near the husband's father.

polyandry Form of **polygamy** in which two or more men are married to one woman.

polygamy Plural marriage; can be either **polyandry** or **polygyny**.

polygyny Form of **polygamy** in which two or more women are married to one man.

power The ability to exert influence on others, whether that influence is seen as legitimate or not.

primary enculturation The process of learning one's first **culture** as opposed to learning a subsequent culture, whether classical or organizational; usually simply referred to as **enculturation**.

private sphere The social sphere that centers on family life and what family members do to provide for their well-being. Also called the domestic sphere.

public sphere The social sphere involved with the broader social world outside the family, especially political activity.

racism A form of prejudice rooted in beliefs of biological superiority and inferiority.

reciprocity A system of exchange in which gifts are given to people who then have an obligation to return gifts.

representations The ideas, beliefs, and sentiments shared by members of a society.

rite of passage A **ritual** marking a person's transition from one life-cycle state to another.

ritual Repetitive, stereotyped behavior (not necessarily religious) characterized by meaning-laden symbolism.

role A set of patterned behaviors associated with a particular status or activity, as in the role of a father or a physiotherapist.

sacred worldview A perspective on the nature of the world that understands causation in personal or spiritual terms.

secular worldview A perspective on the world that accepts only naturalistic mechanisms for explanation.

sedentarization The process of switching from a **nomadic** economy and lifestyle to a more settled way of life.

segmentary lineage system A **hierarchy** of more and more-inclusive **lineages**, capable of coalescing into larger units as the need arises.

self-help system A social system in which individuals and groups must decide what to do when **norms** are broken because there are no formal mechanisms for handling the situation.

shaman A religio-medical practitioner whose powers to heal, find game, and/or divine the future come from spiritual helpers.

sign Something that stands for something else, where the associated meaning is inherent.

small nation A term coined in this text by Donald Bahr indicating a society that is not a state—**band**, **tribe**, and **chiefdom**.

socialization The process of learning how to behave appropriately in a particular society.

sociocentric society A society that values group welfare above individual welfare.

sorcery The use of spiritual **power** applied through physical objects to harm people.

state A complex, hierarchical, autonomous political unit with a centralized government possessing coercive **power**.

status (1) A recognized social position held by an individual. (2) One's relative prestige in a social system with vertical ranking.

subculture An identifiable **culture**, either natural or occupational, within a larger culture.

subsistence (1) All the means by which a society obtains food and the other basic necessities of life, but focusing on the economic strategies of **hunting and gathering**, **horticulture**, **pastoralism**, agriculture, and industry. (2) Those means of making a living that do not involve a **market economy**.

symbol Something that is understood to stand for something else by means of an arbitrary association of meaning within a cultural tradition.

syncretism The blending of two or more cultural traditions into a single new one; most often applied to the fusion of religious traditions.

teknonymy A system of naming people according to their relationship to some other person, as in "Mother of Sam."

transformation In the study of mythology, the idea that neighboring societies imitated each other by performing variations of each other's stories.

transhumance The form of **pastoralism** in which part of the population moves seasonally with the herds while others remain in the home village.

tribe The form of sociopolitical organization associated with **horticultural** and **pastoral** economies. Typically, a tribe is larger than a **band** and has no socioeconomic stratification or centralized rule.

unilineal Pertaining to descent traced exclusively through either the male or the female line.

value A conception of the desirable or the valuable; by extension, the moral and aesthetic aspects of **culture**.

westernization Akin to **modernization**, but with the added implication that the changes involved are not primarily indigenous, but are instead rooted in emulation of the West or in influence from the West.

witchcraft The use of spiritual **power** to harm people without the use of instrumental objects. (Neopagans, including followers of Wicca, have in recent years attempted to reclaim the term on the ground that they are "good witches.")

worldview The overall framework through which a person views life; how people think the world is. An opposition is frequently postulated between a **sacred worldview** and a **secular worldview**.

INDEX